Great Thinkers in Economics

Series Editor
A. P. Thirlwall
School of Economics
University of Kent
Canterbury, UK

The famous historian, E.H. Carr once said that in order to understand history it is necessary to understand the historian writing it. The same could be said of economics. Famous economists often remark that specific episodes in their lives, or particular events that took place in their formative years attracted them to economics. Great Thinkers in Economics is designed to illuminate the economics of some of the great historical and contemporary economists by exploring the interaction between their lives and work, and the events surrounding them.

More information about this series at
http://www.palgrave.com/gp/series/15026

Ramesh Chandra

Allyn Abbott Young

palgrave
macmillan

Ramesh Chandra
Glasgow, UK

ISSN 2662-6276　　　　　　ISSN 2662-6284　(electronic)
Great Thinkers in Economics
ISBN 978-3-030-31983-0　　ISBN 978-3-030-31981-6　(eBook)
https://doi.org/10.1007/978-3-030-31981-6

© The Editor(s) (if applicable) and The Author(s) 2020
This work is subject to copyright. All rights are solely and exclusively licensed by the Publisher, whether the whole or part of the material is concerned, specifically the rights of translation, reprinting, reuse of illustrations, recitation, broadcasting, reproduction on microfilms or in any other physical way, and transmission or information storage and retrieval, electronic adaptation, computer software, or by similar or dissimilar methodology now known or hereafter developed.
The use of general descriptive names, registered names, trademarks, service marks, etc. in this publication does not imply, even in the absence of a specific statement, that such names are exempt from the relevant protective laws and regulations and therefore free for general use.
The publisher, the authors and the editors are safe to assume that the advice and information in this book are believed to be true and accurate at the date of publication. Neither the publisher nor the authors or the editors give a warranty, expressed or implied, with respect to the material contained herein or for any errors or omissions that may have been made. The publisher remains neutral with regard to jurisdictional claims in published maps and institutional affiliations.

Cover illustration: © History collection 2016 / Alamy Stock Photo

This Palgrave Macmillan imprint is published by the registered company Springer Nature Switzerland AG.
The registered company address is: Gewerbestrasse 11, 6330 Cham, Switzerland

Also in the *Great Thinkers in Economics* Series

Forthcoming:
Alan Kirman
Vilfredo Pareto
Harald Hagemann
John Hicks
Esteban Perez
Roy Harrod
Robert Dimand
Tjalling Koopmans
Available:
James Forder
Milton Friedman
Robert Dimand
Irving Fisher
David Reisman
Thomas Robert Malthus
Peter Boettke
F.A. Hayek
David Reisman
James Edward Meade
David Cowan

Also in the *Great Thinkers in Economics* Series

Frank H. Knight
Nahid Aslanbeigui and Guy Oakes
Arthur Cecil Pigou
David Reisman
James Buchanan
Robert Scott
Kenneth Boulding
Robert Dimand
James Tobin
Peter E. Earl and Bruce Littleboy
G.L.S. Shackle
Barbara Ingham and Paul Mosley
Sir Arthur Lewis
John E. King
David Ricardo
Esben Sloth Anderson
Joseph A. Schumpeter
James Ronald Stanfield and Jacqueline Bloom Stanfield
John Kenneth Galbraith
Gavin Kennedy
Adam Smith
Julio Lopez and Michaël Assous
Michal Kalecki
G.C. Harcourt and Prue Kerr
Joan Robinson
Alessandro Roncaglia
Piero Sraffa
Paul Davidson
John Maynard Keynes
John E. King
Nicholas Kaldor
Gordon Fletcher
Dennis Robertson
Michael Szenberg and Lall Ramrattan
Franco Modigliani

Also in the *Great Thinkers in Economics* Series

William J. Barber
Gunnar Myrdal
Peter D. Groenewegen
Alfred Marshall

Preface

Charles Blitch who authored Allyn Young's biography wrote to me in 2005 before his death urging me to write an intellectual biography of Young. He said that his own work was more in the nature of a factual biography and less about his thought. It is true that Young's thought, apart from his growth theory, is not widely known even within academic circles. This book is intended to fill this important gap in the literature. The idea is to present his thought in a systematic way so that it can be understood by as wide an audience as possible.

Allyn Young stated that there was much confusion surrounding the notion of increasing returns. There was no problem where there had been more loose thinking than in increasing returns. His 1928 paper on increasing returns was an attempt to dispel this loose thinking on the subject and is widely quoted in the literature on growth theory. What are not well known are his other ideas. This book is written in a simple and straightforward manner so as to bring out his entire thought, including his growth theory, clearly in the form of thematic chapters. This book is largely about Young's economics—his contribution to monetary economics, value theory, distribution theory, business cycles, growth theory, applied economics, index numbers and imperfect competition. An attempt has also been made to present Young's opinion of some of his contemporaries and earlier economists.

Allyn Young was a great and profound thinker. He was an inspiring teacher and mentor to famous students such as Frank Knight, Edward Chamberlin and Lauchlin Currie. He had studied the whole literature of economics. He had a wide range and depth of knowledge. He commented on well-known economists—past as well as those of his own generation. He was neither a revolutionary nor a reactionary, *but had an evolutionary perspective of society*. He thought of an economic system as an organon, anxious to study the economic phenomenon in its togetherness. He believed neither in complete *laissez-faire* nor in undue interventions. He had an optimistic vision about capitalism and its future. Capitalism will not fail because of its contradictions (as in Karl Marx) nor because of its success (as in Joseph Schumpeter), but would be reformed by the endogenous forces of the system. He had great faith in institutions, which acting in the public interest would save capitalism from its excesses. His ideas need to be clearly and systematically stated along with their deeper implications. This book is an attempt in that direction and is primarily aimed at students and teachers of the history of economic thought. But others interested in the subject such as social scientists (including economists), politicians, journalists, administrators, professionals, businessmen or thinking persons in general can also draw benefit. Some amount of repetition in the book is inevitable because of the interconnectedness and overlapping nature of the various themes.

This book is dedicated to Charles P. Blitch who urged me to undertake this task. I have never met Professor Blitch personally, and at the time when he wrote to me I was hard pressed for time. But now with much more time at my disposal, this task has been easier to undertake. This book is also dedicated to Roger J. Sandilands, my Ph.D. supervisor and later my colleague at Strathclyde University, as it is he who introduced me to Allyn Young. He has also been my co-author who has collaborated with me on a number of journal papers on Young. Besides, he read through all earlier draft chapters of the book.

I am deeply indebted to Anthony P. Thirlwall, the great thinker series editor, for painstakingly going through the entire manuscript and offering constructive criticisms and comments. My special thanks also to Rachel Sangster, Laura Pacey and others at Palgrave Macmillan for their help in shaping this volume in various ways.

Finally, a word of thanks to my family who were patient with me while I worked on this project.

Glasgow, UK
September 2019

Ramesh Chandra

Contents

1 Introduction 1
2 Intellectual Influences on Allyn Young 33
3 Nature, Scope and Method of Economics 69
4 Allyn Young's Contribution to Growth Theory 95
5 Allyn Young's Contribution to Economic Theory 127
6 Allyn Young on Applied Economics 175
7 Allyn Young on Money, Banking and Business Cycles 207
8 Allyn Young's Role as an Author, Teacher and Mentor 235
9 Young's Estimate of His Contemporaries and Earlier Economists 261

10 Concluding Remarks	303
Author Index	327
Subject Index	335

1

Introduction

This book attempts to present Allyn Young's thought in the form of thematic chapters. Since many of his ideas, apart from increasing returns, are not well known, it is hoped that these thematic chapters will lead to a better appreciation of his thought. In this introductory chapter, we shall briefly first make some preliminary remarks about Young and his thought, and then his life and times, his personality, and the scheme of the book.

Allyn Young: Preliminary Remarks

The 1990s have seen a revival of interest in Young with the publication of his first authoritative biography by Charles Blitch (1995). His work, which was largely scattered in obscure journals, newspapers and encyclopaedias, was collected, and a bibliography consisting of about 100 entries was compiled by Perry Mehrling and Roger Sandilands (1999). His monetary thought was pieced together by David Laidler (1993, 1998) and Mehrling (1996, 1997). Some of Young's earlier papers were collected by himself in a volume *Economic Problems: New and Old* (Young 1927). It had been thought that Young published very little, but with the compilation of a bibliography of a hundred items, it became obvious that his work was quite substantial. However, he has largely remained a forgotten figure in the history of economics with some early references emerging about his paper on increasing returns and economic progress (Young 1928) in the writings of the post-WWII development economists such as Paul Rosenstein-Rodan (1943, 1961), Ragnar Nurkse (1953) and Lauchlin Currie (1974). Later, new trade theorists and new growth theorists made him the starting point of their own theories (see Krugman 1993; Romer 1986, 1989; Murphy et al. 1989).

Blitch (1995) portrays Young as a central figure in the development of American economics. Mehrling and Sandilands (1999, p. xi) suggest that modern interest in Young is more due to his economic thought than due to his contribution to the economics profession:

> His fingerprints are everywhere: co-author of a best-selling textbook *Outlines of Economics* (Ely et al. 1908, 1916, 1923, 1930) and of two others besides (Riley 1925; Reed 1925), patient builder of professional infrastructure as head of the Stanford economics department (1906–1910) and Secretary of the fledgling American Economic Association (1914–1920); devoted public servant, most notably as the chief economist and statistician of the American Commission to Negotiate the Peace at Paris; inspiring teacher of a generation of economists, most notably Frank Knight and Edward Chamberlin but including also Holbrook Working, Lauchlin Currie, James Angell, Arthur Marget, and Nicholas Kaldor.
>
> Modern interest in Young stems less, however, from his contributions to the economics profession, than from his contribution to economic thought. Young's 1928 presidential address … has never lacked fans … and the recent flurry of interest in theories of endogenous growth … has brought Young's thinking on growth to the attention of a much broader audience… Only recently with the work of Laidler (1993, 1998) and Mehrling (1996, 1997), has Young begun to come into focus as a figure of fundamental importance in the field of monetary economics, and this side of Young, it is fair to say, is still much less well known than the side concerned with economic growth.

Young was a deep and original thinker. He appeared to resemble an iceberg; what he wrote was just a small part of what he carried inside his mind. Even his writings testified to the same iceberg phenomenon, for what was visible on the surface was just a small part of the full range of his implications. His style was simple; his writings to the unguarded reader appeared commonplace. But they carried a depth uncommon among his contemporaries. Young was a first-rate critic and commented on many of his contemporaries and past economists. He also carried on a lively correspondence with his contemporaries such as John M. Keynes, Joseph A. Schumpeter, Wesley C. Mitchell, Thomas S. Adams, Irving Fisher, Richard T. Ely, Frank W. Taussig and Frank H. Knight. He also wrote on a large variety of subjects such as the nature, scope and method of economics, value theory, distribution theory, rent, wages, interest and profits, Marxism and socialism, increasing returns, imperfect competition, monopoly, concentration of economic power, and applied problems such as railway pricing, farm relief and index numbers. He also made his mark as an original and inspiring graduate teacher. From his writings, comments, teachings, criticisms and correspondence, it would appear that he not only had a very wide range but also uncommon insight. Often he appeared a step ahead of many of the authors he commented on.

Young is best known for his seminal paper on increasing returns and economic progress published just before his untimely death.[1] In this paper, for the first time, he spelt out the disequilibrium paradigm in contrast to the equilibrium paradigm of the neoclassical theory—both of the partial equilibrium type (Marshall 1890) and of the general equilibrium variety (Walras 1874; Pareto 1906). He had made a deep study of the neoclassical theory and had come to the conclusion that there was nothing much in it worth saying which could not be said in a few pages. In a letter to Knight (dated 6 October 1928), in response to Knight's comments on the Presidential address shortly before his death, he stated that he wanted to depart from the equilibrium method in favour of increasing returns. He further maintained that equilibrium rate of change afforded just as appropriate a hunting ground for pure theory as conditions of static equilibrium did.

---

[1] This paper was first delivered as a Presidential address to Section F of the British Association for the Advancement of Science at the University of Glasgow on 10 September 1928, and later appeared in the December issue of the *Economic Journal* along with a graphical appendix.

Although Young was opposed to the partial equilibrium method and its one-thing-at-a-time theorising, he resented the general equilibrium method even more. In his opinion, the partial equilibrium method was eminently suited to dealing with practical problems and was easy to understand especially for beginners. The general equilibrium method, on the other hand, was highly abstract and gave nothing concrete except a truism. Young did not like highly abstract methods that had little bearing on the practical problems of economic life.

Young had mastered the whole of the literature in economics. He was not beholden to a single school or a single way of thinking. He drew his ideas and views from several schools of thought for he believed that each school had its strong points. In his opinion economic truth was not the monopoly of a single method or school. While the historical method gave wisdom, the abstract method of the English political economy supplied us with the instruments to solve communal problems. Any economic doctrine which had existed for long had some truth in it. Rival theorists were generally both right except when denouncing each other. Moreover, different methods were to be treated as complements in the pursuit of knowledge. For example, if deduction and induction are used separately, they would only give us partial results. One was incomplete without the other. Both had to complement to arrive at a fuller picture.

He regarded the distinction between theoretical and applied economics as largely artificial. According to him, theory was useless unless it was capable of dealing with practical problems. He was deeply influenced by English political economy as it dealt with practical national concerns of the time.[2] Moreover, it had an instrumental value in supplying a method to deal with any problem and come to a reasoned conclusion. These economists took their data from real life. Their premises were based on commonplace facts and observations, and it was only superficially that they appeared abstract and deductive.

---

[2] For example, Adam Smith dealt with the relationship between the division of labour and market size and criticised mercantilist restrictions for hampering this relationship and hence prosperity. David Ricardo dealt with the problems arising in the aftermath of the Napoleonic wars. He clearly saw that the Corn Laws (protectionism) would raise food prices, raise rents, reduce profits and therefore growth.

Himself a competent mathematician and statistician, Young was excited by the new developments in mathematics and statistics and their use in economics. But Young regarded a perfectly abstract economics as impracticable. For him a system built on variables defined only by their mathematical attributes was not economics. The results obtained from the use of mathematics and statistics in economics had to be integrated into the existing fabric of knowledge. Averages and aggregates and their interrelationships by themselves provided a weak basis of inductive inference unless supported by other knowledge. Since statisticians were uncovering new facts every day, to use them the theorists would have to make room for new abstractions and conceptions. Theorists and statisticians, therefore, needed to work together to bridge the gap between themselves.

For Young the field of economics was wide open. No doctrine or economic proposition was to be treated as final. Each was to be ruthlessly examined in the light of new facts, observations and information. Economic truth was not something marked in stone and fossilised forever. Young had an evolutionary perspective on economics. What was true in a particular stage of history was not necessarily true in another. His thinking also evolved overtime. Initially, he was fascinated by the equilibrium economics of Antoine Cournot, Alfred Marshall, Léon Walras, Vilfredo Pareto and William Jevons. But later he wanted to abandon equilibrium economics in favour of the disequilibrium method. He was interested in formulating a disequilibrium theory of price formation which linked the theory of value, trade cycles and growth, all with the same theory. Such a theory would not treat money as a veil but would be integral to the theory of value. In fact Young saw money as central to an economic system and not just a 'convenience' to be tolerated. Once money is taken as the prime factor in value theory, price becomes antecedent to value, and not vice versa (Young 1911).

Young was also fascinated by the market form lying between pure competition and pure monopoly as better conforming to the observed realities. For him imperfect competition, which took the form of product differentiation, goodwill, trade marks, brand names, selling costs and so on, was a part of the broader competitive process. Here, competition took the form of non-price competition rather than price competition. At the same time, he was not interested in a static theory of price formation that appealed to some of his Ph.D. students such as Chamberlin and Knight. Although he made a beginning in sketching out his disequilibrium paradigm in his famous paper on increasing returns and economic progress, he did not live to complete the project. At the time of his untimely death in 1929 aged 52, he was working on two treatises, one on theory and the other on money. All his papers pertaining to the two treatises were lost after his death.

Although influenced by Adam Smith, particularly the relationship between the division of labour and market size, he drew the conclusion that the main lesson from Smith was competition rather than laissez-faire. In the evolutionary perspective, the state could not confine itself to just a few basic tasks such as defence, justice and public works. The state had an important role to play in institutional development geared towards the promotion of public interest. Unless independent institutions were developed, control of credit or monopoly could not be accomplished. Moreover, WWI had brought new responsibilities on the state such as mobilising men and materials for the war effort, dealing with post-war reconstruction work, collection and analysis of statistics to deal with the emerging problems more thoroughly, and international institutional arrangements for the orderly conduct of international trade and financial flows (including debts). He believed that sectional interests should (and could) be subordinated to the larger national interest, and narrow national interests should (and could) be curbed to promote larger international welfare. So capitalism would not fail due to its contradictions (as in Marx), nor would it fail because of its successes (as in Schumpeter), but would be reformed by appropriate institutions acting in the public interest.

Smith had decried mercantilism, but Young did not reject it out of hand. He trusted the mercantilist instinct of businessmen and their persisting search for markets. He stated that the businessman's mercantilist emphasis had a sounder basis than an economist steeped in comparative statics was prone to admit. He insisted that it was the commercial revolution which had made possible the industrial revolution. The industrial revolution had not been caused by inventions and technical improvements but by the creation and expansion of markets. He also praised Walter Bagehot for his flash of insight in characterising the English economic system as the 'great commerce' by which England had become rich. Under this system people had learned to govern their activities by contractual agreements, and this profoundly altered the social structure.

Schumpeter (1937, p. 514) stated that Young was first and last a teacher, and his fame largely rested on his influence as a graduate teacher and mentor. Many of his former students testified that he was a much sought-after graduate supervisor and made his name more as a teacher and mentor than as an author. His famous students included Kaldor, Currie, Knight and Chamberlin. He was very generous with his time and ideas; and many books which became well known like *Uncertainty, Risk and Profit* (Knight 1921), *Theory of Monopolistic Competition* (Chamberlin 1933) and others not so well known such as *Increasing Returns* (Jones 1933)[3] and *Marx's Interpretation of History* (Bober 1927) originated with him.

Life and Times

Young was born on 18 September 1876 in Kenton, Ohio. His parents Sutton E. Young and Matilda Stickney Young, who came from New England stock, were both school teachers. Young was the oldest of three children born to Sutton and Matilda. When Young was five, the family moved to Sioux Falls, South Dakota, where his father worked as superintendent of public schools. In 1890, when Young was 14, the family returned to Ohio, and Young was enrolled at the Hiram College where both his parents had studied. Young graduated from the College four years later in 1894, at the age of 17, the youngest graduate on record. In his final year at the College, Young studied economics from the newly published *Outlines of Economics*, written by Ely (1893), who later became his graduate supervisor at Wisconsin.

---

[3] G.T. Jones was one of Young's research students who was killed in a car accident in 1928, and the job of editing his manuscripts fell on Colin Clark, Young's research assistant at the LSE. Clark, in a letter to Blitch dated 7 December 1972, stated that "Jones's methods were greatly in advance of his time, and I think clearly show Young's influence." Schumpeter (1951/2003, p. 108) also stated that the Marshallian long-run industrial supply curves, although untidy to a theorist, open up statistical possibilities which were partially exploited by Jones (1933).

After graduating from Hiram College, Young worked as a printer for four years saving up money for his graduate studies at Wisconsin. He owned 'Allyn A. Young and Company, Printers, Binders and Stationers of Hiram, Ohio' but the business was not successful, so he became a job printer for several companies in Cleveland and Minnesota. He was working as superintendent of the printing department of J.R. Watkins Medical Company in Winona (Minnesota) before joining the graduate school at Wisconsin (Blitch 1995).

He enrolled at Wisconsin in 1898 for a Ph.D. degree in Economics with minors in statistics and history. His economics teachers at Wisconsin were Ely and William A. Scott. He was taught statistics by E.D. Jones and history by Frederick J. Turner and Charles H. Haskins. At Wisconsin, Young took a year off to work at the US Bureau of Census in Washington under Walter F. Wilcox of Cornell. At the Bureau he also met students from other universities such as Wesley C. Mitchell from Chicago and Thomas S. Adams from John Hopkins. They became his lifelong friends. Later, Young returned to Wisconsin to write his dissertation *A Discussion of Age Statistics* based on the data collected at the Bureau. Although his thesis was nominally supervised by Ely, Wilcox was his de facto supervisor and advisor.

After graduating from Wisconsin in 1902, Young chose the life of an academic although he could have chosen a well-paid and more secure government job. He started his academic career at the Western Reserve University, Cleveland. After that Young changed several universities—Dartmouth College, Stanford, Washington, Cornell and Harvard. Interspersed with these posts, Young also held visiting positions at Wisconsin and Harvard. In 1927, Young obtained a three-year appointment at the LSE as the successor to Edwin Cannan, but before completing his assignment, he tragically succumbed to an influenza epidemic in London and died on 7 March 1929, at the age of 52. In his own words, he remained a 'peripatetic economist' throughout life, never settling down in one place, always on the move, much like the disequilibrium economics he advocated. He constantly changed jobs either because there were inadequate library facilities, or inadequate graduate teaching, or the teaching involved subjects which did not interest him, or the administration was simply unhelpful and unsympathetic to his concerns.

He had a streak of adventure in him, a very American quality. He often placed himself in new situations and settings. A part of the reason why he changed jobs so frequently was this sense of adventure. His last job at the London School of Economics gave him immense pride to be the first American economist to be invited for a chair in a European institution. In the words of Taussig (Taussig et al. 1930, p. 550): "At each institution he left an abiding mark, and from each he was drawn to the next not only by the prospect of higher position and more congenial work, but by a certain spirit of adventure. His was a wide-roving disposition; the trait showed itself not only in the many shifts of his career but in the range of his scholarly work. It was this trait which explains the very last move, which ended so tragically… It proved tempting, not only because of the attraction which a new sphere of work always had for him, but because of a natural pride in being the first American economist invited to a high Academic post in European countries."

Young had a history of respiratory ailments, and it was at a printing house at Minnesota that he first developed. This ailment at that time consisted of catarrh and inflammation of the mucous membrane of his nose and throat, but later in 1929 caused his death. Young's influenza in London in the winter of 1928–1929 soon degenerated into a virulent form of pneumonia (Blitch 1995, p. 182). Just before his death, he went into bouts of delirium, and in his final delirium, he lectured to an imaginary class (ibid., p. 182). This showed his immense love for teaching; at the time of his death he was thinking of nothing else but of his class and students. Lionel Robbins (1971, p. 121) in his autobiography describes Young's death as follows:

> He was a big, burly thickset man of the type which is notoriously susceptible to the onset of certain kinds of illness. Antibiotics had not been invented; thus, when he was attacked what must have been a particularly virulent pneumonia in the influenza epidemic of 1929, he just collapsed and expired in a matter of two or three days—a private and public tragedy, since he left behind him a blind wife not very well provided for.

Young had married Jessie Bernice Westlake, the daughter of a businessman, in August 1904. Young had known Jessie since his graduate days in

Madison. The Youngs not only had their own son Jack but also took responsibility for John Westlake, Jessie's father, in his old age. When Jack Westlake, Jessie's brother, died in 1921, the Youngs took responsibility for his two children as well. This was despite the fact that Jessie's eyesight, which was already poor before marriage, deteriorated further soon after, and by the time they moved to Harvard she was completely blind. So Young had a large family to care for and was always looking for opportunities for additional income to support his large and growing family. Many of his writings, which were probably written with an eye on additional income, were later collected from little-known journals, and anonymously, in an encyclopaedia *The Book of Popular Science* (1924). When Young died, President Lowell of Harvard had to make a special provision for a pension for Young's impoverished widow as Young had not completed the mandatory 30 years of service required for a university pension. Young never owned a house renting accommodation wherever his job took him.

Young's death caused something of a stir in the academic world. He had made his reputation as a graduate teacher to whom students flocked in large numbers for guidance in their theses. He had worked at first-rate universities in the US such as Cornell and Harvard before accepting a three-year offer at the LSE, another world-class institution. In fact the position was filled after a prolonged and thorough search of the English-speaking world.[4] As many of his students attested, he was a revered teacher who was generous to a fault in sharing his time and ideas with them. He had built up an international reputation through his role as an advisor to the American Commission to Negotiate Peace at Paris, and along with his British counterpart, J.M. Keynes, he resigned in protest at harshness of the peace that was being imposed on Germany. Just before his death, he had received an offer to head the economics faculty at Chicago, which he had politely declined in person on a visit to Chicago

---

[4] In this regard Robbins (1971, p. 119) stated: "At the time of Cannan's retirement it had been felt that the whole organization of teaching of economics was in need of substantial overhaul… It was therefore decided that the appointment to the new chair should be so eminent as to be the basis of a major expansion; and after a prolonged search of the English-speaking world, the choice fell on the American economist, Allyn Young, already a name to conjure with on account of his standing at Harvard."

in December 1928, where he also attended a meeting of the American Economic Association as a discussant of a paper by Oliver Sprague on Reserve Bank credit policies. He was a "faithful son of America and Harvard" and had made it clear to his employers at the LSE to not count on him for continuing in London beyond the contracted three years (Beveridge 1929).

Coming back to Young's early life, his mother exercised a strong influence on Young, reading to him from early childhood. He was very attached to her, and after her death in 1910, he admitted in a letter to his friend Mitchell that "she was a woman of very exceptional width of interest & mental power", and that "she had always been a stimulating & encouraging factor for me" and that "I shall miss her sorely". His father was a supporter of a free silver movement and his interest in monetary economics, as noted by Mehrling (1997, p. 13), may well have started from conversations at home.

Young's major extracurricular activities at Hiram College included music and declamation.[5] He was a member of the Delphic Literary Society which acted as a forum for speeches by members and guests. He was also interested in music and was an accomplished organist.[6] His interest in music was both a source of pleasure and relaxation throughout his life. He also owned a hand press and helped pay his expenses by doing printing jobs. He also designed and printed many college programmes at Hiram. He was a voracious reader, reading not only for education but also for pleasure and relaxation. This habit lasted throughout his life, and in his chosen field of economics, became well versed with the whole literature of economics over the years. Young also read aloud to his blind wife and children: stories to the children and biographies and Harvard classics to his wife (Blitch 1995, p. 120).

At Wisconsin he was influenced by Ely and his 'look and see' method. In Young's opinion, any hypothesis was to be tested by observation and

---

[5] Regarding Young's interest in sports, Blitch (1995) points out that in his initial years Young was inclined towards athletics and tennis, but in the later years took to golf.

[6] "Not least, he had a deep warm interest in music, was no mean performer on the organ, and at one stage in his career supplemented a slender income by playing that instrument. He knew all the great composers and their works, enjoyed and judged a great interpretation. Here, as in intellectual outlook, he valued the old without belittling the new" (Taussig et al. 1930, p. 551).

facts. If facts and observations were at variance with the hypothesis, the hypothesis needed to be modified or changed. From Turner and Haskins, Young learnt the use of history as a tool of economic research. E.D. Jones provided Young with a solid statistical background and an interest in business cycles. Young also inherited a strong propensity for public service from Wisconsin where the faculty members were deeply interested in redistributive taxes, labour problems, cleaning up or reforming of municipalities and charitable organisations, and public control of big businesses and public utilities.

Because Young's mind was oriented to public service, he had a desire to give back to society in return for what he had received. Therefore, he took up responsibilities as an office bearer of the American Statistical Association (President 1917–1918), American Economic Association (Secretary-Treasurer 1914–1920; President 1925) and Section F of the British Association for the Advancement of Science (President 1928–1929). He also acted as an advisor to the Federal Reserve Bank, advisor to the Massachusetts Committee on Pensions, advisor to the Director of Census, Director of Statistical Research (War Trade Board), member of the American Commission to Negotiate Peace at Paris in 1919 and advisor to the Council of the League of Nations.[7] He also served as a Chairman of the Tax Law Revision Commission (New York) as well as of the Committee of Academic Freedom and Tenure. Young also gave a series of public lectures on varied topics such as socialism, railway pricing, public service regulation, the Sherman Anti-trust Act, the British National Insurance Act and the unshrinkable dollar. As a member of the 'Inquiry',[8] he acquired national fame, and after his work in Paris on the American Commission to Negotiate Peace, he shot into international prominence.

---

[7] On behalf of the League, Young assisted in working out a reconstruction plan for Hungary. The League also asked him to plan a world economic conference to be held in Geneva in 1927. As President of the American Economic Association, his address in 1925 'Economics and War' argued for international institutional arrangements for world economic cooperation for the restoration of world trade and growth after the disruption caused by WWI. See also Emmett (1999).

[8] 'Inquiry' was an organisation created under Colonel Edward M. House to study the post-WWI problems and to prepare the groundwork for the peace negotiations at Paris. See also Chap. 6.

In his intellectual makeup, Young was influenced by authors such as Smith and other classical economists, Marshall, Ely, Karl Knies and Thorstein Veblen to name a few. But he never accepted them uncritically. He always added his own variations, modifications and interpretations. He loved economics because it had an instrumental value and helped solve social problems. He always drew his ideas from a variety of sources, viewing them as complements. Because his focus was always communal welfare, he was neither a blind laissez-faire economist nor in favour of undue government intervention particularly where the market was useful. In his opinion, the state's role had expanded over time because of war and other developments. Institutions acting independently in the public interest were the surest guardians of both democracy and capitalism and could be relied upon to save them from their excesses.

Young's Personality

In a letter (dated 17 March 1929) to Young's widow after his death, Keynes talked of Young's "outstanding personality in the economic world and the most lovable". Young was very generous with his time and ideas not only to his graduate students but also with his colleagues and friends. He wrote introductions and prefaces for his students and colleagues' books. He was extremely generous and found it difficult to say no. Young was also a stimulating teacher and developed his ideas as he went along. His class lectures were often punctuated with long pauses, as he took time to think and develop his ideas. He also shared with his students his current research interests or current problems. He was among the most original of thinkers and teachers. He also had the habit of reformulating the questions asked by students in the class in a way which was made to reflect the depth of his students; by this trick even the most foolish of questions was made to appear profound. He treated his students as his equals, was sensitive to their feelings, and tried to see merit in their most stupid questions by reformulating and then answering them.

Young tended to be an absent-minded professor. Many of his students have testified to his habit of lapsing into brown study or carving a turkey or roast beef for his family while lecturing.[9] He often forgot umbrellas, hats or gloves. His lectures were filled with long pauses and silences and gave the impression of a lack of preparedness or knowledge or both. He also did not use lecture notes in his classes and developed creative ideas as he went along. As noted by Blitch (1995, p. 115), he frequently had to be reminded of his class meetings by his students or colleagues as he was often lost in thought about some current interest. Although most of his students thought him to be a stimulating, creative and innovative graduate teacher, some authors have doubted his lecturing abilities. For example, Robbins (1971, p. 120) writes: "[H]e was not a good general lecturer. The sentences were loaded with fruits of much learning. But they came slowly and heavily, with long pauses for due consideration. The more frivolous spirits in the audience would compile betting books on the length in seconds of the longest interval; and the common run of students were neither stimulated nor enlightened."

Moreover, Young was highly disorganised and, in Robbins's opinion, not a good administrator. "He did not know the background or the tradition of the School and for that reason was ineffective in committees. As for his paperwork in this connection, I, who inherited his desk after his untimely death, can testify to a condition of almost unimaginable confusion, no order or system anywhere. While therefore the effect of the appointment was to enhance the outside reputation of the School and the scholarly weight of its professoriate, the internal effect was very far from what had been hoped and certainly no basis of the wished-for expansion and reorganization. I am fairly clear that Young himself was conscious of this" (ibid., p. 120).

Young, by all accounts, was also a very humble person. Schumpeter wrote of his habit of hiding rather than highlighting his best ideas. Similarly, Keynes wrote of his habit of sharing his best ideas with others and placing his own work last. William Beveridge also wrote about him being the last person, not the first, to be persuaded of his own successes. In his famous paper on increasing returns, Young modestly described himself as a minor composer in comparison to Smith, whom he likened

---

[9] 'Brown study' refers to lapsing into intense thought with the mind going into some other time and place including 'carving a turkey or a roast beef for his family'.

to as one of the masters. It was again his humility which saw merit in every school of thought, and every side of the argument. Although he had developed advanced ideas about imperfect competition, he was prone to attribute to Cournot for most of what he said in class. The *London Times*, 8 March 1929, wrote that he had none of the intellectual arrogance which sometimes accompanied great mental gifts.

Young was a reluctant publisher and refrained from publishing before his own ideas had matured in his own mind. This was partly because he was a top-rate critic and found it difficult to pass his own critical tests before writing. When Young died in 1929, he was at the height of his powers and at last had felt ready to complete two treatises on money and theory he had earlier started. But that was not to be. Moreover, much of what Young wrote, as mentioned above, was scattered in obscure and inaccessible publications, as these writings earned him additional income to provide for his large family.

Although Young had an astonishing range of knowledge, his colleague at the LSE T.E. Gregory (1929) mentions that he was unable to confine himself to a given range of problems for a sufficient length of time. Since economic truth for him was not the monopoly of a single school or a single way of thinking, and that the first duty of a teacher and thinker was to see the strong points in every point of view, this coupled with his great personal modesty made for unsystematic writing, and for scattered papers and articles rather than a comprehensive treatise.

Since Young had a wide range, he did not consider himself to be a specialist; as a generalist, he considered himself to be more suited to writing a textbook than a treatise. Moreover, he did not place any special importance to the writing of a treatise as he considered it narrowed one's interest. He was more at ease as a freelancer than as confining himself on a narrow range of problems. He often compared himself with Edgeworth who had achieved success on the basis of his profound and innovative articles without writing a treatise.

Despite the lack of a treatise, he was a man of very wide attainments. As Taussig (Taussig et al. 1930, p. 551) writes: "Within the range of economics there was hardly a field in which he was not eminently competent. From the most refined theoretical niceties to the most complicated realistic situations, his grasp was secure and his judgement keen. He was a mathematician of the first order; a statistician attentive to the concrete phenomenon underlying the bare figures as well as to the most exacting requirements of refined technique; conversant with economic history; alive to the remarkable and often unique phenomena which have unrolled themselves before our eyes during these first three decades of the twentieth century; above all, a master of the principles of economics, steeped in the great literature of the subject, its method, its relation to other disciplines. With this complete grasp of his chosen subject, he combined an interest and comprehension in a wide range of others,—not only history and politics, but natural science, philosophy, and literature."

In his writings, it was his talent as a critic which stood out. He reviewed many authors such as Jevons, Fisher, Marshall, Keynes, Mitchell, Knight, Edgeworth, A.C. Pigou and Ralph G. Hawtrey. Young used criticism as a method to advance or refine theory. For example, Young criticised Marshall's notion of consumer surplus. In Young's opinion it was a general equilibrium concept and could not be analysed by partial equilibrium tools of demand and supply. Moreover, the concept was not additive, and for a consumer, over all his expenditures, it summed up to zero. According to Young, consumers benefitted not through the demand side but through the lowering of costs made possible by increasing returns. Young also criticised Marshall for confusing the demand curve with the marginal utility curve. After a long correspondence with Irving Fisher on index numbers, he came to the conclusion that an index number was both an average of ratios and ratio of averages. Young also disagreed with Fisher on the need to stabilise the general price level as business cycles are caused by distortion of relative prices. He agreed with Veblen on the need for an evolutionary method for economics, but he disagreed that economics necessarily needed hedonistic or psychological postulates. While reviewing Pigou's *Wealth and Welfare*, he detected a slip in his reasoning. Increasing cost industries did not need to be taxed, as Pigou had suggested, as they did not use up more resources but paid more for their specialised inputs, involving transfers rather than real social costs. Some authors, however, take the view that Young's role as a critic made for his temporary or limited influence. For example, Peter Newman (1987, p. 939) wrote: "He was above all a great critic, and great critics, like great journalists and great wits, seldom survive into posterity."

The Scheme of the Book

In this section chapter-wise outlines are presented:

Chapter 2

This chapter discusses the intellectual influences on Young, and also the points where Young differed. As stated earlier, Young first learnt his economics from Ely's *Outlines of Economics*, and later became his Ph.D. student at Wisconsin. Ely in turn was a student of Karl Knies, and Young was influenced by both. Young had an appreciation of the German historical school, particularly Knies, who did not succumb to the temptation of deciphering binding universal laws akin to physical sciences from the historical studies. Young made Adam Smith's theory of growth as his starting point and developed it further in terms of disequilibrium and cumulative causation. Young used Marshall's *Principles of Economics* as a textbook to teach his classes, but added his own refinements and modifications. He was also influenced by Marshall's concept of external economies and made it an important part of his theory of growth. Young was also influenced by the concept of cumulative causation used by Veblen (1898) in 'Why is economics not an evolutionary science?' and explained the process of growth in these terms without explicitly using the term. But Young disagreed with Veblen that the capitalist system always produced monopoly, unemployment and social wastes and that economics was based on the assumption of hedonistic psychology. As mentioned above, Young was influenced by the method of English political economy, which, although appearing abstract and deductive, had an instrumental value in solving real-life problems. According to Young the main contribution of the English political economy was not that it gave us a finished set of doctrines, but supplied us with the method to attain economic knowledge.

Chapter 3

This chapter discusses the nature, scope and method of economics. Young regarded economics as a study of wealth-generating and wealth-using activities of man, but only in relation to solving communal (or social) problems. He regarded economics as a branch of a broader science of society, so economics was useful if studied in relation to other social sciences. For him economics was more an art than a science if communal welfare was to be the focus. He also envisaged an increased role for the state as well as other institutions created by it in response to changing economic realities. He welcomed the increasing use of mathematics and statistics in economics, but cautioned that each new finding had to be woven into the existing system of knowledge, otherwise these new findings would themselves be suspect. The final terms of each chain of economic inferences reach out into other systems of relations often non-economic in character from which they get their final meaning. So the mathematical symbols cannot always be defined in terms of their algebraic meaning so as to exhaust all other possibilities. Young discounted the notion of rational economic man or the notion that economics was based on rational psychological postulates. English political economists had always taken their data from real life, and the so-called assumed premises were commonplace observations of daily life. Moreover, deduction and induction go hand in hand in every research as there is a constant give and take between the two. Although these economists appeared to be a priori in their reasoning, they were largely dealing with practical national concerns, and doing so in a practical way. Young had a great interest in methodological questions and felt that much confusion existed among the American economists in this regard. So he wanted to bring out a book on methodology consisting of selected readings from such diverse authors as John Stuart Mill, Henry Sidgwick, Max Weber, Heinrich John Rickert, Knies, Cournot and Pareto. Unfortunately, like many other undertakings he had in mind, this too was not to be.

Chapter 4

Chapter 4 takes up Smith's and Young's growth ideas, the important similarities and differences, as well as the later developments by Kaldor and Currie, post-war development economists and 'new growth' and 'new trade' theorists. As already stated, Young made Smith's relationship between the division of labour and market size, together with Marshall's distinction between external and internal economies, the starting point of his growth theory. He held that the dominant tendency in an economic system was disequilibrium as forces of disequilibrium were continually defeating those of equilibrium. He interpreted Smith's aphorism in terms of cumulative causation and came to the conclusion that the division of labour in large part depends on the division of labour itself. He was of the opinion that economic growth will not be negated by its costs, as in that case no real economic progress was possible, a conclusion repugnant to common sense. It was the prior expansion of markets, rather than inventions and innovations, which were mainly responsible for economic progress. He highlighted the togetherness of economic phenomena and stressed macro *increasing returns* rather than micro *economies of scale*. Young held that increasing returns result not from any relationship between supplementary (fixed) and prime (variable) costs but from external economies. An important difference between Smith and Young was that the former had laid great stress on institutional arrangements promoting growth, while the latter explained the growth process more fully. For in Smith's time terms like disequilibrium, external economies, cumulative causation, macroeconomics and so on, which we take for granted today, had not been formulated. Young's students, Currie and Kaldor, developed Young's growth ideas further: while Currie stressed a leading-sector strategy, Kaldor stressed the importance of manufacturing growth and Verdoorn's law. While Kaldor interpreted Youngian increasing returns arising only in manufacturing, Currie had a generalised notion of increasing returns. Currie's interpretation of Young was that the main cause of growth is growth itself. Young was also appropriated by post-war development economists, new growth theorists and new trade theorists. The new growth theory makes Young the starting point and claims to present his ideas with greater rigour, clarity and depth. Since Young's presentation was largely verbal, these theorists use mathematical models in an essentially supply-side production function framework. This chapter will also discuss how far these theorists understood Young's message and how far they misrepresented him.

Chapter 5

Here we discuss Young's important contributions to economic theory. He held that exchange values are determined in the process of exchange, and there they emerge as prices. So prices were antecedent to values. He insisted that the theory of demand and supply was more properly a theory of rate of demand and rate of supply, so prices referred to only the marginal units exchanged. For valuation of the rest, it was more appropriate to use imputed values rather than prices. Young regarded the marginal productivity theory of distribution as only a partial explanation of factor rewards. Factor prices and their overall use are determined at the macro level by their relative scarcity, that is, their supply in relation to demand. For Young scarcity and productivity meant the same thing. He was also deeply interested in the analysis of various market forms. He stated that in the real world competition was the rule rather than exception. If a business grew beyond a point disadvantages accumulated faster than advantages, so it was difficult to find a 'capitalistic' monopoly. He put forward an interesting solution to the duopoly problem—each producer will charge monopoly price without combination if their cost curves were the same. Regarding monopoly, he felt that if increasing returns exist, a monopolist would not maximise his net returns in the short run; the longer the time period he considers, the lower the price he would set. A monopolist was not fully aware of his cost and supply curves, and this ignorance led him to increase his price slowly. Moreover, a monopolist was receptive to public opinion and feared regulation by the government, so monopoly prices were not as high as the theory suggested. He also made a distinction between social dividend and annual product and linked this discussion with the circular flow of income and the problem of distribution (in the form of rent, wages and interest as claims against the social dividend). He stated that just as marginal utility is at the same time cause and effect of price, so marginal productivity is at the same time cause and effect of wages, interest and rent. Regarding concentration of economic power, he stated that concentration and diffusion processes occurred simultaneously, and statistics of concentration merely show the extent to which forces of concentration were ahead of those of diffusion at a given time. He stated that the course of events had belied Marx's forecast—neither the small property owner had disappeared nor the capitalist system had been destroyed. The scale of a business depends on the nature of business and the market in which it operates. There were advantages as well as disadvantages attached to scale, so there was no magic formula for business success.

He advanced other interesting ideas regarding demand and supply. If one abstracted from the distinction between producers and consumers, then each supply curve could be represented as the reciprocal of the demand curve, so could be represented by the ordinary demand curve for money. In the short run, there was no distinction in principle between demand and supply curves as both were downward sloping. One could postulate neither a constant demand curve nor a constant supply curve for the long period. The demand curve would shift as a result of the very forces which shift the supply curve. Seeking equilibrium under these conditions was a hopeless task; it was therefore more appropriate to have a theory of equilibrium rate of progress which would keep the supply curve close up to the demand curve.

Young's ideas on socialism and Marxism are equally illuminating. He made a distinction between socialism as a philosophy and socialism as a programme. In both cases it was difficult to say what socialism really was. Socialism as a philosophy was defined in contrast to individualism where individualism is identified with selfishness and socialism with altruism. Young stated that society in the final analysis was an abstraction, and there was danger in vague abstractions. Just as there were crimes in the name of liberty, there could be crimes in the name of society. Socialism as a programme was also imprecise. On the one hand, there was Fabian Socialism which sought to achieve collective (or public) ownership of the means of production through gradual or legislative methods. Then there were scientific or evolutionary socialists like Marx who did not talk of desirability of collective ownership but its inevitability as the next stage of social evolution. Young stated that the term 'scientific' did not apply to Marx as he was as much utopian as those he criticised; his theory of the class struggle was an invitation to participate in it. For Young class struggle was an ugly and repellent doctrine. Marx by nature was a 'passionate revolutionist'; socialism would realise itself better, not through revolution, but through the democratic process geared towards specific social reforms.

Chapter 6

This chapter discusses Young's interest in applied problems. He was against dividing theory and practice in watertight compartments. Theory was useless unless it was of value in solving practical problems. He dealt with several applied problems such as depreciation and rate control, railway rate making, Sherman Act and other anti-trust laws to control monopoly, the 1925 McNary-Haugen Bill for farm relief and enumeration of children. Regarding his ideas on depreciation for railway rate control, he felt that the practice of compulsory reserve ordered by the Interstate Commerce Commission was alright in businesses with one dominant asset; but in a property of varied assets which was maintained in good condition with repairs and replacements carried out from operating expenses whenever required, there was no need to accumulate a depreciation reserve in advance. For the purposes of rate control, an investment should be appraised at its original value irrespective of whether provision had been made for depreciation or not before the new accounting rules kicked in; and returns should be based on the original value of the property, not on its depreciated value. Since all costs are variable in the long run, Young advocated a cost-of-service principle for railway rate making, departure from which would then have to be justified by the special circumstances of the case. As Chairman of the Tax Law Revision Commission of New York, Young recommended a mix of personal and impersonal taxation in the ongoing work of remodelling the general property tax. To bring consistency and order to the taxation system at the state and local levels, Young recommended impersonal taxation on property, wherever it was located, to be supplemented with personal income taxation on all incomes above a certain exemption limit on all taxpaying residents of a state irrespective of where their properties were located.

Young made a thorough study of anti-trust laws and felt that that the 1890 Sherman Act was least effective against industrial combinations because the government lacked facilities for proper research and investigations. These shortcomings were remedied under President Theodore Roosevelt in 1910 when two successful suits were brought up for dissolution against the Standard Oil Company and the American Tobacco Company. In 1914 two new statutes were passed—the Clayton Act and the Federal Trade Commission Act. None of these new statutes was as good an example of draftsmanship as the Sherman Act. While the Clayton Act freed labour combinations from the anti-trust laws, the Federal Trade Commission Act provided a prompt and efficient procedure to businesses regarding unfair trade practices and allowed relief more quickly than the slow-moving courts. Young stated that although the American anti-trust laws had blundered in several respects, for example, in forcing competition in natural monopolies or giving too much weight to a mere fact of combination, their general direction was not at fault. In his study of under-enumeration (undercounting) of young children, Young came to the conclusion that it was due to overstatement of age rather than faulty enumeration procedure of the census. In 1890 the overstatement of age was more than in 1880 due to change in the census question from 'age at last birthday' to 'age at nearest birthday'. Young estimated that the comparative deficiency in the counting of children was 15.8 per cent for Massachusetts, 9.7 per cent for Connecticut and 10 per cent for Rhode Island. As a member of the Massachusetts Commission on Pensions, Young recommended a system of old-age pension for the poor of Massachusetts. Young criticised the system of discriminatory pricing of the McNary-Haugen Bill. Such a system provided for a farm tariff (thus pushing up domestic prices of farm produce), procurement of farm produce at inflated prices and then selling it at a loss abroad. He stated that the real problem was ensuring adequate return for the capital invested. But this was difficult in agriculture as even in public utilities the invested capital had been difficult to measure. Young also stated that the Haugen proposals were aimed at legitimising artificially the high land values resulting from the post-war boom. Young felt the proposals of the Bill were basically unsound and the farmer had an interest in sizeable tariff reduction *as well as* maintenance of stable conditions. All the problems discussed by Young re-emerged after the proposals, which were rejected under President Calvin Coolidge, resurfaced under the Agricultural Adjustment Act of 1933. Finally, Young also played a key role as an advisor to the American Commission to Negotiate Peace at Paris after WWI.

Chapter 7

Here Young's monetary views are discussed. For Young, money was at the centre of an economic system, and no development in modern economics was of more importance than an increased emphasis on the purely monetary aspects of economic problems. Schumpeter was of the view that it was in money and banking that Young came closest to giving full expression to his views. For Young, money was more than a convenient medium of exchange; it was a monetary standard whose value was fixed in terms of a commodity such as gold, is itself exchangeable in gold, and thus can be used for settlement of balances within and outside the country. Young stated that modern business is in the hands of men who have come to think in terms of money, and the price-making process is largely in their hands. He held that exchange value is derivative to the phenomenon of price, and by recognising this fact the theory of exchange is not substantially altered. A change in the money supply causes distortion of relative prices; hence explanation of a crisis does not lie in the mismatch of aggregate demand and aggregate supply, but in maladjustments of individual demand and supply in specific industries. As prices rise the distribution and amount of income changes in favour of luxuries, where overcapitalisation and overinvestment results. When the structure of installed capacity becomes out of line with the structure of demand, crisis results. Young thus saw money affecting relative prices, distortion of which caused business cycles, and business cycles were themselves placed in the context of growth. Young's project was to link the large volume of banking statistics he had collected to dynamic price formation, and hence to business cycles and growth. Once again his untimely death meant that he never completed this project.

Young's contemporaries in the US included James Laurence Laughlin representing the banking school and Irving Fisher representing the currency school; Young took strong points of both rejecting their weak points. For example, Young agreed with the gold standard approach of Laughlin but rejected his advocacy of laissez-faire and passive monetary accommodation policies. Likewise, he agreed with Fisher's interventionist monetary policy but disagreed that it was the general price level which needed to be stabilised. For Young it was the exchange rate rather than the price level which needed to be stabilised. He also rejected Fisher's varying dollar standard in favour of a fixed gold standard and also his rule-based approach to monetary policy. Young was also influenced by Hawtrey's monetary views and agreed with him on the gold standard and that credit (defined as banks' demand deposit liabilities) was an unstable component of the money supply. Young, like Hawtrey, considered central banking an art and was in favour of discretionary policy. But unlike Hawtrey, Young favoured public works on their own merit; and again unlike Hawtrey, he did not offer a purely monetary explanation of the business cycle. Also unlike Hawtrey, Young had little faith in the discount rate as an instrument of control particularly in the American context. Young favoured independent central banks, and expected them to set and uphold their own traditions, and act in the public interest without undue political or business influence. Central banks were responsible not only for their own solvency but also for the solvency of the entire banking system. Young also favoured international central bank cooperation in pooling of gold reserves for the growth of production and trade without a fall in prices. Young stated that if central banks tried to maintain their separate hoards of gold then deflationary downward trend in price was probable. Hoarding of gold was a sign of financial nationalism, and financial nationalism was an expensive luxury.

Chapter 8

This chapter discusses Young's role as an author, teacher and mentor. Gregory in his obituary remarked that Young was in many respects like Edgeworth, and if his work was ever collected, it would amount to a considerable achievement. When Young's bibliography was compiled, it was found that Gregory was correct in his assessment. Young never wrote a treatise, he himself never gave special importance to it, and considered himself to be best suited to the writing of a general textbook. As a teacher, we have noted that Young was revered by his students and was much sought after, particularly by graduate students who wanted to write their theses under him. Although his lecturing style included long pauses, many of his students pointed out that this was because he developed his ideas as he went along. For him the field of economics was wide open for improvements, and his students always got the sense that they were participating in this process. By most accounts he was an inspiring and creative teacher. His range and depth of knowledge was astounding; he was a voracious reader and always kept in touch with latest developments. As a mentor he shared his original ideas freely with his Ph.D. students. For example, his two famous students Chamberlin and Knight benefitted generously from his time and ideas. Young, from various accounts, had already developed original ideas on imperfect competition—product differentiation, trade marks, brands, selling costs, excess capacity, goodwill, entry of other firms, availability of close substitutes and so on, even before Chamberlin published his *Theory of Monopolistic Competition* (1933) or even submitted his thesis. Young viewed imperfect competition as closer to reality, and as a part of broader competitive process where competition takes the form of non-price competition. By some accounts of his earlier students (see also Young 1990, p. 53), every worthwhile idea in Chamberlin's book originated with Young. His other Ph.D. student Knight, who wrote *Risk, Uncertainty and Profit*, also benefitted immensely from his supervision. Young stated that Knight's thesis was the ablest to pass through his hands, and it would make his reputation as an economist. Young was right in this assessment, for it soon became one of the most read and discussed academic works. However, both Chamberlin and Knight had a static view of competition, and Young was more interested in developing a dynamic theory.

Chapter 9

Chapter 9 gives Young's estimate of his contemporaries and earlier economists. Keynes and Young both represented their respective countries at the Paris peace conference. Both arrived at the same estimate of US$10 billion as German maximum capacity to pay. Young reviewed Keynes's *The Economic Consequences of the Peace* in which he had criticised the peace terms as unduly harsh on Germany. Young reminded Keynes that he had forgotten the political context of the peace as it was a true reflection of the prevailing sentiment at the conference. Keynes had also criticised President Wilson's role at the conference but again Young reminded him that it was a democratic peace, and Wilson did not have the backing of public opinion to force his point of view even though he held all the cards. Young had a high regard for Edgeworth and reviewed his *Papers Relating to Political Economy*. He praised Edgeworth for 'high scientific standards' and 'unflagging intellectual energy', but stated that Edgeworth's indeterminate solution to the duopoly problem was not the last word. Other solutions were possible depending on the assumptions made. Young, in his growth theory, made use of the Marshall-Edgeworth idea of offer curves (based on reciprocal demand) as he criticised the use of the conventional supply-demand apparatus in the analysis of economic growth. In his review of Pigou's *Wealth and Welfare*, Young criticised his advocacy of taxing increasing cost industries as increase in costs did not represent a use of more resources but only higher input prices. Regarding public regulation of monopolies and public utilities, Young felt that Pigou could have learnt from the work of American public utility commissions. Young had a high regard for his close friend Mitchell, particularly his work on business cycles. Young had gone through Mitchell's *Business Cycles* in manuscript form and stated that the book was ideally suited to make a scholar's reputation, and that it was the best piece of work an American economist had produced for many years. As a student of Veblen at Chicago, Mitchell believed that economics was based on hedonist psychology. Young criticised this position in Mitchell's (1924) paper 'Prospects of Economics' stating that economics got its data from experience, not from psychological postulates. Young also carried on a long correspondence with Mitchell on index numbers. Young reviewed Fisher's *Stabilising the Dollar*. Fisher had proposed varying the amount of gold per unit dollar in proportion to the changes in the price index—decreasing it if prices fell, increasing it if they rose. Young criticised this plan on the grounds that Fisher had not worked out the full implications of his plan, and also it may lead to a situation where gold reserves may be exhausted.

Young also carried on extensive correspondence with Fisher on index numbers, and he also reviewed Fisher's *Making of Index Numbers*. There was a fundamental difference in their positions; while Fisher thought an index number to be an average of ratios, Young thought that it was a ratio of averages. Young in the review stated that when index numbers are properly weighted and properly constructed, the average of ratios, the ratio of averages and the ratio of aggregates all come to about the same thing. There is no special advantage of then using the geometric mean, and an ideal index number is unattainable, and the choice of an index would depend on the problem at hand. Young lauded Fisher's work as a landmark in the history of index numbers and a notable scientific achievement.

Young and Schumpeter were discussants of B.H. Meyer's paper 'Certain Considerations in Railway Rate Making' at the December 1913 American Economic Association Meeting at Minneapolis. While Schumpeter was of the view that the railways should charge discriminatory rates in accordance with 'what the traffic could bear', Young advocated the cost-of-service principle as a rule. Despite their differences, Young and Schumpeter became friends, and Young recommended Schumpeter as his replacement when he accepted a three-year appointment at the LSE. Walras was one of the economists, apart from Jevons and Carl Menger, to independently discover the concept of marginal utility. In his *Elements of Pure Economics*, Walras developed a mathematical general equilibrium system. Young felt that the use of mathematics was useful to the extent that it showed the interdependence of factors determining demand, supply, prices, costs, distributive shares and so on and brought to the fore all assumptions implicitly made, but felt that perfectly abstract economics was impracticable; and the general equilibrium approach gave us nothing beyond what was not a truism. Pareto, along with Walras, was one of the leading lights of the Lausanne general equilibrium school. Young had used the collective indifference curve in the mathematical appendix to his 1928 paper on increasing returns. He stated that Pareto was not responsible for the collective curve and held that the conception was not free from difficulties as each point on it represented a different income distribution. But these issues could be sidestepped in the problem at hand. Young stated that Pareto had made a slip while interpreting his index of inequality which decreased as inequality rose contrary to what Pareto had expected. Young also stated that Pareto was one of the first to put forward an explanation of industrial fluctuations in terms of psychological factors as waves of optimas and pessimas. Young was also impressed with Pareto's sociological writings and wanted to include a chapter from them in his proposed book on methodology. Cournot was initially ignored in Britain but his influence was later admitted by Walras, Jevons and Marshall. Young was fascinated by Cournot's treatment of the field intermediate between pure monopoly and pure competition as closer to reality. Although Young had developed many original ideas on imperfect competition, he credited Cournot for most of what he said. He also wanted to include Cournot's chapter on the social environment in his proposed book on methodology.

Young was impressed with the Ricardian stress on value and distribution after Smith, particularly his theory of rent. This stress on value and distribution appeared more abstract than the earlier theory, but Young held that English political economists were dealing with practical problems arising in the wake of the Napoleonic wars in what was intended to be a practical way. He agreed with Ricardo that rents were high because price of corn was high; to reduce rent the free import of corn was a solution. He included the Ricardian theory of rent in his *Outlines of Economics* both at the extensive and intensive margin. According to Young the phrase unearned increment was misleading. Young criticised Henry George for attributing all improvements to labour and for stating that they all go to rent; one might as well attribute all improvements *to land or capital*. Young criticised Ricardo for displaying excessive pessimism regarding growth prospects due the operation of diminishing returns in agriculture. The law of diminishing returns as a tendency could be overcome by more powerful forces like improvement in the means of transport and technical improvements in agriculture.

In his review of Jevons's *Theory of Political Economy*, Young thought the book was unsystematic, lacking even the skeleton of an economic system, and that the first four chapters were more completely elaborated than the remaining four. He stated that Jevons was the first to blend utilitarianism with abstract economics, but that his hedonism could be eliminated from his work without altering the essential features of his theory. Jevons's most important contribution was the concept of 'final degree of utility' and in its mathematical form amounted to the 'equation of exchange' which assumed barter. But equilibrium in barter was indeterminate as shown by Edgeworth. Young stated that the book gave mathematical garb to the results reached by non-mathematical reasoning. He agreed with Marshall that the book would be much improved if mathematics was left out but the diagrams retained. Young stated that despite the shortcomings, the book would still be counted as one of the top four or five books in political economy in the nineteenth century. The body of economic doctrines would have been different had Jevons not written. Jevons's influence in England was reflected in the works of Edgeworth and Wicksteed.

References

Beveridge, William (1929), 'Allyn Abbott Young', *Economica*, 25 (April), pp. 1–3.
Blitch, Charles (1995), *Allyn Young: The Peripatetic Economist*, Basingstoke and London: Macmillan Press Ltd.
Bober, M.M. (1927), *Marx's Interpretation of History*, Cambridge: Harvard University Press.
Chamberlin, Edward (1933), *The Theory of Monopolistic Competition*, Cambridge: Harvard University Press.
Currie, Lauchlin (1974), 'The 'leading sector' model of growth in developing countries', *Journal of Economic Studies*, 1, pp. 1–16.
Ely, Richard T. (1893), *Outlines of Economics*, New York: Hunt and Eaton.

Ely, Richard T., Thomas S. Adams, Max O. Lorenz and Allyn A. Young (1908), *Outlines of Economics*, New York: Macmillan.
Ely, Richard T., Thomas S. Adams, Max O. Lorenz and Allyn A. Young (1916), *Outlines of Economics*, New York: Macmillan.
Ely, Richard T., Thomas S. Adams, Max O. Lorenz and Allyn A. Young (1923), *Outlines of Economics*, New York: Macmillan.
Ely, Richard T., Thomas S. Adams, Max O. Lorenz and Allyn A. Young (1930), *Outlines of Economics*, New York: Macmillan.
Emmett, Ross B. (1999), 'Allyn A. Young', *American National Biography*, Vol. 24, New York: Oxford University Press, pp. 146–48.
Gregory, T.E. (1929), 'Professor Allyn A. Young', *Economic Journal*, 39(154), 297–301.
Jones, G.T. (1933), *Increasing Returns*, Cambridge: Cambridge University Press.
Knight, Frank H. (1921), *Risk, Uncertainty and Profit*, Boston: Houghton Mifflin.
Krugman, Paul (1993), 'Toward a counter counterrevolution in development theory', *Annual Conference on Development Economics*, 1992, pp. 15–38.
Laidler, David (1993), 'Hawtrey, Harvard and the origins of Chicago tradition', *Journal of Political Economy*, 101(6), 1068–1103.
Laidler, David (1998), 'More on Hawtrey, Harvard and Chicago', *Journal of Economic Studies*, 25(1), pp. 4–24.
Marshall, Alfred (1890), *Principles of Economics*, London: Macmillan.
Mehrling, Perry G. (1996), 'The Monetary Thought of Allyn Abbott Young', *History of Political Economy*, 28(4), pp. 607–32.
Mehrling, Perry G. (1997), *The Money Interest and the Public Interest*, Cambridge and London: Harvard University Press.
Mehrling, Perry G. and R.J. Sandilands (1999), *Money and Growth: Selected Papers of Allyn Abbott Young*, London and New York: Routledge.
Mitchell, Wesley (1924), 'The prospects of economics', in Tugwell, R.G.(ed.), *The Trend of Economics*, New York: Alfred A. Knopf.
Murphy, K. M., A. Schleifer and R. Vishny (1989), 'Industrialisation and the big push', *Journal of Political Economy*, 97(5), pp. 1003–26.
Newman, Peter (1987), 'Young, Allyn Abbott', in John Eatwell, Marray Milgate and Peter Newman (eds.), *The New Palgrave Dictionary of Economics*, Vol. 4 (Q to Z), London: Macmillan, pp. 937–39.
Nurkse, Ragnar (1953), *Problems of Capital Formation in Underdeveloped Countries*, Oxford: Basil Blackwell.
Pareto, Vilfredo (1906/1971), *Manuel of Political Economy*, New York: A.M. Kelly.

Reed, Harold Lyle (with Allyn A. Young) (1925) *Principles of Corporate Finance*, Boston: Houghton Mifflin.
Riley, Eugene B. (with Allyn A. Young) (1925) *Economics for Secondary Schools*, Boston: Houghton Mifflin.
Robbins, Lionel (1971), *An Autobiography of an Economist*, London: Macmillan.
Romer, Paul (1986), 'Increasing returns and long-run growth', *Journal of Political Economy*, 94, pp. 1002–38.
Romer, Paul (1989), 'Capital accumulation in the theory of long run growth', in R. J. Barro (ed.), *Modern Business Cycle Theory*, Cambridge: Harvard University Press, pp. 52–127.
Rosenstein-Rodan, Paul (1943), 'Problems of industrialisation in eastern and south-eastern Europe', *Economic Journal*, 53, pp. 202–11.
Rosenstein-Rodan, Paul (1961), 'Notes on the theory of the big push', in H.S. Ellis and H.C. Wallaich (ed.), *Economic Development of Latin America*, London: Macmillan.
Schumpeter, Joseph A. (1937), 'Allyn A. Young', *Encyclopaedia of Social Sciences*, New York: Macmillan, pp. 514–15.
Schumpeter, Joseph A. (1951/2003), *Ten Great Economists From Marx to Keynes*, San Diego: Simon Publications.
Taussig, Frank W., Charles J. Bullock and Harold H. Burbank (1930), 'Allyn Abbott Young (1876–1929)', *Proceedings of the American Academy of Arts and Sciences*, 64(12), pp. 550–53.
Veblen, Thorstein (1898), 'Why is economics not an evolutionary science?', *Quarterly Journal of Economics*, 12(4), pp. 373–97.
Walras, Léon (1874/1954), *Elements of Pure Economics*, Homewood: Irvin.
Young, Allyn (1911), 'Some limitations of the value concept', *Quarterly Journal of Economics*, 25(3), pp. 409–28. Reprinted in Young (1927), pp. 198–212.
Young, Allyn (1927), *Economic Problems: New and Old*, Boston and New York: Houghton Mifflin Company.
Young, Allyn (1928), 'Increasing returns and economic progress', *Economic Journal*, 38(152), 527–42.
Young, Allyn (1990), 'Nicholas Kaldor's notes on Allyn Young's LSE lectures 1927–29', *Journal of Economic Studies*, 17(3/4), pp. 18–114.

2

Intellectual Influences on Allyn Young

In this chapter, we examine intellectual influences on Young. Richard T. Ely was the earliest influence as Young learnt his initial economics from his book *Outlines of Economics* and later was his Ph.D. student at Wisconsin. Adam Smith's growth theory, based on the relationship between the division of labour and market size, influenced Young as he made Smith as his starting point in his famous paper on increasing returns and economic progress. English political economy exercised a deep influence on Young as it provided the equipment to deal with practical problems. Alfred Marshall's *Principles of Economics* was used by Young not only for teaching his classes but also to update Ely's *Outlines* so as to reflect latest advances in theory. Young made use of Thorstein Veblen's evolutionary perspective and his concept of cumulative causation in his theory of growth.

It will be noted that Young did not follow any of these thinkers blindly. He himself was an original thinker and always added his own variations, modifications and nuances. He was also a great critic. He did not hesitate to criticise them if there was some flaw in their reasoning, or if he held a different opinion. He was always looking to refine the ideas of these thinkers and to make his own contribution through this process. He accepted ideas from many schools of thought and realised that they had their strengths. In fact many of these schools were complements, and as a result, made economic science much richer.

Richard T. Ely (1854–1943) and the German Historical School

Richard T. Ely was a doctorate student of Karl Knies, who was one of the founders of the German historical school.[1] After graduating from Columbia in 1876, Ely went to Heidelberg (Germany) where he spent three years for his Ph.D. work. In 1881, he joined the faculty of John Hopkins University, which was modelled on German universities. In 1885, Ely, along with E.R.A. Seligman and Henry C. Adams, founded the American Economic Association. In 1892, he moved to the University of Wisconsin as head of economics, political science and history. At Wisconsin, the faculty included Frederick J. Turner and John R. Commons. In 1893, Ely brought out the first edition of his *Outlines of Economics* which became an extremely popular economics textbook in American universities. Young was to revise and co-author this book with Ely and others for its second edition published in 1908 and three further editions.

Ely is regarded by some as the grandfather of the American institutional school as he was teacher and mentor of both Commons and Wesley C. Mitchell. He also taught Thorstein Veblen political economy at John Hopkins. Ely also had an activist bent of mind and socialist leanings. For example, in trying to promote German historicism at John Hopkins University, he came into sharp conflict with his conservative colleague Simon Newcomb. Despite warning from President Gilman, Ely resumed his advocacy of socialism in 1891 and ultimately quit in 1892. At Wisconsin he again got into trouble and was accused of spreading socialism and inciting labour strikes. He was saved by sympathetic American scholars who united in the defence of academic freedom. Although

---

[1] Knies's other American students included John Bates Clark, E.R.A. Seligman, Herbert Baxter Adams and Andrew Dexter White. His students also included many famous Austrians such as Eugen von Bohm-Bawerk and Friedrich von Wieser.

exonerated in the hearing, he had to admit that he did not hold the views ascribed to him. Ely turned conservative in later years, giving up on the labour movement, and concentrating mostly on land economics.

Ely was a man of varied interests. Apart from the American Economic Association, Ely founded several organisations such as the Institute of Land Economics and Public Utilities and the American Bureau of Industrial Research (along with Commons) to collect and publish source materials. He also had several business interests such as the promotion of the University Heights residential area of Madison, investment in real estate development known as Madison Park in Charlottesville, speculation in western orchards through the North-western Land and Improvement Company of Tacoma, the financing of the Wisconsin Chapter of Alpha Delta Phi and financing of several small businesses. He also took keen interest in the role that churches and religious organisations played in socio-economic development.

Young, at Hiram College, studied economics from the 1893 (first edition) of *Outlines*. There, in the winter term of 1894, he took one course in political economy securing 96 per cent (Blitch 1995, p. 5). Young not only learnt his initial economics from Ely's book but later became his Ph.D. student at Wisconsin. Young was also influenced by his 'look and see' method. No theory or doctrine was to be accepted blindly but only in relation to facts and observations made available through induction. In an evolutionary system where new facts are emerging all the time, a theory was valid for a particular stage of society, and not for all times or all places. As noted by Blitch (1995, p. 9), Ely favoured a broad general approach to economics through grounding in other social sciences. Young was aware of the interconnections of various social sciences, so economics needed to be studied in relation to the other social sciences. At the same time like every social science, economics had its own orientation, so a complete synthesis of all social sciences was not possible. Every social science, including economics, retained its own orientation, scope and viewpoint.

Ely, through Karl Knies at Heidelberg, was deeply influenced by the German historical school. The founders of this school—Wilhelm Roscher, Karl Knies and Bruno Hildebrand—vigorously assailed the doctrines of the classical school and its deductive method. As Ely (1893/1900, pp. 389–90) wrote: "They went back of the old premises—self-interest, private property, demand and supply—and analyzed and explained them. Tracing out historical development, they naturally came to the conclusion asserted by Knies that economic policies were not absolutely but relatively true. There are two ways in which a doctrine may be stated absolutely. We may claim that it is good for all time (perpetualism), and we may claim that it is good for all places (cosmopolitanism). Both of these Knies denied, holding that policies are relatively good or bad; that policies must vary with time and place. The Germans thus took a new attitude with respect to free trade and protection, holding that neither was absolutely good nor absolutely bad, but that the correct policy for a country cannot be told without acquaintance with the particular circumstances of a country."

The historical school had many adherents especially in Germany and Italy. Later it also became influential in America and England. There were thinkers who adopted a moderate line combining deduction and induction, chief among them being Adolf Wagner in Germany. Alfred Marshall and Henry Sidgwick in England favoured a middle ground thus endeavouring to unite English and German thoughts. "The German writers, while not failing by any means to use the deductive method, and not neglecting altogether pure theory, laid chief emphasis upon inductive methods, and gave their attention successfully to the description of institutions and the collection of a vast mass of historical and statistical facts" (ibid., pp. 390–91).

Young, like Ely, was influenced by the historical method but subscribed to a more balanced view. For one, he also appreciated the deductive or a priori method of the English political economy. According to Young, though it appeared to deduce from assumed premises, it actually took its data from real life. At any rate, this was the only scientific method to arrive at generalisations. At the same time, he also appreciated the role of the historical method in drawing attention to institutions, which, in his view, were both masters and servants of men. As a result, economists have now generally come to accept that a given order is in no way permanent or final. Young also praised the historical method for providing us with wisdom and aesthetic quality.

And wisdom, as wise men have told us, is not to be had by contemplating only those measurable or numerable aspects of things with which the abstract or mechanistic sciences deal. Wisdom requires also a balanced view of the concrete diversities of life. So far as this important element in wisdom can be gained or imparted, it must largely be through historical studies. (Young 1928a; Mehrling and Sandilands 1999, p. 25)

Further,

History explains the present in terms of its specific relations to the past, and in so doing it reinterprets the past in terms of the interests and problems of the present. Its quality … is aesthetic, rather than … scientific. (Ibid., p. 26)

Young was appreciative of historical studies to the extent they regarded the structure of a nation's economic life as a 'historical category', something peculiar to a given nation at a given time, a product of the past, and to be understood, therefore, only by the study of that past. But in Young's opinion, most historicists were guilty of overreach and overkill. As Young (1929a; Mehrling and Sandilands 1999, pp. 124–25) writes: "The wisdom of particular economic policies is relative to place and time, and the general or supposedly universal 'laws' of abstract economics need to be supplemented by or even subordinated to an analysis of the concrete facts of each nation's economic growth. If they had gone no further these critics would have found many to agree with them. But the founders of the school (Karl Knies, whose work, *Die politische Oekonomie vom Standpunkte der geschichtlichen Methode*, appeared in 1853, is a notable exception) made of what they called the historical method something peculiarly arbitrary and doctrinaire. Instead of looking to history for the particular antecedents of those concrete differences of economic structure in which they professed to be interested, they proposed to derive from history universal and binding laws, akin to the laws of the physical sciences."

Ely, at Wisconsin, was so impressed with Young's abilities that he secured for him a place in the US Bureau of Census under Walter F. Wilcox beginning in September 1900 (Blitch 1995, p. 10). At the Bureau, Young established lifelong friendships not only with Wilcox but also with Thomas S. Adams and Wesley Mitchell. Wilcox, like Ely, was impressed with Young's intellect and offered him another year of employment at the Bureau. Young turned it down in order to complete his Ph.D. at Wisconsin. He was awarded his Ph.D. in 1902 on 'A Discussion of Age Statistics', which was the direct outgrowth of his work at the Bureau. Although Ely was his official advisor for the thesis, Wilcox was the de facto advisor not only reading it but also advising Young on its contents. He also got it published as a bulletin of the Bureau in 1904 for which Young was paid $400. Wilcox also recommended Young to his friend David Starr Jordan (President of Stanford) for a position at Stanford and later helped him secure an appointment as a professor at Cornell.

Ely and other faculty members at Wisconsin influenced Young in forming a strong commitment to public and business service. The faculty members there worked to improve the lives and working conditions of labour, to remedy municipal abuses, to renovate charitable and penal institutions, to redistribute and readjust taxes, to establish greater public control over utilities and corporations, all making Wisconsin the most progressive state (ibid, p. 10). Young carried this attitude of public service, imbued at Wisconsin, throughout his life. For example, as mentioned in Chap. 1, he served on President Woodrow Wilson's team to negotiate peace at Paris after WWI. He also served as the President of the American Economic Association, the American Statistical Association and Section F of the British Association for the Advancement of Economic Science. While at Cornell, he also served as a chairman of a tax law revision commission and was also elected as a chairman of the committee for academic freedom and tenure.

Ely, on Young's application, appointed him at Wisconsin for a year (1905–1906), and it was at Wisconsin, along with Thomas Adams and Max Lorenz who were also among the teaching faculty, that Young felt that Ely's textbook was sorely in need of revision. For one thing, the empirical part had become outdated. For another, major advances in economic theory had occurred with the publication of Alfred Marshall's *Principles of Economics*. Ely consented to the revision provided the other three co-authored the book with him. Thus began an association for Young with the *Outlines of Economics* starting with the 1908 edition, and was to last for three further editions in 1916, 1923 and 1930. In the 1908

2 Intellectual Influences on Allyn Young

edition, Young contributed 12 chapters (out of 36) amounting to one-third of the book, all of which except the one on business organisation (Chap. 10) were theoretical in nature. Young patterned these chapters along the lines of Marshall's theories. He asked his publishers to send a presentation copy to Marshall and wrote the following letter to him (dated 3 February 1911):

> I imagine that the publishers have sent you a copy of the revised edition of Ely's Outlines of Economics. If you have the time to examine it you will note that the chapters on Economic Theory, especially those on Value and Price, Distribution, Rent, Wages, and Interest, show more clearly than any other American textbook the influence of your work in Economics… I wish to take this opportunity of saying that to my mind the general view of the economic process embodied in your writings is one which is bound to have an increasing influence in American writing… [A]mong the younger men there is a strong feeling that an excessive use and development of the marginal utility analysis will not get us very far away from argument in a circle, and that we have got to apply ourselves to that careful analysis of the forces of demand and supply which has its best presentation in your writings.

Charles Blitch (1995, p. 28) notes that Young's chapters were not copycat versions of Marshall, for he added his own interpretations and criticisms. During 1909–1910, *Outlines* sold more than 6000 copies—more than the combined sales of the next two competitive textbooks in the market.[2] Regarding the next edition of *Outlines*, Young was willing to join provided he was given the final say regarding his chapters and any other chapters assigned to him.[3] But Ely wrote back saying that Young's chapters posed the most difficulty in terms their not being in harmony with the rest of the book. He also said that Adams objected more and more to the whole productivity theory.[4] Young suggested that Ely should secure some new co-authors adding: "You do not like my treatment of theory and I am so stubborn to change its essential features."[5] Ely tried to

---

[2] Ely to Young dated 8 July 2010.
[3] Young to Ely dated 3 November 1913.
[4] Ely to Young dated 16 March 1914.
[5] Young to Ely dated 24 November 1914.

mollify Young saying that his chapters were the most original and the success of the book was largely due to them.[6] Finally, after this long discussion, it was decided that Young was to be the general editor, not only writing his own chapters, but soliciting those of others, and often rewriting some of them. The third edition, published in October 1916, was an immediate success, with MIT and Cornell adopting it. For the fourth edition, Young was reluctant to participate as he had never been especially interested in it. Moreover, he wanted to write his own book and introduce a very different kind of economic theory. But he showed willingness if it was on his own terms.[7] Ely, although taken aback by Young's tone, quickly replied saying that he would agree to Young's terms. Young was again given the responsibility of overseeing the new edition. It appears that despite being busy Young agreed to the revision because of the extra money—he was paid $1000 for the supervision—he needed because of his growing family responsibilities. When it was published in September 1923, it retained its place as the country's leading textbook. Though for the fifth edition which came out in 1930, Young had committed to revising only the money and banking chapters,[8] he had actually revised the first 13 chapters before his untimely death in 1929.[9]

According to Perry Mehrling (1997, p. 23), Young's attempts to bring in elements of classical political economy into Ely's text were "an attempt to sharpen Ely's message and to broaden its appeal by rooting that message in economic theory rather than Christian ethics". They were not entirely a conservative move designed to blunt Ely's progressive ideas or his message of social reform as some like Joseph Dorfman (1959) and Edward Ross (1991) had interpreted (Mehrling 1997, pp. 22–3). In a letter to Ely, on the 1923 edition, Young stated that at the time of the first (1893) edition, progressive message was required; but now there was a danger that progressivism may go too far.[10] In the 1908 edition, Ely had objected to Young's stress on income distribution as it appeared too close

---

[6] Ely to Young dated 16 March 1915.
[7] Young to Ely dated 14 July 1920.
[8] Young to Ely dated 28 June 1927.
[9] See preface of 1930 edition, p. v.
[10] Young to Ely dated 14 November 1921.

to J.B. Clark's income inequality arising from his marginal productivity theory. Also, he did not want to yield ground to advocates of laissez-faire, as he believed income distribution could be influenced through institutional intervention.[11] In the 1908 text, on Ely's insistence, Young explained that it is only about the relationship between production and distribution and had no ethical implications. Ely, in the preface, repeated the same message (Ely et al. 1908, p. vi).

The revision of various editions of the *Outlines* was not the only point of contention between Young and Ely. When Young was on a leave of absence from Stanford for a year's appointment at Harvard during 1910–1911, Ely had offered a professorship to Young, as he himself wanted to secure a position on the Wisconsin Tax Commission. But later it emerged that this was conditional on William Scott's resignation, but since he failed to get appointed to Wisconsin Railroad Commission, the situation had changed. In the meantime, Young had asked for a salary increase to $3500 from David Starr Jordan (President of Stanford) on the basis of this offer, on the surface appearing to use a fictitious offer to get a raise in salary. When Jordan wrote to Charles Van Hise, President of Wisconsin University, it emerged that Hise knew nothing about Ely's offer to Young.[12] Although Jordan ultimately realised that Young was not at all at fault,[13] the whole episode left a bitter taste in Young's mouth as he felt that Ely had not only misled him but also failed to take full responsibility in the matter.

But despite these differences, Young continued to be in touch with Ely and in fact sought his advice while at St Louis about an offer from Wilcox of a Professorship at Cornell for a salary of $4000. Although Ely advised him to stay put at St Louis for the time being, Young decided to go to Cornell as otherwise he felt that he may go to seed as far as scientific work

---

[11] In this regard, according to Mehrling (1997, p. 20), Ely's (1914) *Property and Contract* is concerned with the way the evolving socio-economic order, in particular the evolving institutions of private property and contract, affects the evolving distribution of wealth.

[12] In letter to Jordan, dated 13 February 1911, Hise confidentially stated that Dr. Ely was very sanguine and that Jordan should accept Young's account of the conversation between Ely and Young in which the offer was made.

[13] In a letter to Young, dated 19 March 1925, he stated: "Please do not worry about this matter in the least for it does not 'rankle' in the mind of anyone else except yourself."

was concerned.[14] And despite these differences, Young continued to cooperate in the revision of *Outlines* till he died. But Young's friendship with Ely had been severely tested and when in 1917 the latter requested Young for some 'war work' on the War Trade Board, Young replied: "The difficulty is, as I see it, the land problem is not yet a 'war problem'."[15]

This would appear to relate to Ely's preoccupation with issues related to land. Earlier, Ely had sought Young's help in reading through the manuscript of his *Property and Contract*, with suggestions for its improvement. Young was initially reluctant not because he did not want to help Ely but because he felt he had no special expertise in the subject. In his letter of 13 March 1912 to Ely, Young stated: "This is to be taken as meaning that I would be pleased to read the book if you still desire it, but that I could give it only such criticisms as would occur to the 'general reader'." Young in his letter of 8 January 1913, while offering criticisms, also praised Ely for the wholesomeness of the point of view and simplicity of presentation. But at the same time, he advised Ely to tone down explanations and repetitions, that reflected his class notes to make himself clear to the students. He also advised Ely to make it clear in the preface that he was presenting, not an original study, only economic and social aspects of institutions. Since his work and social point of view had already become widely diffused through his students, it might not strike the reader with a sense of freshness than if it had been published 15 years earlier. Ely took Young's criticisms seriously and revised his manuscript thoroughly even delaying its publication. Ely also sought Young's advice whether he should bring out the book in one or two volumes. Young in a letter dated 18 December 1913 replied: "I do not think that the volume of sales will be perceptively less for a two volume work. The work is one that all of your friends and former students have for a long time anxiously awaited. It represents, it seems to me, your most important work, and I am confident it will have a large sale whether published as two volumes or one." Before *Property and Contract*, Young had helped Ely (1905) with the revision of *Labour Movement in America* (Mehrling 1997, p. 19). As

---

[14] Young's letter to Ely dated 4 February 1913. See also Blitch (1995, pp. 39–40).
[15] Young's letter to Ely dated 23 August 1917. See also Blitch (1995, p. 68).

a result, Ely felt growing respect and personal attachment to Young on account of his intellectual gifts.[16]

The book was finally published in 1914, and on receiving a copy of the two volume work, Young in a letter to Ely dated 14 December 1914 wrote: "It is only recently that I received the copy of your new two volume work from Macmillan. It is immensely improved since I saw it in manuscript and I have no doubt that it will be regarded as your *magnum opus*. Its publication must be a source of much pride and satisfaction to you. To those who studied under you at Wisconsin the book must have a peculiarly personal appeal. More than anything else you have done[,] it is the crystallization of your teaching."

Adam Smith (1723–1790)

Adam Smith is widely regarded as the father of economics. Born in Kirkcaldy (Scotland), he studied first at the Glasgow University and later won a scholarship to study at Balliol College, Oxford. At Glasgow he was influenced by moral philosopher Francis Hutcheson. After returning from Oxford, he spent some time at Edinburgh where he befriended David Hume and other leading lights of the Scottish Enlightenment. Although trained to be a clergyman, he became a professor at Glasgow in 1751. There he first taught logic and then moral philosophy. His first treatise was *The Theory of Moral Sentiments* (1759). In this he tried to find a middle ground between Hume and Hutcheson through the device of the 'impartial spectator'. His lecture notes from 1762–1763 and 1763–1764 became *Lectures on Jurisprudence*. His 1762–1763 private lectures on rhetoric in Glasgow were published as *Lectures on Rhetoric and Belles Lettres*. In 1764, he resigned his post at Glasgow to accompany the young Henry Scott, Duke of Buccleuch, on a European tour. In Paris, he met Physiocrats like Francois Quesnay and Jacques Turgot. On his return to Scotland, he composed his masterpiece *The Wealth of Nations* (1776), the core of which had already been articulated in the early 1760s in his *Lectures on Jurisprudence*. The purpose of this treatise was to influence

---

[16] Ely to Young dated 16 March 1914.

government policy—to repeal Mercantilist-era laws which impeded internal and external commerce. The *Wealth of Nations* was not only a scathing attack on mercantilism, but it also expounded the economic principles underlying the system of natural liberty. It provided the British public with a new way of thinking—how a nation's economic life and policy should be organised. Citing this book as his inspiration, William Pitt, after becoming the prime minister in 1784, began dismantling much of Mercantilist-era apparatus. In 1778, Smith became Scottish commissioner of customs and spent the remaining years of his life in Edinburgh.

In his 1928 paper on increasing returns and economic progress, Young built on Smith's aphorism that the division of labour is limited by the size of the market. As Young (1928b, p. 529) writes: "That theorem, I have always thought, is one of the most illuminating and fruitful generalisations which can be found anywhere in the whole literature of economics. In fact, as I am bound to confess, I am taking it as the text of this paper, in much the way that some minor composer borrows a theme from one of the masters and adds certain developments and variations of his own." Young defined market in an inclusive sense, not as an outlet of goods for a particular industry, but as an outlet of goods in general. In this sense the market is defined by the total volume of production. This at once leads to the notion that capacity to buy depends on the capacity to produce, and Smith's dictum amounts to the theorem that the division of labour in large part depends on the division of labour. Young insisted that this was more than a tautology for the forces of disequilibrium are continually defeating those of equilibrium. Every advance leads to further advances leading to further unsettling effects. Thus, according to Young, change becomes progressive and propagates itself in a cumulative way (ibid., p. 533). Although he did not use the word, Young cast Smith's dictum in terms of cumulative causation. From this Currie (1981, 1997) drew the conclusion that the cause of growth is growth itself.

Smith talked about many factors such as the proportion of productive labourers employed, the rate of saving and capital accumulation not only to employ more productive hands but also to equip them with better equipment and tools, institutional arrangements facilitating or hindering growth, the role of foreign trade in enlarging the market, and public investment in transport and communication in integrating the domestic market. All were important in so far as they advanced the relationship between market size and economic growth. This led Joseph Schumpeter (1954) to remark that for Adam Smith, the division of labour is the only factor in growth. Young, therefore, in building on this relationship went to the crux of the growth problem.

Smith also stated that because of the nature of agricultural operations, the division of labour was not as complete as in industry. In agriculture, the same person was a tiller, the sower, the reaper and the harvester at different times in a year. So specialisation of tasks was not as advanced as in manufacturing. He also held that what became known as the law of diminishing returns was especially operative in agriculture. Young, on the other hand, had a macroeconomic or generalised notion of increasing returns. For him, the law of diminishing returns operated in an extremely elastic manner and was not a binding constraint on growth. He also defined the market in an inclusive sense of an outlet for goods in general, an aggregate of economic activities tied together by trade.

Smith held that man's self-interest could be used to society's advantage. If each man is engaged in furthering his own self-interest, he unintentionally ends up promoting public interest. But Smith had a very broad approach to self-interest as a desire to better one's condition; it is a desire which we are born with and it stays with us till we die. Man's self-interest propels him to save, accumulate and become rich. Young agreed with this broad approach to self-interest but rejected the later concepts of hedonism, utilitarianism, rational economic man and psychological postulates as the basis of economics. He was also of the opinion that man is self-regarding only with respect to certain dealings pertaining to buying and selling, or lending and borrowing.

In *The Wealth of Nations*, Smith regarded political economy as an art—a study with a practical end: "Political Economy, considered as a branch of the science of a statesman or legislator, proposes two distinct objects: first, to provide a plentiful revenue or subsistence for the people, or, more properly, to enable them to provide such a revenue or subsistence for themselves; and secondly, to supply the state or common weal with a revenue sufficient for the public service. It proposes to enrich both the people and the sovereign" (Smith 1776/1976, I, p. 449). Young thought of political economy as a science as well as an art, but considered it more an art when addressing communal problems of economic life.

Smith was very much sceptical of the vested business interests. According to him business men are driven by monopoly spirit and often conspired to subvert the public interest by raising prices. Proposals of law from this group should always be examined with great precaution before being adopted. In order to keep these classes in check, Smith suggested their members be made to compete with each other. Thus, to keep domestic monopolies in check, he advocated free trade. He also called for the dismantling of mercantilist apparatus based on favours and handicaps. He advocated "the obvious and simple" system of natural liberty which establishes itself once all favours and handicaps are dispensed with. In this system the state has three basic tasks—defence, justice, and public works and institutions.

Was Smith a laissez-faire economist? He was a complex economist who favoured self-interest as long as it was a means to the promotion of public interest. If self-interest came in conflict with the larger public interest or if public interest was inadequately promoted, Smith favoured intervention. For example, he favoured public investment in transport and communication to integrate the domestic market. He favoured publicly funded education for the poor to counter the ill effects (e.g., monotony of repetitive work or operations) of the division of labour. He also favoured publicly funded public health measures to check offensive diseases like leprosy.

According to Young, Smith was not a blind follower of laissez-faire. His main message was competition rather than a completely hands-off approach to economic matters. Young himself was neither a laissez-faire economist nor did he like undue intervention in economic matters. He was a great believer in institutions in solving communal problems. This included appropriate institutions to help competition work better. For example, he favoured Federal Reserve control of credit because it was inherently unstable and at the root of business cycles. Similarly, he advocated measures of monopoly control to check the subversion of public interest. In an evolutionary system, newer problems are always emerging which cannot be dealt with by hands-off approaches.

Smith talked of *natural* order and its manifestations as a guide to human action. For example, he stated that the state had no business in superintending the industry of private people as capital would be diverted from its *natural* course to inefficient production, affecting growth. Similarly, he stated that in the long run the market price of a commodity had a tendency to gravitate towards its *natural* price. Further, since industry of a country cannot be out of proportion to its total capital, capital should be left free to find its *natural* employments. The *natural* course of capital was first agriculture, then industry and finally commerce. Lastly, he also talked about the system of *natural* liberty which comes into being on its own accord once all restraints and preferences are removed. It is clear that his effort was to discover natural laws as a practical guide to human action.

Young thought that economists of the second half of the eighteenth century got two kinds of natural orders badly mixed up. Though they did not base their case for laissez-faire because it was natural, that was the way they dressed it up. Later economists like Ricardo and Mill favoured laissez-faire in specific areas which gave practical advantages. In a letter to Frank Knight, dated 9 September 1926, Young wrote:

> One [kind] was the Newtonian order—something which would prevail in spite of all men might do; the other was the natural order of the 'natural law' writers—something which had to be discovered and attained. Because of Adam or some other good reason men had fallen away from the natural order and it had to be regained, either through grace, or, as the 18th century preferred to believe, by the exercise of reason. It is perfectly clear to me as I read Quesney that to him the natural order was the 'best conceivable' order, and it also happened that he thought that the laissez-faire policy gave the best results. One finds the same confusion in Adam Smith, but I do not believe for a moment that either Quesney or Smith really based their case for laissez-faire because it was 'natural'. That is, as I see it, was merely the way in which they dressed the thing up. Smith, it is clear, did not like the special favours the capitalist employers (business men) of his day retained, nor did he like the special favours for which they continued to ask. In fact he did not like business men at all, and thought that they were monopolists in spirit and that, in some way, they ought to be made to compete… [I]f Smith had been writing in the middle of 19th century, I am pretty sure he

would not have advocated laissez-faire… Ricardo, Mill, and the rest argued for laissez-faire in respect of international trade and in some other specific fields, but here they based their conclusions on what they thought were the positive advantages laissez-faire gave. Practically all of these so-called laissez-faire economists were, as you know, favourable to labor legislation.

Smith's main concern in the *Wealth of Nations* was growth. Since the division of labour depends on the size of the market, an open market overcomes the narrowness of the domestic market and furthers the division of labour. So a discussion of foreign trade was integral to political economy. As for Young, economics without foreign trade was like Hamlet without the prince of Denmark. In his review of *The Trend of Economics* (by Tugwell 1924), Young (1927a, p. 249, f.n.1) deplored that neither the articles that Tugwell included nor his bibliography indicated the importance of international trade in economics. He viewed trade as a source of wealth. In his article on 'The creator of wealth', Young (1929b; Mehrling and Sandilands 1999, p. 151) stated that in the growth of our economic civilisation, it has been commerce, rather than agriculture or industry, that has led the way. Further, "Men do not produce or manufacture goods in the blind hope that in some way buyers will be found. In manufacturing and agriculture alike production increases only when larger markets are available. History of commerce has been the history of the growth of markets" (ibid., p. 151).

English Political Economy

Young displayed very broad catholicity of views. He was not only influenced by the German historical school, but even more by the English political economy and its method. While the historical school had its aesthetic value, gave us wisdom and understanding, it did not provide the apparatus to solve the communal problems of economic life. It would therefore appear that Young was attracted to the English political economy chiefly because of its instrumental value in dealing with practical problems.

English political economy was a practical subject arising out of the efforts of this school to deal with issues of national concern. For example, the rise in food prices and the consequent rise in rents after the Napoleonic wars prompted Ricardo to undertake a thorough investigation into these issues based on scarcity of land and the operation of the law of diminishing returns. As inferior grades are brought under cultivation, the conflict between landlords and capitalists received attention. Similarly, frequent labour riots against the use of machinery brought the conflict between labour and capital into sharp focus. Thus Smith's message of harmony of interests could not be taken for granted, nor his optimism that the stationery state was too far away to call for serious analysis.

Many of these economists were social reformers. Smith concerned himself with reforming governments of the errors of mercantilism. He was also of the opinion that governments were unproductive spenders par excellence. So a nation was never ruined by private prodigality and misconduct as sometimes it was by public extravagance and misconduct. He advised governments to mind their own business rather than superintending private people's industry. He advocated the system of natural liberty because in it even an ordinary worker enjoys a standard of living many times higher than a savage king. All these economists, as Young noted, were favourably inclined towards labour legislation to protect the interests of workers. Many of them advocated voluntary restraint in checking their numbers so as to ameliorate their condition. Mill held that the problem of distribution could be influenced through human institutions. Some were also concerned with the problem of the business cycle and its effect on society in terms of unemployment and deterioration of living standards of the poor.

Many had faith in the power of education in improving the life of the poor. Smith, as already noted, advocated publicly funded education to counter the ill effects of the division of labour. "In a similar way J. S. Mill and other Malthusians proposed to improve the economic status of wage-earners by acquainting them with the relation between the increase of population and movement of wages" (Young 1925, 1927a, footnote 1, p. 234).

The second characteristic of the English political economy related to its abstract deductive method proceeding from assumed premises. Young stated that although they presented their doctrines as if flowing from first principles, in reality the real soundness of the system was due to its internal consistency. This would be true of any system whether deductive or institutional. Their emphasis on deduction was merely an expositional form.[17]

Young held that these postulates of deductive economics were just common sense. "One cannot tell just how many 'postulates' deductive economics requires. Nor would there be any practical purpose in trying to find out. The postulates change and grow as experience grows and as experience is better formulated. A very considerable part of our postulates can never be found anywhere else than in that direct and subtle kind of knowledge we call 'common sense'" (Young 1925, 1927a, p. 257).

In Young's opinion, induction and deduction are terms properly applicable to forms of exposition and verification, not to thinking. "I hazard a guess that in the actual construction of economic science analogies and 'models' have had much to do with the form generalizations have taken. Thus our generalizations relating to diminishing and marginal utility are not deductions from psychological postulates, but appear to be organizations of our knowledge of a larger field of economic behavior upon the analogy of or after the model of generalizations already successfully established with respect to the behavior of the market place" (Young 1925, 1927a, footnote 2, pp. 258–9).

Moreover, Young disliked the distinction between theory and practice or pure and applied economics. Since political economy is a practical subject, the divorce between theory and practice appears contrived. Quoting Lane Cooper's *The Greek Genius and its Influence*, Young (1925, 1927a, p. 257, footnote 1) stated: "The distinction between theory and practice we owe, indeed, like many another distinction, to the Greeks, but the divorce is our own contrivance. Accordingly, a theoretical

---

[17] "For exposition's sake, or because they thought logical consistency required it, or for some more subtle and obscure reason, economic theorists have often presented their doctrines as though they flowed from some first principle. But the first principle is generally purely ornamental, like the meaningless 'desire for wealth.' The real soundness of a system of thought depends upon its internal consistency and upon the accuracy with which it summarizes the pertinent parts of experience. These considerations hold true not only for so-called deductive economics (the 'deduction' is only a matter of expositional form) but also for 'institutional' or any other variety of economics" (Young 1925, 1927a, pp. 256–7).

knowledge of human, as of animal, behavior would mean to them the sort of knowledge that corresponds to the facts, and enabling one to deal with the facts in a practical way."

The third point regarding the English political economy relates to its insular character. Despite the criticisms of the opposed schools, it carried on in its own way working on its own problems rarely mindful of these criticisms. The other schools criticised its method or findings, but English political economy remained at the centre. These schools defined themselves in relation to it not vice versa.[18]

Despite the cross-fire from other schools, English political economy continued to grow and show extraordinary vitality. This was due to its inherent internal strengths without which its importance would have declined. It was in fact pronounced dead several times and was also referred to in the past tense. Yet its influence continued to grow because of these lasting sources of strength. Some critics have decried its doctrines as lacking in moral values, others have criticised it for not ridding itself of non-scientific elements. But these large non-scientific elements are inevitable in a discipline not content with ways and means but also concerned with questions of policy. English political economy has never made much use of history in any formal way, and whatever use it has made of history has been unsystematic and casual. "But historical elements are woven, almost indistinguishably, into its general contexture" (Young 1928a; Mehrling and Sandilands 1999, p. 26).

In Young's opinion, the most important thing which English political economy gives us is not finished economic truth or finished doctrines but a method which allows us to face any new problem and reach some reasoned conclusion. Whatever imperfections English political economy may have had, its method was not at fault. It was and is the only method through which new scientific knowledge can be acquired.

---

[18] "English political economy, through all its own changes, held a central place in the midst of the various currents of nineteenth century economic thought. The other 'schools,' for the most part, took over its doctrines and built upon them, modifying here and rejecting there, or seized upon some of its obscurer elements or upon elements to which it seemed to give too little weight and elaborated them into what appeared at first to be competing systems, or frankly defined their own position largely in terms of opposition to its method and disagreements with its findings. The central position which English political economy held was in fact a position of the storm centre" (Young 1928a; Mehrling and Sandilands 1999, p. 18).

Alfred Marshall (1842–1924)

Marshall was the founder of the Cambridge school of the neoclassical theory and authored its most successful textbook *Principles of Economics* (1890). Born in London, he studied mathematics at St John's College (Cambridge), but later developed interest in political economy. He was a lecturer at St John's during 1868–1875. After inheriting a small fortune from his uncle, he toured the US extensively and upon his return married Mary Paley who had been one of his students. In 1878, the couple moved to Bristol at the newly created Bristol University College where Marshall had been appointed as Principal and Professor of Political Economy. Both co-authored the book *Economics of Industry* (1879). Marshall also got two of his tracts *Pure Theory of Foreign Trade* and *Pure Theory of Domestic Values* printed for private circulation among economists. The first contained the famous 'offer curves' and the latter 'demand and supply' diagrams. In a letter to J.B. Clark in 1900, he claimed that he had come up with neoclassical theory even before reading W. Stanley Jevons's (1871) *Theory of Political Economy*. In 1885 he was elected as Professor of Political Economy at Cambridge where he presided over Cambridge economics till his retirement in 1908.

In 1890, he published his *Principles of Economics*, which appeared to occupy the middle ground between narrowly theoretical Ricardian economics and the inductive historical school. He emphasised the need to first decipher economic laws before applying them to practical policy problems. His famous supply-demand diagrams are presented in the inverted form taking price on the vertical and quantity on the horizontal axis. This was in contrast to Cournot who took price (the independent variable) on the horizontal axis and quantity (dependent variable) on the vertical axis. Moreover, Marshall took each market in isolation—the 'one thing at a time' approach which Young would later criticise—making use of the ceteris paribus assumption, and was the founder of partial equilibrium analysis. This contrasts with the general equilibrium approach where all markets are taken together. Below the title of the book, *Principles of Economics*, words '*Natura non facit saltum*' are mentioned meaning 'nature does not make jumps'. This neatly sums up the essence of the marginalist revolution led by Marshall at Cambridge.[19] After retirement, Marshall concentrated on *Industry and Trade* (1919) and *Money, Credit and Commerce* (1923). The second of these was probably put together by Mary Paley as his health by that time had declined considerably.

Young was impressed by Marshall (1890) and he not only used the *Principles of Economics* to revise Ely's *Outlines of Economics* but also used it as a text to teach his students. In his copy of the sixth edition of the *Principles*, Young made extensive notes on the margins and probably used this edition for teaching purposes. The publication of the *Principles* brought about major advances in economic theory and it became inevitable that universities upgraded their teaching to take them into account. As noted above, Young's theoretical chapters in *Outlines* were not a mere carbon copy of Marshall's theories, for Young, himself an original thinker, added his own comments and criticisms.

In his *Principles*, Marshall made a distinction between internal and external economies and combined this with the notion of a representative firm. As the representative firm expands its operations, not only internal economies of scale become available but also external economies which are associated with the growth of a group of related industries. Young took this distinction between internal and external economies as the starting point of his 1928 paper on increasing returns and economic progress. As Young (1928b, pp. 527–8) says: "This distinction has been useful in at least two different ways. In the first place it is, or ought to be, a safeguard against the common error of assuming that wherever increasing returns operate there is necessarily an effective tendency towards monopoly. In the second place it simplifies the analysis of the manner in which the prices of commodities produced under conditions of increasing returns are determined."

However, Young maintained that this distinction is necessarily a partial view as all external economies cannot be accounted for by adding up internal economies of separate firms. In the external field, change is quantitative as well as qualitative, and a representative firm loses its identity.

---

[19] Schumpeter (1951/2003, p. 96) highlights the influence of Cournot and Thünen on Marshall's *Principles*. Marshall himself, in the preface to the first edition, acknowledges the help of both Cournot and Thünen. Schumpeter further suggests that Marshall, given his reading habits, was unlikely to be aware of Jevons's or Léon Walras's works before 1890.

Equilibrium analysis assumes a condition of comparative stability, but when disequilibrium is the dominant force, such analysis becomes meaningless.

Thus in Young's opinion, presence of increasing returns does not lead to breakdown of competition nor necessarily imply a tendency towards monopoly. In fact economists of standing, as pointed out by Young (1928b, p. 531), had "suggested that increasing returns may be altogether illusory or maintained that where they are present they must lead to monopoly".[20] These economists made the error of looking for increasing returns under the equilibrium (and microeconomic) notion of economies of scale and ignoring (or forgetting) the role of external economies.

Marshall studied each market individually, ceteris paribus. He thus employed a two-variable diagrammatic approach which is essentially a partial equilibrium analysis. Although Young ranged himself against the partial equilibrium methods which made use of ceteris paribus assumptions, he also realised that this approach had a practical significance and was especially suitable for undergraduates. In a letter to Frank Knight, dated 5 March 1921, Young while discussing the "alltogether [sic]" and one-thing-at-a-time methods stated: "Now I am convinced of two things: One is that from the point of view of exposition,—especially for undergraduate students,—the Marshall method is better. The other is that the Marshall technique affords a better tool for handling a wide range of concrete economic problems. Of course you have to be careful to know just what you are doing, and to remember the ceteris paribus (Marshall himself forgets them when he is talking about consumers' surplus). The alltogether view is better as a final synthesis than as an introduction to economic theory." Further, "And I have yet to be convinced that for any except adepts the alltogether method is as good as the logically inferior method of one thing at a time." He also praised Marshall for making the oneness of the whole thing as clear as anyone can using this method.

Although Young disliked the partial equilibrium analysis, he disliked the general equilibrium approach even more. At least the partial

---

[20] Perhaps the reference was to Piero Sraffa (1926) as noted by Blitch (1995, p. 170), and Young's 1928 address "was partially an answer to Sraffa's contention that increasing returns are compatible only with monopoly".

equilibrium approach was easy to understand and dealt with practical problems. But, in his opinion, the general equilibrium method was even worse as it did not give us anything useful or anything which was not a truism. Comparing the general equilibrium method of Léon Walras and Vilfredo Pareto with the partial equilibrium approach, Young (1929a; Mehrling and Sandilands 1999, p. 130) wrote: "Other writers, notably Alfred Marshall … have shown that it is possible to put a proper emphasis on the interdependence of economic phenomenon while yet examining more closely and realistically the operations of the different parts of the economic mechanism, and while taking account of factors which make for change as well as of factors which make for stability."

In Young's opinion, partial equilibrium tools were unsuitable for the study of economic growth or for arriving at the social picture. "One cannot apply an additive process, and find a picture of the whole economy" (Young 1990, p. 73). Further, "Marshall's supply and demand curves hold ceteris paribus, and cannot be integrated to give the whole economic structure" (ibid., p. 26). In the adding-up process, there was a fallacy of composition involved. The social picture was much more than the sum of its parts. Therefore, all internal economies when added up do not give us all available external economies. Moreover, inputs are subject to diminishing returns at the micro level, but at the macro level when we allow for *ceteris non-paribus*, they combine to produce increasing returns. According to Young, diminishing returns may be a reality at the micro level under ceteris paribus conditions but meaningless at the macro level. "Following Von Thünen, modern economists, assuming land and machinery as given, draw decreasing productivity curves to labour. But what significance does this have? To what extent is this diminishing productivity a matter of the individual firm? Would integration give a good social picture?" (ibid., p. 73).

Young (1924) criticised Marshall's concept of consumer surplus. He felt that it was a general equilibrium concept and could not be analysed with the partial equilibrium demand-supply curve apparatus. He criticised Marshall for forgetting his own assumptions.[21] Young felt that

---

[21] "Marshall's was a one-thing-at-a-time method … there were times when he overlooked the full significance of the limitations he had put on himself" (Young 1924, p. 147).

Marshall had confused the demand curve with the marginal utility curve.[22] He also neglected the fact that expenditure on a commodity in question is conditioned by his other expenditures. That is, Marshall assumed that the marginal utility of money was constant over the entire range of a consumer's expenditures. Surplus in one commodity gets cancelled by others, so the concept was not additive. For a consumer, its sum would be zero.[23] Young, however, felt that consumers do gain but the nature of such gains must be sought in the analysis of costs, not in demand schedules. Thus, his conclusion was that there was really nothing in the concept.[24]

Young was appreciative of Marshall's offer curves where goods exchange for goods, and where a country's offer of a good at different rates of exchange (or prices), is also demand for the other country's goods.[25] Thus the idea of reciprocal demand is inbuilt in them and they come closest, among all neoclassical techniques, in capturing the essence of exchange. It is therefore obvious that intersection of two countries' offer curves would determine the quantities exchanged as well as the exchange ratios. Young applied the idea of reciprocal demand underlying offer curves to his theory of increasing returns. Given that "commodities exchanged are produced competitively under conditions of increasing returns and demand for each commodity is elastic, in the special sense that a small increase in its supply will be attended by an increase in the amounts of other commodities which can be had in exchange for it", there is no limit to the process of expansion even with stationary population and in the absence of any new discoveries in pure and applied sciences (Young 1928b, p. 534).

---

[22] "Marshall made an elementary slip. He confuses his own demand curve with a utility curve. Utility curves go back to Jevons who introduced the notion. They are made up by adding 'uses'… If you make it a curve, any point shows or measures the addition made to total satisfaction as the quantity of the good increases" (Young 1990, p. 39).

[23] "The different surpluses attributed to the consumer in his purchases of different commodities blot out one another. Consumers' surplus as Marshall measures it, is not additive. Its sum, for any consumer, comes precisely to zero" (Young 1924, p. 147).

[24] "Really there is nothing in the concept at all, except that we all gain when improvements in industrial processes make costs less, and we are able to demand a larger supply of goods with the same amount of sacrifice or exertion. We are better off, but how much better off is unmeasurable" (Young 1990, p. 41).

[25] Offer curves were first introduced by Marshall and later extended by Edgeworth.

Marshall made a distinction between the market period, the short run and the long run. In the market period, supply is vertical (since whatever is brought to the market has to be sold) and price is demand determined. In the short run, an increase in demand leads to increase in price as supply response is limited. In the long run, all factors become variable, firms can expand capacity and entry and exit also becomes feasible. So, supply and cost factors become dominant in price determination. This led to the conclusion that the shorter the period, the greater the role of demand in determining price. Advising Knight on his thesis regarding the need to redefine his short-time view, Young in a letter, dated 5 March 1921, stated: "Hasn't Marshall said about all that is worth saying on this particular point, when he suggests that the shorter the period of time that is taken into account, the larger the relative importance of demand as compared to supply?"

Because of the predominance of supply and cost factors in the long run, Marshall drew downward sloping supply curves as one of the possibilities. According to Marshall, the cost per unit of output falls as output grows, given time for reorganisation of industry. But as Young (1990) observed: "[T]hat is exactly the problem: how much time? The Marshallian statement is really meaningless. The 'period of time' is relative to costs, and costs are relative to period of time… A long-period supply curve is meaningless apart from the particular length of time considered: the curve is relative to the rate at which increasing returns exist. On the other side you cannot postulate a constant demand curve for a good over a long period. It would shift as a result of the very forces which shift a supply curve. *We need a theory of an equilibrium rate of progress. Probably, the optimum rate of progress which will keep the supply curve close up to the demand curve*" (pp. 47–8, emphasis added). There was no other problem where there was so much loose thinking as in the field of increasing returns. Young's overall conclusion was that reduction in cost in the long run is not due to any connection between prime and supplementary costs as Marshall had suggested. Nor are the advantages of increasing returns due to consolidation. Young emphasised that it is large production (at the macroeconomic level), not large-scale production (at the firm level), which leads to increasing returns (ibid., p. 54).

Young was influenced by Marshall in his distinction between internal and external economies, his two-variable method as a practical tool, his *Principles of Economics* which ushered in major advances in economic science and his concept of an offer curve based on the principle of reciprocal demand. But at the same time, Young was quick to point out flaws in his concepts and reasoning, as for example, in consumer surplus or increasing returns arising from the relation between prime and supplementary costs, or a falling supply curve due to expansion of the scale of firms at the micro level. Young used Marshall's book for classroom teaching, not blindly, but by adding his own variations. Similarly, he used new advances in the *Principles* to upgrade *Outlines* again with his own additions and modifications.

Thorstein Veblen (1857–1929)

Veblen was unconventional and quirky not only in his personal life but also as an academic. He always appeared as an outsider in both social and academic life. He was born of Norwegian immigrants and grew up at the family farm in Minnesota. Perhaps his Norwegian background and his relative isolation from American society are crucial factors to understanding his writings. For he was not only cut off from his parents' original culture, but also living in Norwegian society within America meant that he was not able to assimilate himself completely into American society. He spoke Norwegian at home and did not learn English until he was a teenager.[26] He graduated from Carlton College (Minnesota) in 1880 where he studied economics and philosophy under J.B. Clark. Then he moved east to John Hopkins and studied under the pragmatic philosopher Charles S. Peirce. Unable to obtain a scholarship there, he shifted to

---

[26] There is some controversy on Veblen's acquisition of English and his social and cultural isolation. While Joseph Dorfman's *Thorstein Veblen and His America* said that Veblen learnt his English well when he was an adult, Thorstein's older brother Andrew, in letters to Dorfman, countered this view by stating that he had bilingual training in speech from the start and was better equipped in English than his schoolmates or even some of his instructors. The myth that Thorstein knew no English until he was an adult, according to Andrew, may have been deliberately cultivated by him for reasons of his own. Also, Dorfman had greatly exaggerated his cultural isolation. See Rick Tilman (1992, pp. 4–5).

Yale where he studied under evolutionist William G. Sumner and obtained his Ph.D. for the thesis 'Ethical Grounds of a Doctrine of Retribution' in 1884. With a Ph.D. in Philosophy he was unable to find employment for seven years, perhaps because there was not much demand for the subject. After spending this time at his farm, he returned to Cornell to study economics under J. Laurence Laughlin in 1891. After a year, he moved to Chicago along with his mentor Laughlin, who was appointed to head the economics department, and became his teaching assistant. He spent 14 years there, rose to become an assistant professor and also became the managing editor of the *Journal of Political Economy*. He spent the next three years at Stanford where he was forced to resign because of his extramarital affairs with female students.

Steven Pressman (1999, pp. 88–9) describes Veblen's wanderings from university to university, his difficulties everywhere, and his quirky lifestyle as follows:

> After leaving Chicago, Veblen moved constantly from school to school, usually encouraged by college administrators to seek employment elsewhere. Part of the problem was the affairs he had with young co-eds and faculty wives. Another problem was that his caustic criticism—especially of academia (Veblen 1918) and other economists—did not endear him to his colleagues. A further difficulty was that Veblen had no regard for academic rituals like department meetings, taking attendance in class, holding office hours, and grading. He usually gave all his students a 'C' regardless of the quality of their work. Finally, there was the problem with Veblen the teacher. According to Dorfman (1934, p. 234f.), Veblen 'mumbled, he rambled, he digressed. His classes dwindled; one ended up with but one student....'
>
> Veblen was also renowned for his quirky lifestyle. Dorfman (1934, p. 239) reports that Veblen furnished his living quarters with boxes that served as tables and chairs. Mundane household chores such as making up a bed, were deplored as a waste of time. Dirty dishes were stacked in a tub until no clean dishes remained; then Veblen hosed them down. According to Diggins (1978, pp. 33–8), while teaching at the University of Missouri in the 1910s, Veblen lived in the basement of a friend's house, entering and leaving through the basement window.

He is best known for *The Theory of Leisure Class* (1899a). In this book he criticised the conspicuous consumption of the leisure class which does not do sufficient productive work and also consumes high priced goods as a social status. In fact status goods, also known as Veblen goods, became one of the exceptions to the law of demand as the higher the price, the higher the quantity demanded. In this book, apart from conspicuous consumption, he also introduced terms like conspicuous leisure and pecuniary emulation. The conspicuous consumption of the rich is emulated by other classes in a race to be one up, resulting in waste of resources, money and time. Veblen is also known for his other works such as *The Theory of Business Enterprise* (1904), *The Instinct of Workmanship and the State of the Industrial Arts* (1914) and *Engineers and the Price System* (1921). He believed that capitalist institutions produced monopoly, unemployment and business cycles rather than stable economic equilibrium. He castigated the classical and the neoclassical theory for neglecting evolutionary and cumulative change and confining itself to stable equilibrium. Since one's consumption is dependent on emulating others, rational behaviour is ruled out. In fact man's behaviour is conditioned by culture, habits and often irrational factors. Veblen had socialistic leanings but, unlike Marx, he did not believe that the proletariat would overthrow the capitalist system. Instead he thought they would emulate the rich. The challenge to the present system would come from engineers who, unlike the business class whose only interest was in profits, understood the industrial system. In his opinion they would manage it more efficiently and work for the general welfare of society. Business, on the other hand, negatively impacted the system by restricting output, raising prices and through higher unemployment. Veblen hoped that the machine process, when the engineers take over, would in fact replace the price system and would eliminate the twin wastes of unemployment and conspicuous consumption (Pressman 1999, p. 91). Because of his contributions to institutional economics, as also his scathing criticism of neoclassical economics, Veblen is widely regarded as the father or originator of the alternative institutional economics.

When Jordan, President of Stanford, asked for Young's opinion on hiring Veblen in 1906, Young's response was favourable. Young, in successfully recommending Veblen for Associate Professorship, stated: "I understand that he is thoroughly successful with advanced and especially graduate students... I do not think he has an equal among American economists in breadth of scholarship and subtlety of analysis... I mean to imply that I would strongly favour his appointment if the University could meet his conditions."[27] However, when Young requested Jordan for specialised books in anthropology and ethnology for Veblen's research, Jordan refused.[28] Young also recommended Veblen to full professorship in 1908, but again Jordan refused.[29] Veblen applied for leave of absence during 1909–1910. Though regulations only permitted such leave after six years of service, Young requested Jordan to make it a special case,[30] but Jordan turned it down. Young on 27 September 1909, in a letter to Jordan, again recommended Veblen to full professorship, but before any action could be taken, Veblen was forced to resign as one of his female friends from the east had moved in with him (see also Blitch 1995, p. 26). Veblen chose to resign rather than face dismissal for moral turpitude.

In his famous article 'Why is economics not an evolutionary science?', Veblen (1898) wanted the economic process to be studied in terms of cumulative causation rather than natural laws or tendencies towards stable equilibrium. He was opposed to the static method of economics and in its stead advocated an evolutionary (dynamic) approach. Young was probably influenced by Veblen,[31] and although he did not use Veblen's term cumulative causation, his explanation of growth is very much in this spirit. Young (1928b) stated that forces making for disequilibrium are constantly defeating those making for equilibrium. The change therefore becomes progressive and propagates itself in a cumulative way. In that paper he therefore effectively cast Smith's dictum that 'the division of labour is limited by the size of the market' in terms of cumulative causation and concluded that "the division of labour in large part depends on the division of labour". Later, Gunnar Myrdal (1957) also used the concept of cumulative causation, but came to different conclusions.

---

[27] Young's letter to Jordan dated 14 April 1906. See also Blitch (1995, p. 22).
[28] Young's memorandum to Jordan dated 23 January 1908.
[29] Young to Jordan dated 15 June 1908.
[30] Young to Jordan dated 23 March 1909.
[31] Young made reference to almost all major works of Veblen in his 1930 edition of *Outlines* for which he revised the first 13 chapters. See Ely et al. (1930, p. 19, 44, 137, 155).

According to Myrdal, the operation of circular cumulative causation produced international and interregional inequality, and not growth.

Veblen thought that the capitalist institutions produced monopoly and unemployment rather than growth. Young disagreed. In his analysis of growth, he showed that industrial fragmentation was the predominant tendency rather than industrial consolidation. As the size of the market expands, industrial operations split themselves into a large number of specialised firms and industries. The basis for increasing returns is specialisation rather than economies of scale. Each firm's scale was not a matter for the individual firm alone and was dependent on the size of the overall market. Product differentiation is also a manifestation of competition in which each producer tries to compete on the basis of a different product specification. Selling costs incurred in the process do not amount to industrial wastes as they are miniscule in relation to gross sales of the industry as a whole.

Veblen thought that consumption does not depend on individual rational behaviour but on custom, habit, social and even irrational factors. When each man is trying to up the other, the law of demand goes out of the window, at least in so far as the status goods are concerned. Young thought that man was rational in some aspects of his behaviour, for example, in his market behaviour or in his money-making business. Man was self-regarding in a broader Smithian sense of bettering one's condition.

Veblen (1899b, p. 242) stated that the character of economic science is determined by its preconceptions. "The main canons of truth on which the science proceeded: (a) hedonistic-associational psychology, and (b) an uncritical conviction that there is a meliorative trend in the course of events, apart from the conscious ends of the individual members of the community." Young (1925, 1927a, pp. 251–2) criticised this position: "Veblen made no attempt to prove or even illustrate this thesis respecting the first 'canon.' It was and has merely remained a bland assertion." He further stated that economics was a study of human behaviour getting its data from experience and not from psychological postulates. He also held that deduction is merely a matter of expositional form valid for any variety of economics including institutional.

Veblen's second proposition was also equally untenable. Young (1925, 1927a, pp. 251–2, footnote 1) stated:

> So far as English economics after Adam Smith is concerned, it rests only upon Veblen's adroit fumbling of the distinction between normative (meliorative) trends and specific tendencies… On any ground the thesis is untenable. Even Smith's 'system of natural liberty' could be achieved only by conscious effort. By general consent Ricardo's view of the general trend was pessimistic. Mill's famous thesis that 'distribution of wealth is a matter of human institutions only' might conceivably be ruled out, as something apart from the main body of his doctrines. Consider, therefore, the concluding sentence in his discussion of the stationery state. 'Only when, in addition to just institutions, the increase of mankind shall be under the deliberate guidance of judicious foresight, can the conquests made from the powers of nature by the intellect and energy of scientific discoverers become the common property of the species, and the means of improving and elevating the universal lot.'

Mitchell (1924), in his paper 'The Prospects of Economics', stated that while older forms of institutional economics for one reason or another were defective, the newer unorthodox type of economic theory deals with a range of problems undreamt of in the field of value and distribution. Moreover: "Sidney Webb in England, Werner Sombart in Germany, and Thorstein Veblen in America were studying the evolution of economic institutions in a scientific, as opposed to an historical or propagandist, spirit. Further they were claiming that work of this kind is economic theory." In response to this, Young (1925, 1927a, pp. 259–60) stated that Veblen was a genius but the word scientist did not fit him. He painted an impressionistic picture which no one else saw.

According to Young, the institutional method was just one of the valid ways to seek economic truth, but it did not have a monopoly in this regard. Young (1927b; Mehrling and Sandilands 1999, pp. 6–7) writes: "Now it is capital error to hold (with Thorstein Veblen and some of his followers) that explanation of things in terms of their historical antecedents is in some special sense a scientific mode of explanation; that, as Veblen puts it, modern sciences are characteristically 'evolutionary sciences,' and concern themselves primarily with 'unfolding sequences' and 'cumulative causation.' The truth is, of course, that the goal towards which natural sciences are always pressing—even though it may be an unattainable goal—is the explanation of this world of changing and evolving forms and types of organisation in terms of some simple and stable mechanism. Mathematical Physics has not abdicated to descriptive genetics its place as the perfect type of science, and in a manner the ultimate type."

Veblen criticised conspicuous consumption and conspicuous leisure. Smith earlier had taken a very balanced view of conspicuous consumption. Although he lauded the virtues of frugality and went to the extent of branding every spendthrift a public enemy and every frugal a public friend, he did admit that it is the desire for 'baubles and trinkets' and desire to display one's wealth to gain approval of others, which was the motivating force to acquire riches. Desires for necessaries are very easily satisfied, and even an ordinary worker is able to satisfy them. But if this desire to display wealth to gain approval of other fellowmen is taken away, the motivating force of the system is destroyed. In *The Theory of Moral Sentiments*, Smith admits that consumption of the rich is a way of distributing necessaries to the poor.

As for Young he stated that one could not conclude that expenditure over and above necessaries was merely a form of competition that Veblen called 'conspicuous consumption'. As Young (1929c; Mehrling and Sandilands 1999, p. 258) says: "There are many people who love diamonds and other precious stones, not because they are expensive, but because of their real beauty. And doubtless the great majority of those who listen to grand opera will continue to go there because of the real appeal of that combination of musical and dramatic art and not for any less worthy reason. It is easy to be cynical, but the thorough cynic rarely sees more than the surface of economic life."

Young also criticised Veblen's instinct for workmanship. William McDougall (1910) in his article 'Rationality of economic activity' had stated that political economy rested on hedonistic postulates, and instinctive propensities would afford a better basis, giving support to Veblen. In a similar vein, Mitchell (1924) gave further fillip to Veblen, by arguing that one of the major problems before economists was to trace "the processes by which habits and institutions have grown out of instinct". Young

(1925, 1927a, p. 253) criticised this position stating that "Veblen's instinct of workmanship had turned out not to be an instinct, and a new thing, behaviorism, had made its appearance."

David Reisman (2012, p. 75) quoting Donald Walker held that the hypothesis as stated was untestable. "Instincts modify habits. Habits contaminate instincts… History is a sequence of setbacks and spurts… Veblen makes no attempt to decompose the causal impact of the innate as compared with the social. The result is a hypothesis which is untestable: 'It is framed in such a way that it is consistent with any behavior. For example, if behavior is workmanlike, it displays the operation of the instinct of workmanship. If behavior is unworkmanlike, as in the case of Veblen's businessmen, it is because instinct is contaminated or distorted' (Walker 1977, p. 78)."

Young and Veblen were similar in many ways. Both had an evolutionary approach to economics. Both abandoned the static equilibrium approach in favour of dynamic disequilibrium economics. Both favoured 'cumulative causation' or 'cumulative change'. Both disliked the assumption of ceteris paribus or other-things-remaining-constant. Both discounted rational behaviour or rational economic man. Both combined insights from other social sciences for the study of economics. Both disliked laissez-faire economics. But they had their differences. Young regarded institutionalism as one of the many valid approaches to economics. In his opinion, conspicuous consumption was not necessarily a bad thing. For him capitalistic institutions produced endogenous growth and industrial differentiation rather than consolidation and monopoly. Young, like Smith, advocated competition as the best tonic for growth. But at the same time, he favoured strong independent institutions for credit or monopoly control. In his opinion, institutions could be consciously created by human action to meet human ends. For Young the present system was quite resilient and would be overthrown by neither the proletariat nor engineers. It could be reformed through democratic action geared towards the public interest.

References

Blitch, Charles P. (1995), *Allyn Young: The Peripatetic Economist*, Houndmills and London: Macmillan Press Ltd.

Currie, Lauchlin (1981), 'Allyn Young and the development of growth theory', *Journal of Economic Studies*, 8(1), pp. 52–61.

Currie, Lauchlin (1997), 'Implications of an endogenous theory of growth in Allyn Young's macroeconomic concept of increasing returns', *History of Political Economy*, 29(3), 413–43.

Diggins, John P. (1978), *The Bard of Savagery*, New York: Seabury Press.

Dorfman, Joseph (1934), *Thorstein Veblen and his America*, New York: Augustus M. Kelley.

Dorfman, Joseph (1959), *The Economic Mind in American Civilization*, Vol. 1–5, New York: Viking Press.

Ely, Richard T. (1893/1900), *Outlines of Economics*, New York: The Macmillan Company.

Ely, Richard T. (1905), *Labour Movement in America*, New York: Macmillan.

Ely, Richard T. (1914), *Property and Contract*, New York: Macmillan.

Ely, Richard T., Thomas S. Adams, Max O. Lorenz and Allyn A. Young (1908), *Outlines of Economics*, New York: The Macmillan Company.

Ely, Richard T., Thomas S. Adams, Max O. Lorenz and Allyn A. Young (1930), *Outlines of Economics*, New York: The Macmillan Company.

Jevons, W. Stanley (1871), *The Theory of Political Economy*, London: Macmillan.

Marshall, Alfred (1890), *Principles of Economics*, London: Macmillan.

Marshall, Alfred (1919), *Industry and Trade*, London: Macmillan.

Marshall, Alfred (1923), *Money, Credit and Commerce*, London: Macmillan.

Marshall, Alfred and Mary Paley (1879), *Economics of Industry*, London: Macmillan.

McDougall, William (1910), 'The rationality of economic activity', *Journal of Political Economy*, 18pp.

Mehrling, Perry G. (1997), *The Money Interest and the Public Interest*, Cambridge and London: Harvard University Press.

Mehrling, Perry G. and Roger J. Sandilands (1999), *Money and Growth: Selected Papers of Allyn Abbott Young*, London and New York: Routledge.

Mitchell, Wesley (1924), 'The prospects of economics', in Tugwell, T. G. (ed.) (1924) *Trend in Economics*, New York: Alfred A. Knopf.

Myrdal, Gunnar (1957), *Economic Theory and Underdeveloped Regions*, Oxford: Gerard Duckworth.

Pressman, Steven (1999), *Fifty Major Economists*, London and New York: Routledge.
Reisman, David (2012), *The Social Economics of Thorstein Veblen*, Cheltenham: Edward Elgar.
Ross, Edward A. (1991), *Social Control: A Survey of the Foundations of Order*, New York: Macmillan.
Schumpeter, Joseph A. (1951/2003), *Ten Great Economists from Marx to Keynes*, San Diego: Simon Publications.
Schumpeter, Joseph A. (1954), *History of Economic Analysis*, London: Allen and Unwin.
Smith, Adam (1759/1976), *The Theory of Moral Sentiments*, Oxford: Clarendon Press.
Smith, Adam (1776/1976), *An Enquiry into the Nature and Causes of the Wealth of Nations*, Chicago: University of Chicago Press.
Sraffa, Piero (1926), 'Laws of returns under competitive conditions', *Economic Journal* (December), pp. 535–50.
Tilman, Rick (1992), *Thorstein Veblen and His Critics, 1891–1963*, Princeton: Princeton University Press.
Tugwell, T.G. (ed.) (1924), *Trend in Economics*, New York: Alfred A. Knopf.
Veblen, Thorstein (1898), 'Why is economics not an evolutionary science?', *Quarterly Journal of Economics*, 12(4), pp. 373–97.
Veblen, Thorstein (1899a), *The Theory of Leisure Class*, New York: Macmillan.
Veblen, Thorstein (1899b), 'The preconceptions of economic science', *Quarterly Journal of Economics* (January), pp. 121–50.
Veblen, Thorstein (1904), *The Theory of Business Enterprise*, New York: Charles Scribner's Sons.
Veblen, Thorstein (1914), *The Instinct of Workmanship and the State of the Industrial Arts*, New York: Macmillan.
Veblen, Thorstein (1918), *The Higher Learning in America: A Memorandum on the Conduct of Universities by Business Men*, New York: B. W. Huebsch.
Veblen, Thorstein (1921), *The Engineers and the Price System*, New York: B. W. Huebsch.
Walker, D. A. (1977), 'Thorstein Veblen's economic system', *Economic Inquiry*, 15, pp. 213–37.
Young, Allyn (1924), 'Marshall on consumers' surplus in international trade', *Quarterly Journal of Economics*, 39(1), pp. 144–50.
Young, Allyn (1925), 'Review of The Trend of Economics', *Quarterly Journal of Economics*, 39(2), pp. 155–83. Reprinted in Young (1927a), pp. 232–60.

Young, Allyn (1927a), *Economic Problems: New and Old*, Boston and New York: Houghton Mifflin Company.
Young, Allyn (1927b), 'Economics as a field of research', *Quarterly Journal of Economics*, 42(1), pp. 1–25. Reprinted in Mehrling and Sandilands (1999), pp. 3–16.
Young, Allyn (1928a), 'English Political Economy', *Economica*, 8(22), pp. 1–15. Reprinted in Mehrling and Sandilands (1999), pp. 15–28.
Young, Allyn (1928b), 'Increasing returns and economic progress', *Economic Journal*, 38(152), pp. 527–42. Reprinted in Mehrling and Sandilands (1999), pp. 49–61.
Young, Allyn (1929a), 'Economics', *Encyclopaedia Britannica 1928*, London: The Encyclopaedia Britannica Company, pp. 925–32. Reprinted in Mehrling and Sandilands (1999), pp. 115–34.
Young, Allyn (1929b), 'The creator of wealth', *The Book of Popular Science*, New York: The Grolier Society, pp. 110–16. Reprinted in Mehrling and Sandilands (1999), pp. 149–52.
Young, Allyn (1929c), 'The meaning of value', *The Book of Popular Science*, New York: The Grolier Society, pp. 4097–105. Reprinted in Mehrling and Sandilands (1999), pp. 252–60.
Young, Allyn (1990), 'Nicholas Kaldor's notes on Allyn Young's LSE lectures 1927–29', *Journal of Economic Studies*, 17(3/4), pp. 18–114.

3

Nature, Scope and Method of Economics

Allyn Young was as much interested in the method of economics as in economics itself. Although one could theoretically make a distinction between deduction and induction, in any practical research both were complementary, and there was a constant give and take between the two. Young, as stated in the last chapter, was impressed with English political economy not because it provided finished doctrines but a method which enabled one to arrive at a reasoned conclusion. This chapter first discusses the nature and scope of economics, then its method (including the use of mathematics and statistics in economics) and finally the methodological writings of John Stuart Mill, Walter Bagehot, Henry Sidgwick and Max Weber and also their influence on Young's thinking. John Neville Keynes or J.E. Cairnes are not discussed as Young did not want to include them in his proposed book on methodology (which he never wrote) as he did not find anything in them which was not commonplace.[1]

---

[1] However, Young included both in the reference list to chapter 1 'The Nature and Scope of Economics' in the 1930 edition of the *Outlines of Economics* (see Ely et al. 1930, pp. 18–9).

© The Author(s) 2020
R. Chandra, *Allyn Abbott Young*, Great Thinkers in Economics,
https://doi.org/10.1007/978-3-030-31981-6_3

Definition, Nature and Scope

Young (1929a; Mehrling and Sandilands 1999, p. 115) defined economics as "a science which is concerned with the communal problems of economic life". Economics should be defined not so much by its subject matter but by the particular problems it deals with or particular questions it tries to answer. This, according to him, is a better definition than merely defining it as a "science of wealth" or "wealth-getting and wealth-using activities of men". Thus the older name "political economy" still gives the right impression of the kind of problems which economics deals with. "How men acquire wealth and how they use it are matters of fundamental importance for economics, but its principal concern is with the intricate interrelations of various wealth-getting and wealth-using activities and with the ways in which these activities affect the welfare of the community" (ibid., p. 115).

Note that this definition places man or mankind at the centre; it deals with human relationships arising in various wealth-getting and wealth-using activities and also takes into account the ways such activities affect human welfare. In this definition he was also influenced by Richard T. Ely (1893) who thought that economics treats of man, in society, and in the process of development. Since economics deals with human relationships, it is a social science, and not an exact science. Unlike physical sciences, the experimental method is not available to social sciences, the phenomena they deal with are more complex, their data less exact, and they face problem of orientation which is peculiar to them (Young 1927a; Mehrling and Sandilands 1999, p. 4). Moreover, the knowledge they yield, to the extent it has instrumental value, serves human ends and helps modify human arrangements. "The social scientist cannot … put himself, as an observer, outside of society, so as to get a view of social processes as a connected whole. His interests, his values, his ends, lie within the connected whole" (ibid., p. 4).

Since economics is one of the social sciences, some writers regard it as a part of sociology, the general science of society (Ely et al. 1930, p. 9). Economists generally refrain from expressing ethical or moral judgements. Economists analyse economic aspects of practical problems and the final judgement depends on a synthesis of moral, political, economic and other considerations. Moreover: "Above economic man stands the political man, free to limit and define the field of economic man's activity, to impose conditions upon him, to prevent him from doing certain things, to encourage him to do others" (Young 1927a; Mehrling and Sandilands 1999, p. 4).

Since economics deals with man as he actually is, and not with an artificially constructed economic man, it cannot be completely divorced from ethics and politics. For example, in setting of fair and reasonable railway rates, apportionment of taxes, restrictive regulations and sumptuary laws, economic questions get interwoven with ethical, legal and political considerations. Although economics does not undertake a systematic study of law, ethics and politics, its conclusions may almost always be supplemented by non-economic factors which an economist may not have fully taken into account.

Young viewed economic relations as a part of larger social picture (Mehrling and Sandilands 1999, p. xiv). Economics is just one of the social sciences, and the final terms of economic inferences reach out to other systems of relations often non-economic in character. It is from these other relations that final terms of economics get their meaning and significance. Thus, if economics is to remain practically useful, these final terms need to be handled very carefully.

Every social science is defined in terms of its problems but has its own orientation, scope and viewpoint (Young 1927a; Mehrling and Sandilands 1999, p. 5). Thus, political science may study the political man, educational science the learner, and criminology the law breaker. An economist may view a citizen as a free agent; political scientist may regard his behaviour, to some extent, as determinate; while an educationist may regard him as a malleable material. But there is no necessary conflict between these views as each is partial. In Young's opinion, although a social scientist working in his own field needs to be aware of different orientations of others, a complete synthesis of different social sciences is not possible, as the enquirer with his interests stands amidst society and its processes (ibid., p. 5).

An interesting question is whether economics is an art or a science.[2] In a letter to Frank Knight, dated 11 March 1927, Young took a position that it is both: "I am more and more impressed with the fundamental soundness of the position which we both take, namely that social sciences must be art as well as science, and rather more so." Young's pragmatic approach to economics implied that economics, apart from being a science, was an art in solving practical (or communal) problems. Young realised that in an evolving society, institutions had to be created through human actions and made to serve human ends.

Economics, as a practical subject, is profoundly influenced by its legal, institutional and social foundations such as the right to private property; right of contract; right to freedom of movement and occupation; right to manufacture and sell (within reasonable limits) what one pleases; absence of slavery and imprisonment for debt; competition; cooperation and interdependence through the division of labour and exchange; industrial specialisation; and use of money and credit. A competitive exchange economy leads to a framework of social cooperation and interdependence and this in turn determines the essential nature of economics. "*It is above all a science of human relations.* This important truth should be noted by those readers who assume that because economics is 'practical', it is concrete and material. On the contrary its subject matter is largely intangible and its conclusions largely abstract" (Ely et al. 1930, p. 18). Further, "It is the business man, the engineer, the factory inspector, for instance, who are particularly interested in the mechanical and material aspects of factories and machinery. The economist as such is specially concerned with such questions as the influence of factories and machinery upon wages, hours of labour, unemployment, cost of production, prices and profits, in

---

[2] John Stuart Mill (1844/2009, p. 108) made a distinction between science and art: "Science is a collection of *truths*; art a body of *rules*, or directions for conduct. The language of science is, This is, or, This is not; This does, or does not, happen. The language of art is, Do this; Avoid that. Science takes cognizance of a *phenomenon*, and endeavours to discover its *law*; art proposes to itself an *end*, and looks out for *means* to effect it." Mill further added: "If, therefore, Political Economy be a science, it cannot be a collection of practical rules; though, unless it be altogether a useless science, practical rules must be capable of being founded upon it… Rules, therefore, for making a nation increase in wealth, are not a science. Political Economy does not of itself instruct how to make a nation rich; but whoever would be qualified to judge of the means of making a nation rich, must first be a political economist" (ibid., p. 108).

short upon relationships between men as affected by the material conditions under which they earn their living" (ibid., p. 18).

Since economics deals with communal problems of economic life, the role of the state (and institutions) is indispensable to this task. Young neither believed in completely laissez-faire economics nor in undue state intervention in economic matters; but he considered the role of the state as flexible, responding to the evolving nature and needs of society. Overtime, it was expected to assume new roles in line with the changing needs. For example, the Federal Reserve was required to control credit in view of the business cycles. In times of war, government was expected to assume new roles, not only geared towards moving men and materials, but also towards collecting data, information and statistics for a more effective role in this regard. "If war continues it is certain that the field of activity over which public interest will be deemed to extend must be much further widened" (Young 1918; Mehrling and Sandilands 1999, p. 30). Further, "Political organization has not kept pace with economic organization" (Young 1926; Mehrling and Sandilands 1999, p. 43). To improve international economic and trading environment, it was necessary to rise above narrow national interests and devise new forms of international organisation. Both at the national and international levels, Young was a great believer in the role of institutions in solving the communal problems of economic life.

Method

Young rejected psychological postulates of economics such as hedonism, utility or profit maximisation. He was of the opinion that psychologists could learn more from economics than economists from psychology. He held that economics drew its data from real life and not from psychological postulates. "The psychologists and their contributions to economics are receding into the background. It might even be inferred that the (behaviouristic) psychologists have more to learn from economics than economists have to learn from psychology. The truth is, of course, that economics not only should be or is, but always has been a study of human behaviour, getting its data from experience, not from psychological postulates" (Young 1925, 1927b, p. 255).[3] Nicholas Kaldor (1972, p. 1238), one of Young's students at the LSE, observed that the basic assumptions of economic theory are either unverifiable (such as profit or utility maximisation) or directly contradicted by experience (such as perfect competition, perfect divisibility, perfect knowledge or perfect foresight).

Young, influenced by Smith, also rejected the notion of rational economic man.[4] He wanted to study man as he really is and not an artificially simplified rational economic man. Adam Smith in his *Wealth of Nations* had taken a very broad approach to self-interest as bettering one's condition "a desire which, though generally calm and dispassionate, comes with us from the womb, and never leaves us till we go to the grave" (Smith 1776/1976, Vol. I, pp. 362–3). This propels a man to save, accumulate and grow richer. Man does not maximise his self-interest in a single-minded way always targeting maximum pleasure at minimum pain. In the *Wealth of Nations*, man's greed for profits is kept in check by the operation of competition; in the *Theory of Moral Sentiments*, his self-interest is balanced by the opposite motive of sympathy. Knight (1960) observed that purely rational economic man is premised on an absence of personal relations, with humans treating each other like vending machines.

Young believed in blending deduction and induction methods in economic research. But the first task is formulating significant research questions or hypotheses. "The really important thing is that research be directed towards answering of significant questions, and it is hard to frame significant questions except in the light definite hypotheses. Formulating questions and hypotheses is the first and the most important

---

[3] In his review of W.S. Jevons's *The Theory of Political Economy*, Young (1912, 1927b, pp. 121–22) credited Jevons as the first significant author to consciously blend the theories of English utilitarianism with abstract economics. But, at the same time, he stated that his theories would be closer to reality if they were divorced from utilitarianism and hedonism.

[4] "The 'economic man' was a fiction, not of economics, but of the sterile formal logic of economic method, for much of which economists themselves have been responsible. What the economists really abstracted was one special class of human relationships … the impersonal types of relationships that are to be found in the market places of countries where modern commercial institutions have been developed… But their method was not at fault, for, outside of the field where controlled experiments are possible, it is the only method science knows. A better knowledge of general psychology might have helped them here and there. It could not substantially have changed their postulates" (Young 1927b, pp. 258–59).

task of the investigator" (Young 1927a; Mehrling and Sandilands 1999, p. 9).

No method, deduction or induction, in itself is complete unless supplemented with the other. There has to be a constant give and take between the two. "Just because we can make a formal logical distinction between deduction and induction, we are prone to exaggerate the difference between deductive and inductive methods of enquiry. In the practical work of getting knowledge, we pass from a generalization to facts and from facts back to generalizations in a way that blends deduction and induction… In any really creative research, however modest in scale, there is this process of continuous give and take between the search for general relations and the scrutiny of particular details, between thinking and concrete observations" (ibid., pp. 9–10).

Young, as noted by Charles Blitch (1995, p. 8), and Mehrling and Sandilands (1999, Editors' preface, p. xiv), was influenced by the 'look and see' method of Richard T. Ely, who was his economics teacher at Wisconsin. A theory or doctrine was not to be accepted blindly without putting it to test against real-life facts. If the facts were not in accordance with a given hypothesis, the hypothesis needed modification. So hypotheses and observations were crucial. Since an economy was in a continuous flux (or evolution), new facts are emerging all the time and changing our view of the general or abstract relations. Thus a hypothesis was valid for a given stage of economic life. Young was also influenced by his history teachers at Wisconsin, namely, Frederick J. Turner and Charles H. Haskins. From them he learnt that history could be used as a tool of economic research. This is clear from the following passage in Young's 1927 QJE article on economics as a field of research:

> The economic theorist does not "deduce" his results from a few simple premises. Even when he controls his findings by using statistics, he works in the midst of a context of experience, and the system of general relations which constitutes his theory is empty of meaning unless it is consistent with that body of experience, and explains and organizes some part of it. Similarly, whatever new views of the structure of society we get by looking backward to its development must supplement and be consistent with that abstract and general view of economic relations which we call economic

theory. *Every economic theorist ought to be something of a historian, and every student of development of economic institutions ought to be something of a theorist.* (Young 1927a; Mehrling and Sandilands 1999, p. 8, emphasis added)

In the same article, Young (ibid., pp. 5–7) made a distinction between the contractual (or mechanistic) and historical (or institutional) view of society. In the first view, social arrangements are arrived at through voluntary agreements and, in the second, they appear as social habits, products of history, and not shaped by rational actions of men. In the first, institutions, representing the structure of society, are social expedients; in the second, man himself is the product of living in society. In Young's opinion both views are complementary, and social sciences must allow for both types of investigations. In the first, the search is for uniform and dependable relations (or laws); in the second, we look for specific events, particular institutions and unique situations. While the first is essentially an instrumental view and can help us frame practical working rules, the second can add to our experience, understanding and wisdom concerning the things which are worth accomplishing, but cannot give us the means and technical equipment for successful accomplishment.

In Young's view, it would be incorrect to say that the traditional political economy implies a wholly mechanistic view of society because while the instruments of control it provides can be used as the communal interest dictates, they have to pass through the political processes. "All that it implies is a particular orientation with one particular set of social processes viewed as a mechanism by free agents who want to understand the workings of the mechanism because they want to know how best to control it and use it. They want to know how far to control it and how far to leave it alone, and it is desirable that they should be able to predict the more remote as well as the immediate effects of particular measures of control. Agents, mechanism, instruments, and ends are all in the picture. Doubtless they are seen in a one-sided and partial way, and yet this view of things has proved itself to be practically serviceable, and the traditional political economy which embodied it was one of the great intellectual achievements of the nineteenth century" (ibid., p. 5).

English political economy has, however, been criticised on the grounds that it was essentially deductive, was based on questionable premises about human nature, and assigned an important role to the *economic man*. In Young's opinion, this is not the case. "Now the truth is that English Political economy has never been, in any real sense, deductive or a priori, and that it has never put a heavy burden upon the economic man" (Young 1928a; Mehrling and Sandilands 1999, p. 20). Economists did not proceed by drawing inferences from questionable assumptions about the nature of man or of the universe. They collected the commonplace facts of the world, drew upon their own observations about themselves and their neighbours, made occasional use of history and records, used such statistics as were easily available, and drew upon the shrewd observations of other writers. But the facts were not collected blindly but in relation to the thesis under examination. They did go forth and back from hypothesis and facts and facts to hypothesis as every science does. So "the method, as distinguished from the technique, of the English political economy of the nineteenth century was in no sense peculiar to it, but was and is the method—the inevitable method—not only of the sciences generally, but of all intelligent inquiries into the general aspects of the relations of events" (ibid., p. 21). It did proceed on the contractual view of society as the great commercial revolution had changed the world, and conditions were ripe for men to govern themselves on the basis of voluntary agreements. Some order was discernible for a systematic economic enquiry.

So Young regarded the English political economy as an eminently practical subject. It was not created to fill up some existing gaps left uncovered by other sciences, but to deal with large questions of national concern. It came into being to deal with the communal problems of economic life. For this reason, Young held that the distinction between pure economics and applied economics is largely artificial. Pure analysis and description cannot be divorced from human interests and problems. Purely abstract and general modes of analysis have their uses. "I suspect, however, that in the future the largest contributions to economic theory will be made, as they have been made in the past, not by professional 'theorists', but by men who have set themselves the task of forging instruments that will help towards a better knowledge of how to deal with communal problems of organized economic life. English political economy has been built up for the most part in precisely that way, and its instrumental and pragmatic character has always been one of its dominating qualities" (ibid., p. 20).

The most significant contribution of political economy is not a set of doctrines but a set of instruments which help the investigator to find his way through the intricate mazes he has to explore. "The most important thing a student of political economy gets from his training is not the possession of a body of 'economic truth' but command of an intellectual technique. Confronted by a new problem he knows how to find his bearings and how to work his way through to some sort of reasoned conclusion" (ibid., p. 27). Further, "English political economy will not be preserved by its guardians but by men whose interest is not so much in political economy as in the problems with which political economy has to do" (ibid., p. 27).

Young, being catholic in his views, was sympathetic to various schools of economic thought. As Perry G. Mehrling (1997, p. 26) puts it: "The various schools of economics are not so much alternatives as they are complements, indeed not so much complements as supplements to the central strand of economic thought." Young thought that each school had something important to contribute. Therefore, he was appreciative of such diverse thinkers as Adam Smith, David Ricardo, J.S. Mill, Karl Marx, Walter Bagehot, Alfred Marshall, Antoine A. Cournot, Vilfredo Pareto, W.S. Jevons, F.Y. Edgeworth, Karl Knies, Heinrich J. Rickert, Max Weber and Thorstein Veblen. He also understood the need to master the whole literature of economics. As economics is a practical subject, this could be practically useful, so long as the specific context of that literature is kept in mind. He further held that "No theory which has received support for long is ever entirely wrong. 'Rival' theorists are generally both right, except when denouncing the other" (Young 1990, p. 99). The same catholicity applied to various methods of economics: deductive and inductive, contractual and institutional, abstract and historical. All had their place and were useful supplements in arriving at the economic truth. In this regard, neither any particular school of thought nor any specific method of investigation had a sole monopoly.

Use of Statistics and Mathematics

Young considered the use of statistics as the most promising new development (Young 1928a; Mehrling and Sandilands 1999, p. 22). Young felt that although Jevons wanted to revolutionise economic theory, his statistical enquiries may count for more towards that end than his theory of political economy. However, these new developments in statistics did not constitute a revolution. For one thing, they were wholly consistent with the spirit and method of the older political economy. While economic science would give larger place to the study of averages and aggregates in the immediate future, it could not be altogether statistical—a new kind of political arithmetic (Young 1929a; Mehrling and Sandilands 1999, p. 127).[5]

A statistician brings new facts to attention. Also, he deals with the behaviour of averages and aggregates and their interrelations. There is a danger not so much of overestimating the importance of this new tool as of misinterpreting its significance. Some enthusiasts have hailed the new developments as some kind of economic mechanics, not as exact and precise as the celestial mechanics, but reliable enough for prediction purposes and for estimating the effect of planned interventions into economic activities. Young warned that such expectations are bound to be disappointed. "They rest upon a misapprehending of the character of the empirical foundations of scientific knowledge. Such knowledge is not made up of separate bits, each bit supported merely by an isolated series of experiments or by the observation of a series of detached facts. *Each new finding has to be fitted into the existing system of knowledge. If it does not fit, its own special credentials become suspect*" (ibid., p. 23, emphasis added). Taken by themselves, and without the support of other knowledge, averages and aggregates generally provide a weak basis for inductive inference.

Averages and aggregates and their relationships are merely historical facts, and like other historical facts they may be unique. Even if these facts show some stability, and therefore have some predictive value, they

---

[5] The term 'political arithmetic' was used by William Petty to denote the use of the quantitative method in economics.

may at best suggest tendencies, hardly ever defining them. They need to be explained and woven into the general texture of knowledge. They may provide fresh materials for economic theory but cannot be expected to perform the task of weaving its fabric (ibid., p. 24).[6] Economic theory increasingly will have to perform the task of explaining the statistical averages and aggregates; and for that very reason, it will not be able completely to turn away from scrutinising the common experience of life with which it was occupied in the past.

But bridging the gap between economic statistics and useful economic theory of the past is not going to be easy. While economic theory has been based on the interplay of a limited number of important factors, statistical facts are the net resultants of all the factors and of special factors pertaining to particular times and places. While economic theory has never claimed to deal with inter-temporal and interspatial circumstances, statistics does not deal with much else. But the statistician and the economist would have to work together if this gap is to be bridged. "Economics will have to make room for new conceptions and new sorts of abstractions if it is to make effective use of the new facts which statisticians are uncovering. If theorist and statistician continue to work apart, the gap between them will not be bridged, the structures built out from one side and the other will not meet, and neither structure alone will reach across the opposite bank" (ibid., p. 24).

Sometimes the benefit of the statistical method is sought to be conveyed by catchy terms like the 'quantitative method' or the 'exact method'. Young was sceptical whether this approach was suitable for solving all the social problems. In a letter to his friend Frank Knight, dated 11 March 1927, he observed: "I am a little bit bewildered at the rate at which plans for solving all of our social problems by 'quantitative research' are growing.

---

[6] Young (1929a; Mehrling and Sandilands 1999, p. 127) stated: "Every average or aggregate is in some measure unique, the resultant of the play of a particular combination of circumstances, such as may never be encountered again. In order that we may know just how dependable and how significant the variations of these magnitudes are, we need to analyse them so that we can explain them. That is, we need to weave them into the general texture of knowledge, so as to relate them to other things which we know. In short, although economics is beginning to utilize new materials effectively, and although some of these materials call for the use of a new technique, it cannot change its general logical method, for outside the field of experimental sciences there is no other method of getting useful and reliable knowledge."

The Laura Spelman Rockefeller Foundation, the Social Science Research Council, and the rest, are going to 'apply' a good many million dollars during the next few years in an effort to make the social sciences really scientific. Rapidly diminishing returns are going to be encountered for two reasons: (1) the supply of skilled labourers is inelastic; (2) the area which can be successfully cultivated is surprisingly small. It is all very discouraging."

Young (1927b, p. 244, footnote 1) made a distinction between rational economic man and the use of rational (logical) method in economics. While the rational economic man was largely a fiction, the rational (or logical) method used in arriving at theorems of pure economics is a valid scientific method. In criticising Henry L. Moore's *Laws of Wages*, which held that the theorems of pure economics were mere "hypotheses" which needed to be put to statistical verification before they could be called "scientific laws", Young (1914, p. 282) opined: "[T]he theorems of pure economics, if reached in accordance with the rules of logical inference and interpreted with due regard to the limitations implicit in the premises, have a right of their own to rank as 'scientific laws'."

Although much of political economy may consist of abstract general relations, it has been built up by a persistent and patient examination of the complicated facts of economic life. But in 'mathematical economics', there was a high degree of abstraction. "The great advantage of the use of mathematics in economics is that in that way alone is it possible to depict the variety, the complexity and most of all the interdependence of the factors which determine prices, costs, supply, demand and distributive shares. Elaborate mathematical formulations of the conditions of 'general economic equilibrium' have been devised, notably by Leon Walras … and Vilfredo Pareto… The principal value of these elaborate and highly abstract systems is that they put the enquirer on his guard against oversimplifying his problems, as for example, by forgetting that a change of almost any economic variable has its indirect as well as direct effects" (Young 1929a; Mehrling and Sandilands 1999, pp. 129–30).

In his review of A.L. Bowley's (1924) *The Mathematical Groundwork of Economics*, Young (1925, pp. 133–4) observed that the mathematical method supplies to economic theory a highly important critical apparatus. Quoting H.L. Moore, Young agreed that "Attempts at symbolic precision precipitate the assumptions tacitly and unconsciously made in ordinary reasoning."

Although mathematical economics is useful in bringing out the hidden assumptions and logical flaws, it makes for highly abstract economics, tending to make it impractical. Final terms of all economic inferences reach out into other non-economic systems from which they derive their meaning. Economics ceases to be practically useful if these final terms are handled loosely, treated as mere algebraic symbols, exhausting all other meanings. Young (1928a; Mehrling and Sandilands 1999, p. 25) writes:

> A perfectly abstract economics is impracticable. A system concerned merely with the relations of variables which are defined only by their mathematical attributes is not economics, any more than pure mathematics is mechanics… The final terms of every chain of economic inferences reach out into other systems of relations, often non-economic in character, and it is from these other relations that the final terms get their meaning and significance. Except within a very narrow field, no economics can be practically useful in which these final terms are handled loosely, or in which difficulties are evaded by treating them as though they were mere algebraic symbols, or as though a single set of relationships could exhaust their meaning.

In a similar vein, in a letter to Knight, dated 9 December 1922, Young observed that the highly abstract general equilibrium method does not give us anything at all that gets us anywhere as opposed to the two-variable method which lends itself to dealing with practical problems. "The two variable method lends itself to analysis of practical problems. I have yet to see that the method of general equilibrium gives us anything at all that gets us anywhere. Perhaps we cannot get anywhere. It is extremely hard to frame a statement of the economic system viewed as a system of many variables that does not seem to be just truism."

Young's overall conclusion was that the growing use of quantitative methods is the most promising development in contemporary economics. "But it will prove relatively sterile if it does not lead to renaissance of theory" (Young 1927b, p. 244). Experience and theory have to go hand in hand. While inductive findings will give accuracy and concrete meaning to the theorems of rational economics, theory will continue to analyse, interpret, relate and support the results of inductive studies. However, the use of quantitative methods needs to be seen in perspective. Neither their importance needs to be overestimated nor their significance misinterpreted.

Book on Methodology

Young in his letter to Knight, dated 25 February 1927, mentioned that he wanted to bring out a book of classic readings on methodology in social sciences. He felt that most American authors of the time, writing on methodology, had such an inadequate background that such a book was sorely needed. The book would not represent a single point of view nor was he anxious to include every point of view. But every item included should appear in its own right, as a contribution which deserved to be reckoned with seriously.

> For example, I would include a paper by Tschuprow on the statistical method which is about the best single thing ever done on that subject. Again, I should include Cournot's extraordinary chapter on social environment (this is the first chapter in the second volume of his '*De L'Enchainement Des Idées Fondamentales*). There is also a chapter from Pareto's 'Sociology' which I should want to put in. Then there is one chapter by Knies, and I think I might be able to extract something from Rickert. Also, I shall include the first chapter of Bagehot's 'Postulates of Political Economy'. There are about a dozen other things which I have in mind, and out of which I shall probably select half… I do not find anything in Cairnes or J. N. Keynes[7] that is not fairly commonplace. The first three chapters of Sidgwick, '*Principles of Political Economy*', appear to me to be better. I wonder if you have access of Max Weber's '*Gesammelte Aufsatze zur Wissenschaftslehre*'. I think I should like to put one of these, but I do not know just which to include. The one on 'Methodological Foundations of Sociology' is short and pretty good. The one on the objectivity of social-scientific and social-political knowledge is also good, but rather long and

---

[7] However, Schumpeter (1951/2003, p. 261) regarded J.N. Keynes's *Scope and Method of Political Economy* as one of the best methodologies of economics ever written.

wordy. Think this over and help me if you can. I should like to make the collection, in its way, a work of art.

In the handwritten postscript, Young added: "I think I shall include J. S. Mill's early paper on scope and method."

As noted by Blitch (1995), the proposed book on methodology was never published. In what follows, we discuss a few of the above authors to see how they compare with Young's method which we have already discussed and how they influenced him.[8]

First there is J.S. Mill (1844/2009), *Essays on Some Unsettled Questions of Political Economy*, 'Essay V, On the Definition of Political Economy; And on the Method of Investigation Proper to it'.[9]

Mill made a distinction between science and art: while science was a collection of truths, art was a body of rules. Since Smith's time political economy has been viewed as both a science and an art. While the science part deals with regularities, uniformities or laws, the art part deals with discharge of government functions particularly pertaining to taxation and provision of public services. Young took the view that political economy was both a science and an art. But since economics deals with communal problems of economic life, the role of economics as an art was indispensable. In his 11 March 1927 letter to Frank Knight alluded to earlier, Young went a step further and argued that economics was more an art in dealing with practical problems. For Young the evolutionary character of society meant that complete laissez-faire was out of the question. The government, directly or indirectly, had to assume newer roles like utility pricing and regulation, control of monopoly, control of credit,[10]

---

[8] The four we discuss—J.S. Mill, Walter Bagehot, Henry Sidgwick and Max Weber—are chosen pragmatically because they either wrote in English or their English translation was easy to obtain.

[9] This essay also appears as one of the references for the chapter on 'Nature and scope of economics' in Ely et al. (1930, p. 19).

[10] Young felt that government could speed up change through institutional development by creating independent regulators like the Federal Reserve and through creation of appropriate legal framework for this to happen.

subordination of sectional interest for larger national interest,[11] and subordination of narrow national interest for larger global welfare.[12]

Mill held that the distinction between political economy and physical science has to be deeper than the subject matter. Both deal with the objects of man's enjoyment, but are distinct branches of knowledge. Influenced by Mill, Young held that economics is better defined, not in terms of its subject matter, but in terms of the problems it deals with. "Every social science has to be defined in terms of its problems, and accordingly includes agents, instruments, ends, as well as a mechanism, among its postulates" (Young 1927a; Mehrling and Sandilands 1999, p. 5).

Mill stated that political economy does not deal with production and distribution of wealth in all states of mankind but only in his social state. And it deals with human nature in so far as it is concerned with the pursuit of wealth. These considerations made political economy a branch of social economy or speculative politics. Young also favoured the study of economics in relation to other social sciences. The final terms of economics may thus be modified by ethical, moral, political and legal considerations which an economist may not have taken into account.

According to Mill, political economy is essentially an abstract science, and its method is essentially a priori. The a posteriori method could be applied in the aid of the a priori method and must be considered an indispensable supplement to it. Further it was not possible to conduct experiments in political economy. So the only mode of scientific reasoning

---

[11] Young (1926; Mehrling and Sandilands 1999, p. 43), in his article 'Economics and war', quotes his history teacher at Wisconsin F.J. Turner (1925, pp. 275, 279) in this regard: "Statesmanship in this nation consists not only in representing the special interests of the leader's own section, but in finding a formula that will bring the different regions together in a common policy."

[12] Young (1926; Mehrling and Sandilands 1999, p. 43) stated: "But the nation, in its larger relations, is itself a section. Outside of its own borders its interests, real or supposed, conflict with the interest of other nations. Here statesmanship becomes sectional leadership." Young favoured international agreements for the revival of the European economies devastated by WWI. The so-called economic causes of war are not inevitable and unyielding expressions of permanent traits of human nature. "They are forms or patterns of conduct and are correlated with particular modes of organization" (ibid., p. 48). Further, "No sensible person expects that sectional interests or international economic antagonisms will disappear. But it is not unreasonable to hope that some day they may be subordinated to new and larger interests which will grow out of new forms of organization. At any rate, the only way to secure economic peace is to turn our eyes towards it" (ibid., p. 48).

was to proceed on the basis of assumed premises and arrive at generalisations. But Mill was also clear that allowances have to be made in proportion as facts diverge from the premises. Further, the deductive method has to be supplemented with induction or experience, and the results of deduction have to be properly qualified. Moreover, due allowance has to be made to disturbing causes, further qualifying the results of deduction.

Young had an admiration for English political economy and its abstract character. But he agreed with Mill that induction must supplement deduction. The results have to be stated with proper allowances and qualifications. Disturbing causes point to even more caution in interpreting the results. To go a step further, the disturbing causes may become so dominant that the conclusion itself may change. For example, the law of diminishing returns may be counteracted by other powerful forces such as cheapening of the means of transport and communication or technical change in agriculture. So the law of diminishing returns may be true as a tendency but not as a prophecy (Young 1929a; Mehrling and Sandilands 1999, p. 122). Similarly, equilibrium may be true as a tendency, but since the countervailing forces of disequilibrium are so powerful and unsettling, the net result is disequilibrium, particularly in the context of growth (1928b, p. 528).[13]

Next, there is Walter Bagehot (1895), *Economic Studies*, Chapter 1, 'Postulates of English Political Economy'.[14]

Bagehot makes the point that what were accepted as axioms and common sense for the nation in England, making it a rich country, appeared strange and curious on the European continent. The doctrines of free trade and a hands-off approach to government intervention in economic matters were unpopular on the continent. Free trade there was viewed with suspicion and a clever device by the English to ruin them. The English political economy continued to grow in its own way unmindful of developments elsewhere. Young believed that this tradition remained

---

[13] See also R. Chandra (2004) who argues that equilibrium economics was neither Smith's main contribution nor his chief concern.

[14] Young (1929a; Mehrling and Sandilands 1999, p. 134) includes Bagehot in the reference list to his article 'Economics'.

insular during a considerable part of its history.[15] Had this tradition not contained inherent methodological strengths, it would not have survived and grown.[16]

Bagehot points out that the real reason it was unpopular outside of England was its abstract character. In England it was defined as a "science of business" and analysed a world so familiar to Englishmen—the "great commerce". It assumed the principal facts which made this commerce possible and simplified them. It also abstracted and simplified human nature and assumed that man is basically guided by motives of business or making money. Each man behaved rationally, produced at the least cost, sold at the highest profit and tried to gain all possible advantage. This fooled not only foreigners, but many people in England as well, as man was unlike the caricature as depicted. English political economy did not apply to all societies, only where commerce was well developed as in England.

Young (1928a; Mehrling and Sandilands 1999, p. 21) characterised Bagehot's depiction of English political economy as an analysis of the "great commerce" as a "flash of insight". He also did not accept that man was rational and was always guided by motives of furthering his economic advantage. Young held that English political economy took its data from real life; the money-making behaviour of man only applied to his business dealings or his behaviour in the market place. Young further

---

[15] Elsewhere, referring to American sociologist Charles Cooley, Young (1929b; Mehrling and Sandilands 1999, p. 150) stated: "[I]n isolation ... ideas descend vertically, that is, they come down from the past, transmitted from generation to generation. Thus they are old ideas. With free communication between communities ideas tend more and more to come in sidewise, that is they come from the outside. They are new ideas. Communities without commerce stagnate." See also Young (1990, p. 110).

[16] "Despite the virtually continuous cross-fire of criticism directed against it by ... hostile schools, English political economy has continued to show extraordinary vitality. More than once it has been pronounced dead or moribund, and it has sometimes been the fashion to allude to it only in the past tense. But its influence has continued to grow and to become more widely diffused. Even where its findings are mostly rejected, its general method, its categories, its modes of thought, its way of resolving complex problems into manageable elements, are commonly part of the working apparatus of competent economists. It has been a fortunate circumstance, I suspect, that British economists (never a large group) have rarely given more than passing attention to the controversies of the opposed schools, but have continued to work at their own problems in their own way... The comparative insularity of British economics would have been its undoing if it had not within itself lasting sources of strength" (Young 1928a; Mehrling and Sandilands 1999, p. 19).

held that economics did not need psychological postulates, theories of hedonism or utilitarianism. In fact, as mentioned earlier, psychologists could learn more from economists than vice versa.

Young further felt that the abstract method was not a drawback. This is the only method, the 'inevitable method', for any scientific investigation. But since controlled experiments were not possible in economics, its theorems needed to be stated with due qualifications. They needed to be supplemented with observation and experience obtained from induction. As mentioned, Young did not believe in drawing a sharp distinction between deduction and induction, for in any practical research there was a constant give and take between the two. So there was a need to blend both. "The economist, like any other inquirer, goes from hypothesis to facts and from facts back to hypothesis" (ibid., p. 21).

Young observed that the emergence of 'great commerce' in England led to the emergence of some sort of order and balance in the new economic system making possible its systematic exploration. The new forms of economic activities and the new nexus of contractual relations became its dominating elements. Thus English political economy was not deductive or a priori in any real sense, nor did it put a heavy burden on the economic man. It had its orientation based on the newly emerged world. "Its method was determined by the circumstance that it proceeded upon the basis of a mechanistic or contractual as contrasted with an historical or institutional view of the structure of economic society" (ibid., p. 20). It is the contractual view, which is essentially an instrumental view, that helps us to frame practical working rules and supplies us the technical equipment for solving the communal problems of economic life.

Bagehot further stated that, though the English political economy was much more concrete than the mathematical theories regarding it put forward by Léon Walras or W.S. Jevons, it was far from *perfect*. It did not apply to all societies particularly where 'friction' or counteracting forces were strong. Moreover, English economists had neglected to supplement their doctrines with facts or to verify them with the available evidence, which, had they looked for it, was close at hand. Young, similarly, held that English political economy does not give us a finished set of doctrines. The most important thing which the political economy gives us is not a body of economic truth but an intellectual technique. It provides us with an apparatus to confront new problems and to reach reasoned conclusions.

According to Bagehot, free circulation of labour and capital were the basic postulates of English political economy. Factors like the caste system or slave labour prevented free movement of labour even within a country. Free movement of labour also presupposes the presence of different employments and a strong government to maintain not only internal law and order but also capacity to defend against aggression by other nations. Similarly, free circulation of capital presupposes sufficient division of labour and a medium to calculate profits—money and money substitutes. It also requires a strong and fair government and the emergence of a capitalist class to organise factors of production in line with human wants. Young generally agreed that the emergence of the great commerce was a precondition, as some order and balance was necessary, before any systematic exploration could be carried out. He further regarded commercial revolution as a precondition for industrial revolution. It is not the growth of technology or production methods, but the prior expansion of markets which makes progress possible. "[I]n the growth our economic civilization it has been commerce, rather than agriculture or industry, that has led the way. Production is limited by the market. It can advance only as markets are increased" (Young 1929b; Mehrling and Sandilands 1999, p. 151).

Next, Henry Sidgwick (1887, 2nd Edition): *Principles of Political Economy*, Introduction, Chapters 1–3.[17]

The first point made by Sidgwick relates to the settled state of political economy in the third quarter of the nineteenth century. This was preceded and then followed by controversy for similar periods. The settled state itself resulted from prosperity in England due to free trade and to Mill's masterly exposition in which he stated the doctrines with due qualifications and explanations. According to Sidgwick, there was a need to restate the doctrines of political economy in a more guarded fashion to avoid unnecessary controversy. A sharp distinction between deduction and induction could be avoided by applying both methods—inductive

---

[17] Sidgwick's *Principles of Political Economy* is also included in the reference list of the chapter on 'Nature and scope of economics' in Ely et al. (1930, p. 19).

method to the theory of production and deductive method to distribution and exchange. On practical matters dogmatic statements could be avoided. Since sound reasoning was required even in practical matters, Mill's approach regarding the deductive method in *Some Unsettled Questions in Political Economy* needs to be carried further. As we have seen, Young favoured a constant give and take between deduction and induction. In his opinion, there is a tendency to exaggerate the difference between the two.

Regarding the scope of the subject, Sidgwick stated that the general propositions concerning production, distribution and exchange are science while practical rules to attain certain ends constitute art. More specifically, principles of taxation and limits to governmental interference constitute art. But this sharp distinction is neither fully accepted in England nor is it accepted by continental writers. Young also did not believe in a sharp distinction between theory and practice on one hand, and between pure and applied economics on the other. "Economic theory, divorced from its functional relations to economic problems, or with those relations obscured, is no better than an interesting intellectual game. It gives endless opportunities for dialectical ingenuity. But it cannot advance knowledge, for it leads up a blind alley" (Young 1928a; Mehrling and Sandilands 1999, p. 20). Further, "The distinction some economists make between 'pure economics' and 'applied economics' is largely artificial" (ibid., p. 20).

As far as the method of political economy is concerned, Sidgwick raises two questions. The first is whether the science of political economy can be treated apart from the general science of society. Mill stated that as an organ in a body, although influenced by other organs, could be studied separately, production of wealth could be pursued as a separate branch of sociological speculation. Young also believed that political economy, although a part of sociology, was also a separate subject. Since every social science had its own orientation, "no complete *scientific* synthesis between them is possible, if only for the reason that … the inquirer, with his interests, stands somewhere *within* society and its processes" (Young 1927a; Mehrling and Sandilands 1999, p. 5).

The second issue again is whether the proper method of political economy is deductive or inductive. As far as the treatment of production by

Mill is concerned, the deductive element is quite subordinate. When Mill talks of deduction as the only mode of scientific investigation, what he has in mind is the theory of distribution and exchange, and that too is the static part of the theory. According to Sidgwick, the use of abstract deductive method needs to be supplemented by induction and observation. The assumptions need to be stated very clearly along with the cardinal terms. And a generalisation from limited experience should not be interpreted as a universal law. Although deductive method has its limitations, it cannot be accepted that the traditional method of English political economy is faulty or misleading. As we have seen, Young felt that its method was in no way peculiar to it—it was 'the' method, the 'inevitable' method—common to not only all scientific enquiries but all intelligent inquiries into general aspects of relations and events (Young 1928a; Mehrling and Sandilands 1999, p. 21). So Young deeply admired the nineteenth-century English political economy as an "extraordinary intellectual structure" and as an important element in the English "common scientific heritage" (ibid., p. 18).

Max Weber (1947): *The Theory of Social and Economic Organization*, Chapter I.1(a): 'The Methodological Foundations of Sociology'.

Weber stated that in scientific analysis it is convenient to treat irrational or emotionally determined elements of human behaviour as deviations from conceptually pure (or ideal) type of rational action. The influence of irrational factors can be better understood in comparison with this ideal type. Further, it is for reasons of methodological convenience that the methodology of sociology is 'rationalistic'. Young also believed that the abstract deductive method of English political economy was a matter of orientation and sprang from the contractual view of society. The theorems of pure economics arrived at by deduction from a few assumed premises had the right to be called scientific laws but needed to be interpreted with due regard to the limitations implicit in the premises. It was only for methodological convenience that the proper method appeared abstract or rational. But in actual fact, English political economy took its data from real life, dealt with real problems, and was an eminently practical subject.

Weber further stated that the laws of pure economics were examples of pure or ideal type, were based on rational human actions unaffected by emotional factors, and were based on human behaviour directed towards the pursuit of economic advantage. In reality such rational action is unusual and may happen on a stock exchange or in a market place. He further pointed out that it would be erroneous to regard psychology as the foundation of sociological interpretation. Young also rejected psychological postulates as the basis of economics. Assumptions of hedonism, utilitarianism or maximising behaviour could be left out without loss of generality. Similarly human behaviour may sometimes be regarded as strictly rational only in so far as money-making business is concerned, but man in general was not like that.

According to Weber, Gresham's Law (that bad money drives out good money) is an example of generalisation from experience. The facts of experience were known beforehand and generalisation was arrived at later. But in general any theoretical formulation without empirical verification would be worthless. Further, such generalisations were in fact typical probabilities to the effect that under certain conditions, under clearly defined ends, with no other means available, and given rational motives, certain course of action would follow.

As already noted, for Young, there was a constant mutuality between deduction and induction. One was incomplete without the other. Young also emphasised the theory of probability as an important tool in methodology and praised J.M. Keynes's *Treatise on Probability* in this regard (Young 1928a; Mehrling and Sandilands 1999, p. 24).

For Weber, it is a gross misunderstanding to suggest that an *individualistic* method involves individualistic system of *values* or there is a predominance of *rationalistic* motives underlying sociological concepts. Further, even the socialistic economy had to be analysed in individualistic terms, like the free exchange system is, in terms of marginal utility. Similarly, collectivities such as states, corporations or foundations had to be seen as resultants of individual actions. As we have seen, in Young's opinion, an individualistic method based on a contractual view of society[18] is a matter of methodological convenience. "Economics is indeed

---

[18] Young (1929a; Mehrling and Sandilands 1999, p. 125) contrasts the contractual view with the institutional (or historical) view of society: "Despite the extremes to which they pushed their contentions, the historical economists gave a needed emphasis to what may be called the institutional as contrasted with the free or contractual aspects of economic activities. Their work, and that of

abstract, as any science must be, but it has never been in any real sense deductive or a priori, *and the 'economic man' will be found upon scrutiny to be a fairly complex sort of person, whose behavior is taken to be self-regarding only in respect of certain aspects of relationships into which he enters as buyer or seller, borrower or lender*" (Young 1929a; Mehrling and Sandilands 1999, p. 126, emphasis added).

References

Bagehot, Walter (1895), *Economic Studies*, London and New York: Longmans, Green and Co.
Blitch, Charles P. (1995), *Allyn Young: The Peripatetic Economist*, Basingstoke and London: The Macmillan Press Ltd.
Bowley, A. L. (1924), *The Mathematical Groundwork in Economics*, Oxford: Clarendon Press.
Chandra, Ramesh (2004), 'Adam Smith and competitive equilibrium', *Evolutionary and Institutional Economic Review*, 1(1), pp. 57–83.
Ely, Richard T. (1893/1900), *Outlines of Economics*, New York: The Macmillan Company.
Ely, Richard T., Thomas S. Adams, Max O. Lorenz and Allyn A. Young (1930), *Outlines of Economics*, New York: The Macmillan Company.
Kaldor, Nicholas (1972), 'The irrelevance of equilibrium economics', *Economic Journal*, 82, pp. 1237–1255.
Knight, Frank (1960), *Intelligence and Democratic Action*, Cambridge: Harvard University Press.
Mehrling, Perry G. (1997), *The Money Interest and the Public Interest*, Cambridge and London: Harvard University Press.
Mehrling, Perry G. and Roger J. Sandilands (ed.) (1999), *Money and Growth: Selected Papers of Allyn Abbott Young*, London and New York: Routledge.
Mill, John S. (1844/2009), *Essays on Some Unsettled Questions of Political Economy*, Rockville: Serenity Publishers.
Schumpeter, Joseph A. (1951/2003), *Ten Great Economists from Marx to Keynes*, San Diego: Simon Publications.

---

their successors, has made economists more mindful of the way in which institutions are the masters as well as the servants of men, and less ready to assume that the particular economic order with which their analysis is mostly concerned is inevitably permanent or final."

Sidgwick, Henry (1887), *The Principles of Political Economy*, London: Macmillan and Co.mpany.
Smith, Adam (1776/1976), *An Enquiry into the Nature and Causes of the Wealth of Nations*, Chicago: University of Chicago Press.
Turner, F. J. (1925), 'The significance of the section in American history', *Wisconsin Magazine of History*, 13(March), pp. 275–79.
Weber, Max (1947), *The Theory of Social and Economic Organization*, New York: Oxford University Press.
Young, Allyn (1912), Jevons's *Theory of Political Economy*, *American Economic Review*, 2(3), pp. 576–89. Reprinted in Young (1927b), pp. 213–31.
Young, Allyn (1914), 'Review of Moore, Henry L., *Laws of Wages*', *Annals of the American Academy of Political and Social Science*, 51 (January), pp. 282–84.
Young, Allyn (1918), 'National statistics in war and peace', *American Statistical Association*, 16(121), pp. 873–85. Reprinted in Mehrling and Sandilands (1999), pp. 29–37.
Young, Allyn (1925), 'Review of *Trend in Economics*', *Quarterly Journal of Economics*, 39(2), pp. 155–83. Reprinted in Young (1927b), pp. 232–60.
Young, Allyn (1926), 'Economics and war', *American Economic Review*, 16(1), pp. 1–13. Reprinted in Mehrling and Sandilands (1999), pp. 38–48.
Young, Allyn (1927a), 'Economics as a field of research', *Quarterly Journal of Economics*, 42(1), pp. 1–25. Reprinted in Mehrling and Sandilands (1999), pp. 3–16.
Young, Allyn (1927b), *Economic Problems New and Old*, Boston and New York: Houghton Mifflin Company.
Young, Allyn (1928a), 'English political economy', *Economica*, 8(22), pp. 1–15. Reprinted in Mehrling and Sandilands (1999), pp. 17–28.
Young, Allyn (1928b), 'Increasing returns and economic progress', *Economic Journal*, 38(152), pp. 527–42. Reprinted in Mehrling and Sandilands (1999), pp. 49–61.
Young, Allyn (1929a), 'Economics', *Encyclopaedia Britannica 1928*, London: The Encyclopaedia Britannica Company, pp. 925–32. Reprinted in Mehrling and Sandilands (1999), pp. 115–34.
Young, Allyn (1929b), 'The creator of wealth', *The Book of Popular Science*, New York: The Grolier Society, pp. 110–16. Reprinted in Mehrling and Sandilands (1999), pp. 149–52.
Young, Allyn (1990), 'Nicholas Kaldor's notes on Allyn Young's LSE lectures, 1927–29', *Journal of Economic Studies*, 17(3/4), pp. 18–114.

4

Allyn Young's Contribution to Growth Theory

Allyn Young's (1928) paper on increasing returns and economic progress is a seminal contribution on the subject. About this paper, Joseph Schumpeter (1954, p. 875) remarked that one can form some idea about a lion from this single claw. It came at a time when the mainstream thinking on equilibrium economics predominated. Two predominant schools of thought—general equilibrium and partial equilibrium held sway. Young's paper went against the main current and saw the economic process not in terms of equilibrium but disequilibrium as, realistically, the predominant tendency in the economic system.

Young made Adam Smith's relationship between the division of labour and market size and Alfred Marshall's (1890) distinction between internal and external economies as his starting point and cast his theory of growth in terms of cumulative causation. Rejecting one-thing-at-a-time theorising, he advocated an all-together approach where all factors are allowed to vary at the same time. Once this is combined with the external field where change is both quantitative and qualitative, the conclusion that disequilibrium is a predominant tendency in the economic system is inescapable. Movements away from equilibrium and departures from past trends then become central to the economic process. Diminishing returns and unidirectional relationships, so popular in neoclassical static equilibrium theory, then give way to increasing returns and cumulative causation.

In this chapter we start with Smith's analysis of growth. Young, building on Smith, highlighted the role disequilibrium—and hence cumulative causation plays in the process. While discussing Young's contribution to growth theory, we shall also highlight the role of pecuniary external economies (as opposed to internal economies of scale), industrial differentiation (as opposed to industrial integration) and macro increasing returns (as opposed to micro increasing returns). We then discuss the similarities and differences between Young and Smith. Two of Young's students—Lauchlin Currie and Nicholas Kaldor—also made important contributions to growth theory. We shall discuss their contributions and bring out how they compare with the Smith-Young framework.

Young was also appropriated by modern endogenous growth theorists (e.g., Paul Romer, Robert Lucas and Kevin Murphy, etc.), modern trade theorists (e.g., Paul Krugman) and post-WWII development economists such as Paul Rosenstein-Rodan and Ragnar Nurkse. We shall examine to what extent they properly understood his message. It will be seen that these authors, although claiming to be inspired by Young, actually misunderstood his message and misrepresented him in important ways.

Smith's Growth Theory

The relationship between the division of labour and market size lies at the heart of Smith's growth theory. In this regard, Smith also stressed the role of systems, institutions and laws facilitating the exchange process, the proper role of the government in the system of natural liberty, the role of international trade, the role of competition, the role of productive and unproductive labour, the role of saving and investment (or capital accumulation), and the motive power of self-interest in bettering one's condition. However, the system of natural liberty, guaranteeing both liberty and security for the accumulation of private property, remained the big picture for Smith. Indeed he devoted much time and effort in analysing various systems to arrive at the one best suited for growth.

Smith noted that the division of labour arises in the process of exchange. It therefore becomes limited by the power which gives rise to it. In other words, the division of labour is limited by the size of the market. The larger the exchange nexus, the larger is the division of labour. So the key to growth lies in increasing the size of the market, by integrating it internally through public investment in transport and communication and opening it up to free trade externally.

Smith gave the example of pin manufacture to illustrate the concept of the division of labour. If each man is involved with all the operations of pin making, his output would be minimal. But if each man specialises in some particular aspect of pin making, there is a dramatic increase not only in total output but also output per man. Smith listed three advantages flowing from the division of labour—increase in the skills and dexterity of each worker, saving of time which is wasted by moving from one operation to another, and invention of machinery which promotes the division of labour. It may be noted that the pin-factory example is for illustrative purposes only as there is a broader process of the *social division of labour* at work.

To illustrate this larger social process, Smith describes the manufacture of a coarse woollen coat where many arts and crafts have to cooperate to render it possible. Smith stated that the shepherd, the sorter, the carder, the dyer, the scribbler, the spinner, the weaver, the fuller, the dresser, along with many others have all to come together to complete even this homely production. Smith again linked the social division of labour with the size of the market. For example, in the vicinity of a big city many trades thrive, but in the Scottish highlands it is difficult to find any for miles. There every farmer has to act as butcher, baker and brewer for his family. Further, with the growth of the market, a trade gets subdivided into many special types. While in the countryside it is difficult to find different types of smiths or carpenters, in the vicinity of a big city, there are various specialisations even within a single trade.

Smith was of the opinion that the division of labour was more fully carried out in manufacturing than in agriculture. Agriculture was different as it did not allow as complete a subdivision of occupations as in manufacturing. "It is impossible to separate so entirely, the business of the grazier from that of a corn-farmer, as the trade of a carpenter is commonly separated from that of the smith. The spinner is almost always a distinct person from the weaver; but the ploughman, the harrower, the sower of the seed, and the reaper of the corn, are often the same" (Smith 1776/1976, I, pp. 9–10). If the division of labour is better carried in industry, it did not imply that Smith advocated favours to industry over agriculture. In fact, he stated that in the natural course of development, the capital of a country first gets attracted in agriculture, then in manufactures and finally in foreign commerce.[1]

International trade is central to Smith's theory of growth.[2] Through international trade a country can overcome the smallness of its domestic market and the division of labour can be carried to the highest perfection. The productive powers of a nation are thereby increased and its capital gets deployed in the most productive lines. That is why Smith opposed mercantilist policies of interference in economic affairs and the accumulation of gold and silver by giving bounties on exports and putting handicaps on imports. Apart from ensuring higher growth, free trade has many other benefits. It not only keeps domestic monopolies in check but also benefits the consumer in the form of lower price and better quality. Smith did not cast his explanation of international trade in static terms or comparative advantage but in terms of the division of labour.[3]

Smith stated that national wealth did not consist of hoards of precious metals such as gold and silver but output of real goods. Therefore, to make the annual produce of a country as large as possible, governments should mind their own business rather than superintending private people's industry. Since the industry of a country could not be out of proportion to its capital, any artificial direction of economic activity through tariffs or other import restrictions misdirects its capital from more

---

[1] This apparent priority to agriculture arose because of differential rates of profit in different sectors (a reflection of disequilibrium) as noted by many scholars such as Gavin Reid (1989) and Samuel Hollander (1971, 1973).

[2] For Smith economic growth and international trade were two sides of the same coin. See, for example, Hla Myint (1977, p. 231) who argued that his theory of foreign trade is so closely interwoven with his theory of economic growth that both have to be considered together.

[3] David Ricardo's explanation of trade was in terms of static comparative advantage theory. A nation suffering absolute disadvantage in every commodity could still trade on the basis of its comparative advantage. It is possible that while Ricardo may have used it as an additional argument for free trade, the subsequent neoclassical literature made it the central focus of international trade.

profitable lines to less. The annual produce of a nation is thereby lower, affecting its saving, investment and growth rate.

Markets work on the principle of self-interest but in the end promote public interest as an unintentional outcome. "It is not from the benevolence of the butcher, the brewer or the baker, that we expect our dinner, but from their regard to their own interest" (ibid., I, p. 18). Self-interest is a very powerful principle—it becomes a means to the promotion of larger public welfare. However, Smith did not favour unbridled pursuit of self-interest. He was critical of organised business interests[4] who often conspired to raise prices and secure the passage of laws that favoured them. So any proposal of law coming from such classes needed to be viewed with great caution and scepticism before being passed. Moreover, self-interest did not mean a single-minded pursuit of some hedonistic principle such as utility or profit maximisation. In Smith, self-interest took a broader form of bettering one's condition—a desire which comes to all of us from the womb and never leaves us till we die.

While Smith saw that self-interest of man can be used to society's advantage, he favoured competition to keep his excessive greed in check. In Smith, competition is a process or a race in which the state acts as a referee, that is, lays down the rules of the game as well as enforces them in a manner to ensure fair play. It is not the job of the state to distribute favours or patronage to a selected few. In the system of natural liberty which Smith advocated, all favours and handicaps are withdrawn, the playing field is levelled for everyone, and winners and losers emerge from the competitive race. In this system each individual is free to follow his own interest in his own way provided he does not violate the laws of justice.

The desire to better one's condition prompts one to save, accumulate and become rich. Thus Smith emphasised the role of capital accumulation in growth: "Capitals are increased by parsimony, and diminished by prodigality and misconduct" (ibid., I, p. 358). Capital serves two purposes: it helps employ productive workers, and it equips them with better

---

[4] Smith (1776/1976, I, p. 144) stated: "People of the same trade seldom meet together, even for merriment and diversion, but the conversation ends in conspiracy against the public, or in some contrivance to raise prices."

tools and equipment. In both cases capital helps promote the division of labour. Smith even went to the extent of branding every spendthrift a public enemy and every frugal a public friend. From this it should not be concluded that capital accumulation is an independent engine of growth. Capital accumulation is important because of its link with the division of labour. Since the division of labour is limited by the size of the market, the use of capital in production also becomes market determined. Although Smith emphasised the importance of capital accumulation in growth, he did not say that it needs to be promoted through artificial means or by subverting the market.

Smith linked his theory of growth with his theory of evolution. He believed that the market system contains the seeds of its own growth.[5] The development process can be thought of an evolution from one stage to another where change is both quantitative and qualitative. These different stages are hunting, pasturage, farming and commercial society. Raphael (1985) held that this historical picture is geared to explain the emergence of law and government. Law and government are first needed in the age of shepherds when the concept of private property first arises.

Indeed the progress of society is crucially linked to the emergence of private property and the emergence of a civil government to protect it. In the system of natural liberty, the state has to guarantee private property and ensure a secure climate for its accumulation. The state also has to establish a system of justice which can punish or chastise the law breakers. While the working of the invisible hand can be relied upon to ensure growth and riches, the state confines itself to three basic tasks—defence, justice, and public works and institutions.

Smith dwelt at great length on various institutions and systems and their link with growth.[6] While all systems based on restraints and encouragements such as agricultural systems, slavery and mercantilism were inferior from the point of view of growth, the system of natural liberty which ensured both liberty and security was the best. It not only ensured

---

[5] This view should be contrasted with Karl Marx who held that the market system contained the seeds of its own destruction. While Smith emphasised harmony of interests, Marx was more interested in developing a theory of class struggle.

[6] See, for example, R. Chandra (2004) for Smith's emphasis on the role of proper institutions and systems in growth.

growth but also a standard of living for an ordinary worker many times higher than a savage king. Despite the inequalities inherent in the system, the system of natural liberty was not unfair to the labouring classes in terms of equity.

Although Smith decried state intervention in the private industry of people, he was not a laissez-faire economist, nor did he coin the term. Whenever self-interest promoted public interest, he advocated non-interference. Whenever self-interest led to subversion of public interest or where public interest was inadequately promoted, he advocated intervention. For example, he advocated free trade to keep domestic monopolies in check. He also advocated public investment in transport and communications to integrate the domestic market. He advocated public health measures to check offensive diseases like leprosy. He also advocated public education for the working class to counter the ill effects of the division of labour (or of repetitive work). It is obvious that Smith was a complex economist, and it is best to regard him as a champion of competition rather than a champion of laissez-faire.[7]

Young on Growth

Young built on Smith's dictum that the division of labour is limited by the size of the market. If market is considered in an inclusive sense as an outlet of goods in general, and not as an outlet of goods for a particular industry, the size of the market is defined by the volume of total production. This at once suggests that capacity to buy depends on the capacity to produce, and "Adam Smith's dictum amounts to the theorem that the division of labour depends in large part on the division of labour" (Young 1928, p. 533). Young stated that this was more than a tautology as "the counter forces which are continually defeating the forces which make for economic equilibrium are more pervasive and more deeply rooted in the constitution of a modern economic system than we commonly realise"

---

[7] "Smith's real concern was for establishing and maintaining competitive conditions rather than vigorous observance by governments of a hands-off policy in respect of economic matters" (Young 1929a; Mehrling and Sandilands 1999, p. 119).

(ibid.). Although Young did not use the word cumulative causation,[8] his explanation of growth was in this spirit:

> Every important advance in the organisation of production, regardless of whether it is based on anything which in a narrow or technical sense, would be called a new 'invention,' or involves a fresh application of the fruits of scientific progress to industry, alters the condition of industrial activity and initiates responses elsewhere in the industrial structure which in turn have a further unsettling effect. Thus change becomes progressive and propagates itself in a cumulative way. (Ibid., p. 533)

In making use of Marshall's concept of external economies in his explanation of growth, Young stated that change in the external field is both quantitative and qualitative. New products, new tasks, new materials and new industries are always appearing. So analysis of economic equilibrium will not serve to illuminate this field "for movements away from equilibrium, departures from past trends, are characteristic of it" (ibid., p. 522). In response to external economies, a firm or an industry loses its identity. "Its internal economies dissolve into the internal and external economies of the more highly specialised undertakings which are its successors, and are supplemented by new economies" (ibid., p. 538).[9]

Although Marshall's distinction between internal and external economies is useful against the common error of assuming that whenever there are increasing returns, there is an effective tendency towards monopoly, it is essentially partial view of the matter. "This will be clear, I think, if we observe that, although the internal economies of some firms producing, let us say, materials or appliances may figure as external economies of other firms, not all the economies which are properly to be called external can be accounted for by adding up the internal economies of all the separate firms" (ibid., p. 528). In other words, increasing returns are such that

---

[8] 'Cumulative causation' was first used by Thorstein Veblen (1898) in 'Why is Economics not an evolutionary science?', but Young applied it in the explanation of growth.

[9] In the rare case where a firm may not lose its identity, the conception is that of dynamic economies of scale as long-run average cost curves continuously shift downwards in response to the external field. So the movement is not along the same curve but from a higher to a lower curve.

they do not follow the law of simple addition. The social picture is more than the sum of its parts.

With increasing specialisation at firm and industry levels, as the size of the overall market expands, increasing returns take the form of reduced costs and prices. In other words, increasing returns take the form of pecuniary external economies[10] and a competitive market system is essential to their transmission. Thus in Young increasing returns are not mainly based on internal economies of scale or to any relationship between prime (variable) and supplementary (fixed) costs.[11] Smith's pin-factory example gives the misleading notion that internal economies of scale are the mainstay of increasing returns. As already pointed out, Smith used the pin-factory example for illustrative purposes as all the operations of pin making can be observed under one roof, but he did talk of the wider process of social division of labour in which not only new trades come into being but within a trade there is further subdivision as the market expands.

Young maintained that scale of a firm or industry was incidental to the broader phenomenon of increasing returns. Scale at the micro level may be important if the product is standardised and processes can be simplified.[12] It is also true that when the scale of a firm expands, its fixed costs are spread over a larger output leading to reduction in per unit cost. Internal economies of scale are basically the economies of capitalistic and roundabout methods of production. But the important point is that these are limited by the size of the market. So the scale on which a firm or industry is able to operate is not independent of the size of the market, and thus the scale on which a firm (or industry) operates is not entirely a matter for it to decide. Moreover, in an expanding market, costs are not

---

[10] In the literature two types of external economies are distinguished: (1) technological which operate through the production function and (2) pecuniary which operate through the price system. It has been pointed out that it is the concept of pecuniary external economies which is more relevant from the point of view of development. See, for example, Tibor Scitovsky (1954).

[11] For the details of the role played by pecuniary external economies, as opposed to internal economies of scale, see Chandra and Sandilands (2006).

[12] Young felt that 'rational' economic reforms or catchwords such as 'mass production', 'simplification and standardisation', 'reorganisation of industry' have their limits. "Pressed beyond a certain point they become the reverse of rational" (Young 1928, p. 531).

just spread over the output of a firm but the whole industry, indeed, the whole economy.

> The output of the individual firm is generally a relatively small proportion of the aggregate output of an industry. The degree to which it can secure economies by making its operations more roundabout is limited. But certain roundabout methods are fairly sure to become feasible and economical when their advantages can be spread over the output of the whole industry… The scale of their operations (which is only incidentally or under special conditions a matter of the size of the individual firm) merely reflects the size of the market for the final products of the industry or industries to whose operations their own are ancillary. (Ibid., p. 539)

Young also emphasised the role of large production (at the macro level) as contrasted with large-scale production (at the micro level) in increasing returns. We are likely to miss these economies if we focus too much on the scale of a firm or industry. "In fact, these economies lie under our eyes, but we may miss them if we try to make of *large-scale* production (in the sense of production by large firms or large industries), as contrasted with *large* production, any more than an incident in the general process by which increasing returns are secured and if accordingly we look too much at individual firm or even … at the individual industry" (ibid., p. 531).

When Smith wrote about the division of labour, what he mostly had in mind was job specialisation at the firm level and the emergence of specialised arts and crafts as the market expanded. Young went a step further to include specialist firms and industries which emerge as the broader process of the industrial division of labour unfolds. Young stated that as the market size expands, increasing returns mostly take the form of industrial differentiation as opposed to integration. "Much has been said about industrial integration as a concomitant or a natural result of an increasing industrial output… But the opposed process, industrial differentiation, has been and remains the type of change characteristically associated with the growth of production. Notable as has been the increase in the complexity of the apparatus of living, as shown by the variety of goods offered in consumers' markets, the increase in the

4 Allyn Young's Contribution to Growth Theory

diversification of intermediate products and of industries manufacturing special products or groups of products has gone even further" (ibid., p. 537). In this process, he also stressed that "the division of labour among industries is a vehicle for increasing returns" (ibid., 538).

He gave the example of the printing trade, which he thought was not exceptional, but characteristic of industry in general. As the market expands, printing splits up into a number of specialised producers of wood pulp, paper, inks and their ingredients, type metal and type, technical parts used for illustrations, specialised tools and machines.[13] Similarly, in automobiles, manufacture under one roof gives way to a number of specialised undertakings and industries manufacturing parts like wipers, mirrors, different types of glasses, batteries, bulbs, clutches, brakes, wheels, tyres, radiators, engine parts, axles, chassis and numerous other components. The older industry thus splits up into a number of specialised undertakings which taken together constitute a new industry. For Young, it is this process of splitting up which is at the heart of increasing returns rather than integration.

Furthermore, the makers of specialised appliances need not produce at full capacity to reap increasing returns provided their costs can be spread over a large volume of final products. "The derived demands for many types of specialised production appliances are inelastic over a relatively large range. If the benefits and the costs of using such appliances are spread over a relatively large volume of final products, their technical effectiveness is a larger factor in determining whether it is profitable to use them than any difference which producing them on a large or small scale would make in their costs" (ibid., p. 530).

Young also decried the use of the usual demand-supply apparatus in the study of increasing returns. It may divert attention to partial or incidental aspects of a process which should be seen as a whole. If however one insisted in using these demand-supply formulas, the best way then was to use them in the reciprocal sense. Given that the commodities exchanged are produced competitively under conditions of increasing

---

[13] "It is sufficiently obvious ... that over a large part of the field of industry an increasingly intricate nexus of specialized undertakings has inserted itself between the producer of raw materials and the consumer of the final product" (Young 1928, p. 538).

returns, and assuming elastic demand[14] for each commodity in the sense that a small increase in its supply are attended by increase in other commodities in exchange for it, then:

> Under such conditions an increase in supply of one commodity is an increase in demand for other commodities, and it must be supposed that every increase in demand will evoke an increase in supply. The rate at which any one industry grows is conditioned by the rate at which other industries grow, but since the elasticities of demand and supply will differ for different products, some industries will grow faster than others. Even with a stationary population and in the absence of new discoveries in pure or applied science there are no limits to the process of expansion except the limits beyond which demand is not elastic and returns do not increase. (Ibid., p. 534)

Young points to two obstacles to this unhindered process of expansion: (1) human material is resistant to change and (2) accumulation of necessary capital takes time. Those habituated to the equilibrium way of thinking may maintain that economies of increasing returns may be offset by their costs, but Young stated that this would amount to saying that no real economic progress was possible due to forces endogenous to the system—a conclusion repugnant to common sense. "To deal with this point thoroughly would take us too far afield. I shall merely observe, first, that the appropriate conception is that of *moving* equilibrium, and second, that the costs which (under increasing returns) grow less rapidly than the product are not the 'costs' which figure in an 'equilibrium of costs and advantages'" (ibid., p. 535).

Young stated that while the causal links between the progress of science and growth of industry run in both directions, it is difficult to determine where the preponderant influence lies. While growth of population,

---

[14] Young placed great stress on elasticity of demand for the smooth working of Say's Law. "There is a sense in which supply and demand, seen in the aggregate, are merely different aspects of a single situation. It is for this reason that some of the older economists held that general overproduction is impossible – a theorem which, though not really erroneous, has proved to be misleading… Only so far as the demand for a particular commodity is elastic is it true in any significant sense that an increase of its supply is an effective increase of demand for other commodities" (Young 1929b; Mehrling and Sandilands 1999, p. 145).

under most circumstances, needs to be counted as a factor in larger per capita income, it needs to be qualified by the fact that increasing returns may still be secured without growth of population. Young further stated that it is dangerous to assign to any single factor the leading role in that continuing economic revolution which has taken the modern world so far away from the world of a few hundred years ago. But there was no other factor which had a better claim to that role than the persisting search for markets. No other hypothesis so well united economic history and economic theory (ibid., p. 536).

Smith and Young: Similarities and Differences

There were many similarities between Smith's and Young's approaches to growth. Young built on Smith's dictum that the division of labour is limited by the size of the market. Both had an endogenous view of growth. Both had an evolutionary perspective in the sense that an economic (and social) system was viewed to be in a state of continuous dynamic motion. Both emphasised competition. But Young went a step further and couched his explanation of growth in terms of disequilibrium, cumulative causation, external economies, macroeconomic increasing returns, industrial differentiation and industrial specialisation. In fact, such vocabulary did not exist in Smith's time. Therefore, Smith could not have been expected to couch his explanation of growth in quite these terms as these concepts came much later. Many of these ideas are implicit rather than explicit in Smith. This section will argue that while Smith emphasised the role of institutions in growth, Young explained the growth mechanics more fully.

For Smith the system of natural liberty was the big picture and most of his other analyses can be fitted into this framework. Smith lived at a time when mercantilist institutions and restrictions were pervasive and therefore the system of natural liberty could not be taken for granted. Smith spent much time and energy in analysing various systems such as agricultural systems, slavery, mercantilism and the commercial society in order to arrive at the best system for growth. Smith's conclusion was that the system of natural liberty was the best as it ensured liberty and security.

Once these are provided, then the natural effort of each individual to better his own condition is such a powerful principle that it cannot only propel him but the whole nation to wealth and riches.

Smith was of the view that laws and institutions were paramount in determining whether a country would be able to acquire the full complement of riches. For example, China had long become stationary without acquiring its full potential as the laws and institutions there were oppressive. Holland, on the other hand, was close to reaching its full potential because of its superior laws and institutions. To take another example, Smith regarded security, and not bounty on corn, as the main reason for Britain's prosperity while lack of security and liberty in Portugal and Spain were responsible for their relative poverty (Smith 1776/1976, II, pp. 49–50).

Smith viewed slavery as inadequate from the point of view of growth as it is free labour, not slavery, which is conducive to technical improvements and innovation. Similarly, agricultural systems, by preferring agriculture and imposing restraints on manufactures, make the rude produce relatively cheaper, and ultimately end up discouraging their own favourite industries. The mercantile system, by focusing on production rather than consumption, as the object of industry and commerce, sacrifices the interest of the consumers, breeds monopolies and misdirects a country's capital. Moreover, it views the principal benefit of foreign trade as importation of gold and silver rather than (1) the importation of valuable goods in exchange for a country's superfluities and (2) the fuller division of labour through widening of its market.

So all systems based on artificial encouragements and restraints retard rather than accelerate the progress of society. "[E]very system which endeavours, either, by extraordinary encouragements, to draw towards a particular species of industry a greater share of capital of the society than that would naturally go to it; or, by extraordinary restraints, to force from a particular species of industry some share of the capital which would otherwise be employed in it; is in reality subversive of the great purpose which it means to promote. It retards, instead of accelerating, the progress of society towards real wealth and greatness; and diminishes, instead of increasing, the real value of the annual produce of its land and labour" (ibid., II, p. 208). The system of natural liberty, by ensuring liberty as

4 Allyn Young's Contribution to Growth Theory

well as security, was not only best from the point of view of growth, but also provided a reasonable standard of living even to an ordinary worker.

Given natural liberty, Young explored the mechanics of the growth process more fully. As mentioned before, Smith's pin-factory example gave the misleading impression of the relative importance of microeconomic increasing returns. Young emphasised the need to view industrial operations as an *integrated whole*.[15] For him increasing returns were *generalised* rather than sector specific, *macroeconomic* rather than microeconomic. They were based more on the economies of *industrial specialisation* than on economies of scale. *Differentiation* rather than integration characterised industrial change. He also emphasised the role of *pecuniary external economies* in the theory of increasing returns and the role of competition in their effective transmission. He also emphasised that the counter forces of *disequilibrium* were deeply rooted in an economic system and were continuously defeating those of equilibrium. He restated Adam Smith's dictum in terms of *cumulative causation* as: "the division of labour depends in large part on the division of labour". He also made use of the concept of *reciprocal demand* to suggest that each industry will grow at different rates depending on the *elasticity of demand and supply*.

Young (1928, p. 529) while comparing himself with Smith described himself as a "minor composer" and Smith as "one of the masters" from whom he had borrowed a theme to add "certain developments and variations of his own". This gives the impression that while Smith's contribution was great, Young's was minor. As we noted, while Smith's main concern was the establishment of institutions for a competitive exchange economy, Young explained the growth process more fully and explicitly. Moreover, Young was a very modest person as noted by several persons associated with him such as J.M. Keynes, William Beveridge, T.E. Gregory, Oscar Morgenstern and Earl J. Hamilton in the letters and obituaries written after his death.[16] Schumpeter (1954, p. 876) also noted that

---

[15] "[T]he mechanism of increasing returns is not to be discerned adequately by observing the effect of variations in the size of an individual firm or of a particular industry, for the progressive division and specialisation of industries is an essential part of the process by which increasing returns are realised. *What is required is that industrial operations are seen as an integrated whole*" (Young 1928, p. 539, emphasis added).

[16] See, for example, Charles Blitch (1995, p. 185) and Roger Sandilands (1999, p. 454, 457, 469).

Young had the "habit of hiding rather than emphasizing his own points". So while undoubtedly Smith's contribution was great, as he painted on a much wider canvass, Young's contribution was not "minor".

Smith's concern, as the title of his book *Wealth of Nations* suggests, was to enquire how nations could become rich. Though he was aware of the scarcity of land and the law of diminishing returns in agriculture, he did not, like his successors such as Malthus and Ricardo, make this the focal point of his enquiry. Similarly, Young also did not emphasise the scarcity aspect of economics. Firstly, he thought that the growth process once started was self-sustaining even with a stationary population and the existing stock of scientific knowledge—both pure and applied. Secondly, for him the law of diminishing returns was true as a statement of tendency but not as a prophecy. Revolution in the methods of transport and improvements in agricultural technique meant that this law was often overcome by other powerful countervailing forces. He thus appeared optimistic about the general prospects in agriculture despite gloomy prophecies to the contrary (Young 1929a, p. 122). Finally, he viewed scarcity as synonymous with productivity and thought that earnings of capital or labour could be attributed to both their productivity and scarcity. If viewed from the supply perspective, scarcity of resources appears as a formidable constraint on the satisfaction of human wants, yet viewed from a demand perspective scarcity becomes productivity. It appears that Young was planning a new vision which, unlike the neoclassical economics, saw economics more in terms of opportunities provided by a growing market than in terms of constraints arising out of scarcity.[17]

In the current development context, both approaches are relevant. Many developing countries, which still suffer from the mercantilist type of restrictions and institutions, can greatly benefit from Smith's institutional emphasis. To reap Youngian-style increasing returns, they first need to develop appropriate institutions, systems and conditions.

---

[17] For the elaboration of this point, see Chandra (2002, 2003).

Currie and Kaldor

Lauchlin Currie was a student of Young at Harvard but completed his Ph.D. under John H. Williams after Young departed for the London School of Economics. Currie (1974) was deeply influenced by Young as his leading-sector strategy of growth is based on Sayian or Young's intersectoral demand. Expansion of one sector constitutes demand for the products of other sectors, and expansion of these sectors in turn fuels growth in the original sector. Since reciprocal exchange characterises the overall economy, economic growth can be stimulated by expanding the chosen sector. It is important to note that demand here does not mean Keynesian aggregate demand but intersectoral demand in the Youngian sense.

Currie identified two leading sectors—housing as the internal leading sector and exports as the external leading sector. Both sectors had latent demand which if actualised by removing the institutional barriers would stimulate the overall growth rate. This would set off what Currie termed the 'Young multiplier' and Roger Sandilands (1990, pp. 320–21) as the 'Currie-Young multiplier'. This should not be confused with the Keynesian multiplier as it is based on Young's reciprocal supply-demand approach.

Currie identified two criteria for choosing a leading sector. First, it should have a large latent demand. Second, the increase in the sector's growth rate should be capable of being exogenous or independent of the overall growth rate. After discussing several sectors—textiles, transport, consumer durables such as automobiles, intermediate goods—which are either too small, have low elasticities of demand, cannot grow independently from the final goods sector, or are otherwise dubious in an economy with other important unmet needs, Currie selects two, namely, housing and exports.

Currie interpreted Young's conclusion that "the division of labour in large part depends on the division of labour" as "the main cause of growth is growth itself". Given the institutional and policy framework, the same rate of growth tends to perpetuate itself. That is, a low growth would perpetuate a low growth rate and a high growth rate would perpetuate a high growth rate. If an economy is caught up in a low growth trap, it could be extricated by exogenous changes in institutions and policies. He justified efforts aimed at these changes as they have a tremendous absolute effect because of compounding: "The tremendous gain resulting from high rates of growth sustained over a period justifies great effort to attain a higher rate of growth, especially for countries in the process of development, to capture the tremendous exponential gains from compound interest" (Currie 1983, p. 45).

Apart from the power of the compounding, Currie justified this strategy on the grounds that it would shift people from low paid jobs in agriculture to higher paid jobs outside it. Moreover, slack in the system is due to institutional barriers to mobility, low utilisation of equipment and inappropriate factor combinations. In such circumstances it is not the Keynesian monetary demand but "measures to ensure better mobility or better combination of factors" that would raise real incomes (Currie 1974, p. 4). In other words, this strategy was also justified as it would enhance the mobility mechanism of the economy.

Currie borrowed the term 'leading sectors' from W.W. Rostow (1960) who had talked about textiles, heavy industry or railroads as the leading sectors in the historical context of the take-off. But Currie was more interested in how to make things happen rather than what happened in history. "My interest is not to explain the historical growth process but rather to develop a strategy of accelerating growth. Most of the cases mentioned by Rostow 'happened once upon a time'. My interest lies rather in developing a strategy to make things happen, and for that purpose to identify large sectors where growth can be stimulated independently of the overall rate of growth" (Currie 1974, p. 14).

Chandra (2006) has argued that Currie's leading-sector strategy is neither based on the logic of sector-specific increasing returns nor on a policy of favours to the chosen sectors. Taking the first point, Currie did not have a sectoral view of increasing returns nor did he think it was possible to identify increasing returns sectors for policy purposes. Any attempt to identify such sectors would result in J.M. Clapham's (1922) empty economic boxes. Currie also stated that Clapham's position was close to Young "who was reluctant to speak of an industry of increasing returns even as a hypothetical example" (Currie 1981, p. 54). Further: "This strategy is more consistent with Young's overall or reciprocal supply-demand approach than with those who operate on same sectors by filling Clapham's empty economic boxes and stressing the internal economies of those sectors. Also it provides a means of passing from a constant low to constant high rate of growth" (ibid., p. 56).

As regards the second point, the term 'leading-sector strategy' is a misnomer in the sense that it does not envisage any favoured or privileged treatment to the chosen sectors, only removal of institutional barriers or policy handicaps facing a particular sector. Exports suffer from overvalued exchange rates. Housing suffers from a lack of suitable financial products which can spread repayment over a long period.[18] If these barriers are removed, the latent demand in these sectors can be actualised and these sectors can take off, pulling the rest of the economy with them. The idea is to make the market work in these sectors which was earlier frustrated by structural barriers or inappropriate policies. However, the logic of handicap removal need not be confined to the chosen sectors but can be extended to the whole economy. The field can be levelled for all sectors in the framework of "no favours, no handicaps" and the winners and losers then emerge from the growth process.

Currie's strategy is often compared with Rosenstein-Rodan's 'big push'. Currie (1974, p. 14) himself stated: "The use of leading sectors to achieve a Big Push (Rosenstein-Rodan's phrase) in developing countries occurred to me in 1960 and was published in *Operation Colombia* in the following year. It was further elaborated in *Accelerating Development*." Although Currie was fascinated by the idea of the 'big push' as an objective, his means of achieving it were very different from those of Rosenstein-Rodan (Chandra 2006). First, Rosenstein-Rodan emphasised the role of saving, investment and capital accumulation in growth. Currie on the other hand thought of capital accumulation as derivative to growth.[19] "The higher the rate of growth, the larger the saving and investment… The dynamic element is not saving, but the increase in real demand, which in

---

[18] Otherwise there is a front-end loading problem as repayments of the principal and interest get bunched together towards the front.

[19] There is considerable evidence to suggest that capital accumulation is not the cause but the effect of growth. See, for example, A. Montenegro (1989), M. Blomström et al. (1996), R. Lipsey and I. Kravis (1987) and Chandra and Sandilands (2003).

the longer term is dependent on improvements that reduce real cost and improve quality" (Currie 1997). Second, Rosenstein-Rodan talked about market intervention through a centralised investment board, with the need to step up rates of saving and investment as the market could not be relied to achieve optimal results, and industrialisation was seen in an inward-looking framework. Currie, on the other hand, relied on the market to boost exports and housing by removing handicaps where market forces are frustrated. Third, while Rosenstein-Rodan talked about the need to create a market by coordinating investment decisions on a wide front, this in actuality required large resources of both domestic capital and foreign aid. For Currie resources were not a constraint because if growth begets growth, it begets also the financing of growth, out of retained earnings and depreciation accounts of the businesses themselves. Thus growth was largely self-sustaining. Moreover, Currie did not stress foreign aid. Rather he relied on exports to finance a country's import needs. Finally, unlike Rosenstein-Rodan, Currie did not frown upon consumption as 'bad' and investment as 'good'. In his opinion, poverty in low income countries could be removed by producing what the masses needed—housing, textiles and consumer goods. But the sequence has to be right. By making housing and exports as leading sectors, increased incomes there would give a boost to consumer goods. By getting the sequence right, the 'big push' automatically becomes a reality.

It is possible that Currie may have used the 'big push' as a counterweight to Albert Hirschman's (1958) unbalanced growth.[20] Particularly, he did not like the ideas of forward and backward linkages, the principle of the hiding hand, and deliberate creation of artificial tensions, shortages and imbalances advocated by Hirschman. He thought that the principle of the hiding hand which involved exaggerating the benefits and understating the costs was immoral. He also disliked the idea of a steel plant in Colombia based on forward and backward linkages in view of its small

---

[20] Currie thought that the real issue was not balanced vs. unbalanced growth as authors such as Rosenstein-Rodan, Nurkse and Scitovsky were not specifically dealing with it, nor did they propound a theory of economic growth. Hirschman first made big push synonymous with balanced growth and then demolished it. The real issue, according to Currie, was to make a critical minimum effort (or big push) to overcome the obstacles inherent in a low equilibrium trap situation. This was elaborated in a manuscript written in 1970 but published posthumously much later (Currie 2018).

market and poor quality iron ore. To be fair to Hirschman, his approach resembles Young's disequilibrium economics, eschews detailed centralised planning, economises on the decision making, and appears more market friendly than Rosenstein-Rodan's centralised planning. Moreover, the idea of backward linkages is not totally missing from Currie because once the housing sector takes off, it will buy construction materials such as steel, cement, furniture, bricks, timber, tiles, glass and so on—an important backward linkage.[21]

Nicholas Kaldor was another of Young's students at the London School of Economics who, along with his classmate Maurice Allen (later an Executive Director of the Bank of England), took extensive lecture notes in Young's classes, and these were later published in the *Journal of Economic Studies* (Young 1990). Kaldor was initially influenced by Young and many of his papers showed Youngian influence but later converted to the Keynesian way of thinking. He was also attracted to Gunnar Myrdal (1957) who viewed the market forces and international trade as promoting interregional and international inequalities. In line with Myrdal, he subscribed to an inward-looking import substitution model of development in a planned framework. Kaldor was also a member of the Labour Party and subscribed to its ideology of Fabian Socialism, that is, the use of democratic means to bring about change. His biographer Anthony Thirlwall (1987, p. 6) mentions that when the Labour Party came to power in 1964, he was appointed as Special Advisor to the Chancellor of the Exchequer, and during 1964–1970 exerted more influence on policy making than any other economist except Keynes. His appointment along with that of Thomas Balogh as adviser to the Prime Minister was depicted by the press as the "Hungarian Mafia" or the "Terrible Twins" about to impose the East European experiment on the British people by squeezing out the capitalist class.

In his famous article 'The irrelevance of equilibrium economics', Kaldor (1972) launched a scathing attack on the neoclassical equilibrium economics as well as the assumptions on which it was based. He stated that the main task of economic theory should be to study cumulative

---

[21] However, unlike in Hirschman, Sandilands (2018) maintains that Currie focused more on the demand potential of a sector rather than on its supply-side, input-output coefficients.

change rather than the optimum allocation of resources. He emphasised the creative function of markets as opposed to their allocative role. He also thought that economic theory went astray from the middle of Chap. 4 of the *Wealth of Nations* when Smith suddenly got interested in the distinction between value in use and value in exchange on the one hand and between real and money prices on the other. His attack on neoclassical theory clearly reflected Young's (1928) influence.

Kaldor interpreted the Smith-Young approach to increasing returns in sectoral terms. While Smith did say that agriculture was a diminishing returns sector while manufacturing was the increasing returns sector, he did not say that manufacturing should be promoted through protection or subsidies. Any artificial direction to economic activity was anathema to him. Buchanan and Yoon (1999, 2000) have shown that in its minimalist formulation, the Smithian proposition does not require any distinction between various sectors or industries, but that a larger economic nexus is more efficient than a smaller. As for Young, he viewed the economy as an interrelated whole and had a generalised notion of increasing returns. Increasing returns for him arose largely through pecuniary external economies which required competition for their effective transmission. The Smith-Young approach leads to a framework of "no favours no handicaps". Kaldor, on the other hand, thought that increasing returns are confined to manufacturing which therefore needs to be promoted.

Perhaps Kaldor's emphasis on manufacturing owes something to Verdoorn's Law which states that there is a strong positive and causal relationship between manufacturing growth as an independent variable and manufacturing productivity growth as a dependent variable. Kaldor later conceded that there could be a two-way causation between the two in a framework of circular cumulative causation. He further suggested that manufacturing growth could itself be driven by export growth.

Young had stated that, assuming commodities are produced competitively under conditions of increasing returns and demand for each commodity is elastic, an increase in supply of one commodity is an increase in demand for other commodities and it must be supposed that every increase in demand will evoke an increase in supply. While Kaldor agreed that an increase in demand would evoke an increase in supply, the reverse may not necessarily hold. He felt that elasticity of demand by itself was insufficient to perpetuate the Youngian growth mechanism. Particularly, it needed to be supplemented by Keynesian monetary demand through "induced investment". Kaldor felt that an increased supply of elastically demanded goods may divert purchasing power to these commodities leading to accumulation of stocks of other commodities. These accumulated stocks would have to be financed by the banking system through credit expansion.

Currie in a letter to Kaldor dated 16 January 1978 (Sandilands 1990, pp. 298–303) criticised him for this position. Kaldor had assumed that there was no slack in the system, and this was contrary to reality especially in developing countries. "If the increased supply came from the work of previously underutilized factors, there need be no diminution in the aggregate production of goods and hence, in the Sayian sense, in the aggregate demand nor a shift in demand… So it is not the increase in investment in the Keynesian sense that is the key but the increase in output arising from (a) the economies of scale induced by actual growth (b) the taking up of slack (unemployed labour) or (c) the possible economies of more roundabout production (a special Harrod-Domar case of increased productivity from division of labour and specialization)."

Currie (1997) was also critical of Kaldor's one-thing-at-a-time thinking. While Young thought in terms of barter, Kaldor shifted the premises by introducing a money economy. Currie agreed that provision of additional money may help in smoother working of the barter system, the barter system had its own importance. Even in a period of recession, there were continuous improvements and cost reductions thereby increasing real demand. While money flows were important, things like 'economies of scale', 'the spread of knowledge' and 'the catching-up process' involving millions of producers were more important. It appears that Kaldor had underestimated the importance of the reciprocal supply-demand mechanism in self-sustaining growth.

Kaldor had a dirigiste mindset to policy making—even more than Keynes, as noted by Thirlwall (1987, p. 11). He believed that manufacturing was an engine of growth and should be promoted through protection and subsidies. He opposed Britain's entry to the EEC because if a country started weak in its growth, it would always be disadvantaged by the law of circular cumulative causation. He seemed to agree with Myrdal that international trade perpetuated international inequalities. In his opinion protectionism was good not only for developing countries but also for Britain. To boost manufacturing exports, Kaldor (1964) advocated a dual exchange rate system—official rate for primary commodities and free market rate for manufactured goods. As a tax advisor to many developing countries, he recommended an expenditure tax which favoured saving and penalised consumption. Kaldor (1966) identified labour shortages as the major constraint in manufacturing in the UK and recommended selective employment tax (SET) on services to speed up the transfer of labour to manufacturing.[22] It is obvious that Kaldor deviated substantially from the Smithian system of natural liberty, the Smith-Young stress on competition and their "no favours, no handicaps" policy framework. He felt that Smith had nothing much to contribute beyond the first three and a half chapters of *The Wealth of Nations*. Kaldor forgot that by analysing various systems, Smith was trying to arrive at the best one from the point of view of growth and the proper role of government in it.

Post-WWII Development Economists and Modern Endogenous Growth Theory

Post-war development economists such as Paul Rosenstein-Rodan (1943, 1961) and Ragnar Nurkse (1953) were influenced by Young's increasing returns paper. They agreed with Young that the problem of real demand (or market size) needed to be tackled if the underdeveloped countries were to break free from the vicious circles of poverty. Rosenstein-Rodan gave the example of a shoe factory. While an isolated act of investment in a shoe factory would not enlarge the size of the market, coordination of investment over a wide front was expected to solve the demand problem as workers would then act as each others' buyers.

Nurkse (1953) mentioned the vicious circles of poverty on the demand side as well as the supply side. He also quoted Smith with approval to

---

[22] Later in 1967, Kaldor changed his mind regarding the role of labour shortages in constraining the UK growth rate.

conclude that inducement to invest was limited by the size of the market—a variant on Smith's famous relationship. But his final view was that though capital formation was not entirely a matter of capital supply, but this was the more important part of the problem. To finance 'a more or less synchronised application of capital to a wide range of different industries', a high saving ratio as well as foreign aid would be necessary. Nurkse (1962), in principle, agreed that trade could serve as an engine of growth but that world trade had considerably slowed down during 1928–1958, so the trade option was no longer available to the contemporary developing countries. In the absence of this option, these countries were advised to follow import substitution policies including protectionism.

Rosenstein-Rodan highlighted the role of indivisibilities and complementarities in the production process. While the individual investment decisions would be frustrated by the forces of inertia, a 'big push' or a coordinated investment programme would launch these countries into self-sustaining growth. The size of the investment programme had to be big to overcome the obstacles to growth, and this again required not only massive domestic resources but also large foreign aid. In his 1961 paper, he also included social overhead capital in his big push programme. Though a sensible idea as it would integrate the domestic market, it would make the size of the big push even bigger. Rosenstein-Rodan also advocated a centralised investment board to coordinate the investment programme. He argued that the entire industrial sector needed to be planned and created as if it were one huge firm or trust.

Moreover, many of these development economists thought of pecuniary external economies as a cause of market failure. "Given an imperfect investment market, pecuniary external   economies have the same effect in the theory of growth as technological external economies. They are a cause of a possible divergence between the private and social marginal net product. Since pecuniary, unlike technological, external economies are all pervading and frequent, the price mechanism does not put the economy on an optimum path" (Rosenstein-Rodan 1961, p. 58).

While these development economists talked about the constraint posed by the small domestic market, the offered solution was capital formation or the supply of capital. They also talked about import substitution, protectionism, the lack of adequate trade opportunities and the need for foreign aid. Whereas in Young the growth process is self-generating, these economists viewed capital as a missing component, which if applied in proper amounts, would kick-start the growth process. While Young viewed pecuniary external economies as a vehicle for transmitting increasing returns in the form of reduced costs and prices, these economists thought of pecuniary external economies as a sign of market failure. While Smith and Young emphasised the role of competition in a market system, these economists advocated an interventionist policy in a framework of protection and import substitution. It appears that they misunderstood the basic message that increasing returns are facilitated in a well-functioning market, not in an anti-market framework.

Modern endogenous growth theorists such as Paul Romer (1987, 1989, 1990), Robert Lucas (1988), Murphy et al. (1989a, b), Paul Krugman (1990, 1993), G.K. Shaw (1992), and P. Aghion and P. Howitt (1998) were also influenced by Young's concept of increasing returns as well as Marshall's distinction between internal and external economies. They discarded the neoclassical notion of unexplained, exogenous technical progress. However, within the same production function framework, they made technical change endogenous by introducing such features as investment in human capital and R&D expenditures. They then claimed to explain what Young had in mind with greater rigour, clarity and depth.

Romer thought that Young was referring to some kind of competitive equilibrium in the presence of increasing returns. "The idea that increasing returns are central to the explanation of long-run growth is at least as old as Adam Smith's story of the pin factory. With the introduction by Alfred Marshall of the distinction between internal and external economies, it appeared that this explanation could be given a consistent, competitive equilibrium interpretation. The most prominent such attempt was made by Allyn Young in his 1928 presidential address" (Romer 1986, p. 1004).

Romer further thought that fixed costs and market power were essential ingredients in endogenous growth models. "The degree of specialisation, or equivalently, the number of different firms that are available at any point in time or location, is limited by the presence of fixed costs… Although Marshall and Young choose to describe specialization in terms of competitive equilibrium with externalities, it is now clear that a more rigorous way to capture the effects they had in mind is in a model with fixed costs. In equilibrium with nonnegative profits, price must exceed marginal cost to be able to recover these fixed costs, so the model must contemplate some form of market power" (Romer 1989, p. 108).

Krugman (1993) highlighted the role of economies of scale and imperfect competition in growth. Invoking Hirschman's (1958) concept of backward and forward linkages, he stated: "I would argue, then, the central concept of high development theory circa 1958 was the idea that economies of scale at the level of the individual plant translated into increasing returns at the aggregate level through pecuniary external economies" (Krugman 1993, p. 22). Moreover: "As long as there are unexhausted economies of scale in the modern sector, which are crucial to the argument, one must face up to the necessity of modelling the modern sector as imperfectly competitive" (ibid., p. 20).

The endogenous growth literature also stresses some form of market power such as patents, copyrights, protectionism, imperfect competition and strategic trade policy on the pretext that R&D, human capital and innovation costs would otherwise not be covered. This market power has to be policy-induced to promote higher growth.

This literature has been criticised by a number of authors. B. Fine (2000) suggests that there is little new in this literature as it draws heavily on the microeconomic foundations of neoclassical theory. What was earlier exogenous is now explained. Thirlwall (2003) also finds nothing essentially new in this literature since externalities arising out of R&D and human capital expenditures had earlier been emphasised by T. Schultz (1961), E. Denison (1967) and many others. Sandilands (2000) is sceptical about the stress on *new* knowledge as opposed to greater use of the already *existing* knowledge in response to new opportunities.

Chandra and Sandilands (2005) have shown that this literature misrepresents Young in important ways. Young did not talk about competitive equilibrium, fixed costs, economies of scale[23] or deliberately created market power as the source of increasing returns. While Young supported

---

[23] In Young, increasing returns are not due to any connection between prime (variable) costs and supplementary (fixed) costs but due to entirely different causes. "Large production, not large scale production, permits increasing returns" (Young 1990, p. 54).

copyrights, he was against all other artificial privileges including patents.[24] The production function framework employed is essentially an extension of the neoclassical supply-side view of the matter, albeit now yielding endogenous technical change. Young, by contrast, emphasised real demand. He also stressed the role of competition in achieving increasing returns rather than policy-induced favours or handicaps.[25] In his opinion a policy of favours and handicaps ends up distorting intersectoral relationships based on reciprocal exchange. In Young there is no end to increasing returns even with a stationary population and in the absence of new additions to the existing stock of scientific knowledge.

While Young was against deliberately created market power, he thought that some form of market power, product differentiation or imperfect competition could emerge from the growth process itself. The first innovators normally reap supernormal profits, but as others enter the field or new substitutes are developed, these tend to disappear. Young also stated that in the long run, pure profits were probably zero or negative. Moreover, product differentiation was a part of the normal competitive process in which each producer tries to be a bit different from others in order to compete. Selling costs are thus not market wastes but competitive investments. While some market power may emerge from the normal market process itself, it does not imply that an artificially induced market power is a sound policy to promote growth. Imperfect competition in the real world meant imperfect working of competition rather than absence of competition.

References

Aghion, P. and P. Howitt (1998), *Endogenous Growth Theory*, Cambridge: MIT Press.

---

[24] Young (1990, p. 52) favoured copyrights as otherwise it would not be possible for publishers to give adequate royalties to the authors.

[25] Young criticised A.C. Pigou's tax-cum-subsidy approach to promote increasing returns industries and to discourage decreasing returns industries as it "may stand in the way of a clear view of the more general or elementary aspects of the phenomenon of increasing returns" (Young 1928, p. 527).

Blitch, Charles P. (1995), *Allyn Young: The Peripatetic Economist*, Houndmills and London: Macmillan.

Blomström, M., R.E. Lipsey and M. Zejan (1996), 'Is fixed investment the key to economic growth?', *Quarterly Journal of Economics*, 111 (February), pp. 269–73.

Buchanan, James M. and Yong J. Yoon (1999), 'Generalised increasing returns, Euler's theorem, and competitive equilibrium', *History of Political Economy*, 31(3), pp. 511–23.

Buchanan, James M. and Yong J. Yoon (2000), 'A Smithian perspective on increasing returns', *Journal of the History of Economic Thought*, 22(1), pp. 43–48.

Chandra, Ramesh (2002), 'Thinking about development: going back to the basics', *Strathclyde Papers in Economics*, Glasgow: University of Strathclyde.

Chandra, Ramesh (2003), 'Allyn Young revisited', *Journal of Economic Studies*, 30(1), pp. 46–65.

Chandra, Ramesh (2004), 'Adam Smith, Allyn Young and the division of labour', *Journal of Economic Issues*, 38, pp. 787–805.

Chandra, Ramesh (2006), 'Currie's leading-sector strategy of growth: an appraisal', *Journal of Development Studies*, 42, pp. 490–508.

Chandra, Ramesh and Roger J. Sandilands (2003), 'Does investment cause growth? A test of an endogenous demand-driven theory of growth applied to India 1950–96', in Neri Salvadori (ed.), *Old and New Growth Theories: An Assessment*, Cheltenham: Edward Elgar.

Chandra, Ramesh and Roger J. Sandilands (2005), 'Does modern endogenous growth theory adequately represent Allyn Young?', *Cambridge Journal of Economics*, 29, pp. 463–73.

Chandra, Ramesh and Roger J. Sandilands (2006), 'The role of pecuniary external economies and economies of scale in the theory of increasing returns', *Review of Political Economy*, 18(2), pp. 193–208.

Clapham, J.M. (1922), 'On empty economic boxes', *Economic Journal*, 32, pp. 305–14.

Currie, Lauchlin (1974), 'The 'leading sector' model of growth in developing countries', *Journal of Economic Studies*, 1, pp. 1–16.

Currie, Lauchlin (1981), 'Allyn Young and the development of growth theory', *Journal of Economic Studies*, 8, pp. 52–60.

Currie, Lauchlin (1983), 'The 'multiplier' in economic literature', *Journal of Economic Studies*, 10(3), 42–8.

Currie, Lauchlin (1997), 'Implications of an endogenous theory of growth in Allyn Young's macroeconomic concept of increasing returns', *History of Political Economy*, 29, pp. 413–443.

Currie, Lauchlin (2018), 'The 'Big Push' and balanced and unbalanced growth', in Sandilands (2018), pp. 11–25.

Denison, E. (1967), *Why Growth Rates Differ: Post-war Experience in Nine Western Countries*, Washington, DC: Brookings Institution.

Fine, B. (2000), 'Endogenous growth theory: a critical assessment', *Cambridge Journal of Economics*, 24(2), 245–65.

Hirschman, Albert O. (1958), *The Strategy of Economic Development*, New Haven: Yale University Press.

Hollander, Samuel (1971), 'Some implications of Adam Smith's analysis of investment priorities', *History of Political Economy*, 3, pp. 238–64.

Hollander, Samuel (1973), *The Economics of Adam Smith*, London: Heinemann.

Kaldor, Nicholas (1964), 'Dual exchange rates and economic development', *Economic Bulletin for Latin America*, September.

Kaldor, Nicholas (1966), *Causes of the Slow Rate of Economic Growth in the United Kingdom*, Cambridge: Cambridge University Press.

Kaldor, Nicholas (1972), 'The irrelevance of equilibrium economics', *Economic Journal*, 82, pp. 1237–55.

Krugman, Paul (1990), *Rethinking International Trade*, Cambridge: MIT Press.

Krugman, Paul (1993), 'Toward a counter-counterrevolution in development theory', *Annual Conference on Development Economics*, 1922, pp. 15–38.

Lipsey, R. and I. Kravis (1987), *Saving and Economic Growth: Is the United States Really Falling Behind?* New York: The Conference Board Inc.

Lucas, Robert E. (1988), 'On the mechanics of economic development', *Journal of Monetary Economics*, 22(1), pp. 3–42.

Marshall, Alfred (1890), *Principles of Economics*, London: Macmillan.

Mehrling, Perry G. and Roger J. Sandilands (1999), *Money and Growth: Selected Papers of Allyn Abbott Young*, London and New York: Routledge.

Montenegro, A. (1989), Inversion y PIB: relaciones de causalidad, *Desarrollo y Sociedad* (CEDE, Bogota), 24(September), pp. 53–61.

Murphy, K. M., A. Schleifer and R. Vishny (1989a), 'Income distribution, market size, and industrialisation', *Quarterly Journal of Economics*, 104(3), pp. 537–64.

Murphy, K. M., A. Schleifer and R. Vishny (1989b), 'Industrialisation and the big push', *Journal of Political Economy*, 97(5), pp. 1003–26.

Myint, Hla (1977), 'Adam Smith's theory of international trade in the perspective of economic development', *Economica*, 44, pp. 231–48.

Myrdal, Gunnar (1957), *Economic Theory and Underdeveloped Regions*, Oxford: Gerard Duckworth.

Nurkse, Ragnar (1953), *Problems of Capital Formation in Underdeveloped Countries*, Oxford: Basil Blackwell.

Nurkse, Ragnar (1962), *Patterns of Trade and Development*, Oxford: Basil Blackwell.

Raphael, D.D. (1985), *Adam Smith*, Oxford and New York: Oxford University Press.

Reid, Gavin (1989), *Classical Economic Growth*, Oxford: Basil Blackwell.

Romer, Paul (1986), 'Increasing returns and long-run growth', *Journal of Political Economy*, 94, pp. 1002–38.

Romer, Paul (1987), 'Growth based on increasing returns due to specialisation', *American Economic Review*, 77(2), pp. 56–62.

Romer, Paul (1989), 'Capital accumulation in the theory of long run growth', in R. J. Barro (ed.), *Modern Business Cycle Theory*, Cambridge: Harvard University Press, pp. 52–127.

Romer, Paul (1990), 'Endogenous technological change', *Journal of Political Economy*, 98(5), S71–S102.

Rosenstein-Rodan, Paul (1943), 'Problems of industrialisation in eastern and south-eastern Europe', *Economic Journal*, 53, pp. 202–11.

Rosenstein-Rodan, Paul (1961), 'Notes on the theory of the big push', in H.S. Ellis and H.C. Wallaich (ed.), *Economic Development of Latin America*, London: Macmillan.

Rostow, W.W. (1960), *The Stages of Economic Growth*, Cambridge: Cambridge University Press.

Sandilands, Roger J. (1990), *The Life and Political Economy of Lauchlin Currie*, Durham and London: Duke University Press.

Sandilands, Roger J. (1999), 'New evidence on Allyn Young's style and influence as a teacher', *Journal of Economic Studies*, 26(6), pp. 453–80.

Sandilands, Roger J. (2000), 'Perspectives on Allyn Young in theories of endogenous growth', *Journal of the History of Economic Thought*, 22(3), pp. 309–28.

Sandilands, Roger J. (2018), 'Albert Hirschman, Lauchlin Currie, 'linkages' theory, and Paul Rosenstein-Rodan's big push', University of Strathclyde, Department of Economics, *Discussion Paper*, 17(17).

Schumpeter, Joseph A. (1954/1982), *History of Economic Analysis*, London: Allen and Unwin.

Scitovsky, Tibor (1954), 'Two concepts of external economies', *Journal of Political Economy*, 62, pp. 143–51.
Shaw, G.K. (1992), 'Policy implications of endogenous growth theory', *Economic Journal*, 102(412), pp. 611–21.
Schultz, T. (1961), 'Investment in human capital', *American Economic Review*, 51(March), pp. 1–17.
Smith, Adam (1776/1976), *An Inquiry into the Nature and Causes of the Wealth of Nations*, Edwin Cannan (ed.), Chicago: University of Chicago Press.
Thirlwall, Anthony P. (1987), *Nicholas Kaldor*, New York: New York University Press.
Thirlwall, Anthony P. (2003), 'Old thoughts on new growth theory', in N. Salvadori (ed.) *Old and new Growth Theories: An Assessment*, Cheltenham and Northampton: Edward Elgar.
Veblen, Thorstein (1898), 'Why is economics not an evolutionary science?', *Quarterly Journal of Economics*, 12(4), pp. 373–97.
Young, Allyn (1928), 'Increasing returns and economic progress', *Economic Journal*, 38(152), 527–42.
Young, Allyn (1929a), 'Economics', *Encyclopaedia Britannica 1928*, London: The Encyclopaedia Britannica Company, pp. 925–32. Reproduced in Mehrling and Sandilands (1999), pp. 115–34.
Young, Allyn (1929b), 'Supply and demand', *Encyclopaedia Britannica 1928*, London: The Encyclopaedia Britannica Company, pp. 579–80. Reproduced in Mehrling and Sandilands (1999), pp. 143–46.
Young, Allyn (1990), 'Nicholas Kaldor's notes on Allyn Young's LSE lectures 1927–29', *Journal of Economic Studies*, 17(3/4), pp. 18–114.

5

Allyn Young's Contribution to Economic Theory

Young made important contributions in the analyses of value, distribution, market forms (such as competition, monopolistic competition, duopoly and monopoly), social dividend and circular flow model, concentration of wealth and growth of big business, Marxism and socialism, and demand and supply. This chapter discusses all these topics except monopolistic competition which is discussed elsewhere (Chap. 8). Young also commented on Alfred Marshall's notion of consumers' surplus and one-thing-at-a-time theorising, A.C. Pigou's notion of social cost and so on. In the process, he used criticism as a method to advance theory. These aspects however will not be discussed in this chapter as these are taken up elsewhere in the book (Chaps. 2 and 9).

Theory of Value

Classical economists regarded value as antecedent to price. By value they meant value in exchange or ratio of exchange. Adam Smith made a useful distinction between value in exchange and value in use. While diamonds had a high value in exchange and low value in use, water on the other hand commanded low value in exchange and a high value in use. This paradox was later resolved with reference to marginal utility; while the marginal utility of diamonds is high, that of water is low. Hence high exchange value depends not on total utility but on marginal utility.

In the classical world, values are determined not with reference to money but in a regime of pure barter. Money is brought in at the end as a common denominator of the values reached through barter. In his paper 'Some Limitations of the Value Concept', Young (1911, 1927, pp. 199–200) criticised this position: "The concrete facts are the exchanges of goods and services for money and money substitutes. Prices, not values, are the primary elements of the situation with which the economic theorist has to deal… This subordination of price to value puts aside the fact that exchange values emerge only from the actual process of exchange (and there emerge as prices) as of minor import for the purposes of pure theory. The only excuse for this procedure is that value is the more general of the two concepts. But this greater degree of generality is purchased at the expense of precision and reality."

Young stated that even historically speaking pure barter was "probably a sheer work of imagination". One could override this objection, according to Young, if it could be shown that an idealised scheme of barter made for simpler analysis. But as Wesley C. Mitchell, an American institutionalist, had shown the money concept was itself an active factor in giving purpose, system and rationality to economic activity. Young believed that modern business was conducted by men who had learned to think in terms of money, and the price-making process was largely in their hands (ibid., pp. 201–2).

Young further pointed out that in pure barter there was no efficient tendency towards definite equilibrium. Between two commodities an equilibrium point might be reached if the market was fairly large. "But it would be quite unreasonable to expect that the $n(n-1)$ ratios of exchange thus established would be mutually consistent" (ibid., p. 202).

The subordination of price to value started from Smith who was interested in "the real measure of value". Young (ibid., p. 203) observed that this led to two divergent streams of theory. First was "the ultimate standard of value" which had a practical orientation dealt with in the literature on index numbers and standard of deferred payments and had no direct relation with economic equilibrium. The second was "the exact measure of value" where the marginal utility concept held sway. But in this analysis there was nothing which prevented a frank recognition of the role of money prices in economic equilibrium.

Young suggested that frank recognition that exchange value was derivative to price would not lead to any substantial modification of the theory of exchange. We had gone long past the point of diminishing returns as far as harvesting the concept of static equilibrium was concerned. "What is needed is an analysis of the actual mechanism of the price-making process. There should be no room for crudities as even an implied determination of prices by the comparison of the 'value of commodities' and the (independently determined) 'value of money'" (ibid., p. 204).

Young further believed that prices measure value in the process of exchange, and if applied to a stock of goods led to nothing but imputed value. Cournot had stated that the current prices could only be maintained if the market was not overcrowded. If additional quantities bought and sold affected the market price, valuation of a stock of goods would be problematic. Since exchange values are marginal values, price only applied to marginal units bought and sold. Thus, Young agreed with Jevons that the theory of demand and supply was properly a theory of the rate of demand and rate of supply. From this Young deduced the outline of a dynamic theory of price which would analyse the forces affecting the rates of flow of commodities and the rates of flow of money streams which were equated in the market. Such a theory would not lead to substantially different conclusions but would be definitely more cumbersome. But the use of the static method falsified our view in important ways. Young writes:

> Seizing a moment when the two streams are running smoothly and steadily (corresponding to the condition of static equilibrium), we imagine them, in effect, to be suddenly congealed. Then, with this tactical advantage, we devote ourselves to a painstaking analysis of the proximate factors determining the prices of the goods which happened to be thus arrested at the very moment when they were passing through the narrow channel of exchange. But to be satisfied with this achievement would be to fall short of the opportunity for system making. So we examine the upper reaches of

the congealed stream of goods, imputing value to everything we find, on the basis of price units discovered at the point of exchange. Going still farther we subject to the same Midas-like touch the upper reservoir of goods that are usually drawn upon only when the stream is running dry. And finally, by a supreme *tour de force*, we convert into value units those outlying pools of intimate personal belongings, not ordinarily appraised in terms of money value, even by those who prize them most, and from which normally only a thin rivulet trickles to join the stream of goods passing through the market place.

In short, for the system's sake, the whole material equipment of human living is recast in molds fashioned after the notions of catallactics. This view of things is implicit in a large part of the body of systematic economics. (Ibid., pp. 208–9)

Young in this paper on 'Some Limitations on the Concept of Value' confined his criticisms of the concept of value within the conventional limits of equilibrium economic theory. He felt that there was reason for questioning the elimination of money from the valuation process. Recognising exchange value as derivative to price would not substantially alter things. The introduction of money was not to be viewed as a concession but a prime factor in the situation, and this led to a wholesome change of emphasis. New developments such as the index number problem or the concept of marginal utility do not change the dominant role played by money in economic equilibrium. "From utility, up through marginal utility, subjective value, and exchange value, to price, is a long slippery road. Marginal utility, like price, is a relatively simple notion, close to the concrete facts of experience. Exchange value is a looser and thinner abstraction" (ibid., p. 203).

However, if premises are changed to a disequilibrium price-making process, the theory is substantially changed. Money emerges as a link connecting the theory of value to trade cycles where trade cycles are themselves seen as a subset of the broader phenomenon of growth. Thus, for the study of a modern exchange, economy money is indispensable. It links up the dynamic price-making process to trade cycles and growth.

Analysis of Various Market Forms

Nicholas Kaldor's notes on Young's (1990) LSE lectures from 1927–1929 show that Young had developed a full range of ideas on various market forms such as competition, monopoly, duopoly and imperfect competition.

Young believed that in the real world, competition[1] was the rule rather than an exception. He discounted the Marxian doctrine that competition everywhere was self-destructive and inevitably led to monopoly. Marxian interpretation of history was based on the assumption that, as competition was self-destructive, control would pass into a few hands. Even some courts, as pointed out by Young, had suggested that every competitor wanted to be monopolist. But is it really true that every competitor was a monopolist in embryo form?

Young argued against this view. First, the limiting form of pure competition was agriculture, and no farmer sought to monopolise the world wheat supply. Second, when a firm grew beyond a certain point, disadvantages accumulated faster than advantages. "So a 'capitalistic monopoly' is not to be found, nor can there be other than a short-lived monopoly of such a type" (ibid., p. 51). Third, price fixation under competition is shaky. A producer tries to maximise his product and, unlike a monopolist, does not have a price policy.

Young outlined three conditions for competition to be self-destructive: (1) there is no opportunity for goodwill to develop, that is, the commodity is standardised; (2) technical and physical conditions are such that there are a limited number of competitors; and (3) the proportion of fixed (or supplementary) to variable (or prime) costs is high.

Young introduced the concept of normal price which is the price just needed to cover the long-run expenses. Yet, at any given time, there are great deviations from it. Cost curves of different firms are also different. It would, therefore, appear that some producers could benefit if they cut prices and increased output. A good many writers had suggested that

---

[1] By competition Young did not mean pure competition but as it prevailed in the real world. Like Adam Smith, he had a process view of competition rather than an outcome (or end-state) view such as Pareto optimality.

underproduction was a chronic disease of modern industry. Young insisted that underproduction was not a disease but rather an inherent feature of growth in the system. "[S]urplus productive capacity is a normal and necessary condition of economic progress. We must build in advance when we invest for the future, and wait for demand to catch up" (ibid., p. 54).

How do firms actually determine their output? They grow up to a certain point but after that an outlay on plant and machinery is needed. Otherwise costs will rise sharply. "Plant cannot grow by infinitesimals; the representative firm generally has more power than is necessary for immediate needs. It shows progress rather than depression and is evidently, in the long run, productive and economical or it would not be done (e.g. a new railway where underproduction is a normal concomitant of growth)" (ibid., p. 48).

To illustrate self-destructive competition, Young took the example of railways. In a standardised product, a relatively small difference in price would divert trade as long as there is no goodwill. As the others also cut price, the process continues till prime (or variable) costs are covered. The prices may even go lower in a situation of trade war. For example, the Lake Eyre Service price of a journey from Cleveland to Detroit gradually fell from $2 to $1 to 75c to 50c to finally 25c with a free dinner. This resulted in a combination and agreement.

When a railway firm reduces its price below the normal price, then in the short run its total revenues obviously increase, but its net excess over total costs is lowered. In the long run, supplementary (fixed) costs have to be covered. When traffic grows, 'supplementary costs' become prime costs, that is, all costs are prime costs if a right period of time is taken. "When railways do compete they compete on the basis of prime costs, which leads to bankruptcy or monopoly (as the American railway history shows). The same holds good for local public services. In America, an attempt was made to regulate its public services by competition. The only result was that various people took advantage of it" (ibid., p. 49). Thus, railways and public utilities are examples of natural monopolies, and cannot be run according to the rules of competition. "With public services, the duplication of services is generally impossible, or evidently wasteful" (ibid., p. 50).

Young defined monopoly as unified control especially in respect of price. "The criterion is always price, as other aspects are ultimately reducible to this" (ibid., p. 51). He distinguished between three kinds of monopolies: (1) artificial monopolies which are created by the state like the GPO and railways (but these two tend to be monopolies anyway), (2) natural monopolies such as some unique natural resource or mines (e.g., Kimberley mines of South Africa), and (3) those arising from conditions making competition self-destructive. Under artificial monopolies, one can also include fiscal monopoly (where the objective is to collect revenue, e.g., salt or tobacco) or non-fiscal monopoly (e.g., copyrights and patents). Young held that copyrights are more defensible as otherwise it will not be possible to give adequate royalties to authors to encourage the production of good books. Patents, on the other hand, are unjustified as with the development of industry one patent is valueless without another. Developments in pure and applied sciences were not patentable anyway. Patents also did not fit the modern industrial situation and the system was so intricate that: "We can probably do away with patents and not much retard development" (ibid., p. 52).[2]

Young pointed out that reduction in costs under monopoly should not be confused with increasing returns. Most advantages of increasing returns can be had in those industries which are not consolidated. Increasing returns arose from increased specialisation, from reorganisation, not merely from increase in the size of operating units. A monopoly reducing its price to capture the market based this on the relationship between prime and supplementary costs. Increasing returns on the other hand were not based on this relationship but were due to different causes such as external economies which arise with the growth of an industry or a group of related industries.

Young pointed out that English laws were founded not on the statute of monopolies but on restrictions regarding restraints of trade. Combination of two or three individuals into partnership was generally legal. English laws were more lenient to combinations than American laws.

---

[2] To a modern reader, Young's views on patents may appear odd but it has to be borne in mind that Young, like Smith, stressed on competition as the best tonic for growth.

Young further stated that it was not possible to sustain an artificial monopoly against competitive forces unless there was an underlying natural monopoly. The question was whether these monopolies were in accordance with general economic welfare. "The advantages attributed to a large-scale industry are sometimes productive, sometimes competitive. So far as they are productive they are economies socially. But competitive advantages are not necessarily social. For example, buying raw material at low prices through large-scale buying" (ibid., p. 56).

Young also put forward interesting ideas regarding monopoly price. Young stated that a monopolist will maximise his net profits where marginal cost equals marginal revenue. If the cost curves are such that increasing returns exist, then a monopolist may not try to maximise his net returns in the short term. The longer the time period he considers, the lower the price he will set. Moreover, a monopolist is not fully aware of his demand and supply functions. This ignorance makes him raise his prices slowly if at all. Finally, public opinion also counts for much, so that monopoly prices are not as high as the theory suggests. There is always a fear that too high a price may attract public regulation.

Young also discussed four solutions to the duopoly problem in which there are two producers. Each solution is correct depending on the premises—it depends on how far each producer takes account of the actions of the other. The four solutions are (1) price is set between competition price and monopoly price; (2) they combine; (3) the problem is indeterminate; and (4) they will set a price, without combination, as if they had been in combination as a monopoly. Francis Edgeworth had suggested that the solution is indeterminate. Young, on the other hand, had suggested the fourth solution. In his review of A.L. Bowley's *The Mathematical Groundwork of Economics*, Young stated that if the cost curves of the two producers are alike, the price "will be fixed at the point where it would be put by a monopolist who could produce 2x units at just twice the cost incurred by either competitor in producing x units" (Young 1925, p. 134).

Young also discussed a case of price discrimination between the domestic and foreign market. A cartel charges lower price in the foreign market and higher in the domestic market. Those who oppose cartels claim that foreigners are unduly benefitted from this combination, while apologists argue that home consumers benefit in the long run as otherwise the same level of output could not be maintained and domestic prices would be still higher. If increasing returns are secured by an industry, the required capital is supplied by domestic consumers in the form of an imposed levy through higher prices. This is different from the infant-industry case where increasing returns set in sharply after a certain point has been reached. In the present case, the assumption is that the community's discount rate is lower than the individual's.

Theory of Distribution

Young (Ely et al. 1923) made a distinction between the distribution of income among persons and the distribution of income among productive factors. The first concerns the distribution of income or wealth among individuals and families and deals with questions of individual fortunes, poverty and wealth. It also involves ethical aspects of the problem. The second concerns the apportionment of the product to different factors of production such as land, labour and capital. "This is not a question of wealth versus poverty, but of wages versus interest, profits, and rent. Of course this kind of distribution affects the personal distribution of wealth, but the two are by no means identical" (ibid., pp. 382–3).

To explain factor prices—wages, rents and interest—there are special and distinguishing characteristics concerning each. For example, the conditions governing the supply of labour are very different from the conditions governing the supply of land. However, there are some common elements entering into each of these prices such as diminishing productivity and equality of marginal product and expense of each additional unit of a factor employed.

According to the law of diminishing productivity, when more and more units of a variable factor are employed, other factors remaining unchanged, total output will increase but after a point at a diminishing rate. So each factor will be employed to a point where its price equals the marginal product it contributes. That is, for each marginal unit employed, a labourer should earn his wages, land its rent and capital its interest. "In order to achieve maximum profits, each entrepreneur will endeavor, so far as is practicable, to apportion his use of different classes of productive agents so that the value of the increment of product attributable to the marginal unit of each will about equal its expense" (ibid., p. 392).

Further, given free competition, different entrepreneurs in the same market will pay the same wages for the same kind of labour, the same price for the same kind of capital goods, and the same rent for the same kind of land. "Moreover, *any one unit* of the aggregate amount of a productive agent of any one kind employed at any one time may be deemed to be the marginal unit" (ibid., p. 393).

But it cannot be supposed that equality of factor price with the value of its marginal product is a complete explanation of factor rewards.[3] "In fact, from one point of view, marginal productivity itself depends upon the prices which the entrepreneur has to pay for the services of the factors in production… The demand for the use of land, labor, and capital goods is ultimately a demand for their products—the goods that satisfy human wants[4]… The wages, rent, and interest that are actually paid for the services of the factors in production are the resultants of the demand of entrepreneurs, on the one hand, and the supply of these factors on the other hand… The principle of marginal productivity is thus an illuminating way of stating the problem of distribution of wealth, rather than a solution to it" (ibid., p. 396).

Young also insisted that the statement that rewards tend to equal products has no ethical significance. First, the ethical side of the problem relates to personal distribution of income. Second, efficiency of an

---

[3] The marginal productivity theory of distribution, due to J.B. Clark, can be seen as an answer partly to Karl Marx who regarded labour as the only source of value (and therefore spoke of the exploitation of labour through surplus value), and partly to Henry George, who regarded rent as unearned and rise in land values as an unearned increment. J.B. Clark suggested that provided there was competition factor reward in line with a factor's marginal contribution was a fair outcome as each factor got what it contributed. Later on, Knut Wicksell demonstrated that the total product will be exhausted if constant returns to scale are assumed, and thus constant returns to scale came to be linked with competition.

[4] The demand for factors of production is a derived demand. The value of productive agents depends on the value of final products produced by them. "The problem of distribution, viewed from this particular angle, is the problem of discovering the general relations between the values of the final products of trade and industry and the values of the productive agents" (Young 1929b, Mehrling and Sandilands 1999, p. 128). Young further stated that if the factors of production are combined in fixed proportions to produce final goods, the problem is relatively simple. The problem becomes exceedingly complex because goods can be produced in several ways using simple or highly roundabout methods, and given the fact of factor substitutability.

individual worker, which is one of the things determining his productivity, often depends on the *opportunity* to realise his potential.[5] Third, the marginal product of a factor is itself the result of forces affecting supply of factors and the conditions which affect their suitability in producing things currently in demand. Finally, the doctrine is a statement of normal tendency and is subject to economic friction, inertia, custom, haggling of the market as well as social control in the form of labour and usury laws. "Actual wages may differ from the normal wages measured by marginal product just as contractual rent may differ from economic rent" (ibid., p. 399).

Just as there are free goods in consumption, so there are free production goods like wind, oceans, lakes and natural forces of all kinds, but they cannot be called productive. For example, wind is not productive, windmills are. Oceans are not productive but vessels and docks are. Productivity can only be attributed to goods or services which are objects of property rights or other analogous rights of control. "We harness natural forces for the work of production, but we impute productivity only to the harness" (ibid., p. 398).

Marginal productivity cannot be attributed solely to the marginal unit of a factor. It has social aspects as well. If a nation is faced with immigration, without corresponding increase in land and capital, its total output may increase as also the marginal product of land and capital, but the marginal product of labour may decline. So rents and interest may rise but wages may fall. If the supply of capital in a country goes up, land and labour remaining constant, rents and wages are likely to go up while remuneration of capital may fall. "In a very real sense the same labourer is more productive in a country where land is relatively plentiful than in a country where land is relatively scarce. A labourer may gain no technical efficiency by migrating from Europe to America, but the increment of product attributable to his work is likely to be considerably larger in the United States than it was in Europe" (ibid., p. 400).

Young was generally critical of neoclassical marginal productivity theory of distribution as it was a partial explanation of factor rewards. While

---

[5] "What a man can produce depends not only on his capacities, but on his various opportunities, past and present, including mobility" (Young 1990, p. 73).

factor payments depend on a factor's marginal contribution, they also depend on its relative scarcity. By relative scarcity he meant demand for a factor in relation to its supply. In fact, he stated that there is no fundamental difference between scarcity and productivity; they are merely two aspects of a single situation.[6] "Capital would not be deemed productive if its supply were not limited, nor would it be deemed scarce if it were not productive. Whether the earnings of capital are attributable to its productivity or to its scarcity is therefore a meaningless question" (Young 1929a; Mehrling and Sandilands 1999, pp. 137–8).[7]

Marginal productivity may be a useful tool at the micro level and may help an entrepreneur to apportion his expenses to different factors but the additive process does not give a good social picture. "One should not fix one's eyes too narrowly on the way the individual entrepreneur apportions his expenses. One cannot apply an additive process, and find the picture for the whole economy" (Young 1990, p. 73). While diminishing productivity to a factor may be a reality at the micro level, at the macro level increasing returns are generally the norm. So integration does not give a good social picture.

Young's conclusion was that the real significance of the marginal productivity theory, taken by itself, was not that factors are paid in line with what they contribute but as a corrective to the even more misleading notion that there is no relationship between rewards and productivity (Young 1929b; Mehrling and Sandilands 1999, p. 129).

---

[6] "This does not mean that you can create a product by creating scarcity, however" (Young 1990, p. 73).

[7] Young (1929a; Mehrling and Sandilands 1999) stated that neither labour nor capital were inherently productive. Just as land could grow thistles as well as figs, so labour and capital could be used to make things that nobody wanted, and therefore would have no value. Productivity and scarcity had to be seen together. "When we say that capital is productive we imply not only that capital can be used so as to increase the supply of valuable goods but also that the supply of capital itself is in some degree limited or inelastic" (p. 137).

The Rent of Land

Young (Ely et al. 1923, p. 402) defined rent as the price paid for the services of land. Young noted two features about land—its quality and its location. As regards quality, there were different fertilities of different types of land which are seen by some (e.g., Ricardo 1817/1971, p. 91) to depend on the "original and indestructible powers of the soil". But some other writers have denied the significance of this factor arguing that soil was not indestructible as it could be exhausted or replenished by fertilisation. There was no other indestructible property than standing room. Young noted that while "soil" or the top layer could be carted on and off at will, there were many properties that still remained indestructible or unproducible such as whether land was hilly or plain, or whether located on the north side of a mountain or the south, whether it received adequate rainfall or not and so on. The ownership of land carries with it all the conditions attached to it. So the expression 'original and indestructible properties of the soil' may be inadequate and misleading but expresses more than 'standing room'. It is therefore better to define the quality of land in terms of 'irremovable conditions affecting its productiveness'.

The location of land is closely connected to climate but usually refers to its situation with respect to markets. Land nearer the market centres would be worth much more than that far away from them. This however is a matter of accessibility rather than mere distance. The availability of transportation facilities and their cost is also an important factor. For example, revolution in ocean transport had a dampening influence on rent in England and brought distant lands very near her shores. While the quality of a piece of land affected its physical product, its location affected the price of the product.

Young also talked about the extensive and intensive margin of cultivation. Settlers in a new country occupy the best lands and pay no rent on it. As long as the best quality land is widely available for free there is no reason to pay rent. As population increases, cultivation of inferior grades is undertaken, and the owner of better lands will be able to demand a rent. With further increase in population, cultivation of land would be extended to lower quality lands till the point where expense of production of the marginal land equals the value of its product. If it is assumed that the same amount of labour and capital is used per acre, then:

> Rent, under these conditions, is a differential which measures accurately the superiority of the rent-bearing land over the *marginal land*—the land which just repays the expenses of production. It is not necessary to the significance of the theory that all, or even any, of the farmers should be tenant farmers. If the farmer owns the land that he operates, the part of his income which may be imputed to the superiority of his land over an equal area of marginal land must, in any accurate accounting, be counted as rent. (Ibid., p. 407)

It is however not necessary to cultivate poorer lands after the best lands have been exhausted. Best lands can be cultivated more intensively by applying increasing amounts of labour and capital per acre. If this is done, the law of diminishing productivity is encountered. "It will pay, however, to go up to the point where the last unit of labor and capital adds barely enough to the product to pay for the increased expense, – a point which is called the *intensive margin*" (ibid., p. 407).

In general: "The rent of any piece of land is measured by the difference between the money value of the products obtained from it by the use of the most advantageous amounts of labor and capital and the money value of the products which could be obtained by the use of the same amounts of labor and capital on marginal land, or at the intensive margin of cultivation" (ibid., p. 409).

Young pointed out that land is valued because of its income-earning power. Land is valued because it commands a rent. It is a fallacy to suppose that high land values lead to high agricultural product prices. "High prices of agricultural products lead to high rents, which in turn make land values high" (ibid., p. 412). In England, where lands are commonly leased, the price of land is its annual rent, and the selling price as the number of years' purchase. Capitalisation is the determination of selling price on the basis of annual income. Common observation shows that the rate of capitalisation—the ratio of income to selling value—is lower in land than for most capital goods.

5 Allyn Young's Contribution to Economic Theory

Young stated that there was a general tendency of rents to increase with economic progress as it was impossible to meet the demands of a growing and wealthier population without resort to more intensive and extensive cultivation. Bound up with this tendency was the law of diminishing returns which had been made as the basis of gloomy prophecies regarding the prospects for continued economic progress. Young stated that the history of the nineteenth century had belied these gloomy prophecies. Despite the increase in population rents, in the older parts of the world had not increased (after making due allowance for changes in the purchasing power of money). Young explains:

> This does not disprove the law of diminishing returns. That law, like other economic laws, is true only as a statement of tendency. If the tendency has not resulted in increased rents, it is not because it has not been operative, but because other powerful factors have counteracted its effects. Two things, at least, have prevented a rise in rents. In the first place, improvements in agricultural methods have greatly increased the product which can be got from a given acre of land… Of much greater importance … has been the revolution in ocean and land transportation, which has enormously increased the available amount of land. Lands in England have gone out of cultivation because the railway and the steamship have brought the great wheat fields of America to her very doors. (Ibid., pp. 414–5)

His view was that the principle of diminishing returns does not pose any fixed or rigid barrier to economic progress. It operates in an exceedingly elastic manner. For example, small increases in prices of lamb, mutton and woollen goods over a long enough period makes it profitable to use the range system if land is abundant and cheap, while in congested regions, sheep-raising on farms becomes important as a part of diversified agriculture. Similar considerations applied to cattle. "Relatively large additions to the annual product of agriculture are available, even without further advances in agricultural technique, at *relatively* small increases in cost per unit" (ibid., p. 417, italics in original). Further, changes in the pattern of demand may shift lands from the present uses to crops for which they are more suited. Young concluded:

> Although it is absurd to suppose that the rent of land will not increase as society continues to increase in wealth and numbers, it is just as absurd to make this fundamental tendency toward diminishing returns in agriculture a basis for pessimistic views regarding the possibility of economic progress. (Ibid., p. 417)

Young further pointed out that the sum total of all rents (as distinguished from rent per acre), and consequently the land values, is much greater today than at any time in the past. The increase in land value which is accompanied by its income-yielding power is often termed as unearned increment. This suggests that the rise in land values is not due to any special efforts on the part of the owner but due to general economic progress, that is, rise in population and average wealth. According to Young, the phrase unearned increment is misleading because, as generally used, it implies that land is rarely produced, so land values are always unearned as compared with produced goods which incur expenses of production. Young stated that an expense is incurred in producing goods because people want them and are willing to pay for them. Similarly: "land commands a price because its supply is naturally limited, and because there are competing users of land who can apportion the available supply among themselves only on the basis of prices and rents corresponding to the advantages which different pieces of land give their possessors" (ibid., p. 419). Moreover, so far as increase in land values can be foreseen or anticipated, it will be discounted. So increase in land values cannot be wholly termed unearned, firstly, because a foreseen increment has to be paid for and, secondly, the expense of buying and holding land is like any other business. Often great sacrifices are involved in settling new lands and making improvements on them which otherwise may not have been made if the anticipated rise in land values had not been counted as earned.

Henry George, an American reformer, had advocated a single tax on land values. His plea was that all improvements in productive powers of labour are reflected in rise in rents and hence land values. All the advantages of economic progress go to owners of land, and wages do not increase. Young criticised this position. Firstly all improvements in the methods of production do not necessarily mean improvements in the productive powers of labour. All factors—land, labour and capital—cooperate in production, so fruits of improvements are due to all three. Secondly, if supply of labour rises faster than the supply of land, rents may rise faster than wages, but this does not preclude an absolute advance in wages too. Henry George did not propose to abolish rent but only its private receipt, as he thought this, by preventing speculative holding of land, would lower rents. In Young's opinion, land held for purely speculative purposes is often overestimated. Prestige of ownership and its use in more profitable and important ways in future have to be taken into account. Further, land in urban areas as elsewhere is subject to true unearned decrements as well as true unearned increments.[8]

Is rent a cost? According to Young (1990, p. 97), 'rent enters into cost' and 'rent does not enter into cost' are both true. From an individual entrepreneur's point of view rent is a cost, but from the social point of view rent is not a cost. The Ricardian principle 'rent is high because the price of corn is high' implies that rent does not cause price, but rather is the result of it. Ricardo was looking at long-run tendencies as well as the social point of view. When rents rise, the distribution of social dividend is affected. Share of landowners increases while that of other factors diminishes. From the social point of view, rent is therefore not a cost but a transfer payment from other factors to owners of land.

Young's (ibid., p. 98) own attitude to rent was closer to J.S. Mill who viewed rent as a purely distributive problem:

> Do landlords gain at the expense of other members of society? The Ricardian attitude showed rent as due to niggardliness of nature. But surely rent is neither a charge nor a bounty, but merely a distributive problem; cff. Mill and other radicals, especially Henry George. The origin of the idea of confiscating unearned increment is not with George, but with the early English socialists. (See Foxwell's introduction to Marx)

---

[8] "Taking the average, the 'increment' in land values is as much earned as any other. But there are reasons for holding the single tax. (1) Private land ownership has had effects on town planning, cff. New York… (2) Private holding of increment does not lead to the best distribution, socially, of the community's resources" (Young 1990, pp. 98–9).

Finally, there is the question of economic rent. It is an income which the owner of a productive instrument gets either by using it himself or by exacting it from another user. According to Young, the income-earning power of an instrument is determined not by its cost but by the value of its productive use, that is, by the laws of rent. Young (1929c; Sandilands 1990) writes:

> The specific hypothesis upon which the significance of the principle of rent depends is that the supply of the productive instruments which yield rent may be assumed to be given or fixed… Rent is generally held to have two distinguishing characteristics: first, it is a differential or graded return; second it is a surplus over costs. That it is a differential return depends on the circumstance that productive instruments are described or measured in units (e.g. acres) which themselves are not units of productive efficiency. It is obvious that if one acre of agricultural land is better (more fertile or nearer to the market) than another it will command a larger rent… That rent may be regarded as surplus over costs is a consequence of a circumstance that the supply of rent-yielding instruments is taken as given. (pp. 134–5)

The Wages of Labour

Wages can be defined as the prices paid for labour services—manual, white collar or professional—though in common usage the term refers to the price of manual work. Price of labour can be thought of as coming under the laws of supply and demand, just like any other commodity, being determined where demand and supply are in equilibrium. According to Young (Ely et al. 1923, p. 423), however, this way of looking at things does not take us very far.

The demand for labour is a derived demand. Labour is demanded not for its own sake but because it helps produce things which are demanded. The proportion of the product attributable to labour depends on the principle of marginal productivity. "The demand for any particular kind of labor is thus influenced by variations (1) in the demand for the products of that particular kind of labor, and (2) in the proportion of the production attributable to labor rather than to land and capital" (ibid., p. 425).

It is with respect to the labour supply that the difference in the determination of wages and commodity prices becomes most apparent. Firstly, in case of labour there is not much difference between actual supply and 'potential supply'. Labour can hold out for higher wages but this power is limited by the necessities arising out of making a livelihood. "In the long run, small wages are better than none. The sale of labour is often a forced sale" (ibid., 427). Secondly, since labour and the person of the labourer are inseparable, labour is not only selling his services but also gives up certain amount of control over his life by agreeing to conditions of work which may often be unpleasant. Thirdly, labour is relatively immobile as it is constrained by family ties, patriotism, religion, custom, language and so on. The supply of labour not only depends on population but also its structure in terms of sex ratio, age composition and so on. Moreover: "The physical strength and vigor, industry, intelligence, ingenuity, and the moral qualities of the laboring population determine the amounts and kind of work they can do" (ibid., p. 429).

Young also discussed Malthusian theory of population, subsistence theory of wages and standard of life theory of wages in relation to labour supply. The Malthusian theory of population postulates that population tends to increase faster than food supplies and is only held back by preventive checks like famine and disease or voluntary restraints exercised by the population by delaying marriage or raising of families till income is sufficient for the purpose. While this theory may apply to countries such as India where population presses very closely upon food supplies, it does not square with some facts in the countries of western civilisation such as the US, Canada or England. Population there does not press very closely on the food supply, and the poor people generally have a higher birth rate. Yet taking a broader view, population has generally increased wherever increase in wealth has given an opportunity. For example, in 1761, on the eve of the industrial revolution, the population of England was 6,700,000 which more than doubled to 14,000,000 by 1831, and by 1921 reached a figure of 38,000,000. After the industrial revolution, average real incomes as well as real wages had increased substantially.

As a corollary to the Malthusian theory of population, English economists advanced a subsistence theory of wages according to which wages, in the long run, tend towards a bare subsistence level. If wages fall below this level, numbers will reduce; if wages rise above it, numbers will increase till wages are pushed back to subsistence. Actual wages determined by demand and supply forces fluctuate around the long-run normal wages determined by the 'cost of subsistence' or 'expenses of production'. Some socialists have interpreted this doctrine in a very rigid form called the 'iron law of wages'. Under such a law, it is impossible to better the condition of the labourers even if alternative schemes of socialists (or Henry George) are adopted. "The subsistence theory of wages, if true, would be just as true under socialism or under national ownership of land as under existing conditions" (ibid., p. 433).

Ricardo had defined the natural price of labour as that price which is necessary for labourers to subsist and to perpetuate their race without increase or diminution. Today real wages are much more than the 'minimum of subsistence'. However Ricardo, unlike the socialists, did not attach any rigid meaning to it. Rather it depends on custom and habits of the people. Under this more flexible form, this 'minimum of subsistence' gets transformed into what is termed as 'the standard of life'. "The number and character of the wants which a man considers more important than marriage and family constitute his standard of life. Whenever wages fall below a point where the standard of life can be maintained for a family, the workman will do without the family and maintain the standard of life for himself alone" (ibid., p. 434).

Another associated idea in the nineteenth century was the wage-fund doctrine where wages are paid out of capital and the demand for labour depends on the availability of capital (or wage fund) for this purpose. Emphasis was laid on the fact that wages were advances paid before the final product reached the consumer. Young stated that the wage-fund doctrine was not altogether untrue but its emphasis was misplaced resulting in misleading inferences. "The doctrine implies a static conception of what, as its proponents recognized in other connections, is essentially a dynamic problem. Wages are paid not out of a fixed fund, but out of a continuing flow of wealth… Through the modern mechanism of credit, moreover, the future value of part of the product of present labour is

5 Allyn Young's Contribution to Economic Theory

discounted, and the proceeds are used in paying present wages" (Young 1929d; Sandilands 1990, p. 138).

In general, Young felt that to look at wages as determined by supply and demand like other prices is not very helpful. An increase in labour supply consequent on an increase in population does not mean that real wages will be lower. In an economy with serious impediments to industrial development (such as India, China and Russia), this may well be true. But in a country where a higher stage of industrial development has been reached, the economies of large-scale production and of the division of labour may be so dependent on the size of the domestic market that any considerable reduction of population may also lead to diminution of the per capita wealth produced. As Young says:

> It cannot be assumed, therefore, that an increase of the aggregate supply of labour will normally have the effect of reducing wages. Nor can it be assumed that a general reduction of real wages would lead to the increased employment of labour … in the way that the reduction of the price of a particular commodity will generally lead to larger sales. Little or nothing is to be gained by looking at the general formula of supply and demand for an explanation of the determination of wages. (Ibid., p. 138)

A worker's wages are actually determined by the agreement between him and his employer. The worker's relative position is generally weak in comparison to that of the employer. For example, an employer knows what he can afford to pay his worker, how much the worker will add to his product, what it will cost him to obtain the added product through other ways such as overtime work of present employees or mechanisation. The worker on the other hand does not have a very accurate idea of what his services are worth to the employer, has limited capacity to hold out for higher wages, may have few alternative employment options or have an unclear idea of how much he may get there.

> Under these conditions wages are likely to be fixed much closer to the minimum which the laborer will take than to the maximum which the employer will pay. Where laborers can bargain in groups rather than individuals, their disadvantages are lessened. The fundamental motive

underlying the development of labor organizations has been to secure the advantages of *collective bargaining*. (Ely et al. 1923, p. 438)

Interest

Young (ibid., p. 490) defined interest as a price paid for the services of capital. It has two forms—loan interest and imputed interest. The former is the amount paid by one person to another for the advances of money, while the latter is that value of the total product of industry which is imputed to the services of capital goods. Sometimes it is said that interest is paid because capital is productive. "The problem of interest relates to the value of the product, not to the amount of the product… It cannot be too strongly emphasized that neither land, nor labor, nor capital produces value. They are simply the instruments used in the production of things that command a price in the market because they satisfy human wants and will not be furnished except at a price… To say that capital produces value is to reverse the true process. Capital goods help to produce other goods, and derive their value from that fact" (ibid., pp. 491–2).

To understand interest, it is important to ask (1) how interest is possible and (2) why interest is necessary. As regards the first, the mere fact that capital goods are productive does not explain interest, but under the guidance of entrepreneurs, they produce goods which people want and get prices sufficient to cover their expenses of using capital. As regards the second, it needs to be pointed out that productivity cannot be attributed to specific units of free goods such as air or wind or oceans because the product is not dependent on utilisation of any one unit of them. Because the supply of capital goods is limited, productivity has to be attributed to specific units used. The supply of capital is limited because some members of the community have to turn aside from producing things required for satisfying immediate wants to the production of capital goods for the future production of consumption goods. This involves postponing of consumption or the sacrifice involved in waiting. Since present consumption is preferred to future consumption, an additional payment in the form of interest is necessary. "To induce the saving prerequisite to using capital in industry, a premium or reward for waiting has to be paid in the form of interest. This fact is the most fundamental thing in the explanation of interest" (ibid., p. 494).

At any given time, the interest rate is considerably higher than is necessary to induce waiting from a large number of savers who supply funds for capital goods. It is however just high enough to induce marginal waiting (or marginal savers who will not save below this rate).

Investment is the process by which savings are made to contribute to maintenance and increase in supply of capital goods. So continuous saving is a prerequisite not only to maintain the existing stock of capital goods but also to the formation of new capital.

According to Young, if a snapshot view of the processes by which wealth is created and distributed is taken, there is no important difference between land and capital goods. While some capital goods yield more than that required to pay for replacement and interest, some earn less than interest and replacement. Capital goods that are barely worth using may be called marginal capital goods and are analogous to marginal land. Income yielded by better capital goods is analogous to rent of land. "For this reason Professor Marshall has called the income from capital goods, when the point of view takes into account only a short period of time, *quasi-rent*" (ibid., p. 501).

However, from the long-term point of view, there is an important difference between income from land and income from capital goods.[9] The society's stock of capital goods is a shifting thing. Capital goods which are not profitable to cover the principal and provide for an interest will be replaced when they wear out. If capital goods yield considerable surplus over and above interest and replacement, there will be a tendency to increase investments in such goods. Thus in the long run, earnings of capital goods will tend towards the common level of interest and replacement. "Just as the expense of producing consumption goods forms a normal price, to which their actual prices (under competitive condition) continually tend to approximate, so the expense incurred in investments in capital goods form a norm toward which their actual earnings

---

[9] "If the static view is taken, and given amounts of land, capital and labour are assumed to exist, then the return to each factor can be regarded as rent… The difference only appears in the dynamic view. The existence, or continued existence, of capital and labour depends upon whether they will pay. Hence we have interest which is needed to call out saving" (Young 1990, p. 99).

continually tend. This expense includes … both the actual money outlay required to produce new capital goods and interest on that amount" (ibid., pp. 501–2). But in case of land, there is no normal price as it has no expense of production. This distinction has an important implication—there is no 'unearned increment' attached to capital goods.

Expenses of production devoted to wage advances can be treated as investment in capital goods. Wages are commonly advanced to labour before the goods can be sold. A lengthy period of time may elapse before this happens. According to Young, all of the various expenses of production (including wages, rent and interest) are really different ways of investing money in capital goods. Thus wages are one of the ways in which money gets invested in capital goods. While wage advances are investments in capital goods, labourers are not in any sense capital goods.

Similarly selling expenses—defined as expenses incurred not in producing what people want but in selling what the entrepreneur has produced—can also be regarded as competitive investments. From the social point of view, not all selling expenses are wasteful. Selling expenses, in some instances, may contribute to creating a market for better things. Moreover, truthful advertising may have an educative effect on the consumer and may help him choose among the perplexing range of alternative choices. On the other hand, selling expenses may sometimes lead to the exploitation of the consumer's weakness or ignorance. In any case, they are not a part of the social process of production of goods as their purpose is not to satisfy existing demand but to shift demand from other channels.

The full role played by capital in production can only be appreciated if an individual entrepreneur is seen only as a link in a continuous chain. "A particular entrepreneur may be interested only in disposing of his product at remunerative prices to the entrepreneurs who stand next to him in the productive series, but this does not affect the essential nature of investment, which, from the social point of view, is a cumulative process" (ibid., p. 506).

If the production of any consumption good is traced back to all the long series of goods and services which have contributed to its making, we find that expenses of production ultimately resolve themselves into rent, wages and interest, and what is left in the hands of the entrepreneurs is profit.

According to Young, business profits in his day were the largest source of investment funds. "In recent years from a third to a half of the net earnings of the average business corporation in the United States have been reinvested in business… Other investment funds come from the rent, wages, and interest into which (together with minimum or 'necessary' profits) the expenses of production ultimately resolve themselves" (ibid., p. 508).

The money incomes received by landowners, labourers, capitalists and entrepreneurs get divided into two streams—one going into payment for present goods which were produced in the past, and the other going as payment for present expenses of forwarding goods for future consumption. "This division represents a kind of social balancing of possible present satisfactions over against the larger future satisfactions which the productive use of capital goods makes possible… The interest rate, like any other competitive price, will normally be fixed at the point where the supply and demand of investment funds is in equilibrium" (ibid., pp. 508–9).

The demand and supply of waiting vary with the interest rate where the interest rate is one of the factors. The demand for waiting depends on the degree of roundaboutness, and the higher the interest rate the greater would be the expense of using roundabout methods. The supply of waiting also depends on the interest rate. The higher the interest rate, ceteris paribus, the larger would be the money income saved rather than spent on immediate consumption.

In the short term, interest rates show marked fluctuations, advancing in periods of rising prices and declining when prices fall. Their movement generally lags somewhat behind the movement in prices. Short-term movements in interest rates are thus linked to business cycles. In the long term, however, interest rates show constancy and are linked to the persistent traits of human psychology such as 'impatience', 'time preference' and the 'sacrifice involved in waiting'.

Just as inflation at the instance of the government involves disguised taxation, periodic expansion of bank credit also involves involuntary saving. High prices spread the burden of saving over the whole body of consumers. In the long run, accumulation of capital goods during the expansion phase of the business cycle is considerably greater in amount but somewhat different in kind. "Banking, therefore, as at present conducted, probably has the net effect of accelerating the rate at which capital is accumulated" (ibid., p. 511).

Profits

Modern production involves estimates of the future—the future prices of commodities, the quantum of demand and the costs of production. If the estimated revenues are more than the estimated costs of production, a manufacturer would undertake production. "This work of forecasting future conditions, of deciding whether they justify production, of assuming responsibility for the speculative risks of the venture, and of assembling or manufacturing the goods—with all that the latter implies in the way of organization and superintendence—is the essential function of the entrepreneur. The compensation or return for this service is *profits*" (ibid., p. 513).

The term 'profits' is used in four senses: (1) *Profits or ordinary profits* are the entrepreneur's money income minus his contractual expenses. They would include remuneration for the entrepreneur's own labour, capital and land (or imputed wages, interest and rent). (2) *Business profits* are ordinary profits minus wages imputed to the entrepreneur (or the wages of management). (3) *Minimum profits* are the sum of imputed wages, rent and interest and can be estimated by the opportunity cost of the entrepreneur's services of owned land, labour and capital. (4) *Pure profits* are the difference between ordinary and minimum profits and constitute the residual element in profits.

It is obvious that an entrepreneur would not continue to perform his function unless he gets profits approximately equal to the going rate of minimum profits. It may be pointed out that even his imputed wages, interest and rent are not always guaranteed. They are subject to the risks his business is subject to. For example, while a hired labourer gets his stipulated wages, an entrepreneur who suffers a loss may not get his full 'wages of management' or get less than what he would have got had he been employed by some other business. Similarly: "In any particular year the entrepreneur assumes a greater risk of losing rent and interest altogether than the man who hires to others his capital or his land" (ibid., p. 517). So imputed wages, rent and interest cannot be equated with contractual (or ordinary) wages, rent and interest, being subject to the risks of business. "They are the resultant of all the forces that tend to bring about inequality between the prices paid for things and the contractual or actual expenses of producing them" (ibid., p. 516).[10]

Prices in the long run must cover minimum profits to keep production going, but minimum profits cannot be precisely measured. They can only be estimated and the estimate at best is an approximation. While minimum profits are an expense of production, they are a flexible category as an entrepreneur may not be able to entirely cover them in the short run nor can he precisely measure them.

Are profits expenses of production from the social point of view? Three points can be noted. First, from the social point of view, and in the long run, most profits resolve into rent, wages and interest. Second, losses of the unsuccessful entrepreneurs have to be set off against the profits of the successful ones. Third, for many practical purposes, it may be more helpful to know the profits of the industry as a whole than profits of an individual entrepreneur.

How about pure profits? While it is true that pure profits are, in large part, a payment for assuming certain 'unavoidable and non-insurable' risks, in the long run they tend to be at best negligible. For example, an American farmer does not get more than his fair wages and fair interest on the capital employed (including land) in the long run. Net business profits during good years have to be set off against the business losses during bad years. "From the social point of view and in the long run, it is probably true that pure profits are a negligible, or possibly even a negative, quantity" (ibid., p. 518).

---

[10] "Profits are about the only form of income which is not contractual but contingent; in fact one might as well define profits as 'that form of income which is contingent and not contractual'" (Young 1990, p. 26). Further: "Profits are not imputable to any particular cause, as is land rent for example. A complete theory of economic change and friction is needed to give a complete theory of profits" (ibid., p. 26).

Are pure profits an expense of production? Young's conclusion was that from the individual point of view they are, but from the social point of view they are not:

> From the standpoint of the individual entrepreneur, under a system of private property and enterprise, pure profits would seem to be a particularly necessary and essential part of the expenses of production. Risk, uncertainty, responsibility: these are disutilities for the assumption of which payment in some form would appear to be unavoidable. But it is more important that pure profits should be obtainable than obtained. To induce even the most intense competition for a prize it is not necessary that each contestant should receive a prize. Considered from the social viewpoint, as a share in the social dividend, pure profits probably do not exist, as a positive quantity. In the aggregate, society probably secures the services of entrepreneurs without paying them anything additional to what would be regarded as a fair estimate of minimum profits. But the chance of securing pure profits must be held out to the individual entrepreneur as a possible and legitimate reward for keeping his expenses of production below the prices which he can secure for his product… Pure profits are at once necessary and non-existent. They represent a potential expense of production to the individual entrepreneur which probably does not constitute an actual social expense of production. (Ibid., pp. 518–9)

Pure profits arise because of imperfect working of competition and can be traced to two general sources: (1) inconsistencies and incomplete adjustment of prices at a given time and (2) changes in the price situation overtime. In most cases, there is a blend of both. In the great mass of business transactions, it is not a question of merely buying a thing and then selling it either immediately or at some other time, but generally of buying factors of production to use them to make a new saleable product. It is the inconsistencies and maladjustments in the general price situation which result in profits. "If competition worked with absolute promptness, smoothness, efficiency, things would sell at prices equal to their expenses of production, and the most the entrepreneur could get would be minimum profits" (ibid., p. 521). The time element also enters the picture because the expenses of production are generally incurred before the product is sold.

In case of standardised products, the most important profits are those which come to the industry as a whole. In agriculture, for example, wheat or corn farmers prosper or lose together. The fortunes of a farmer here depend on the fortunes of the industry as a whole. In case of differentiated products, the situation is very different. The seller of a branded product is able to secure pure profits (or losses) beyond those which are tied up with business fluctuations. The entrepreneur may incur many expenses not related to product creation but to market creation for his product. These expenses are called selling expenses and may result in one competitor gaining while others are losing. Here the fortunes of an individual entrepreneur can be delinked from the general business conditions.

Profits result from successful risk taking. Risk taking does not mean blind dependence on chance though chance may be regarded as one of the elements in profits. "Risk taking is nearly synonymous with business enterprise… In some few cases profits are secured without risk; some (not all) kinds of risks can be eliminated by insurance or shifted to some other risk taker; but, in general, profit seeking and risk taking go hand in hand" (ibid., pp. 525–6).

On the question of profiteering or excess profits, the difficulty is twofold: (1) uncertainty of their existence in the long run and (2) difference of opinion as to what constitutes the normal rate of profits. Going back to the normal conditions which prevailed before the war, courts and commissions took a rate of return between 6 and 8 per cent for regulating the rates of public utility companies as normal. Banks were generally considered to be a safer and a more stable business. The earnings of the national banks averaged 8.64 per cent during 1874–1919, while manufacturing and mercantile companies earned 11 per cent on their invested capital during 1911–1913. Not only is it difficult to determine what a fair or normal rate is, its application in regulating prices in the short term is fraught with pitfalls. Supernormal profits in the short term may represent exceptional efficiency, courage and foresight. They also need to be set off against losses sustained in bad years. "[I]t is the opportunity of securing abnormally high profits which induces business men to run the risk of sustaining the losses which examination may show occur with frequency" (ibid., p. 528). In Young's opinion, there is a need for exercising sound judgement regarding profits which needs to be qualitative rather than quantitative:

> We should look to the manner in which profits were earned rather than their amount or relation to investment. If the entrepreneur has participated in some combination in restraint of trade, or has indulged in unfair trade practices, or has imposed on the weakness or good faith of his customers, he may properly be condemned. But he may make exceedingly high profits in any one year or series of years without being fairly subject to criticism. (Ibid., p. 529)

Young was of the opinion that courts and regulatory bodies had not been generous in their attitude towards public utilities. Limiting their profits to 8 per cent had made them too inelastic. Ingenious plans like reduced rates for consumers and increased dividends for investors had been devised. But, in Young's opinion, there was a need for greater elasticity with respect to profits earned in regulating public utility companies. "Unless this be done, the issue will narrow down even more sharply to a bald choice between government ownership and complete abandonment of the attempt to regulate rates" (ibid., pp. 529–30).

Applying excess-profits tax to supernormal profits in excess of 8 per cent of invested capital violated the theory and caused great hardship in practice. Any measurement of supernormal profits must be based on the average profits realised over a considerable number of years. The gains of the fat years must be merged with the losses of the lean years. The offset should apply not to three years as at present but to much longer periods. "The only normal profits, if they can be said to exist in case of particular entrepreneurs, are long period, average profits" (ibid., p. 531).

Social Dividend and the Circular Flow of Income

In the 1908 edition of *Outlines of Economics*, Young introduced a section on 'social dividend' in the chapter on 'Profits'. Teachers using the book gave the feedback that this discussion was too difficult for beginners.

Young omitted this section in later editions, but the material it contained was so important that he reintegrated parts of it with his chapters on distribution. The discussion of social dividend is not only tied up with circular flow of income but has an intimate bearing on the problem of distribution as well. "The process by which the claims of different individuals against the social dividend are adjudicated is the process of the distribution of wealth" (Ely et al. 1908, p. 448).

Young (ibid., pp. 448–50) made an important distinction between *social dividend* and *annual product*. While the former "is made up of scarce and valuable things (commodities and services) that are of direct use in the satisfaction of human wants", the latter consists of not only things of direct and immediate use but also those things "that will come to a final fruition in the satisfaction of human wants in the more or less remote future". At another place, Young (1929e; Sandilands 1990, pp. 158–9) stated: "This annual flow of income, or *national dividend*, may be conceived of as comprising all of the valuable commodities which pass into the hands of their final consumers during the year, together with the valuable personal services (e.g. the services of the Government, of physicians, of actors, of household servants) rendered during the year, apart from those which come to the consumer embodied, as we might say, in the products of industry and trade. Alternatively, the community's annual flow of wealth may be identified with its *annual product*, which comprises the personal services directly rendered to consumers … together with the results of all that is accomplished during the year in forwarding products towards their final form and destination, and in augmenting the community's productive equipment" (emphasis added).

He also pointed out that the two concepts overlapped for both included the products of the work which came to final fruition during the year. "But one conception includes, in addition, ripened fruits of work done in the past, while the other includes the fruits of present work which will reach their maturity only in future years" (ibid., p. 159). Further: "The money value of what we may call consumers' real income (the first of the two conceptions) will not, in general, be the same as the money value of the annual product. In a prosperous community, where saving is growing relatively to consumption, the money value of the annual product will be the larger of the two… It lends itself better to statistical measurement than consumers' real income does, and it is the better index of the community's economic welfare" (ibid., p. 159).

Young (Ely et al. 1908) then links the discussion of the social dividend with the circular flow of income.[11] Since land, labour and capital have cooperated in the production of final goods, the three claims against the social dividend are rent, wages and interest. They, in fact, are different forms of money income paid for the services of the three factors in the production of valuable things. Entrepreneurs' activities play a crucial role in the valuation a society puts on its productive goods or factor services. "There is thus a continuous flow of money income through the hands of entrepreneurs, appearing first in the form of prices that are paid for an entrepreneur's goods, then emerging in the form of rent, wages, and interest that the entrepreneur pays for the service of factors in production, then reappearing in the prices paid for other goods, and so on in a continually recurring cycle of income and outgo" (ibid., pp. 448–9).

Young further wrote: "While the social dividend is to a large extent the outcome of past work and effort, the annual product is very largely a provision for future wants" (ibid., p. 450). This leads us to the role of interest in the circular flow of money income: "The productive efforts of the past, which satisfy the wants of to-day, were paid for out of past income, while the present work of producing goods that will be ripe for consumption only in the future is paid for out of present income. In this fact lies the explanation of the nature and necessity of the one of the various kinds of claims against the social dividend—interest" (ibid., 451). This implies that the prices which consumers pay today not only cover the past expenses of production but also the interest on them till finished goods reach the ultimate consumer. Interest is the important exception to the statement that the prices paid for the consumers' share in the social dividend constitute the fund that pays for the annual product.

Young then links this discussion with the marginal productivity theory of distribution. Young stated that the claims of the labourers, the landlords and the capitalists against the social dividend depend on their

---

[11] Don Patinkin (1981) partly traced back Frank Knight's famous circular flow diagram to his 1951 entry 'Economics' in the *Encyclopaedia Britannica*, but as Mehrling and Sandilands (1999, Editors' Preface, p. xxiv) point out, this was a lightly edited version of Young's 1929 entry, and in the process Patinkin also missed Young's 1908 discussion on 'social dividend'.

marginal contribution to the annual product. And marginal productivity is not merely a matter of technical efficiency or physical productivity but also of the amount and elasticity of supply of land, labour and waiting. Further, the tendency towards equality between prices paid for factor services and their marginal products is only an illuminating way of stating the real problem of distribution for the causation runs both ways. Young remarks:

> Just as marginal utility is at the same time the cause and effect of price, so marginal productivity is at the same time the cause and effect of wages, rent, and interest. From one point of view it is seen that the competition of producers makes it necessary that specific units of land, labor, and capital should get a reward proportionate to the value of the amounts which they contribute to the social dividend; from another point of view it is equally clear that the necessary expenditures for land, labor and capital are, in the long run, potent factors in determining the value of the things that make up the social dividend. (Ibid., p. 455)

Young further maintained that the word 'productivity' had a limited meaning in economics. Productivity is imputed to those goods which are subject to property rights and not to free goods. For example, boats and ferries have productivity while oceans and lakes, being free goods, have no productivity. Similarly the vast fund of scientific knowledge, which is a common property of mankind, has no productivity but patented methods have. Those who contribute to the vast fund of 'unproductive' scientific knowledge often get no commensurate pecuniary rewards but contribute immensely to the social dividend.

Concentration of Wealth and Growth of Big Business

Young (1917, 1927, p. 95) stated that economic progress yields a disposable surplus. In a dynamic society, more is produced than can be imputed (or attributed) in the form of income. The shares in this surplus are actively contested, and this is at the root of the phenomenon of concentration of wealth or the wide disparities between services and rewards. Young writes:

> Here are the chief sources of the gains of monopoly, of financial manipulations, and of strategic competitive advantages. Here are found most of those capitalized income yielding opportunities which we know under such names as franchise values, corporate excess, and good will. *The fruits of progress are not apportioned at first among all the cooperating producers, nor do they go in major part, to the pioneers of science and industry who have made the largest effective contributions to the knowledge that makes progress possible. They go to those who actively and successfully contend for them.* (Ibid., pp. 95–6, emphasis added)

At the same time, forces of diffusion of the product operate relentlessly. The factor that increases less rapidly commands a higher price. Business advantages may be snatched away by competition. Monopoly may crumble. There is increased demand for labour, for savings and for productive factor services. "Every bit of ground gained by the rank and file is tenaciously held, and becomes the starting point for yet further progress" (ibid., p. 96).

Concentration and diffusion processes work simultaneously. Statistics of concentration merely show the extent to which at any one time forces of concentration are ahead of those for diffusion. The terms 'concentration of wealth' and 'inequality in the distribution of wealth' have tended to be used interchangeably. While any departure from perfect equality is inequality, concentration of wealth is a social problem if it is undue or excessive. Thus, inequality is compatible with concentration which is not excessive. Young stated that the right interpretation of the concentration statistics does not call for "an arbitrary levelling down of fortunes" or "a revolutionary change in the general structure of our economic life". Rather the road towards *equality of competitive opportunity*, though longer and with many turns, is the right one.

Young (1929f; Mehrling and Sandilands 1999, p. 411) also stated that the observable tendency towards the increase in average business size had led some to prophesy the doom of the capitalist system and to the extinction of small businesses. For example, Karl Marx had predicted the extinction of the small property owner with the means of production getting concentrated in a few hands. Young stated that the general course of events thus far had belied Marx's forecast. Railways had not supplanted other modes of transport, as predicted, but on the contrary faced powerful competition from road transport. During 1898–1904, 90 combinations had been recorded, out of which only a few were successful. Many of them were formed to sell their securities at inflated prices. Thus, the emergence of monopoly capitalism was not inevitable.

Young observed that the economic system grows and evolves like a living organism through successive adjustments and adaptations. "But change breeds change, and every new adjustment paves the way for another" (ibid., p. 411). There was no one dominating principle shaping the course of evolution. The situation is forever changing. There were advantages as well as disadvantages attached to large-scale unified management. "Which are preponderant in a particular industry cannot be determined by abstract considerations alone. Everything depends on the characteristics of a particular industry, upon the nature of its products, and the size of its market" (ibid., p. 412). The emergence of the new does not necessarily herald the doom of the old.

When the departmental stores made their first appearance, many foretold the demise of the small trader. Later the emergence of the mail-order houses and the chain stores also led to similar forebodings. Young stated: "The fears, once prevalent, that great department stores would secure a monopoly of all retail trade have pretty completely disappeared. In the first place, anything like an effective monopoly of retail trade is impossible for there is no way in which competition in that field can be effectively suppressed. Even though certain great department stores have been amalgamated, so that they are units or links in 'chains' of stores, competition on the part of department stores themselves remains keen and effective. In the second place, the department store has not displaced the smaller establishment. Not merely do these survive, but with the growth of our towns and cities, their numbers continue to increase. Most of them are comprised in one or the other of two distinct classes: first, the specialized shop, offering a limited and distinct type of goods; second, the neighbourhood store ... conveniently accessible to a fair number of possible customers" (ibid., pp. 416–7).

Young pointed out that the unified managements and large-scale undertakings succeed best when the product is standardised in the sense that any one unit is like any other, and the processes of production can be broken up into a series of routine operations. "Sometimes the various stages of a series of industrial operations are brought together into what is called an 'integrated' industry. The United States Steel Corporation and the Ford Motor Works, are as good examples as can be found anywhere of integrated undertakings. In no case, however, can integration of successive industrial processes be altogether complete. Nor are the conditions common which make any large degree of integration economical or feasible" (ibid., p. 413). Young also gave the example of heavy industries producing 'semi-finished' products as another example of standardisation. These standardised semi-finished or intermediate products are converted by specialised industries into a diversity of finished goods. Some of the industries making finished goods may be large industries, while others small. "As a general rule, however, and as we should expect, the typical establishment which has a specialized product … is not as large as the typical establishment producing semi-finished or 'intermediate' goods" (ibid., p. 415).

Farming, according to Young, though producing standardised products like wheat, corn or cotton, is not carried on at a very large scale.[12] Farming does not lend itself to routine as the farmer has to deal with different qualities of land, vicissitudes of weather and one small emergency after another. Thus farming has to concern itself with a multitude of small details and cannot be spread to a very large field successfully. This is one reason, apart from agriculture being a family industry, why an average farm is not a very large undertaking. Printing, on the other hand, produces a large number of varying products. Book printing, newspaper printing and commercial printing are different trades requiring different kinds of equipment. Each requires a great deal of detailed supervision. Markets for many kinds of printing are local. Because of these reasons, printing is not concentrated in a few large establishments.

The size of the market also exercises an important influence on the size of the undertaking. As the market for a particular product is enlarged,

---

[12] This is not strictly true particularly in the mid-west of the US.

one needs to focus not on the activities of a particular firm but upon the operations of the entire industry or on a whole group of related industries which contribute to a single product. As the size of the market for printing expands, printing trade splits up into a large number of specialised undertakings like type founders, makers of linotypes and monotypes, printing presses and other specialised machines, wood pulp, paper and industries which supply materials and equipment to auxiliary industries. The products of printing trade are not the outcome of large establishments but of a system of industries, *operating in the aggregate*, on a very large scale.

Transportation costs also exercise an important influence on the size of an establishment. For example, if the transportation costs are high and raw materials to be transported are bulky and scattered, it may be more economical to locate a number of small plants to draw upon the local supplies. If the final product is bulky, perishable and difficult to transport, it may be more economical to have a number of small plants near the principal markets. If on the other hand transportation costs have cheapened, so that the raw materials can be obtained from far-off places, and the final products can be sent to far-off markets, the average size of the establishment would be larger.

The advent of the telephone and the automobile also had their influences on retail shopping. With the advent of the telephone, the advantages of location which a small trader had were lost. It became possible to cater to 'better-class trade' in groceries and provisions. "An established reputation for reliable goods and prompt service came to count far more, with certain classes of consumers, than the certainty that the prices asked were as low as the market afforded. The consumer in fact was willing to pay a certain price for relief from the inconvenience of personal shopping. Many grocery stores, although affording facilities for the personal inspection of goods, came to be largely warehouses from which goods were delivered, upon order, to the customer's home. The system of making sales upon credit, already well established, extended still further as a result of the introduction of the telephone" (ibid., pp. 418–9). The advent of the automobile as a quick and flexible means of transport meant that it was not necessary to locate stores in a crowded or important business districts. "The locations selected have generally been away from the crowded business and shopping districts, where access by automobile is difficult and where parking space is not to be had" (ibid., p. 420).

Young concluded that there was no magic formula for business success whether the undertakings are large or small, chain stores or single establishments. The scale of operation depends, first, on the characteristic of a particular industry and, second, on the market environment in which the business operates.

Supply and Demand

Young (1990, pp. 41–3) pointed out that Marshall's particular expenses curve should not be confused with the supply curve. It was not a true supply curve, yet it was upward sloping because not all the producers have the same costs. Those who produce at the lowest cost do not sell at the lowest price. Everyone whether producing at high or low costs sells at the equilibrium market price, and the area under the curve gives the producers' total expenses.

Young also stated that if we abstract from the distinction between producers and consumers, that is, a situation where members deal with each other, the supply curve coincides with the demand curve. "Suppliers are people who want other commodities. Each supply curve is a reciprocal of the demand curve, so it could be represented by an ordinary demand curve for money. There is no difference in principle between the short-period demand and short-period supply curves" (ibid., p. 42).

Drawing a downward sloping supply curve abstracts from the fact that there are no outside improvements or unexpected developments apart from the growth of the industry. Even this supply curve is fraught with difficulties: (1) it relates to a particular industry, and if applied to a firm would result in monopoly; (2) sometimes it cannot even be related to an industry, but to a particular or differentiated product; and (3) sometimes even the product will not do as new substitutes appear serving the same end, for example, an automobile in place of a carriage. Further difficulties arise on the question of its relation to the short-time curves or whether it should be taken to mean average or marginal costs of production. Marshall had stated that in the long run the distinction between average and marginal costs became blurred. He in fact took the average costs in his "representative firm". In Young's view, the representative firm was an expository device which Lionel Robbins (1928) had failed to appreciate.[13]

The demand curve of an industry (say X) is closely connected with the supply curve of other industries. In fact, the demand curve for X is the reciprocal of the supply curves of other industries. If the other supplies are elastic, then increasing the production of the good in question (X) is likely to alter the supply of other goods, shifting the demand curve of X to the right. Young stated that the long-period supply curve is meaningless apart from the length of time considered. The curve is relative to the rate at which increasing returns exist. On the other hand, one cannot postulate a constant demand curve for the long period because it would shift as a result of the forces which shift the supply curve. It is therefore more appropriate to have a theory of an equilibrium (or the optimum) rate of progress which would keep the supply curve close to the demand curve. When the supply and demand curves are both shifting: "Seeking equilibrium conditions under increasing returns is as good as looking for a mare's nest" (Young 1990, p. 45).

Elsewhere, Young (1929g; Sandilands 1990, p. 151) postulated that supply and demand in the aggregate were merely different aspects of a single situation. The theorem that 'supply creates its own demand' is not really erroneous but has proved to be misleading. It will be true only if the demand for a commodity is elastic, not otherwise. Given elastic demand for products, general overproduction is impossible. There may be maladjustments of supply and demand or the overall production may exceed the expansion of incomes. But these will be attended to by fluctuations in the general prices as well as relative prices.

Young also drew attention to the fact that much of scientific economics is largely concerned with supply and demand, and the way variations in these affected prices as well as the production and distribution of wealth. But it was not the economists who invented the formulae of supply and demand; the traders were already aware of the relationship of

---

[13] Robbins (1928) in his *Economic Journal* article was too critical and failed to appreciate that Marshall's 'representative firm' was an expository device. "The question is perhaps one 'hardly worth wasting an article on in the *Economic Journal*'" (Young 1990, p. 45).

supply or demand with prices much before any systematic analysis was carried out.

Socialism and Marxism

In Young's (1912; Mehrling and Sandilands 1999, p. 74) opinion, it was difficult to say anything precise about what socialism was. He distinguished between socialism as a *philosophy* and socialism as a *programme*. Regarding the former Young stated that it was defined in contrast to individualism. "Individualism is identified with selfishness; the social point with altruism. The very essence of the individual is even denied, except as a unit in Society… Society, in other words, is the concrete reality, of which the individual is a mere abstraction… As the social has come to stand for positive values the individual has been relegated to the negative" (ibid., pp. 75–6). Young also stated that at present socialism as a social philosophy seemed to occupy a dominant position with emphasis on such catch words as 'social welfare' and the 'interests of society'.

The new social philosophy had an excuse—after the French Revolution, individualism came to be identified with natural rights, laissez-faire, let-alone-policy of government. Individualism was narrowly and wrongly interpreted to mean privilege, class selfishness, a rallying cry for reaction, and opposed to humanitarian movements in the nineteenth century. So today we talk not of individual rights but of 'social welfare'. But, social welfare is a vague term which can be used to advocate any policy. "In the absence of a clearly defined social ideal 'social welfare' is often meaningless… Too often a symbol of mushy sentimentalism in one's attitude toward social problems. Too often 'social welfare' means the interest of or the supposed interests of the 'masses,' without reckoning the costs to the so-called 'classes' or to the forgotten middle layer of society—most numerous of all" (ibid., pp. 76–7).

Young held that there was a danger in vague abstractions. Just as there are crimes in the name of liberty, there could be crimes in the name of society. Society in the last analysis was only an abstraction, a name for all of us taken together. Even if it is admitted that 'all of us taken together' means more than 'all of us taken separately', and that the individual is a socialised unit, he still is a unit, and counts for one. "It is the individual who feels pleasure and suffers pain, who finds life worth living or not worth living. There are no values, no things worth while, except as they affect the individual and his life, or some other individual and his life" (ibid., p. 77). In his day, it had become dangerous to proclaim oneself as an individualist, as one ran the risk of being termed as reactionary or as one opposed to all progress. However, he also noted that "believers in the socialist program may be, and often are, individualists" (ibid., p. 78).

Regarding socialism as a programme, Young thought that even here there was no one thing which one could call socialism. Socialists themselves defined socialism as the public or common ownership of the means of production. Under this, Young included Fabian Socialism,[14] which is socialism by gradual means, by legislative enactments and by dissemination of socialist opinions. Young also stated that the name 'Fabian' was a misnomer as it did not mean to 'wait' idly, as a Marxist might, but to achieve socialism gradually. Besides the general programme, most kinds of socialism would contain two common elements: (1) communal control of the distribution of income and (2) less reliance on selfishness as the mainspring of human action.

There were considerable socialist movements even before Karl Marx wrote. Modern socialistic doctrine can perhaps be traced to William Godwin's (1793) *Inquiry Concerning Political Justice*. Young (1990, p. 88) noted that the Marxian tradition distinguishes between two kinds of socialism—utopian and scientific. Utopian socialism, associated with the names of Robert Owen, Henri de Saint-Simon, Charles Fourier, Étienne Cabet, Edward Bellamy and others, criticised the evils of the competitive system and proposed collective ownership as a remedy. Many of these writers "conceived oases of socialism in the desert of capitalism". Utopian socialism, also called rationalistic socialism, pictures an ideal state of affairs in which men behave reasonably so that injustice and unhappiness are banished. This kind of socialism demands a complete change in human nature though it is recognised that men's faults are due to faulty social and economic institutions and would disappear once these are

---

[14] Young noted that Fabian socialism was associated with such names as Sidney Webb, Sydney Olivier, Bernard Shaw, William Clark, Graham Wallas, Hubert Bland and Edward Pease.

changed. Robert Owen, who advocated voluntary cooperation, tried an experiment of a colony at New Harmony, Indiana, where there was to be an atmosphere of association, instead of self-seeking, and where no private property or competition would exist. Like most such enterprises, the experiment ended in failure.[15]

Marx and his followers called themselves scientific or evolutionary socialists. They did not talk about the desirability of collective ownership of the means of production but its inevitability as the next stage in social evolution. The main pillars of their doctrine were the labour theory of value, exploitation of the working class through the capitalist's appropriation of surplus value, class struggle and an economic interpretation of history. The Marxian doctrine maintains that labour is the source of all wealth, and labour is paid less than the value it produces. The surplus of the product's value over wages accrues to the capitalist in the form of surplus value. As capitalism matures, it becomes monopoly capital with the means of production getting concentrated in a few hands. The antagonism of capitalists and workers would result in a revolutionary overthrow of the capitalist system once the workers are able to organise themselves as a class. Thus, the emergence of socialism from capitalism is inevitable through a dialectic process since capitalism contains the seeds of its own destruction.

Young (ibid., p. 89) thought that the adjective 'scientific' did not apply to Marx:

> He was not writing in the language of nineteenth century science, and the last adjective to be applied to him is scientific. He is just as much utopian as those he criticises. It is argued that Marx transformed the Hegelian evolutionary process of history, not guided by 'ideas' but by the power of internal factors… (v. M.M. Bober's recent book on Marx's interpretation of history, written under Young at Harvard.) Among these factors Marx emphasises: (1) The institutional factors of economic society… (2) The Techniques of production… So Marx either begs the question of the material guidance of history, or abandons it, since 'institutional factors' must be

---

[15] "Those which were most successful had a 'social cement' generally of a religious nature, and these have generally broken up for non-economic reasons. The highly individual members tend to withdraw" (Young 1990, p. 88).

explained. His doctrine of the 'class struggle' was an invitation to participate in it. His was a suggested pattern of history, rather than any real interpretation.

Young (ibid., p. 89) described scientific or revolutionary socialism as a repellent doctrine:

> Its hope is based the continuance of the class struggle, in which the balance of power passes to wage earners. An ugly and repellent doctrine.

In Young's (1912) opinion, the most notable single thing about the dogma that called itself scientific socialism was its pretentiousness. It was an unsuccessful attempt to prove by dialectics that socialism was inevitable. Although Marx was a passionate revolutionist by nature, there could be no question to his honesty and sincerity of purpose. The book *Das Kapital* was a passionate outcry against injustices both real and imagined. It was as if he was constantly goading and preaching the workers of the world to unite to get rid of their chains. However:

> I am inclined to agree with John Spargo (the latest biographer of Marx) that Marx, despite his obvious pride of authorship, would have been ready to throw overboard his own theories if he were convinced that they stood in the way of the socialist movement. (Young 1912; Mehrling and Sandilands 1999, p. 81)

Young (1990, p. 90) also stated that socialism and anarchism did not differ as much as was generally believed:

> Anarchism and 'socialism' do not differ materially in their concrete proposals. (cff. Proudhon, Marx; Bakunin, Kropotkin; American industrialists; Mussolini, 'corporate state')... The anarchist is not so far from the socialist as is generally supposed. Nor is there much difference between Marx and Proudhon. Marx made the most of these differences, probably jealous of Proudhon lest he assume intellectual leadership of the socialist movement. The emphasis by anarchists is on opportunities for voluntary assistance,

guild socialism[16] with the state removed, and no compulsion. Some industrialists contend that all would be well if the power of monopoly were removed, and labour organised in company unions would identify its interests with capital; *à peu près* Mussolini.

The socialist diagnosis, based on a surface view that private property is the root of all evils in the system, is itself fraught with pitfalls. If private property is abolished, the assertion that each man will get the full product of his labour was itself a guarantee of a kind of property right. After private property is abolished, there will be a problem in adjusting rent and interest. Young stated that these can at best be added on to real wages of labour but could not be a part of it:

> As for the proposed abolition of the 'rent of land' and of the 'interest on capital,' that, I am confident is *inherently impossible*. There will always be land rent so long as the use of better lands gives an economic advantage over the use of poorer lands;—there will always be interest on capital so long as the present use of money is worth more than its future use, so long as the dollar today is valued more highly than dollar ten years from today. Yes, the advanced (revisionist) Socialist will say, but when land and capital are owned by the community, the *private receipt* of rent and interest will have been abolished! But communal receipt of rent and interest involves the ultimate distribution of these forms of income among individuals. Aside from the amount needed to pay the expenses of government ... what will be done with the tremendous fund arising from the real earnings of land and capital? It may be added to the real wages of labor, but it can never be a part of the real wages of labor. How shall the ultimate private property rights ... in rent and interest be adjusted? (Young 1912; Mehrling and Sandilands 1999, p. 83)

---

[16] "**Guild Socialism** ... is a relatively recent development in England. In one aspect, it represents an attempt to find a middle road between the 'tyranny of collectivism' and the planless anarchy of syndicalism. In another aspect, it reflects the same romantic idealization of the industrial system of the Middle Ages which one finds in the writings of John Ruskin and William Morris" (Ely et al. 1923, p. 605).

5 Allyn Young's Contribution to Economic Theory

Although the socialists of Young's day talked about social progress or social welfare or the superiority of the claims of society over those of the individual, their driving power itself arose from democratic rights:

> The socialist movement, in its most general aspects, seems to me to be nothing more or less than the natural and inevitable continuation of that great movement of the eighteenth and nineteenth centuries toward *democracy*. Individual rights are now, as they were hundred years ago, the fundamental things in the situation… [T]he driving power of the social movement today comes from individuals who imagine, or who know, or who are being taught that they, in common, perhaps, with millions of others, have *rights* that are implicit in the very notion of democracy, but rights which, for one reason or another cannot be realized under the existing social arrangements. (Ibid., p. 82)

Young thought that the socialist movement was becoming opportunistic. At one time reforms such as minimum wage laws, factory laws, laws regulating the hours of work, public control of monopolies, taxation reforms, compulsory education laws, universal franchise laws and so on were regarded as palliatives. But now socialism wanted to grab what it could. "*The victory seems to be with Lassalle, with Jaurès, with Fabians, rather than with Karl Marx.* Unless all signs fail, socialism will not come in the form of the abolition of private property. This … would involve (1) a taking away, and (2) a regranting, of private property rights" (ibid., pp. 83–4, emphasis added).

Young objected to the socialist organisation because of the strong governments it involved:

> A socialist organisation of society is compatible only with strong governments. It could not be based on the democratic system of one vote to each individual. And notice that individualism in philosophy is an outcome of commercial change, not vice versa. Modern democracy is the result of economic democracy. (Young 1990, p. 91)

Further, an ordered society is likely to be inefficient in production:

> Just as socialists give too much importance to the problem of interest so do they give too much importance to the question of efficiency in production. But there is nothing in human experience to suggest that any 'ordered' society could be more efficient. In fact the strength of the present system is on its production side. Where the values of society centre on the 'ability to make money', which is correlated approximately with production, there is greater emphasis on production. Under socialism values would change so that productive efficiency would become relatively less important. The serious indictment against the present order is rather in respect of its type and kind of consumption, the uses to which it puts wealth. (Ibid., p. 91)

Young's (Mehrling and Sandilands 1999, p. 84) overall conclusion was that socialism would realise itself better through the democratic process geared towards specific social reforms, and not through revolution:

> But it is fairly certain that socialism will realize itself, not in a revolution, but along the lines of specific social reforms. So far as these reforms represent the unfolding of democracy; so far as they strike at discriminating privileges, and strive merely to remove the handicaps which make the present economic struggle an unfair one,—to that extent they will undoubtedly be given a growing measure of support… Our fundamental institutions are too deeply rooted; too carefully selected in the long process of social evolution, to give way under the pressure of the moment, unless the forces making for change have been dammed and held back by an obstinate and unreasoning reaction. Socialism at work, socialism as the unfolding of democracy is socialism with its teeth drawn. Or, better perhaps, socialism as a doctrine, as a creed, is an abstraction. Give to this abstraction a concrete content, and it ceases to be socialism![17]

References

Ely, Richard T., Thomas S. Adams, Max O. Lorenz and Allyn A. Young (1908), *Outlines of Economics*, New York: The Macmillan Company.

---

[17] Young (1990, pp. 91–2) thought that it was not possible to change an economic order for the better without first changing the human element.

Ely, Richard T., Thomas S. Adams, Max O. Lorenz and Allyn A. Young (1923), *Outlines of Economics*, New York: The Macmillan Company.

Godwin, William (1793), *An Inquiry Concerning Political Justice*, London: C.G.J. and J. Robinson, Paternoster Row.

Mehrling, Perry G. and Roger J. Sandilands (1999) (ed.), *Money and Growth: Selected Papers of Allyn Abbott Young*, London and New York: Routledge.

Patinkin, Don (1981), 'In search of the wheel of wealth', *Essays on and in the Chicago Tradition*, Durham: Duke University Press, pp. 53–72.

Ricardo, David (1817/1971), *Principles of Political Economy and Taxation*, Harmondsworth: Penguin Books Ltd.

Robbins, Lionel (1928), 'The representative firm', *Economic Journal*, 38 (September), pp. 387–404.

Sandilands, Roger J. (1990), (ed.), 'Nicholas Kaldor's notes on Allyn Young's LSE lectures, 1927–29', *Journal of Economic Studies*, 17(3/4).

Young, Allyn (1911), 'Some limitations of the value concept', *Quarterly Journal of Economics*, 25(3), pp. 409–28. Reprinted in Young (1927), pp. 198–212.

Young, Allyn (1912), *Socialism: Lecture Notes*, St Louis: Washington University. Reprinted in Mehrling and Sandilands (1999).

Young, Allyn (1917), 'Do the statistics of concentration of wealth in the United States mean what they are commonly assumed to mean', *American Statistical Association*, 15(117), pp. 471–84. Reprinted in Young (1927), pp. 95–107.

Young, Allyn (1925), 'Review of *The Mathematical Groundwork in Economics* by A.L. Bowley', *American Statistical Association*, 20(149), pp. 133–5.

Young, Allyn (1927), *Economic Problems New and Old*, Boston: Houghton Mifflin.

Young, Allyn (1929a), 'Capital', *Encyclopaedia Britannica 1928*, London: The Encyclopaedia Britannica Company. Reprinted in Mehrling and Sandilands (1999), pp. 125–42.

Young, Allyn (1929b), 'Economics', *Encyclopaedia Britannica 1928*, London: The Encyclopaedia Britannica Company. Reprinted in Mehrling and Sandilands (1999), pp. 115–34.

Young, Allyn (1929c), 'Rent in economics', *Encyclopaedia Britannica 1928*, London: The Encyclopaedia Britannica Company. Reprinted in Sandilands (1990), pp. 134–36.

Young, Allyn (1929d), 'Wages', *Encyclopaedia Britannica 1928*, London: The Encyclopaedia Britannica Company. Reprinted in Sandilands (1990), pp. 137–42.

Young, Allyn (1929e), 'Wealth', *Encyclopaedia Britannica 1928*, London: The Encyclopaedia Britannica Company. Reprinted in Sandilands (1990), pp. 158–9.

Young, Allyn (1929f), 'Big business: how the economic system grows and evolves like a living organism', *Book of Popular Science 1929*, New York: The Grolier Society. Reprinted in Mehrling and Sandilands (1999), pp. 411–20.

Young, Allyn (1929g), 'Supply and demand', *Encyclopaedia Britannica 1928*, London: The Encyclopaedia Britannica Company. Reprinted in Sandilands (1990), pp. 149–52.

Young, Allyn (1990), 'Nicholas Kaldor's notes on Allyn Young's LSE lectures, 1927–29', *Journal of Economic Studies*, 17(3/4), pp. 18–114.

6

Allyn Young on Applied Economics

Allyn Young had a penchant for applied economic problems and he regarded the distinction between theoretical and applied economics as largely artificial. Economics was an eminently practical subject for him useful in solving communal problems of economic life. Bearing this in mind, in this chapter we take up the applied or practical problems Young dealt with. We shall discuss depreciation and rate control, railway rate making, personal and impersonal taxation, the Sherman Act and other Antitrust-laws for monopoly control, census and age statistics, old-age pension for the poor of Massachusetts, the Haugen Bill for farm relief, and his role in the Paris peace conference after WWI.[1] His contributions to index number theory and to the index of inequality have been discussed elsewhere in the book (Chap. 9), so will not be discussed in this chapter.

---

[1] 'Depreciation and rate control' refers to the effect of depreciation provision on railway service pricing and 'railway rate making' denotes the factors to be considered for railway service pricing.

Depreciation and Rate Control

Taking American railroads as an example to illustrate his views on depreciation and rate control, Young (1914a, 1927) stated that in the earlier period, inadequate appropriations for maintenance served as a common method to milk the property and to manipulate the value of securities through payment of unearned dividends. In the latter years, there was a tendency to go to the other extreme of overstating the maintenance costs by counting many betterments and replacements under maintenance. So the Interstate Commerce Commission, acting under the enhanced powers it obtained under the Hepburn Act of 1906, required that the depreciation of rolling stock be counted as an operating expense. The Commission sought to control not only the inflated maintenance costs but also made elaborate rules for the definition and classification of additions and betterments.

Young (ibid., p. 127) observed that the orders of the Commission were in the right direction and there was no reason to doubt the wisdom of the general policy. He wrote:

> Charging betterments to operating expenses builds up a 'secret reserve' which can be brought to light at any time and thus made as effective a means of manipulation as unearned dividends. The arbitrary diminution of the amount available as net income, by reason of swollen maintenance expenses, is unfair to the owners of income bonds or of non-cumulative preferred stock, or to other holders of equities in the business who may be more interested in maintaining present returns than in increasing future profits. Finally, it is not in the public interest that the existing level of rates should appear to be less profitable to the railroads than it really is.

There were, however, certain difficulties in handling the depreciation accounts. First, the Commission did not prescribe the annual rates of depreciation which the carriers should use for different classes of equipment. The depreciation charges continued to be either overstated or understated as there were no reliable statistics on the average life of different equipment under different operating conditions. Second, the disposition of the reserve created by depreciation charges posed a problem. These charges were credited to replacement account, but since replacement expenditure was not sufficient to use up these funds, the continuing growing surplus furnished an opportunity for additional equipment to be charged to replacement. Thus the replacement account became a misnomer. The Commission in 1910 responded by making these accounts as 'reserves for accrued depreciation', which now covered not only depreciation but also additions and betterment. The balances on these accounts were shown in the balance sheet as a deduction from the aggregate investment in infrastructure and equipment to reflect the permanent nature of this reserve.

Young also drew attention to the implications of this new procedure. First, the compulsory annual additions to the reserve for accrued depreciation reduced profits by the full amount of the addition, and hence the amount available for dividends. Second, the writing down of capital assets by the amount of accrued deprecation meant that other assets had to be larger or that liabilities had to be smaller. Third, the requirement of a compulsory reserve implied the control of financial policies of the companies by the Commission.

In Young's opinion, this procedure appeared adequate in an undertaking with one dominant asset such as a steamship or a coalmine where either enough was kept aside annually to replace it at retirement or where the proprietors considered that their investment was being returned to them in instalments. But in a property of varied assets where no single asset was of dominating importance, the case was different. "The periods of use of the different items of assets *overlap*, so that when depreciation is charged from the beginning on each item, a reserve begins to accrue on a given item before the reserves accumulated on account of other items have been diminished on account of replacements. The permanent reserve thus created is not needed" (ibid., pp. 138–9). Further:

> In economic fact the property of a public service undertaking as a whole is a productive unit. Consider it as such—then replacements appear merely as repairs necessary to keep the whole property in a state of efficiency. Repairs in this large sense are of course to be counted as operating expenses, as is true of minor repairs. But if such repairs are fairly regular in amount year by year there appears to be no inexorable reason why a fund to provide

for them should be accumulated in advance and more especially a fund that will provide more than the annual cost of the repairs. (ibid., p. 139)

Those favouring the depreciation reserve could argue that when a property changes from newness to a condition of about half its expected total life, about half the original investment returns to the stockholders, so the investment amount on the balance sheet has to be written down accordingly. In Young's opinion this argument was fallacious because (1) there was no necessary correlation between aging (or wear and tear) and diminution of investment; and (2) if capital goods were replaced promptly when retired the amount of the investment in every real sense remained intact. So there was no case for writing down the value of the property which had not provided for depreciation reserves before the regulation by Interstate Commerce Commission came into force on 1 July 1907. Since the subsequent investments after this date were made with full knowledge of the new accounting rules, whether reserve for accrued depreciation was required was purely a matter of public policy. Young concluded:

> From the point of view of public policy, then, the depreciation rules of the Interstate Commerce Commission and of the various state commissions which have followed its lead are in general reasonable and apparently well advised. They seem open to criticism only in so far as they compel the accumulation of depreciation charges on property acquired *before* the rules were put into operation... It is only the practice of reaching back into the past for whatever depreciation is supposed to have accrued before July 1, 1907, that is open to objection. (ibid., pp. 142–3)

Young's conclusion, unlike those of most commissions[2] and courts, was in line with the ruling of the St Louis Public Service Commission, which held that if replacements and renewals were promptly attended to, no deduction for depreciation should be made. The commission also

---

[2] In this regard, Young stated that the opinions of the Wisconsin Railroad Commission were representative. The Commission had held that if depreciation needed for wear and tear and renewal was not kept aside it was tantamount to payment of dividends out of capital. Young (1914a, 1927, pp. 147–8) countered this by stating that it had failed to see that if a public service property had been properly maintained, an accumulation of a depreciation reserve posed a burden which was neither necessary nor just.

stated that to investigate those companies who had not provided for depreciation before the new rules came into being was to regulate past profits—a task it refused to attempt. Young in his analysis of the issue was also influenced by James E. Allison, a former member of the St Louis Public Service Commission as well as its chief engineer. As Charles Blitch (1995, p. 48) notes, Allison's view was that an investment should be appraised at its original cost (without allowing for depreciation) and earnings should be calculated on this figure. In other words, for purposes of rate control, returns should be calculated on the original value of the property, and not its depreciated value, irrespective of whether a provision for depreciation had been made before the new accounting rules or not.

In summary:

1. If depreciated charges have not been required by public authority, it cannot be assumed that the proprietors of a large public service undertaking should have accumulated a reserve for accrued depreciation.
2. The absence of such a reserve does not necessarily mean that part of the principal of the investment has been returned to the proprietors.
3. In valuation for purposes of rate control no deduction should be made on account of depreciation of large and varied properties, except for depreciation allocated to a period in which depreciation accruals were regularly charged to operating expenses (ibid., p. 151).

Railway Rate Making

B.H. Meyer (1914) of the Interstate Commerce Commission, in an article 'Certain considerations in railway rate making' presented to the American Economic Association meeting in December 1913, held that there could be no one standard which could be adhered to under all circumstances in the interests of justice. Instead the search should be for a set of standards, and each particular case requires the application of a different standard or a different combination of standards to promote justice to all interested parties. The important thing to keep in mind was that justice should be achieved in a large way. "That is why I cannot give you a universal rate yardstick but must content myself with directing attention to a few of its important components" (ibid., p. 80). The three considerations pointed out by Meyer in railway rate making were a fair return on the value of property, cost of service and a sound public policy. Each of these was to be interpreted in the light of others, and wise discretion was to be used with respect to the facts of a particular situation.

Young, along with Joseph Schumpeter and others, was one of the discussants of this article at the meeting. Schumpeter argued for the 'what the traffic will bear' rate system as this represented finding the slopes of the demand curves experimentally. Earnest R. Dewsnup agreed with Francis Edgeworth that a system of moderately controlled discriminatory rate making (rather than a non-discriminatory rate system) would confer greater advantage to the community. Frank H. Dixon, while expressing agreement with the general reasoning of Meyer's article, stated that he was not an irreconcilable enemy of the cost theory as cost was the minimum below which rates should not go. So a more complete and accurate knowledge of costs than what the railways now possessed would be beneficial to them as well as the public. Arthur J. Boynton stated that theories such as cost of service or value of service would remain empty phrases unless some idea as to their content and some units to measure the same are devised. So statistical studies had to precede rate theories because, without their proper unit records and determined standards, they will furnish but a meagre basis for regulation. Lewis H. Haney, while agreeing with the thesis of Meyer's article that rates should be based on cost modified by the principle of public policy, wanted both supply and demand to be taken into consideration. Given monopoly in railways, he wanted to approximate the effect of competition on rates by constructing shippers' demand prices and carriers' supply prices. Since joint expenses would pose difficulty, the heart of the problem was to determine apportioning of expenses to each class of traffic as if under competition.

While Meyer regarded the cost-of-service principle as one of the principles of railway rate making, for Young (1914b) it was the fundamental factor. In the interest of true *laissez-faire*, Young stated, it was necessary to secure the advantages of broader competition and economies bound up with comparative costs. If all costs are fixed, then it could be shown that a discriminatory rate system based on what the traffic would bear would be the most advantageous. But if all railway costs are variable, as they are in the long run, the cost-of-service principle even ceases to be a debatable proposition. Young believed:

> Rates proportional to costs would secure the most advantageous distribution of industrial undertakings. They would lead, not necessarily to a minimum of transportation but to a minimum of aggregate productive and distributive costs for a given national dividend. It is true that certain writers, most recently Professor Edgeworth and Professor Pigou, have tried to show that under conditions hardly realizable in practice certain particular sorts of rate discrimination might possibly be more advantageous, economically speaking, than rates based on cost… With all railroad costs variable costs, the cost principle of rates becomes, I think, generally conceded. (ibid., p. 83)

Young further held that charging according to what the traffic will bear assumed a static view of facts; it assumed that a large part of railway plant and equipment was a given quantum, and was more than ample for present needs. But when increasing population, wealth and transportation needs were considered, not only cost of conducting transportation but fixed charges as well as maintenance all increased. From the long-time, social point of view, fixed charges were apt to be variable charges.[3]

Young observed that the present rate system was characterised by a balancing of competing interests and this delicately balanced system must be disturbed if cost of service was to be consistently adhered to. Besides, there were practical considerations pointing in the same direction. For example, any basis of rates other than cost would be inconsistent with the present judicial decisions which regarded cost as the limit beyond which important rates could not be forced by public control. Moreover, with states having power to determine interstate rates, a chaotic system of rate making could be avoided if the Interstate Commission set a uniform standard based on cost to be then approved by the Supreme Court. This

---

[3] "In the case of railways, when traffic grows, 'supplementary costs' become prime costs, i.e. all costs are prime costs if you take a right period of time" (Young 1990, p. 49).

would lead to an eventual harmony in the rate systems even under a divided system of control.

Young concluded:

> In conclusion let me make it clear that I am not claiming that the cost-of-service principle should be used as the invariable yardstick of rate making. But neither should it be counted as one among the myriad of factors affecting rates. It is, in my opinion, properly to be regarded as a first principle of rate making, departure from which is to be justified only by the special circumstances of the individual case. (ibid., p. 86)

Personal and Impersonal Taxation

Young (1913) had written a report on the vote on the single tax in Missouri.[4] On Walter Wilcox's recommendation he was appointed the Chairman of the Tax Law Revision Commission of New York. His work on personal and impersonal taxation at the state level reflected this experience.

Young (1915a, 1927, p. 108) distinguished between personal and impersonal taxation—while the first was taxation of persons, the second pertained to taxation of things. "Thus indirect taxes, whatever their ultimate incidence, are from this point of view always and everywhere impersonal taxes… [However] it does not follow that all direct taxes are personal taxes. Income taxes, proportional and progressive, falling alike on different classes of income-receivers, are personal taxes. The general property tax is a personal tax in its general purpose and its traditions, although not in all details of its operation. And so with the inheritance tax and habitation tax. But a tax upon one specific kind of property, such as a tax on automobiles or dogs or land, or even upon real estate in general, is not, taken by itself, a personal tax" (ibid., pp. 108–9).

---

[4] The proposed amendment on the single tax in Missouri was rejected by the voters in 1912 although it was limited in nature as compared with Henry George's more thoroughgoing proposals. The voters suspected this to be the starting point of the complete government appropriation of land rent. The proposal for a permanent tax commission was also rejected as it was suspected to conceal some sinister move towards a single tax.

Young appeared inclined towards personal taxation though he recognised that there were particular circumstances where each one had its validity.

> Personal taxation rests more or less solidly upon the ability-to-pay principle of taxation; impersonal taxation finds a slender prop in the benefit principle, or expresses national commercial policy, or is to be considered as sumptuary legislation, or frankly commands support on grounds of fiscal expediency and administrative economy, or, as in the single tax on land, is based upon an alleged public equity in some particular form of property. This is not to say that all impersonal taxation is bad. In particular circumstances one or another of these various principles may have both validity and weight. (ibid., p. 109)

The pressing question then was the extent to which these contrasting principles needed recognition in the American taxation system, and more specifically which one was to be given primacy in the ongoing work of remodelling the general property tax. Personal tax was superior if all property was located in the districts where the owner lived, and if wealth was held in concrete and tangible forms. But if property was intangible (e.g., securities) and the owners of tangible properties resided in different locations than the properties, then the question was: "In this separation of men and their possessions shall taxes follow the man or the property?" (ibid., p. 110).

Young stated that both points of view had their advocates who could put forward weighty arguments for their respective cases:

> The advocate of impersonal taxation is not without weighty arguments. Simplicity, convenience, efficiency in raising revenue, and similar points are things which he is prone to stress... The advocate of personal taxation, in his turn, will have no difficulty in making out a strong case. Personal taxation is an expression of the now dominant ability-to-pay or faculty theory of taxation. It is in line with the origins and traditions of voluntary taxation among English-speaking peoples. There is a wholesome social ideal embodied in the notion that each member of the community should contribute to the public purse in accordance with his means. (ibid., pp. 111–2)

Young suggested that the arguments for personal taxation appeared weightier, yet a thoroughgoing application of the principles of personal taxation was impracticable and undesirable. First, there was no close relation between the personal taxpaying ability among different tax districts and the revenue needs of these districts. Second, all state and local taxation on a personal basis would encounter opposition from the most entrenched part that the tax on real property was not a personal tax. Although in most cases the taxpayer and his property were in the same district, exceptions were important enough to disprove the rule. Where the taxpayer and his property were in different states, the impersonal character of the tax stood out clearly. Although not squaring with the ability-to-pay principle, impersonal tax on property had almost no enemies. Young concluded: "In short, there is no consistent recognition of the principle of personal taxation in our present tax practice, and there are decisive obstacles in the way of re-organizing our tax systems upon a definitely personal basis" (ibid., p. 114).

Young pointed out that despite the ineffectiveness of personal taxation we had stuck to it because the personal property tax was levied at the domicile of the owner. The new tax proposals to replace the personal property tax found their justification in the principle of personal taxation. Instead, Young argued, there was a need to have a system where the personal and impersonal principles were both logically and consistently recognised throughout. He wrote:

> There would be recognition of the right of the State or locality to levy taxes upon all property located within its borders, and there would be equal recognition of the right of the State or locality to tax every resident on the basis of his property, wherever located, or his income whatever the source… If owner and land are in the same taxing district, there should be two taxes imposed, one because the land is located there, and the other because the owner lives there… Double taxation would be eliminated by the simple device of making double taxation the uniform rule… But the general result could be reached just as well by a state income tax, apportioned in part to localities, and falling upon *all* incomes above a low exemption limit. This should not be a special or supplementary income tax, but an *inclusive* tax upon all incomes received by residents of the State, even where such

incomes are derived from property already taxed in the same or other jurisdiction. The tax on real property should be retained in its present form, and such tangible personality as is taxed at all should be taxed where located. (ibid., pp. 115–7)

Young argued that this was a practical way of bringing order and consistency into the American systems of state and local taxation and freeing them from double taxation. While tangible property would be taxed at the place of its location, a thoroughgoing system of personal taxation would be introduced covering all taxpaying citizens of the State. Young felt that the state income tax or the special tax on intangibles should not apply to corporations. Instead, all domestic and foreign businesses should be taxed in the form of a privilege tax or licence fee, and these should not be disguised as general taxes on property or persons.

Anti-trust Laws

Young (1915b; Ely et al. 1923) made a deep study of the prevailing anti-trust laws as contained in the Sherman Act (1890), the Clayton Act (1914) and Federal Trade Commission Act (1914). Young believed that the general revival of interest in the control of trusts was in part bound up with the growth of a general radical movement in politics. Experience showed prosecutions against illegal combinations could only be successful if they were backed by detailed researches.

The federal Sherman Anti-trust Act was based on the federal power to control interstate commerce. It was directed against contracts or combinations aimed at not only "restraint of trade or commerce" among states or foreign nations but also against those who "monopolize or attempt to monopolize" trade and commerce among states or foreign nations. The government could either launch criminal cases against unlawful combinations or proceedings to prevent violations of law. Criminal prosecutions were generally unsuccessful because the offence such as the "restraint of trade" was so abstract, general or common that a jury found it difficult to give conviction. The phrase "restraint of trade" had been taken from the common law where it applied to agreements not to compete. Such contracts were generally considered valid where the restraint of trade was incidental to some legitimate purpose. For example, two competitors might form a partnership or one might sell his business to the other agreeing not to set up another of the same kind—the restraint of competition did not necessarily render them illegal.

Although the Sherman Act was intended against great industrial combinations, the courts also chose to apply it to certain activities of the labour unions. Activities such as strikes and boycotts were seen as interfering with interstate free flow of commerce. Similarly, the courts held that the railroad agreements were in violation of the Sherman Act. These agreements were of a reasonable nature and had been defended by the Interstate Commerce Commission. The courts held that if the direct purpose of these agreements was restraint of competition, they were illegal whether they were reasonable or not. Young stated that since railways were natural monopolies, the attempts by the courts to force competition were unfortunate. Since 1887, the Interstate Commerce Commission had been regulating railway rates on the premise that they were natural monopolies, and this was a more effective method to regulate unfair rates. The effect of the court decisions was to use a holding company as a device in railroads and manufacturing. These holding companies involved undue concentration of financial power, opportunities for unfair treatment of minority shareholders, and were not subject to prosecution under restraint of trade.

The Sherman Act was the least effective against the industrial combinations as the government lacked proper bureaux of research and investigation as well as suffering from the apathy of government officials. These shortcomings were remedied under President Theodore Roosevelt, and, in 1910, two successful suits for dissolution were brought against the Standard Oil Company and American Tobacco Company. The court decisions highlighted certain business practices as evidence of their monopolistic intent. For example, the Standard Oil Company was not a natural monopoly but had consistently pursued a policy of monopolisation either by absorbing its competitors or driving them out of business.

The use of unfair competition[5] by these companies was also found to be illegal under the Sherman Act. Young (Ely et al. 1923, pp. 225–6) stated that it was too early to judge the ultimate effect of reorganisation brought about by the Sherman Act, but there could be no doubt that in a number of industries, including oil and tobacco, there was now a larger measure of normal competition than before the dissolutions.

In 1914, two new Acts were passed—the Clayton Anti-trust Act and Federal Trade Commission Act. Young stated that to some extent the two statutes overlapped, in others they were supplementary. "Neither statute is so good a specimen of draftsmanship as the Sherman Act, while the Clayton Act, with its twenty-six sections and its heterogeneous subject matter, is a particularly formless piece of legislation. In statute-making, defects of form are prone to be associated with defects of substance, and there is reason to fear that there is such an association in the Clayton Act" (Young 1915b, p. 175).

The sixth section of the Clayton Act exempted labour combinations from the condemnation of anti-trust laws. It not only applied to labour organisations but also included agricultural and horticultural organisations. Young stated that agreements to maintain prices or to restrict output were not common among agriculturists. Thus few, if any, would fall under the condemnation of the anti-trust laws. Agricultural organisations were not actively involved with lobbying for these provisions. Young also stated that the Sherman Act applied to labour combinations not because labour unions were themselves monopolies but because their actions such as strikes and boycotts interfered to some degree with the free flow of goods from one state to another. It was not clear that the new section altered the law in this respect. It would have been better to restrict

---

[5] "It includes the use of such devices as (1) cutting prices below cost in a locality in which competition appears; (2) discriminating in favor of merchants who agree to refuse to handle or to discriminate against competitors' products; (3) the use of threats and other forms of intimidation; (4) the employment of spies to ascertain the details of competitors' business transactions; (5) the production of special brands of goods, sold at very low prices for the purpose of driving competitors' products out of the market; (6) the use of subsidiary companies as bogus independent concerns" (Ely et al. 1923, p. 224). Young stated that not all of these methods in themselves were illegal. Some of them like price cutting were common in ordinary competitive trade where the size of the establishment was not large, but when used by large industrial combinations they became "unfair" and dangerously destructive. There was an important difference between trying to gain business under competitive conditions and an effort to destroy competitive conditions.

the Sherman Act to monopolising rather than also to interference with the movement of commerce.

The Clayton Act also prohibited interlocking stockholding (i.e., acquisition by one corporation of the stock in another) and interlocking directorates if the effect was substantially to lessen competition or to tend to create a monopoly between the corporations concerned (although competitive conditions might continue in the industry in general). "But so far as their effect on the industrial combinations is concerned they add little to the Sherman Act, as now interpreted by the courts" (Ely et al. 1923, p. 226).

The Clayton Act further prohibited certain trade practices such as (1) unjustifiable discrimination in the prices charged to different purchasers, (2) sale of goods made with the understanding that the purchaser shall not deal with the goods of a competitor, as well as discounts and rebates associated with such sales. Young stated that in these respects also the Clayton Act did not add much to the Sherman Act as the courts had already counted such trade practices as evidence of monopolising.

The Federal Trade Commission established under the Federal Trade Commission Act succeeded the Bureau of Corporations, which was established for the purpose of making special investigations of particular corporations and combinations, and of conditions in particular industries. The Federal Trade Commission had larger powers of investigation and could also ask for annual or special reports from interstate corporations. It could also investigate any corporation violating anti-trust laws at the request of the Attorney General and could make recommendations for the readjustment of its business. The courts could ask the commission to prepare a decree having a bearing on the dissolution proceedings. For the reorganisation plan not only required technical information but also care and judgement. Further, the Commission had the power to monitor the manner in which decrees were carried out.

The most important power of the Commission pertained to the orders restraining unfair methods of competition in commerce. Young stated that such methods added nothing to the Sherman Act except a new, prompt and efficient procedure. The Commission was also empowered to build and maintain higher standards of competition and to draw a line beyond which the businesses could not go in diverting trade from their competitors. Among the methods condemned by the commission were misbranding, adulteration, bribing, false or misleading advertising, and selling goods below cost to drive competitors out of business. Young stated that many of these practices were already illegal under the law. But through the Commission a businessman got relief more promptly and economically than through the slower process of the courts. Perhaps the most important work of the Commission was the voluntary adoption by businesses themselves of the new and higher standards of competition. Voluntary cooperation of trade organisations had also been secured to get rid of unfair trade practices.

Young pointed out that the US had committed many blunders in formulating and implementing a policy directed against large combinations. For example, the attempt to force competition in the field of natural monopolies (as mentioned above) or giving too much importance to the mere fact of combination or curing many evils rooted in corporate finance through sweeping prohibitions under restraint of trade or monopolising. But the general direction of the anti-trust policy was not at fault:

> Monopoly has yet to prove itself more efficient than competition. And, moreover, it is not entirely a question of economic efficiency. There are differences between monopoly and competition in their effects upon the distribution of wealth, upon the equality of economic opportunity, and upon a host of economic and social relations; and in most of these particulars, it is generally believed, the advantage rests with competition. At any rate, we are proceeding along sound lines in endeavoring to raise the level of competitive methods and to eliminate any advantages which large combinations may have in their power of destructive competition. This will give a fairer field for experimentation with respect to the forms of business organization really best fitted for survival. (ibid., p. 230)

Young suggested that the lack of uniform state laws in corporate governance could be remedied by federal action. Apart from lack of uniformity in state laws, the mere size of modern businesses and their interstate operations made it difficult for individual states to control them effectively. "What is needed is a federal statute dealing thoroughly and systematically with the promotion, organization, and management of corporations engaged in interstate commerce… It would be legally possible and economically advisable to require at least a *federal license* from all corporations engaging in interstate commerce. Moderate and just requirements as to publicity, capitalization, and other things might very well be imposed as the price of a federal license" (ibid., p. 231).

Young also compared the US combinations with those in other countries. He stated that the movement towards combinations in England had made much less headway than in the US. This might be because of their stricter company laws as well as the absence of protective tariff. Before the WWI many important combinations were formed there but only a few succeeded. In Germany and other countries of continental Europe, combinations took the form of the *Kartell* which resembled a pool more than the highly centralised combinations of the US. The *Kartell* controlled the price, output, sales and the distribution of orders and profits while individual companies acted as individual producing establishments. Opinion in Germany appeared divided on the success of the *Kartells*. While some thought that they had eliminated many competitive wastes and captured foreign markets, others thought that they discriminated against the home consumer by charging a lower price abroad.

Enumeration of Children

At the turn of the twentieth century, the US lacked an adequate system of registration of births as only a few states had such a system. The birth rate was determined on the basis of children less than one year old reported by the census. In his pre-doctoral article 'The enumeration of children', which also reflected the findings in his Ph.D. dissertation (Young 1904), Young (1901) pointed out that the census reports were inaccurate in enumerating young children and this could be definitely proved. Under normal conditions it was expected that the number of children in the first year of life in any population would be more than in the second, more in the second than in the third, and so on. The reason was that mortality in the first year of life was so great that the number of children less than one year old was much larger than the one year old. A reversal in this pattern could not be caused by the normal fluctuations in birth and death rates. A simple inspection of the census figures showed that there were more children reported at each of the next higher ages than at under one or one.

There could be two possible causes of underreporting of young children—omission in enumeration and overstatement of age. While most experts were prone to believe that the inaccuracy of the census results was due to wrong enumeration, reflecting rather badly on the truthfulness of the count, Young stated that overstatement of age was the more important cause. The overstatement of age in the 1890 census was more than that in 1880 and this was caused by the change in age question from 'age at last birthday' to 'age at nearest birthday'. Young also compared registration of births in Massachusetts, Connecticut and Rhode Island with the census results in these states and estimated the comparative deficiency of each census in which the age question related to the nearest birthday in 1890. The comparative deficiency was shown to be 15.8 per cent for Massachusetts, 9.7 per cent for Connecticut and 10 per cent in Rhode Island. Young's overall conclusions were as follows:

1. The apparent deficiencies in census reports of children are caused by omissions in the enumeration and by overstatement of age; the latter cause being by far the more important. The omission of a small proportion of children in the enumeration is a matter of general census experience, while overstatement of ages of children seems to be a fault peculiar to those censuses in which the age is obtained by direct question as to the number of years lived.
2. These two causes of deficiency were operative in the United States censuses of 1880 and 1890. It is probable that the increased deficiency of children under one year of age, in 1890, was caused by an increase in the overstatement of ages. There is no trustworthy evidence of an increased omission of children in the census of 1890.
3. It is difficult to measure the absolute deficiency of children in either 1880 or 1890. What evidence we have points toward a probable excess in deficiency of children under one year of age in 1890 over that in 1880, amounting to about 10 percent of the total number…
4. The increased overstatement of children's ages in 1890 was caused by the change in the age question form 'age at last birthday,' to 'age at

nearest birthday,' and does not necessarily indicate that the enumeration was less careful than in previous censuses (ibid. 1901, p. 254).

In a later article 'The census age question' Young (1910) criticised the William Bailey and Julius Parmelee (1910) conclusion that in 1900 where the enumerators were required to ascertain the year and month of birth in addition to age this did not affect the quality of the age statistics of the 1900 census. Young stated that this was at variance with former views on the subject. Young noted that the 1900 census returns were distinctly more accurate than in the past, which, inter alia, was due to decreased overstatement of ages of young children. The date-of-birth inquiry gave far more accurate results than the age inquiry.

Devising a Pension System for Massachusetts

Young was a member of the Massachusetts Commission on Pensions which submitted its report to the state legislature in 1925. It inquired into the economic status of the aged people of the state with a double purpose of (1) establishing the degree of need for old-age pensions (or some other system of relief) and (2) supplying an estimate of the public expenditure involved. In an article 'The aged poor of Massachusetts' Young (1926a), presented the findings based on interviews of 21,594 persons spread across 10 cities and 23 towns. Young stated that the results were robust to any reasonable community-wise weighting scheme used and that the sample was reliable. The findings revealed that by the time people reached old age, most persons had either saved a substantial amount or little (or nothing). Those aged 65 years or over not supported by public funds or private organised charity (i.e., non-dependents) constituted 84.4 per cent of the total. The figure for non-dependents was 79.2 per cent for those aged 70 years or over.

The financial condition of the non-dependent aged population of 65 years or over revealed the following facts. First, 59.2 per cent had property of less than $5000, and 32.4 per cent had an annual income of less than $400. Classification according to the age group revealed that as age advanced the earning power failed and small savings were gradually used up; so relatively larger number found themselves with an exceedingly smaller income or none at all. Young stated that these figures gave an exaggerated impression of the degree of need that existed among the aged people of the state. First, only 35 per cent of the aged with property less than $5000 and income less than $1000 were entirely self-supporting as the others were supported either by their children or friends and relatives. Second, the non-dependent aged had four times as many children living as almshouse inmates—one of the reasons why they themselves were not almshouse inmates. Further, taking the marital status into account, it was found that while 7.1 per cent of the married had no income, the percentage for single or widowed was much greater—15.4 per cent for men and 32.5 per cent for women.

Based on the survey results, Young concluded that the annual cost of non-contributory old-age pension of a dollar a day for all those aged 65 or over would amount to about $58 million; and if the pension age were increased to 70 years or over, the amount would be about $32 million. The cost could be reduced to $10–11 million if only those aged 70 and over with income from all sources (including pension) less than $365, and with property of less than $3000 were included. This figure could be further lowered to $5–6 million if pensions were refused to those whose children were able to support them.

The Economics of Farm Relief

The Haugen Bill proposed a system of discriminatory prices for farm produce (in place of competitive conditions) whereby a tariff would shelter the domestic market, special agencies would procure enough farm produce to push up domestic prices, and sell the surplus in the foreign markets for whatever prices that could be obtained. Since most of the produce would be sold in the domestic market, domestic consumers would lose by paying a much higher price as compared to the foreign consumer. Young (1926b; Mehrling and Sandilands 1999, p. 111) argued that successful price discrimination required a unified monopolistic control of production, something which was absent in agriculture:

The fundamental obstacle to successful price regulation or price maintenance in any purely competitive field of industry is that it is impracticable to regulate output or to close the doors to entry of new labor and new capital. Successful price maintenance calls for something like a unified monopolistic control of production, and that is out of the question in an industry like agriculture.

Even if wheat was singled out for special treatment, the amount of land devoted to wheat would increase at the expense of other crops. Any attempt to control the prices of other products would meet with special difficulties. The demand for meat was much more elastic as compared to wheat, and therefore more sensitive to price changes. The export market for some crops like corn was much smaller than the domestic market, so unsalable export surpluses procured to boost domestic prices would pile up. Other farm products like cotton were raw materials in the domestic manufacturing, and an American manufacturer would have to pay a higher price for the same material than a foreign buyer. This would call for a scheme to refund the American manufacturer the excess paid by him as well as a higher tariff to protect him against the foreign manufacturer. Moreover, increased exports of cotton by the US would only be possible at markedly lower prices; so any profits resulting from higher prices to domestic consumers would easily be offset by losses from foreign sales.

Young further stated that the criteria for 'fair and reasonable' prices were always loose and uncertain, and in the case of agriculture they were virtually non-existent. Some past period, when agriculture was prosperous, was to be taken as the norm or standard, and the authorities would then fix agricultural prices in a manner that would keep them in the same average relation to other prices as obtained in the so-called normal year. Young criticised this scheme as it had several lacunae. For one, it was unclear what the price-fixing authorities would do in case the ordinary demand and supply forces of the market themselves fixed a price above the so-called norm. Moreover, this scheme failed completely in the case of separate agricultural products.

According to Young, the real issue was to ensure a satisfactory return on the capital invested in agriculture. The prices had to be high enough to ensure reasonable profits to the farmer over and above his costs of production. "It is upon some such basis that we regulate the rates and earnings of railways and of public utilities. Is not the American farmer entitled to a fair return upon his capital, quite as much as the public service corporation?" (ibid., p. 113). However, there were difficulties in this task. First, while a public service undertaking was a monopoly, farming was the most competitive of all businesses. Second, the task of determining the invested capital, which was difficult enough in the case of public utilities, was simply impossible in the case of agriculture.

In Young's opinion, the genesis of the problem lay in the post-war agricultural boom and the accompanying rise in land values. The Haugen proposals were, in effect, aimed at legitimising artificially the inflated system of land values resulting from the post-war boom. He wrote:

> If one could effectively control agricultural prices, one would, in fact, control land values. This is the vital fact behind the price-control movement… The unduly heavy overhead costs which the farmer now has to carry, are, in considerable part, a sequel of the postwar agricultural boom and the accompanying rise in land values. It was then that agriculture became heavily overcapitalized and an enormous structure of fixed charges was created. The current proposals for price control, such as the Haugen bill, are, in effect, proposals for the artificial valorization of a part, at least, of what is already an inflated system of land values. (ibid., p. 113)

Young feared that the proposals, although defeated in the Senate, might be revived again. Young felt that the proposals, in large part, were unworkable, and would do more harm than good. Young also felt that agricultural depression was real and one could not disprove it by merely pointing to higher agricultural prices than a few years ago. Agricultural depressions were longer lived than in trade and industry, and liquidation there involved a slower and more painful process.

Young (ibid., p. 114) concluded:

> The present situation is one of the results of war. The burdens of war are never equitably distributed, and an undue proportion of them have fallen upon the landowning farmer. If I knew of any really effective way of redressing the balance, I would support it. As things are, I think, the farmer has a genuine interest in two things: first, sizable tariff reduction; second,

the maintenance of generally stable conditions and, in particular, the avoidance of another period of inflated prices necessitating further readjustment and distressing unrest.

In condemning the bill Young had stated that not since the free silver campaign of 1896 had the American people been asked to agree to an unsounder economic proposal. At the same time Young did not want to judge an economist's competence on the basis of his attitude towards the bill as his friend Frank Knight had supported it on the grounds that its proposals would counterbalance the protective tariff to industry. Blitch (1995) noted that when the McNary-Haugen bill reached President Coolidge, it was promptly vetoed but its provisions resurfaced in the Agricultural Adjustment Act of 1933. "All the problems which Young had discussed have emerged" (ibid., p. 155).[6]

The Paris Peace Conference (1918–1919)[7]

Preparatory to the Paris peace conference Young was appointed as the economics specialist of 'The Inquiry'—an organisation charged with the responsibility to study the post-war problems and to lay the groundwork for the peace conference. The organisation mainly consisted of experts drawn from American universities working under the direction of Colonel Edward M. House—a close confidant of President Woodrow Wilson. Apart from Young, members of the group included James Shotwell (Professor of History at Columbia), Charles S. Haskins (Dean of the Harvard Graduate School), Isaiah Bowman (President of the American Geographical Society), Charles Seymour (Professor of History at Yale), William E. Lunt (Professor of English History at Cornell), Clive Day

---

[6] Because of its agricultural support programme the US accumulated grain surpluses and was forced to ship them to poorer countries as food aid under its PL480 programme. The surpluses which were stored in the US granaries amounted to "a free lunch programme for rats and mice" as Milton Friedman (1965, p. 2) characterised them. Similar support programmes in the EU under its common agricultural policy (CAP) also led to grain and butter mountains as well as milk and wine lakes (see Paul Lewis 1986).

[7] This section is mainly based on Young (1919, 1920), Miller (1928), Shotwell (1937) and Blitch (1995).

(Professor of Economic History at Yale) and Douglas W. Johnson (Assistant Professor of Physiography at Columbia). Walter Lippmann was the organisation's secretary, David Hunter Miller (a prominent New York City Attorney) the treasurer, and Sidney E. Mezes (President of the City College of New York) its head. Because of the internal frictions in the organisation initially, it was decided that Mezes would remain the nominal director and a committee consisting of Young, Bowman and Haskins would look after the executive functions.

The Inquiry, as noted by Blitch (1995, pp. 65–6), was faced with several problems:

> The problems facing 'The Inquiry' were not only enormous in scope, but were completely new because the United States had never taken part in a general peace conference and, even though a world power, lacked a general world view. The major problems of the organization, such as delineating procedures and fields of work, recruiting competent personnel, and securing adequate financing, were never fully overcome… The economics division exhibited in a microcosm all the problems facing the whole organization.

Blitch further noted that out of a small total budget of $15,000, the economics division received about 10 per cent. The division was manned by just six persons. Despite Young's pleas for more staff and funds, there was little recognition of the importance of economic matters outside of the economics division. Young was forced to rely on outside agencies for much of the economic and statistical reports. Since these reports lacked a clear purpose and received little or no remuneration, their quality and usefulness was variable. Young and his staff had the unenviable task of making sense out of them, extracting what was useful, and putting the whole thing in a coherent form. Moreover, the inquiry was organised along geographical lines and excluded the common problems facing Europe as a whole. Young in his memorandum stated that the information gathered should be on subjects rather than on areas, but his pleas were to no avail.

On 30 November 1919, Secretary of State Robert Lansing wrote to Young appointing him as Specialist in Economic Resources at a monthly salary of $600 to the American Commission to Negotiate Peace at Paris. Initially Mezes had recommended Young to Lansing as a regional specialist for Turkey but later changed it to Economic Resources.[8] He thought it better for Young to go under his own colours rather than as a regional specialist for Turkey. The members of the inquiry—Young, Shotwell, Bowman, Day, Haskins, Seymour and Lunt—along with new members—Douglas Johnson, William L. Westermann, George L. Beer, Robert H. Lord and Mark Jefferson—were also named to accompany the delegation led by President Wilson. Young, who had shot into national prominence with his association with the Inquiry, built up an international reputation for his work in Paris.

The ship *George Washington* carrying the President and his team set sail on 4 December 1918 and reached the French port of Brest on 13 December. While on the ship, on 10 December, the President addressed his technical experts—Bowman, Day, Haskins, Lord, Mezes, Seymour, Westermann and Young—in his office, shaking hands with them individually. He stated that the American delegation would be the only disinterested party at the conference and that peace must be based on justice. This might encounter opposition as boundary questions were involved. Regarding German indemnity, he insisted that it should be confined to actual war damages done by Germany as the aggressor to civilian properties. It was not a question of restitution which the other allied powers were probably contemplating but of actual civilian damages to be estimated by a commission. Regarding the League of Nations, he stated that covenants were more important than the actual organisation, and the latter could be worked out in a conference. A League of Nations was essential for lasting peace, otherwise the ideas of great powers and balance of power would re-emerge, and he was sick of this concept. The disposal of German colonies could be mandates of the League. Finally, he hoped to see his advisors frequently to advise him on the justice or injustice of various claims. He asked them to tell him what was right and he would fight for it. On December 12, when the President sent for him, Young told him that Germany's ability to pay damages even for civilian damages was very limited, not to speak of her actual obligations. The President felt

---

[8] Mezes to Lansing dated 14 November 1918.

that the first discussion should be on the basis of Germany's obligations.[9] President Wilson and his team aboard *George Washington* arrived at Brest to a grand reception including a 21-gun salute on 13 December 1918. Young and the other technical advisers arrived in Paris on the 14th morning and were put up at the Hotel de Crillon, the headquarters of the American Peace Commission. President Wilson arrived later on the same day in the special blue train of the French President.

From the outset Young grappled with the problem of German reparations. He met with David Hunter Miller and Paul Cravath, financial and legal advisers to the American Commission, to discuss the latter's memorandum on Germany's indemnity. Cravath had shown this memorandum to J.M. Keynes while in London enroute to Paris. Cravath was keen that Keynes and Young as economists meet each other, and since he was returning to America shortly, he requested Miller to introduce the two economists.[10] Shotwell (1937) recorded in his diary that Young had been placed in charge of the Economic Division, with Colonel Ayres as his collaborator, to deal with the subject of indemnities. He also noted that Young was happy and excited.

Young prepared an article 'A suggestion for American policy with respect to indemnities' as a basis for German reparations (Miller 1928, pp. 121–2). He stated that although indemnity was compensatory rather than punitive, and limited to the amount of injury actually done to civilians and their property, it was equally necessary to use the proceeds of the indemnity for no other purpose than compensating for the losses actually incurred. For example, payment to the French government should be on account of it being a trustee to the French citizens who had suffered losses and not on account of the French national economic fabric being injured. The civilian losses should not only be the basis of the indemnity but also its purpose. In another memorandum 'The determination of the losses resulting from damages to structures', Young stated that the French and

---

[9] Young did not keep notes of this meeting but later wrote to Taussig (on 10 December 1921) to this effect.

[10] Blitch (1995, p. 89) notes that Young and Keynes did not form a close relationship in Paris. But, nevertheless, Keynes had a presentation copy of *Economic Consequences of the Peace* (1919) sent to Young, who in his reply to Keynes, dated 11 February 1920, regretted that "I did not see more of you at Paris". See also Chap. 9 (section on Keynes).

German claims for damages to buildings were estimated on the basis of the pre-war construction costs multiplied by a factor expressing a general increase in building costs since 1914 (ibid., pp. 136–7). This method led to exaggerated estimates of the actual costs of restoration as it was based on the assumption that complete reconstruction de novo was necessary. The actual facts, however, were that in most instances excavations, foundations and much building material remained. Opportunities for improvements (e.g., in street plans of parts of towns and villages) as well as economies should both be utilised. What was required was restoration rather than reduplication. Compensation needed to be fixed by the actual necessities of practicable reconstruction and not in accordance with reduplication of what existed before the war. Indemnification needed to be determined by the amount of damage done, and losses by the cost of actual reconstruction in situ. "Restoration, it must be assumed, is accomplished by replacing a damaged structure by one of equal utility and equal *value*, which need not necessarily be one of equal *cost*" (Miller 1928, p. 137).

Before leaving New York, Young had seen a memorandum prepared by Edwin F. Gay, Director of the Central Bureau of Research and Statistics, stating that the Bureau would be the sole source of economic data and information for the American Commission at the Paris Conference. It also had President Wilson's signatures. Young, offended because it undercut his authority, had the occasion to mention this to President Wilson while aboard *George Washington*. The President admitted that he may have signed a large number of memoranda without reading them in the excitement and confusion surrounding the preparations for Paris. He asked Young to continue with his job of supplying economic information to the American Commission. When John Foster Dulles, along with a group of Gay's men from the Central Bureau, armed with a copy of the memorandum arrived in Paris, Young was upset that his authority may again be undermined. Dulles was moreover Secretary of State Lansing's nephew and might try to use his uncle's influence in the matter. When the controversy heated up, the President once again intervened to say that to the best of his knowledge he had not authorised any arrangement in which Dulles would be the exclusive source of economic information. With the establishment of the Commission on Reparation of Damage

(CRD), on 23 January 1919 by the Council of Ten, the matter got resolved. Dulles was appointed as legal counsel to the American representatives, with Young the economic consultant. Shotwell (1937, p. 118) wrote that Young and Dulles[11] were on friendly terms and were in substantial agreement over reparations and other issues.

In the proceedings of the CRD, the most intense debate took place over the question of the amount Germany was to pay. The French wanted the entire cost of the war, which they estimated to be $200 billion, to be paid. Britain asked for $120 billion. Then there was a debate on what assets could be transferred immediately. Cravath had recommended that $3 billion be paid immediately and an additional $15 billion spread over 28 years. Young in a memorandum 'Tentative valuation of immediately transferrable assets' placed the value of these assets at $6.39 billion—$5.59 billion on private and $0.80 billion on public account (Miller 1928, p. 111). Privately owned property included merchant fleet, property owned abroad (in the US, Latin America and other countries) and property owned in German colonies and ceded territory. Government owned property included rolling stock taken by armistice, property in ceded territories such as railroads and state mines (e.g., coal mines) but excluded gold. Young was against seizing German gold assets as they were needed to stabilise the financial conditions both within Germany and to redeem large quantities of paper marks held in formerly occupied territories (ibid., pp. 116–7).

Writing in the *New York Times* Young (1919), in an article 'Practical basis of Germany's bill', stated:

> A nation has only four ways of making foreign payments: First, by exporting gold; second, by drawing on funds already established in foreign centres; third, by borrowing in foreign centres; fourth, by selling goods and services in foreign markets. Germany's gold would cover only a very small fraction of her reparation liabilities, and to take any large part of it would so unsettle financial conditions in Germany as to lessen that country's power to make reparation payments in a degree wholly disproportionate to the amount of gold taken. Moreover, if the German paper marks now held

---

[11] Later, Dulles's sister Eleanor Lansing Dulles was Young's Ph.D. student at Harvard.

in large quantities in France, Belgium, Poland, and in South-eastern Europe are ultimately to be redeemed, the German gold reserves must be husbanded rather than dissipated. The funds now to Germany's credit in foreign money centres (e.g. in neutral countries) are very small, and with negligible exceptions are already mortgaged for other purposes. Borrowing in foreign markets, even if it were feasible, would not solve the problem. It would merely replace one sort of foreign indebtedness by another.

For most of the other reparation payments, therefore, Germany must rely upon sale of services or property in foreign markets. Here she can utilize two classes of things: First, things now outside of Germany or that can be easily moved outside of Germany; second, things that can be produced in Germany in the future and sold in foreign markets. The first of these two classes of things constitute Germany's cash assets, which will have to be relied upon to meet the first installments of the reparation payments. The second class of things must be relied upon as the source of later successive payments upon the indemnity.

Young argued that securing a surplus of exports over imports posed its own problems. First, in her best pre-war year 1913, Germany had a trade deficit, so to export more than imports, she had to put restrictions on the foreign trade sector to cut down unnecessary imports and government control over industry to prioritise exports. But this might arouse dangerous disaffection and discontent among the German people. Second, Germany had lost much of the goodwill of the world's markets, so to regain the pre-war position would take time. If the allied powers allowed more preferential German exports within their own countries and also allowed access to German exports in neutral countries, the problem could be simplified. But this was highly unlikely; nor could it be expected that these countries would employ German labour or assign contracts for reconstruction work in devastated regions to German firms employing German labour. "Relying, then, only upon shipments of coal and potash and exports of the usual sort of manufactured goods, a trade balance of half a billion dollars a year is likely to be about as much as Germany can be expected to achieve in the near future" (ibid.).

Young estimated that Germany's *liability* to pay reparations was closer to $20 billion and her *capacity* to pay was half of that amount at

$10 billion. Young (1920, p. 388), while reviewing Keynes's *The Economic Consequences of the Peace*, stated:

> I should put the total reparation payment to which Germany is liable under the pre-armistice agreements closer to $20,000,000,000 than to Mr. Keynes' estimate of $10,600,000,000. I put her capacity to pay, as he does at $10,000,000,000. But there is nothing in her economic situation which enables one to say that a payment of twice that size, is impossible. The obstacle is the claimant nations to take so large a payment in the form in which it would have to be made, that is, in German goods or in contracts for reconstruction work let to German firms.

Young, along with the other Americans on the CRD, wanted the German reparations to be a fixed sum to be paid in a given period and based only on the injuries to civilians and their property. "Only in the case of Belgium were pensions sought for families whose civilian breadwinners had been lost through enemy action. Young's estimates of ten billion dollars as the minimum and fifteen billion dollars as a maximum were accepted, and 30 years as the payment period. Both the French and British representatives balked at the fixed sum and pressed for the damage categories to be enlarged to cover military pensions and allowances. By the end of March 1919 the reparation debate had reached an impasse. Suddenly, in early April, President Wilson without explanation, conceded all points to the French and the British. The amount of the indemnity was left open to be determined by the reparations commission after the peace had been concluded. It would provide for military pensions and allowances, and no time limit for payment was set" (Blitch 1995, p. 81).

Young, in a letter to Frank W. Taussig, blamed Colonel House and Thomas W. Lamont for making a mess of things.[12] In another letter to Ray Stannard Baker, he stated that the President's task would have been easier if some of his advisors had stood by him more loyally.[13] He also stated that Colonel House had tried to 'arrange' or 'manage' the President on precisely those points which were of most concern. The Reparation

---

[12] Young to Taussig dated 16 December 1921.
[13] Young to Baker dated 24 December 1919.

Commission fixed Germany's bill at $33 billion in 1921. The Owen D. Young Plan reduced it to $8 billion. Before the moratorium in 1932, Germany paid only $5 billion, of which half a billion was a loan to her under the Dawes and Young Plans.[14]

References

Bailey, William B. and Julius H. Parmelee (1910), 'The age returns of the twentieth census', *Publications of the American Statistical Association*, 12, pp. 110–23.

Blitch, Charles P. (1995), *Allyn Young: The Peripatetic Economist*, Basingstoke and London: Macmillan Press Ltd.

Ely, Richard T., Thomas S. Adams, Max O. Lorenz and Allyn A. Young (1923), *Outlines of Economics*, New York: The Macmillan Company.

Friedman, Milton (1965), 'Transfer Payments and the Social Security System', *National Industrial Conference Board Record 2* (September), pp. 7–10.

Keynes, John M. (1919; 1920), *The Economic Consequences of the Peace*, New York: Harcourt, Brace and Howe.

Lewis, Paul (1986), 'Food surplus may bankrupt European bloc', *New York Times*, December 27.

Mehrling, Perry G. and Roger J. Sandilands (eds.) (1999), *Money and Growth: Selected Papers of Allyn Abbott Young*, London and New York: Routledge.

Meyer, Balthasar H. (1914), 'Certain considerations in railway rate making', *American Economic Review*, 4, pp. 69–80.

Miller, David H. (1928), *My Diary at the Paris Peace Conference*, Washington.

Shotwell, James T. (1937), *At the Paris Peace Conference*, New York.

Young, Allyn (1901), 'The enumeration of children', *Publications of the American Statistical Association*, 7(53), pp. 227–54.

Young, Allyn (1904), *A Discussion of Age Statistics*, U.S. Bureau of Census, Washington: Government Printing Office.

Young, Allyn (1910), 'The census age question', *Publications of the American Statistical Association*, 12(92), pp. 360–70.

Young, Allyn (1913), 'Street car transport in St. Louis', *American Economic Review*, 3(3), pp. 712–14.

---

[14] The issue became known as the transfer problem and is also taken up later in Chap. 9 under the section on John M. Keynes.

Young, Allyn (1914a), 'Depreciation and rate control', *Quarterly Journal of Economics*, 28(3), pp. 630–63. Reprinted in Young (1927), pp. 119–51.

Young, Allyn (1914b), 'Railway rate making: discussion', *American Economic Review*, 4(1), Supplement (March), pp. 82–6.

Young, Allyn (1915a), 'Personal and impersonal taxation', *Proceedings of the Ninth Annual Conference of National Tax Association 1915*, Ithaca, NY: National Tax Association. Reprinted in Young (1927), pp. 108–18.

Young, Allyn (1915b), 'The Sherman Act and the new anti-trust legislation', *Journal of Political Economy*, 23(3–5), pp. 201–20, 305–26, 417–36. Reprinted in Young (1927), pp. 158–97.

Young, Allyn (1919), 'Practical basis of Germany's bill', *The New York Times*, 10th August, pp. 1–8.

Young, Allyn (1920), 'The economics of the treaty', *The New Republic*, 25th February, pp. 388–9.

Young, Allyn (1926a), 'The aged poor in Massachusetts', *Quarterly Journal of Economics*, 40(3), 549–54.

Young, Allyn (1926b), 'The economics of farm relief', *The Independent*, New York. Reprinted in Mehrling and Sandilands (1999), pp. 110–14.

Young, Allyn (1927), *Economic Problems New and Old*, Boston and New York: Houghton Mifflin Company.

Young, Allyn (1990), 'Nicholas Kaldor's Notes on Allyn Young's LSE Lectures, 1927–29', *Journal of Economic Studies*, 17(3/4), pp. 18–114.

7

Allyn Young on Money, Banking and Business Cycles

Classical economists abstracted from the use of money.[1] They thought of money as a veil behind which the real economy lay. Money was regarded as a convenient medium of exchange leaving the relative prices unchanged. The money supply affected the general price level but not the exchange ratios. Value was thought to be antecedent to price and one had to dig below the surface view to get the real picture. Money prices were merely exchange values expressed in money terms.

For Allyn Young, prices were primary and values secondary. Values were determined in the process of exchange and there they emerged as prices. The change in money supply not only affected the price level but more importantly the relative prices. According to him, it was the distortion or mismatch in relative prices which caused business cycles. Young advocated an interventionist monetary policy to control credit. He thought that credit was inherently unstable and needed to be controlled by the central bank to moderate the business cycle. Young also wanted to go beyond the concept of static equilibrium and explore the disequilibrium

---

[1] Their distaste for money perhaps arose as a reaction to mercantilist obsession with hoards of gold and silver to the neglect of the real economy. In the classical conception wealth meant real output rather than gold and silver.

process of price formation. He saw money prices as important to this task. In his opinion price was antecedent to value and not vice versa.

Perry Mehrling (1997) interpreted Young's monetary thought as holding a middle ground between J. Laurence Laughlin's real bills doctrine (or banking school) and Irving Fisher's quantity theory approach (or currency school). While the former advocated the gold standard, passive accommodation by the central banks and laissez-faire, the latter supported active monetary policy, stabilisation of the general price level and a variable monetary standard. Young's approach was to pick the best points of both and marry them with his agenda of disequilibrium price formation. For example, while rejecting Laughlin's passive accommodation and laissez-faire, Young also rejected Fisher's agenda to stabilise the average price level by varying the price of gold in terms of the dollar.

Young was also influenced by Ralph Hawtrey's monetary views. Like Hawtrey he believed credit[2] to be an unstable component of the money supply. Like Hawtrey he believed in the gold standard. Again like Hawtrey he believed in an activist-discretionary monetary policy to keep credit under control to influence the business cycle. But unlike Hawtrey, he advocated public works in their own right as a means of stabilisation. Hawtrey generally did not favour public works unless they led to money creation. Again unlike Hawtrey, he did not offer a purely monetary explanation of the business cycle.[3] For him wrong estimates by businesses of the quantum and composition of future demand played a dominant role.[4]

For Young, money was central to a modern economic system. In a letter to Bruce Blivin, editor of the *New York Globe*, Young argued: "The older economists used to discuss economic problems as though the use of money was merely a convenience, without real effects upon the nature of economic relations. No development in modern economics has more importance than the increased emphasis upon the purely monetary aspects of economic problems."[5] Joseph Schumpeter (1935, 1954) noted

---

[2] In his day, credit was commonly defined as checkable demand deposits.

[3] "Even if not the fundamental cause, the expansion of bank credit is a necessary *condition* of the overexpansion of business" (Ely et al. 1923, p. 337).

[4] Mehrling (1996, pp. 620–1) observes that for Young business cycles were not monetary in origin but definitely monetary in character.

[5] Young to Blivin dated 9 January 1923.

that it was in money and banking that Young came nearest to giving full exposition to his views.[6]

Unfortunately, the treatise on money which Young was working on at the time of his premature death got lost. His monetary thought has to be constructed from various scattered articles; collections like Mehrling and Sandilands (1999) and Young (1927a); Nicholas Kaldor's Notes on Allyn Young's LSE Lectures (Young 1990); secondary literature such as David Laidler (1993, 1999) and Mehrling (1996, 1997, 2002), Laidler and Sandilands (2002); biographies such as Charles Blitch (1995) and Roger Sandilands (1990); Young's chapters in the various editions of *Outlines of Economics*; and *An Analysis of Bank Statistics for the United States* (Young 1928) besides the unpublished correspondence.

Monetary (and Gold) Standard

Young put forward his theory of a monetary standard as an alternative to money as merely a medium of exchange. In a letter to William Foster dated 12 April 1923, Young stated: "Let me say just what I think a monetary standard is. In the first place, it is the one commodity the price of which is definitely fixed in terms of money. In the second place, the monetary standard is itself the money of gold redemption. In the third place, it, or some money directly based upon it, must be used in the payment of balances…whether between individual banks, between different regions, or between different countries." In other words, a monetary standard provides a fixed point for a system of relative prices, is directly exchangeable in gold (or gold coin) and serves as an ultimate reserve to clear all outstanding balances. At the national level, net balances between banks are cleared in the monetary standard and international settlements are made in gold.

After WWI, Young advocated a return to the gold standard as gold already performed the task of international payments. Gold served this purpose because demand for it was elastic whereas the demand for most

---

[6] Schumpeter (1954, p. 876, f.n. 23) stated that "in his [Young's] concise and unassuming analysis of national bank statistics, there is enshrined the better part of a whole theory of money and credit".

necessities of life was inelastic. Because of its elasticity creditors are willing to receive payment in gold. Mehrling (1996, p. 616) notes that Young supported the return to the gold standard not as an ideal monetary system but because it was the only viable standard in that historical stage.[7] Young was aware that limited gold supplies in the face of expanding world output could potentially cause deflation. But he saw the solution in international cooperation of central banks to conserve limited gold supplies.[8] In other words, his support was for the gold-exchange standard.[9] He warned that fiat currency, apart from the problem of overissue, would always be prone to speculative attacks creating difficulties in the way of foreign trade and international settlements. Furthermore, he favoured a return to the gold standard not at pre-war but at post-war parities to avoid deflation.

Young viewed the exchange rate as an anchor which needed to be stabilised rather than the price level. The post-war German inflation was not a conspiracy by the German government to destroy its capacity to make reparation payments. Rather Germans preferred to sell the depreciating marks for goods and foreign exchange. As government receipts and expenditures were affected, the resulting budget deficit forced the government to print more paper money, resulting in a cumulative price spiral. Overexpansion of money supply was the result of depreciation rather than its cause. Thus he believed that the best way to obtain monetary

---

[7] "An ideal monetary system would be that which would give stability in prices. The gold standard, by this test, is far from ideal. Its strongest claim is not that it gives stability in prices, but that it is, one might say, automatic in its operations. If we must have general fluctuations in prices, alternating movements up and down, it is better that these should be governed by the changes in the output of a relatively stable commodity, like gold, than that they should be the outcome of political manipulation or of arbitrary adjustment of any sort whatever. It may be said of the gold standard, not that it is perfect, but that it is measurably 'fool-proof'" (Young 1929a; Mehrling and Sandilands 1999, p. 292).

[8] "There is plenty of gold. Production and trade can grow without there being a general fall of prices, if only the central banks of the world will permit it… To attempt, under present conditions, to build a large idle hoard of gold, whether in London or elsewhere, is generally only an expression of financial nationalism, and financial nationalism is an expensive luxury… A gradual downward trend of prices is probable, not because the supply of gold is or will soon become inadequate, but merely because the central banks of different countries will probably try to maintain their separate hoards of gold" (Young 1929b; Mehrling and Sandilands 1999, p. 373).

[9] Young defines this as a standard where local currency is not necessarily redeemable in gold in the home country, but redeemable in bills of exchange or drafts payable in gold in a foreign country (Ely et al. 1916, p. 270).

stability was to stabilise the foreign exchange rates rather than the price level. The best way to achieve this was to attract capital inflows (and not through export surplus). Allied citizens needed to accept German bonds and claims on German property; Germans needed to be convinced to trade their foreign assets for government debt. In this way intergovernmental debt could be reduced without affecting trade flows. Young thus differed from J.M. Keynes who advocated stabilisation of domestic prices and Gustav Cassel's notion of purchasing power parity which focused on goods flows, ignoring capital flows. Mehrling (1996, p. 620) sums up:

> From the point of view of the theory of banking, it was the strain of wartime capital flows that forced the abandonment of the gold standard and those same flows stood at the root of the postwar monetary disorder. The disorder was caused not so much by irresponsible national money and credit policies as by the normal mechanism of international payments in the face of the extraordinary strains of war and its aftermath. And the solution lay not so much in improving management of the existing fiat currencies as it did in removing the source of the unnatural strain by a reduction of war debts.

The key to the debt problem lay with the US. If the US forgave England then England could afford to forgive France, and France in turn could forgive Germany, then the reparation and inter-allied debt problem could be solved (or mitigated). But the US neither ratified the Versailles Treaty[10] nor was it willing to forgive the inter-allied debts entirely. Secretary of Commerce Herbert Hoover, the most influential figure at the Debt Commission, argued that debts were a moral and contractual obligation and if repudiated would undermine international relations. "Despite Hoover's contention the Debt Commission reduced the debts, in effect, by decreasing the interest rates and expanding the period of amortization. On 11 June 1931, Hoover, then President of the United States, declared a one year moratorium on debt payments by the Allies. No further receipts were received from the Allied Governments during the great

---

[10] Young was the chief US economist at the Versailles Peace Conference in Paris in 1919 but resigned (as did Keynes) because the peace terms were unduly harsh to Germany.

depression of the 1930s, and new debt was created by rearmament for WWII" (Blitch 1995, p. 106).

Exchange Values, Prices and Business Cycles

As already noted, the classical economists thought of value as primary and price as a derivative concept. For the determination of exchange values or ratios of exchange, money was eliminated as an essential mechanism of the market. Values were thought to be determined by the regime of pure barter. Money came in at the end as an expository device to serve as a common denominator of the exchange values reached through barter. According to Young, even historically speaking, barter was a sheer work of imagination. It would be wrong to say that money was invented to overcome the inconveniences of barter; barter and the use of money had gone hand in hand.[11] Referring to Wesley Mitchell, Young pointed out that money concept has itself been a factor in giving purpose, system and rationality to economic activity. "Modern business is conducted by men who have learned to think in terms of money, and the price making process is largely in their hands" (Young 1911, 1927a, pp. 201–2). Young further pointed out that static equilibrium under pure barter cannot be reached unless the market is fairly large. Therefore: "The lucidity which premising of a general medium of exchange adds to economic analysis (as in the theory of supply and demand *at a price*) is only a reflection of the precision and determinateness which the use of money gives to the actual operations of the market" (ibid., pp. 202–3).

Adam Smith may have thought of the real measure of value as a real measure of wealth in his attempt to measure aggregate change over time.

---

[11] "[The] view of things, that men *invented* money in order to rid themselves of the difficulties and inconveniences of barter, belongs, along with much of conjectural history, on the scrapheap of discredited ideas. Men did not invent money by reasoning about the inconveniences of barter any more than they invented government by reasoning about the inconveniences of some mythical primitive state of anarchy. The use of money, like other human institutions, grew or evolved. Its origins are obscure. It is, nevertheless, fairly certain that at no period in history has man ever conducted any considerable volume of trade by means of barter. There was very small gap, perhaps no gap at all, between the beginnings of trade and the origin of money" (Young 1929c; Mehrling and Sandilands 1999, p. 265).

7 Allyn Young on Money, Banking and Business Cycles

Perhaps he was grappling with what is now termed as the index number problem. But today, because of the advances in index number theory and practice, that orientation of value theory is not required. "Frank recognition of the fact that the notion of exchange value is derivative of the phenomenon of price would call for no substantial modification of the theory of exchange" (ibid., pp. 203–4). Furthermore, we are long past the point of diminishing returns as far as the theory of static equilibrium is concerned. "What is needed is an analysis of the actual mechanism of the price-making process" (ibid., p. 204). This theory is sketched by Young in the following words:

> A stream of goods flows through the market from sellers to buyers, and at the point of exchange this flow is equated (in terms of price) to the stream of money flowing in the opposite direction. The vague outlines of a *dynamic* theory of price are easily imaginable. Such a theory might analyze the forces controlling the volumes and rates of particular kinds of commodities, and the volumes and rates of flow of the parts of the money stream to which these are equated in the market. Such a theory would not lead to conclusions substantially different from those reached by the analysis of the forces tending to static equilibrium, and it would be decidedly more cumbersome (ibid., p. 208, emphasis added).[12]

Young also introduced the concept of imputed price. "Prices emerge as concrete facts only in the process of exchange, and only in the process of exchange does money actually 'measure value.' Value as applied to a stock of goods, is nothing more or less than *imputed price*" (ibid., pp. 204–5). This also meant that price only applied to marginal units exchanged. In other cases, imputed price was purely hypothetical or at best an estimate.

Young had an ambition to integrate the theory of relative prices with that of business cycles. As Mehrling (1997, p. 37) notes: "For Young, the practical importance of the theory of the price-making process lay in its potential contribution to the theory of business cycles." As early as 1908 Young recognised that a crisis arose from the mishaps of valuation of things (Ely et al. 1908, p. 267). In 1916, he again argued: "Crises spring

---

[12] Young (1911, 1927a, p. 208) agreed with W.S. Jevons that the theory of demand and supply is more properly a theory of *rates* of demand and supply.

from mishaps in the price process" (Ely et al. 1916, p. 333). These mishaps result when the structure of demand (money flows) and the structure of supply (goods flows) are mismatched. In other words, relative prices become maladjusted.

While discussing the equation of exchange, Young (ibid., p. 320) observed that a change in the money supply for making payments would lead to a proportionate increase or decrease in prices provided other things are kept constant.[13] "It is not necessary for the truth of this theorem that all prices change in the same proportion. The general change in prices may, for example, be upward, but some prices may rise by smaller proportion or may even fall, provided these are offset by sufficiently large increases in prices of other things" (ibid., pp. 320–1). Young was not much interested in the change in the general price level resulting from a change in money supply. He was more interested in the change in the structure of relative prices.

During the credit expansion phase, when will the business expansion come to an end? According to Young the explanation must be found, not in a difference between aggregate demand and aggregate supply, but in maladjustments of demand and supply. As Young (1923a, 1927a) says: "As prices increase the distribution as well as the amount of money incomes changes, and hence the incidence of the demand for different types of consumption and production on goods changes. Without a careful statistical study of the problem it would be hazardous to generalize respecting the precise way in which rising prices shift demand… It is clear, however, that in a period of rising prices the demand for luxuries must increase faster than demand for necessaries. It is also clear that prosperous industries not only attract larger investments, but, just because they are prosperous, have larger funds at their command… The expansion of production does not and cannot shift its direction fast enough to keep pace with the changing distribution of demand… In this way strains accumulate in the industrial system which of themselves would bring

---

[13] However, other things may not remain constant—given unutilized resources the volume of transactions may increase; a sudden increase in the money supply may reduce transactions velocity V; and an increase in M may increase M', the demand deposits.

about its collapse, whether in the course of an ordinary business cycle or in a period of paper money inflation" (pp. 72–3).

Further: "Modern business involves an elaborate system of production for a future market. The ultimate market—the outlet to consumers—is estimated. On the estimated size and character of the market, a vast system of production is built up, held together largely by contracts,—agreements to deliver, to buy or to sell, and to pay. The system of contracts is interdependent. One man's failure to meet his obligations makes it more difficult for others to meet theirs. A crisis comes when a system of contracts breaks down, proving that mistakes *have been made in estimating the quantity and character of the goods* consumers will purchase at prices profitable to producers and dealers. Dealers find themselves overstocked and manufacturing establishments find themselves overexpanded or overcapitalized" (Ely et al. 1923, pp. 334–5, emphasis added).

It was earlier mentioned that in 1908 Young had already formulated the basic idea of the theory of business cycles as a mismatch in valuation of things. Why then did he wait till 1923 to write a full chapter on the subject?[14] Perhaps he wanted to be on a sounder footing by first collecting and analysing bank statistics of the US before committing himself on the business cycle. The bank statistics were published in a series of four articles in the *Review of Economics and Statistics* in Young (1924a, 1925a, b, 1927b). Mehrling (1997, p. 43) observes that Young, because of his premature death, never linked this work on banking statistics with the dynamic theory of price formation to create a theory of business cycles, but that was the direction he was heading.[15]

---

[14] Blitch (1995, p. 134) appears to think that the chapter on business cycles in the 1923 edition of the *Outlines* was written by T.S. Adams, but Laidler (1993) and Mehrling (1997) who reconstructed Young's monetary theory think that it was written by Young himself. If one compares this chapter with Young's treatment of business cycles in *Nicholas Kaldor's Notes on Allyn Young's LSE Lectures 1927–29* (Young 1990), the treatment of the subject appears strikingly similar suggesting that it is probably Young rather than Adams who wrote the chapter.

[15] But Young (1928; Mehrling and Sandilands 1999, p. 356), did state: "I have little doubt but that relations such as we are now considering lie at the very heart of the problem of instability of the modern mechanism of bank credit and of those business activities which depend upon credit." Further: "Under the national banking system, the money forced out of circulation, in periods of low prices and stagnant trade, flowed to New York… The New York banks made advances to investors and to speculative buyers of bonds… But a considerable part of the funds thus secured in New York could not be held there long. Payments had to be made to the *ultimate* borrowers in

Finally, Young placed the business cycle in the context of growth. "Without the business cycle economic change would be distinctly slower, for some of the incentives to daring ventures and experiments in new fields of enterprise would be gone" (Ely et al. 1923, p. 338). Further: "Crises seem to be unpreventable so long as competition and the credit system dominate in industry" (Ely et al. 1916, p. 336). However, Young felt that recent developments (e.g., the setting up of the Federal Reserve system in 1913) may make them less frequent and less serious.[16] "The best way of softening the rigors of a panic and of restoring normal conditions promptly is through a wise use of the lending power inherent in a system of really elastic bank reserves, just as the best way of preventing panics is through a firm control of discount rates when all other conditions are ripe for a period of business inflation. It is in these ways, perhaps, that the new federal reserve system can best serve the country" (ibid., p. 336).

J. Laurence Laughlin and Irving Fisher

Laughlin was a Chicago neoclassical economist whose reputation rested on his work in monetary economics. He represented the banking school in the US. In *Principles of Money* (1903), he attacked the quantity theory of money as well as political movements for cheap money such as those for greenbacks and free silver. He was an ardent supporter of the gold

---

other parts of the country. Deposits were transferred to outside banks. The revival of industrial activity, with which these outside payments probably had something to do, led to increased lending by outside banks. An increase of prices and of the volume of retail trade draws money from New York through the outside banks, into circulation… I see no basis for the belief that these cyclical swings, once under way, were never halted until the resources of the banks had been exhausted… But only in cycles of exceptional magnitude do such limits become effective" (ibid., pp. 356–8). Moreover: "The investment operations of the outside banks were…a factor making for stability of the deposits and their earnings. But in this, as in other respects, the comparative stability of outside banks was purchased by throwing upon the New York banks most of the stresses created by the cyclical flow of money into and out of the banks" (ibid., p. 360).

[16] Young had expressed an early enthusiasm for banks' loan-deposit ratios as key indicators of credit cycles. With the establishment of the Federal Reserve System, the alternation of funds between country banks and New York and back so prominent earlier was now less visible. In a letter to Thomas Adams (18 April 1922), Young admitted: "The relation of bank loans to bank deposits is a hobby of mine, and I may exaggerate its importance."

standard. Since excessive note issue was impossible under this system, he favoured passive accommodation rather than interventionist monetary policy. Laughlin believed in the real bills doctrine and emphasised the importance of bank credit over currency. Credit enabled property to be turned into a means of payment when used as collateral. He thought of deposit banking as a refined system of barter. He also made a distinction between normal and abnormal credits. Through normal credits diverse goods are transformed into mobile form while abnormal credit causes panics and crises. Laughlin also rooted his theory in laissez-faire.

Young disagreed with Laughlin's laissez-faire approach. In his opinion activist monetary policy was needed not only to protect the solvency of the whole system but also to control the business cycle. He rejected the passive accommodation approach of the real bills doctrine and favoured discretionary intervention by the central bank.

While opposed to the cheap money policy as bad in theory, Young was sympathetic to the plight of those who, like his own father, had agitated for cheap money. The cause of the cheap money advocates could best be served by reform of the credit system. For developing new lands and improving the existing ones, capital expenditures were required, and funds were hard to get because individual credit,[17] the foundation of bank credit, was lacking. Populist pressures for bimetallism[18] and fiat currency were better directed towards easier credit than for cheaper money (Ely et al. 1908, p. 233).

Young also rejected the distinction between normal and abnormal credit. Since business cycles are caused by distortion in relative prices, credit in the aggregate may not be mismatched. While the maladjustment of relative prices was dismissed by Laughlin as unimportant, for Young it was central to his explanation of business cycles. Laughlin thought of exchange ratios as determined independently of the medium of exchange, and in some sense immanent. For Young, however, they could be maladjusted as in a business cycle. "Under dynamic conditions

---

[17] Young emphasized individual or personal credit as opposed to collateral and hence for him credit was more than coining of saleable goods.

[18] Young did not favour bimetallism on a further ground that it is difficult to keep the market ratio of gold and silver at the same point as the mint ratio, driving one of them out of circulation. Thus, Gresham's Law would become operative.

there are always, at any given time, large elements of maladjustment from an equilibrium situation" (Young 1990, p. 46).

Young also rejected the notion that a modern economy was a refined system of barter. For him a modern economy was monetary in character and the dynamic price-making process involved money flows meeting the goods flows directly. Exchange of goods and money was direct and not through barter.

Irving Fisher represented the currency school in the US. Like Laughlin he was also a neoclassical economist but advocated interventionist monetary policy to stabilise the price level. His approach to monetary policy was based on the transactions version of the quantity theory of money. An interventionist approach also led him to contribute to index number theory and practice. More specifically he wanted to peg the gold value of the dollar to a general price index. He did not believe in the gold standard but instead in a variable standard. He wanted to fix the general price level and make the price of gold variable, as doing so in his opinion would eliminate the general price changes.

Young agreed with Fisher's interventionist approach to monetary policy but not its aggregative character. He agreed with Fisher that money affected prices but he was more interested in the structure of relative prices rather than the general price level. He was of the opinion that the equation of exchange did not carry us very far into monetary theory.

Money was not neutral with respect to the real economy. All prices did not increase proportionately with an increase in the money supply. Different prices changed by different amounts depending on demand elasticities. Some prices may even fall but the net result is the distortion of relative prices. Even if it is assumed that with an increase in money supply there is a proportionate increase in the price level, it was the effect on relative prices which was more important as it was at the root of a business cycle.

Fisher's work on the ideal index number was aimed at constructing an index of the general price level for controlling business fluctuations.[19] Young, on the other hand, wanted to target a narrow index focusing on commodity prices more sensitive to the business cycle. Young also differed from Fisher in tying the gold value of the dollar to the general price index.

---

[19] For Young's (1923b) review of Fisher's *Making of Index Numbers*, see Chapter 9.

In *Stabilizing the Dollar* (1920), Fisher proposed to correct price instability by increasing the gold weight of the dollar in case of rising prices and reducing its weight in case of falling prices. Fisher thought that this policy would stabilise prices in the same way as clock adjustment is made for daylight saving. This would also stabilise the business cycle as it was caused by price level fluctuations or what Fisher termed as "the dance of the dollar".

Young objected to Fisher's plan. Such a plan could not be implemented without international cooperation, and nor did he like tinkering with the gold standard. He wrote:

> It is clear that no one nation could introduce such a plan, because it would cause highly objectionable fluctuations in the price of foreign exchange and in the domestic prices of imported goods and of important exports. Moreover, like fiat-money schemes, it makes the control of the general level of prices an arbitrary thing. It would constitute a constant and dangerous suggestion of the possibility of using a country's monetary system to achieve political ends. It should be remembered, also, that the most harmful fluctuations in the general level of prices are those which come either from inflation or from the expansion and contraction of bank credit. To attempt to offset or neutralize the effect of inflation or of credit expansion by tinkering with the gold standard appears to be an awkward and unnecessary roundabout way of attacking the problem. The gold standard is far from perfect; but it has the one great advantage that its variations are automatic; the result of market forces rather than governmental manipulation (Ely et al. 1923, p. 318).[20]

Fisher also advocated legislation for the above plan as the Federal Reserve on its own could not be trusted to do so. Young, however, was opposed to legislated rules, as mentioned above, and favoured a discretionary approach to monetary policy whether to stabilise prices or to control the money supply. Young favoured the establishment of strong

---

[20] In a letter to Thomas S. Adams dated 18 April 1922, on the subject of business cycles, Young stated: "I must say frankly that I do not believe that I can get at the matter by tinkering with the monetary standard. This is for two reasons. In the first place, any arbitrary adjustment of the monetary standard would react differently upon different sorts of prices... In the second place, it is easily possible that the mint officials and the Federal Reserve Board might be pulling in the opposite direction... Changes in the production of gold have little or nothing to do with business cycles."

independent institutions and trusted them to establish and uphold sound traditions in the conduct of policy. For him central banking was an art; the Federal Reserve was better suited to managing monetary policy than the legislature or government.

To sum up the discussion of this section, Young, as Mehrling observes, sought a middle ground between Laughlin and Fisher. In doing so, he rejected the weak points of both while retaining their best points. It is clear that he wanted to chart out his own independent path which combined his faith in the gold standard, activist monetary policy based on discretion rather than fixed or legislated rules, and a dynamic theory of price formation. Young also advocated institutional freedom as institutions like the Federal Reserve had to establish and uphold their own traditions for the proper conduct of monetary policy rather than serving a political agenda. Money was central to a modern economic system and not a mere convenience to be tolerated. In fact, the medium of exchange and measure of value were one function, not two.[21] Money was not neutral—while affecting the general price level, the more important effect was on the structure of relative prices.

Hawtrey and Young

Ralph Hawtrey was a British Treasury official who authored influential books such as *Currency and Credit* (1919), *Monetary Reconstruction* (1922) and *The Art of Central Banking* (1932). He was a firm advocate of the gold standard, activist monetary policy based on discretion rather than rules, and a monetary theory of business fluctuations. He was occasionally prepared to advocate public works but only if they were the most efficacious means to increase the money supply. He subscribed to an income velocity version of the quantity theory of money and developed

---

[21] "The general exchange values of commodities that are bought and sold in modern markets are, in fact, merely relations that we derive or infer from their money prices… [M]easuring values and serving as a medium of exchange are only one function, not two" (Young 1929c; Mehrling and Sandilands 1999, p. 268). According to Young, these word-wasting controversies can be avoided by recognizing money as a *means of payment*. This would cover all its uses: medium of exchange, measure of value, a standard of deferred payments and settlement of debts (ibid., p. 268).

the concept of the multiplier. He insisted on the predominance of credit over gold in a modern economy. While credit was unstable, money (or currency) had to perform a stability function. Wholesalers, who financed their inventories by issuing bills of exchange, were central in his system. The discount rate played a crucial role in this process as businesses would expand if the expected profits were higher than the discount rate and contract if vice versa. He also developed the concept of credit deadlock as a situation of excessive build-up of reserves during depression that could require exceptional policy responses.

Hawtrey also traced the transmission mechanism of monetary policy. Here he introduces a set of new concepts such as 'consumers' income', 'consumers' outlay' and 'the unspent margin'. A wholesaler would vary his holding of inventories depending on the profitability of holding them. An increase in bank credit goes into paying the expenses (and profits) of production and distribution and becomes consumers' income. If consumers' outlay (i.e., purchases) keeps pace with consumers' income, business keeps expanding. If outlays lag behind consumers' income then balances of money and credit (the unspent margin) will increase slowing the advance of prices. During a period of depression, because of unutilised productive resources, credit creation may not be accompanied by rise in prices.[22] Prices start rising once credit is increased beyond the point where resources become utilised. The process is cumulative unless bank reserves get depleted or the discount rate is increased.

Young reviewed Hawtrey's *Currency and Credit*, both the first edition (1919) and the second (1923). In the first review, Young stated that Hawtrey's account of the ordinary succession of events during credit expansion was possibly his most substantial achievement. "In particular his analysis of the respective parts played by manufacturers, merchants, and consumers is enlightening and for the most part persuasive" (Young 1920, p. 522). Hawtrey, breaking with precedent, made gold subordinate to credit. Young stated that this may help in giving more realism to his account, but did not materially affect his conclusions. "They are what

---

[22] As Young (1920, p. 525) noted: "A rise in prices results from the use of purchasing power, not from its accumulation."

they would have been if he had chosen to invert the order of functional, or logical, priority between gold and credit" (Young 1920, p. 521).

Young agreed with the idea of inherent instability of credit, as "an expansion of credit once initiated, along with the accompanying upward or downward movement of prices, would tend to continue in a cumulative way, without an effective limit.[23] An expansion of credit would create a higher price level and the higher price level would make possible and even necessary a further expansion of credit. Under favorable conditions this process of reciprocal response might perpetuate itself indefinitely"[24] (ibid., p. 522). But Young could not agree that money of account could be disassociated from money in circulation.[25] "With Mr. Hawtrey's nominalistic views, such as that even where there is no money in circulation a money of account, 'something wholly conventional and arbitrary,' is possible, I cannot agree" (ibid., p. 521). He, however, commended Hawtrey for his dissatisfaction with the conventional quantity theory or the equation of exchange. "Hawtrey is less interested in imagined states of monetary equilibrium than in what Professor Fisher would call 'transition periods,' for these latter seem to Mr. Hawtrey, as to many others, to hold the stage most of the time, and to include the monetary phenomenon most worthy of careful study" (ibid., p. 523). Young further stated: "The equation of exchange does not carry one very far into monetary theory" (ibid., p. 523).

In his review of the second edition of *Currency and Credit*, Young was more profuse in his praise. He wrote: "The first edition of Currency and Credit appeared in 1919. It at once took its place as one of the most significant—possibly the most significant—of the modern treatises on

---

[23] Young (1928; Mehrling and Sandilands 1999, n. 4, p. 361) commended Hawtrey's analysis of instability of credit thus: "I know of no better analysis of the essential instability of the volume of bank credit than is to be found in Hawtrey, R. G., (1923) *Currency and Credit*…"

[24] Laidler (1993, p. 1073) compares Hawtrey's cumulative process of credit expansion with Knut Wicksell's (1898) 'pure credit economy' though he points out that there is no evidence that Hawtrey was aware of this work.

[25] By 'money of account' Hawtrey (1919, p. 2) meant a unit for the measurement of debts which could be served by credit even in the absence of physical money. "In fact a *unit* for the measurement of debts is indispensable. Where a commodity is used as money, it naturally supplies the unit for the measurement of debts. Where there is no money, the unit must be something wholly conventional and arbitrary. This is what is technically called a 'money of account'." That there could be credit without currency was a proposition Young could not agree with.

money" (Young 1924b, p. 349). He also commended Hawtrey for (1) formulating the general principles of the monetary theory in which the monetary unit played a primary and the monetary standard a secondary role; (2) emphasising the cyclical behaviour of credit and inflation; (3) interpreting business cycle as a purely monetary phenomenon; and (4) a historical account of the gold standard and currency upheavals after the war.

Young, however, felt that Hawtrey's analysis was more in tune with the London money market and less readily applicable to the American situation. First, he gave more importance to monetary aspects for manufacturing and trading than for farmers' incomes which played a more important part in the American situation. Secondly, the London money market for the bills of exchange was well developed and financed trade not only in Britain but all over the world. In America this was not the case and American firms were largely self-financing. So the discount-rate policy so effective in England was on a weaker footing in America where stronger measures of credit control were needed.[26] The nature of credit was also different. It was more of long-term credit in the US to finance capital expenditures of agriculture and industry. It was not the discount rate but the longer-term bond yield which was more relevant. Even above the bond yield, it was the expected future profitability of industrial and agricultural investment which was the more important factor.[27] Finally, reserves were more elastic in the US as domestic credit expansion could not come to an end as long as the banks had eligible paper for rediscount at the Federal Reserve.

Young (1924b) also reviewed Hawtrey's (1923) *Monetary Reconstruction*—a volume made up of six essays four of which had already

---

[26] In a letter to T.S. Adams, dated 18 April 1922 referred to earlier, Young stated: "So far as the mechanism is concerned, I am not at all sure about the adequacy of the Federal Reserve discount rate to control matters in a period of rapid business expansion. The analogy with the bank of England is imperfect… By reason of our comparative isolation, it is idle to suggest that we shall hold large quantities of foreign paper, even if our discount rates should become the lowest in the world. It was of course low discount rates which attracted foreign paper to London."

[27] Young was sceptical in the ability of interest rates to influence investment. As opposed to the importance attached by Keynes, Cassel and Hawtrey to the rate of interest, Young (1990, p. 82) stated: "[A]ctual industrialists (and bankers) deny that variations in the rate of interest influence the extent of their operations, providing their competitors pay the same. It is the 'market' on which they count."

been published in journals. Young stated that the one dealing with the Federal Reserve system was "an astonishingly accurate analysis of the outstanding facts in the monetary history of the United States from 1914 to 1922" (ibid., pp. 349–50). He commended Hawtrey's views on the gold standard that any permanent settlement of the world's currencies must be based on gold. Hawtrey also advocated stabilising the exchange rate rather than the price level. "With many others, Mr. Hawtrey believes that the feasible (and probable) way of bettering the monetary conditions is through the development and general adoption of a gold-exchange standard. This would mean in practice the stabilizing of exchange rates rather than of domestic price levels" (ibid., p. 350).

Young's admiration for Hawtrey led him to arrange for his appointment as a visitor at Harvard during 1928–1929 while he himself was on leave for a three-year term at the London School of Economics. But the admiration was mutual, as Hawtrey reviewed his 1927 collection *Economic Problems New and Old* in glowing terms. "In this little book of Professor Young's is to be found the doubly distilled essence of an economic system… Among the best are two critical articles, one on Jevons's *Theory of Political Economy*…and the other a review of *The Trend in Economics*, a collection of economic essays from a number of American economists… Here is to be found a survey of fundamentals in economic theory… Monetary theory and the theory of credit are represented by articles on the Trend of Prices…and the Structure of the Federal Reserve System… Between them they contain a philosophy of central banking" (Hawtrey 1928, p. 601).[28]

Despite wide-ranging agreements with Hawtrey, Young had his differences.[29] For example, Young was sceptical of the discount-rate policy as

---

[28] See also Patrick Deutscher (1990, pp. 195–99) for a discussion of similarities and differences in Young and Hawtrey's views on monetary theory. Deutscher stated that while Young was influenced by Hawtrey, he was himself an independent and influential figure making original contributions in various fields of economics. Thus, Young was not Hawtrey's disciple, and probably, Hawtrey never had any.

[29] In a letter to Charles Blitch, dated 15 October 1973, Overton H. Taylor, one of Young's students at Harvard who took his course in Money and Banking during 1924–1925, wrote: "Our textbook in that course was R. G. Hawtrey's *Currency and Credit*. Young made us understand Hawtrey's version of the Cambridge (Marshallian) 'cash balances' idea (Hawtrey's 'unspent margin') and its uses. He was critical, however, of Hawtrey's stress on the effects of high and low short-term interest rates on 'traders' and thus on the level of economic activity." See Blitch (1995, pp. 61–2).

an instrument of control.[30] As noted by Mehrling (1997, p. 76), Young emphasised intervention at the extremes of the swing as opposed to frequent adjustments advocated by Hawtrey. In other words, he wanted to time the intervention to prevent the cycle going too far. Secondly, Young did not give a purely monetary explanation of the cycle. Although the "inherent instability of the credit" played a part in business fluctuations, mistakes and mismatches which arose in estimating the quantity and composition of demand at prices profitable to the producers or dealers were largely responsible.[31] When this happened the system of contracts broke down and crisis resulted. Finally, Young favoured public works on their own steam as a stabilisation measure without linking them to money creation. He stressed that public expenditure should bring permanent improvements.[32] These should be undertaken at such a time as to bring about maximum public benefits, not when the private expenditures are at their maximum.[33]

---

[30] "Some have suggested that, since credit expansion is a necessary factor the overexpansion of business, the Federal Reserve Board attempt to control credit expansion through its power to modify the rate of discount. It is very difficult to say whether the Federal Reserve Board could accomplish this result. Furthermore, would the Federal Reserve Board wish to use such power even if it possessed that control? In the first place, it is practically impossible to say to what extent the Federal Reserve Board could, by increasing the discount rate, control the expansion of credit at the beginning of the period of credit expansion. Such a policy would undoubtedly be more effective later in the cycle when member banks became dependent on the federal reserve banks for additional funds. The tendency would then be for businessmen to limit such expansion as was highly speculative. However, it should be remembered that that interest is only one of the expenses of production. Secondly, if the Federal Reserve Board could check expansion by raising the discount rate, could it not create prosperity by lowering the rate of discount? After the World War the Federal Reserve Board raised the discount rate. Since then there has been much talk to the effect that the prices of farm products were deflated too rapidly by this means. The possibility of using this power, if the Federal Reserve Board possessed it, for political ends is clear. There might be political pressure from various organized groups for higher prices for their own commodities" (Young 1925c, pp. 140–1).

[31] "Business cycle is largely the result of inaccurate estimates" (ibid., p. 140).

[32] In a letter to Senator William S. Keyton of Ohio dated 25 November 1921, commending him on his bill to tackle future depressions, Young stated: "It is sound economics and it seems to me that it would be sound public policy to attempt to counteract the disastrous periods of business depression, so far as possible, by increasing public expenditures on permanent improvements at such times."

[33] "It is certainly unwise that public expenditures should be at their maximum when private expenditures are also at their maximum... The proposals made in the carefully drafted bill do not look forward, as I understand them, to the imposition of heavier taxes or securing of larger public revenues in other ways in depression. The proposals merely are that such public funds as can be con-

Federal Reserve System and the Art of Central Banking

Young stated that a good deal of wisdom went into creating the Federal Reserve System with the Federal Reserve Board in Washington and 12 semi-autonomous reserve banks in different regions of the country. This fitted well with the economic geography and political structure of the US. "The wisdom of the plan, however, is in these large structural features, not in its detailed specifications" (Young 1927c, p. 77). The actual working of the central banking would obviously be in response to changes in the financial and industrial environment, and therefore every departure from the original "intent" should not be lamented as long as it was consistent with the law. He set out a number of tasks for the Federal Reserve system.

First, a central bank had not only to ensure its own solvency but the solvency of the entire banking system. For this reason they had to hold disproportionate amounts of idle gold and currency. While they stood ready to help other banks with cash and gold on demand, they could not expect the same service in return.

Second, no central bank could pursue a purely passive policy of accommodation in line with the real bills doctrine. If it did so, it would soon be depleted of its gold and currency reserves. So it had to protect itself by a discount-rate policy and open market operations. Even if it conducts its policy of supplying gold and currency on demand without reciprocal help from other banks, it will still have a stabilising influence on trade and industry.

Third, since the end of the war the main aim of their policies had properly been to secure the maximum practical degree of business stability. "There are some who deprecate any interference with 'the natural course of business.' They forget that the operations of central banks cannot but have their effects on business, and that it would be blindly stupid not to take these effects into account when determining just what a central bank shall do and when it shall do it" (Young 1927a, p. 80, 1927c). Young

---

veniently and properly expended at one period rather than another, should so far as possible, be expanded at times when such expenditures will be attended by maximum public benefits" (ibid.).

further stated that the powers of the central banks were not privileges conferred on them but were inseparably bound up with their duties and responsibilities. For example, these banks maintained idle reserves and thereby sacrificed profits which commercial banks did not. In other words, profit maximisation should not be the goal of a central bank.

Fourth, central banks had to follow a discretionary approach to the conduct of policy rather than a rules-based approach. "We can be certain that reliance upon any simple rules would be dangerous. Economic situations are never twice alike" (ibid., p. 81). Further: "What the Federal Reserve Banks need most, therefore, is not more power or less power, or a doctrinaire formulation of what their policy ought to be, but merely an opportunity to develop a sound tradition, and to establish it firmly" (ibid., p. 82). Such a sound tradition would have the following ingredients: (1) a balanced view of the total situation; (2) an intellectual tradition within the Federal Reserve and systems for collecting and analysing relevant information; and (3) immunity from business and political pressures. In Young's opinion it would be the Federal Reserve Banks rather than the Federal Reserve Board who were more likely to become the repositories of accumulated experience and practical wisdom, being closer to the markets and a step removed from political pressures. Further: "It would be the kind of tradition which leaves room for growth, for adjustment to constantly changing conditions, and for occasional experimenting" (ibid., p. 82).

Fifth, the New York Federal Reserve Bank was and will remain first among equals. This special position arose because surplus banking funds tended to concentrate there (and partly be used for speculation), and because of its links with the international money markets. This might have gone against the original intent but should not be lamented as international cooperation in pooling world reserves operates through New York. "Such cooperation has naturally taken the form of cooperation on the central banks of New York, London and Berlin, and other national financial capitals, rather than on the part of Governments" (ibid., p. 92). Further, New York had taken on more responsibilities assigned to it by the national money market and the relations between that market and the world market.

To sum up, much like Hawtrey, Young viewed central banking as an art[34] based on discretion rather than legislated rules (or maxims), on sound traditions than on expedients, on a balanced view of the situation (and accumulated wisdom) than on adhocism, and on institutional independence than on political (or business) influence. In this process, central banks may make mistakes, learn from them, and grow in experience and wisdom.

The Great Depression and After

The great depression of the 1930s, starting with the New York stock market crash in October 1929, caused major upheavals in the western world. It also posed a great challenge to the prevailing doctrines for their failure to anticipate and deal with it. Unfortunately, since Young died in 1929, he did not live long enough to see it. Some authors (e.g., Mehrling 1997) argue that Young was incrementalist in his approach, influenced by Marshallian belief in the dictum that "nature does not make jumps," and even while analysing the events of the first world war it was continuity, rather than change, that impressed him. The institutional arrangements he advocated, involving the gold standard and improved international cooperation, did not go far enough. Moreover, it was by no means obvious that the market system would itself survive even in a drastically altered form. "Even if he had lived, it is doubtful whether Young would have proved an able guide through the wilderness of the 1930s. The motive forces of his thought—the tension between Ely and Marshall, between Laughlin and Fisher, between Fisher and Hawtrey—were about equally irrelevant to a generation that was questioning whether the market system itself was worth saving. Life in the wilderness required a

---

[34] Hawtrey (1932, pp. 208–9) commended Benjamin Strong, Governor of the New York Federal Reserve Bank, to whom Young was a consultant, for following "a policy of stabilisation, which prevented any serious fluctuation of the price level from 1922 to 1929". With Strong's death in 1928, this experiment came to an end. This was in contrast to Bank of England's practice of using the discount rate to protect its gold reserves rather than to stabilise the cycle (see Ely et al. 1923, p. 338).

different kind of mind, one less impressed by continuity and more comfortable with disjuncture" (ibid., pp. 80–1).[35]

What would Young have done had he lived? To answer this question, first we need to know what some of his disciples who were influenced by him (e.g., Lauchlin Currie) and admirers (e.g., Hawtrey) did in the situation.

Currie (1931, 1934a, b) offered a monetary explanation of the great depression. Furthermore, Currie et al. (2002) anticipated several Keynesian ideas such as unbalanced budgets, public works, fiscal inflationism (money-financed fiscal deficits with inclusion of government securities as a legitimate basis of note issue), and abandonment of the gold standard. Currie also castigated the role of the Federal Reserve in the whole episode for curbing the money supply when the real economy had declined. He also castigated the Federal Reserve for its wrong diagnosis in tracing the cause to too much speculation rather than to real contraction. Had the policy mistakes not been made the depression would have lost its severity and recovery have been earlier. Currie as a leading "new dealer" in the 1930s has been highlighted by R.J. Sandilands (1990) and his ideas as "domesticated Keynesianism" by William Barber (1996).[36] In many of his writings there is no doubt that Currie was influenced by Young, his teacher at Harvard, and by Hawtrey, for whom he was a teaching assistant at Harvard.[37]

Hawtrey stressed that public works not accompanied by money creation would not be effective. He also propounded the notion of credit deadlock—an excessive accumulation of reserves as opposed to a Keynesian liquidity trap where bond prices have peaked and the interest rate has fallen to its floor level. However, the fact was that by the early 1930s the bond market had totally collapsed and needed to be revived through purchase of government bonds by the reserve banks. Hawtrey

---

[35] It is worth noting that Fisher damaged his professional reputation by forecasting that stock market prices would keep rising before the Great Crash occurred.

[36] Sandilands (1990) also complained that Milton Friedman and Anna Schwartz (1963) in their *A Monetary History of the United States 1867–1960* paid insufficient attention to Currie's work.

[37] Laidler and Sandilands (2002, p. 522) write: "And in the background here perhaps there stands the shade of Young, who had advocated activist monetary and fiscal stabilization policies during the 1920s."

(1937) thus looked at the notion of a floor rate of interest with scepticism. For him the rate of interest was not independent of the marginal efficiency of capital; if this fell over time so would the long-term interest rate.

Then there is the question whether the Keynesian revolution was really a revolution or whether the building blocks already existed before Keynes put them together in 1936. Keynes himself gave credit to R.F. Kahn, Joan Robinson, Ralph Hawtrey, Roy Harrod and others for their participation in the shaping of the *General Theory* (Schumpeter 1951/2003, pp. 279–80). "While Keynes was remodeling his work, he currently talked about it in his lectures, in conversation, in the 'Keynes Club' that used to meet in his rooms at Kings. And there was a lively give and take" (ibid.).[38] In some accounts, there is also a mention of 'Cambridge Circus' consisting of Kahn, Robinson, Meade and Harrod which discussed drafts of the *General Theory* (1936) shortly after the publication of Keynes's *Treatise on Money* (1930). According to Laidler (1999, p. 3) an element of mythmaking is involved when the phrase 'Keynesian revolution' is deployed. "[T]he rearrangement of ideas to which it refers was neither revolutionary in the usual sense of the word nor by any means uniquely Keynesian in origin" (ibid., p. 3). He further contended that there was no overthrow of any orthodoxy or the established order after 1936, for none had existed. Instead, a new orthodoxy developed. "What happened was altogether more mundane, though a good deal more useful: economics acquired a new formal model, around which there would, in due course, develop an orthodox body of analysis called macroeconomics" (ibid., p. 3). Laidler further points out that had it been really original, President Roosevelt's 'new deal' policies would not have been in place before the publication of the *General Theory* in 1936. To the ideas which already

---

[38] Also see Robert Skidelsky (1992), Keynes biographer, who wrote: "In the 1920s Keynes's good conversations in economics were with Robertson, Hawtrey, Henderson, Gerald Shove, less frequently with Pigou: all Cambridge men, within the Marshallian tradition… In the 1930s his good conversations were with disciples like Richard Kahn, Joan and Austin Robinson, though he continued to have bad ones with his older colleagues" (p. 424). Further: "By May 1935, Maynard's book was in 'retouching' state… Gallery proofs went out to Harrod, Hawtrey, Kahn and Joan Robinson in mid-June. The exchanges with Robertson were not renewed with mutual consent… Neither Henderson nor Pigou received proofs. Thus, of his own generation, Keynes thought only Hawtrey was sufficiently sympathetic to help him in his last stage" (ibid., p. 532).

existed there were many contributors who, among others, included Hawtrey, Young and Currie.

So what would Young have done if faced with the great depression? Any answer to this question is likely to be highly speculative but there is evidence to suggest that his views did evolve overtime.[39] Moreover, like the classical economists, he took his data from real life. Faced with the depression he might have abandoned the gold standard and advocated money-financed fiscal deficits[40] as a stabilisation tool apart from a more activist monetary policy. Perhaps as an advisor to the Federal Reserve he might have rooted for more active purchases of government bonds to revive the bond market. He might have focused more on the real sector and the measures to revive it than on the stock exchange speculation. All this remains in the realm of speculation. However, his faith in international cooperation and institutions was spot on; it was only after the Bretton Woods System came into being in 1946 that the world recovery became more sustainable after the twin disasters of the great depression and the WWII.

References

Barber, William J. (1996), *Designs Within Disorder: Franklin Roosevelt, the Economists and the Shaping of American Economic Policy 1933–45*, Cambridge: Cambridge University Press.

---

[39] In his review of A.C. Pigou's *Wealth and Welfare* he took the view that external economies were not very plentiful. In his article on increasing returns and economic progress he based his growth theory on external economies. To take another example, in index number theory he was initially fascinated by the ideal index number but later changed his views to say that any properly weighted index was just as good.

[40] There is some evidence that Young was aware of pump priming as a tool in depression. One of his students at Harvard Overton H. Taylor, who took Young's course on money and banking, in a letter to Charles Blitch dated October 15, 1973, stated that one of the books for that course was that of W.T. Foster and W. Catchings (1923), "attributing depressions to insufficient purchasing power in the hands of the people, and advocating 'pump priming' through governmental public works expenditures as the remedy". See Sandilands (1999, p. 474). See also Currie (1990, p. 13) who wrote: "It is interesting to speculate on the position he would have taken in the Great Depression. I am sure that he would immediately have seen the fallacy of composition in the argument of the budget balancers… Of all the people at Harvard, I think that he would have been the most open minded to the Keynesian point of view."

Blitch, Charles P. (1995), *Allyn Young: A Peripatetic Economist*, Houndmills and London: Macmillan Press Ltd.
Currie, Lauchlin (1931), *Bank Assets and Banking Theory*, Ph.D. Dissertation, Harvard University.
Currie, Lauchlin (1934a), *The Supply and Control of Credit in the United States*, Cambridge: Harvard University Press.
Currie, Lauchlin (1934b), 'The failure of the monetary policy to prevent the depression of 1929–32', *Journal of Political Economy*, XLII, pp. 145–77.
Currie, Lauchlin (1990), 'Recollections of Allyn Young', *Journal of Economic Studies*, 17(3/4), pp. 10–13.
Currie, Lauchlin, P. T. Ellsworth and Harry D. White (2002), 'Memorandum prepared by L.B. Currie, P.T. Ellswoth and H.D. White (Cambridge, Mass., January 1932)', *History of Political Economy*, 34(3), pp. 533–52.
Deutscher, Patrick (1990), *R.G. Hawtrey and the Development of Macroeconomics*, Ann Arbor: University of Michigan Press.
Ely, Richard T., Thomas S. Adams, Max O. Lorenz and Allyn A. Young (1908), *Outlines of Economics*, New York: The Macmillan Company.
Ely, Richard T., Thomas S. Adams, Max O. Lorenz and Allyn A. Young (1916), *Outlines of Economics*, New York: The Macmillan Company.
Ely, Richard T., Thomas S. Adams, Max O. Lorenz and Allyn A. Young (1923), *Outlines of Economics*, New York: The Macmillan Company.
Fisher, Irving (1920), *Stabilizing the Dollar*, New York: Macmillan.
Foster, W.T. and W. Catchings (1923), *Money*, Boston: Houghton Mifflin.
Friedman, Milton and Anna J. Schwartz (1963), *A Monetary History of the United States 1867–1960*, Princeton: Princeton University Press.
Hawtrey, Ralph G. (1919), First Edition, *Currency and Credit*, London: Longmans, Green and Co.
Hawtrey, Ralph G. (1922), *Monetary Reconstruction*, London: Longmans, Green and Co.
Hawtrey, Ralph G. (1923), Second Edition, *Currency and Credit*, London: Longmans, Green and Co.
Hawtrey, Ralph G. (1928), *Economic Problems New and Old* by Professor Allyn A. Young, *Economic Journal*, December.
Hawtrey, Ralph G. (1932), *The Art of Central Banking*, London: Longmans, Green and Co.
Hawtrey, Ralph G. (1937), *Capital and Employment*, London: Longman Group.
Keynes, John M. (1930), *Treatise on Money*, London: Macmillan and Company Ltd.
Keynes, John M. (1936), *General Theory of Employment, Interest and Money*, London: Macmillan and Company Ltd.

Laidler, David (1993), 'Hawtrey, Harvard, and the Origins of the Chicago Tradition', *Journal of Political Economy*, 101(6), pp. 1068–1103.

Laidler, David (1999), *Fabricating the Keynesian Revolution*, Cambridge: Cambridge University Press.

Laidler, David and Roger J. Sandilands (2002), 'An early Harvard memorandum on anti-depression policies: an introductory note', *History of Political Economy*, 34(3), 515–32.

Laughlin, J. Laurence (1903), *Principles of Money*, New York: Scribner's.

Mehrling, Perry G. (1996), 'The Monetary Thought of Allyn Abbott Young', *History of Political Economy*, 28(4), pp. 607–32.

Mehrling, Perry G. (1997), *The Money Interest and the Public Interest*, Cambridge and London: Harvard University Press.

Mehrling, Perry G. (2002), 'Retrospectives: Economists and the Fed: Beginnings', *Journal of Economic Perspectives*, 16(4), pp. 207–18.

Mehrling, Perry G. and Roger J. Sandilands (eds.) (1999), *Money and Growth: Selected Papers of Allyn Abbott Young*, London and New York: Routledge.

Sandilands, Roger J. (1990), *The Life and Political Economy of Lauchlin Currie*, Durham and London: Duke University Press.

Sandilands, Roger J. (1999), 'New evidence on Allyn Young's style and influence as a teacher', *Journal of Economic Studies*, 26(6), pp. 453–79.

Schumpeter, Joseph A. (1935), 'Young, Allyn Abbott', in Seligman, Edwin R. A. (ed.), *Encyclopaedia of Social Sciences*, New York: Macmillan.

Schumpeter, Joseph A. (1951/2003), *Ten Great Economists from Marx to Keynes*, San Diego: Simon Publications.

Schumpeter, Joseph A. (1954), *History of Economic Analysis*, London: Allen and Unwin.

Skidelsky, Robert (1992), *John Maynard Keynes (Vol.II): The Economist as Saviour 1920–1937*, London: Macmillan.

Wicksell, Knut (1898), *Interest and Prices*, Jena: Fischer. English Translation by Kahn, R. F. (1936), London: Macmillan.

Young, Allyn A. (1911), 'Some limitations of the value concept', *Quarterly Journal of Economics*, 25(3), pp. 409–28. Reprinted in Young (1927a), pp. 198–212.

Young, Allyn A. (1920), 'Review of Currency and Credit by Ralph Hawtrey and Stabilizing the Dollar by Irvind Fisher', *Quarterly Journal of Economics*, 34(2), pp. 520–32.

Young, Allyn A. (1923a), 'The trend of prices', *American Economic Review*, 13(1), pp. 5–14. Reprinted in Young (1927a), pp. 63–76.

Young, Allyn A. (1923b), 'Fisher's *Making of Index Numbers*', *Quarterly Journal of Economics*, 37(2), pp. 342–64. Reprinted in Young (1927a), pp. 276–301.

Young, Allyn A. (1924a), 'An analysis of the bank statistics of the United States I: The national banks 1867–1914', *Review of Economics and Statistics*, 6(4): October, pp. 284–96.

Young, Allyn A. (1924b), 'Review of *Currency and Credit* Second Edition and *Monetary Reconstruction* by R. G. Hawtrey', *American Economic Review*, 14(2), pp. 349–52.

Young, Allyn A. (1925a), 'An analysis of the bank statistics of the United States II: The seasonal and cyclical fluctuations 1901–1914', *Review of Economics and Statistics*, 7(1): January, pp. 19–37.

Young, Allyn A. (1925b), 'An analysis of the bank statistics of the United States III: Regional differences 1901–1914', *Review of Economics and Statistics*, 7(2): April, pp. 86–104.

Young, Allyn A. (1925c), 'Chapters VIII (Money and Credit) and IX (Banking)', in Riley, Eugen B., *Economics for Secondary Schools*, Boston and New York: Houghton Mifflin Company.

Young, Allyn A. (1927a), *Economic Problems New and Old*, Boston and New York: Houghton Mifflin Company.

Young, Allyn A. (1927b), 'An analysis of the bank statistics of the United States IV: The national banks 1915–26', *Review of Economics and Statistics*, 9(3): July, 121–41.

Young, Allyn A. (1927c), 'The structure and the policies of the Federal Reserve System', *The Annalist*, May 6 and May 13. Reprinted in Young (1927a), pp. 77–94.

Young, Allyn A. (1928), *An Analysis of Bank Statistics for the United States*, Cambridge: Harvard University Press.

Young, Allyn A. (1929a), 'Monetary system in the U.S.', *The Book of Popular Science*, New York: The Grolier Society. Reprinted in Mehrling and Sandilands (1999), pp. 277–92.

Young, Allyn A. (1929b), 'Downward price trend probable, due to hoarding of gold by central banks', *The Annalist*, 36, pp. 96–7. Reprinted in Mehrling and Sandilands (1999), pp. 369–73.

Young, Allyn A. (1929c), 'The mystery of money', *The Book of Popular Science*, New York: The Grolier Society. Reprinted in Mehrling and Sandilands (1999), pp. 265–76.

Young, Allyn A. (1990), 'Nicholas Kaldor's Notes on Allyn Young's LSE Lectures 1927–29', *Journal of Economic Studies*, 17(3/4), pp. 18–114.

8

Allyn Young's Role as an Author, Teacher and Mentor

There has been a widespread belief that Allyn Young did not publish much. He neither published a treatise nor did he contribute prolifically in mainstream professional journals. His fame rested more on his style and influence as a teacher, mentor, Ph.D. supervisor and a critic than as an author. Joseph Schumpeter (1937) observed: "Rarely if ever has fame comparable to his been acquired on the basis of so little published work. What there is consists of fragments written in response to chance occasions". Further: "He was first and last a creative teacher, and it was through his teaching rather than his writing that he influenced contemporary thought." In a similar vein J.M. Keynes,[1] in a letter of condolence to Mrs Young after her husband's untimely death, wrote: "His was an outstanding personality in the economics world and the most lovable. His influence as a teacher and a critic and as one who would always share with others all his best ideas was far greater than anyone would suppose who only knew his printed words; for it was his own work—unfortunately perhaps—which always came last."

In a letter dated 4 January 1923, T.S. Adams wrote to Young: "I am doubtful whether you (& I also) are ever going to publish much in

---

[1] Keynes to Mrs Young dated 17 March 1929.

economic science, but that's not conclusive about a big scientific career… You can do your work through your students, occasional articles etc., public service." Young had asked for Adam's opinion about the offer of a deanship at Cornell with an annual salary of $10,000. Adams had advised him to turn down the offer as staying at Harvard, in addition to his European experience and banking knowledge, would put him "in line for the big things". Adams made the above remark in closing but, as Charles Blitch (1995, p. 135) observes, it turned out to be "an accurate prediction of the future of Allyn Young's career".

At the time of his death Young was working on two treatises: one on money and the other on economic theory. His papers were apparently lost when his family left hastily for the US after his death.[2] Blitch (1995, p. 185) observes that there is some mystery surrounding the disappearance of his manuscripts. His room at the LSE was cleared by some staff, his papers packed and sent to Mrs Young in the US, "but no trace of either the manuscript on money or on economic theory was ever found".[3] Blitch also notes that from the available evidence, Young had written the introduction of his treatise on money and possibly outlined its contents and not much more. Wesley Mitchell, in a letter to Young dated 7 January 1927, also refers to this treatise: "Your opening pages mark out the field you intend to cover with masterly clarity and conciseness. I hope that, whatever you decide to do, you will be able to push this job through to a conclusion in the near future."

This chapter explores three themes: (1) his role as an author—whether he wrote very little and the possible reasons thereof; (2) his exact role and influence as a teacher; and (3) his role in mentoring his Ph.D. students such as Frank Knight, Edward Chamberlin and others.

---

[2] Referring to Blitch, David Laidler thinks that Young's papers were "presumably destroyed" when his office was cleared at the LSE. Lionel Robbins (1971, p. 120) who inherited his desk after his death wrote of "almost unimaginable confusion, no system or order anywhere". Perhaps it is possible that Robbins got the room cleared of all unwanted papers or materials to restore order.

[3] In a letter to Charles Blitch dated 14 February 1973, Earl J. Hamilton, one of Young's students at Harvard, wrote that the LSE had bought his books and installed them along with his portrait in a room called the Allyn A. Young Room. He further wrote that he did not know but suspected that Young's papers were in that room too. However, as Roger Sandilands (1999, p. 478) notes: "There is no longer any trace of Young's books or papers at the LSE."

Young as an Author

Theodore E. Gregory (1929), in his obituary piece 'Professor Allyn A. Young', stated: "In many respects he resembled Edgeworth, for whose work he felt a growing admiration; and if Young's work is ever collected, it will be seen that, like Edgeworth's, it amounts in sum to a very considerable and impressive achievement." After 70 years, with the publication of Perry Mehrling and Roger Sandilands (1999), a bibliography of about 100 items was compiled, and it was seen that Gregory was correct in his assessment. It was not that Young wrote little; it was more a case that whatever he wrote was scattered all over in obscure journals, encyclopaedias, chapters to the bestselling textbook *Outlines of Economics*, and introductions/forewords to books by his students or colleagues. Many of his pieces on varied topics were found in the Grolier Society's *Book of Popular Science*, *Encyclopaedia Britannica*, *The Cornell Civil Engineer*, *The Independent* and *The Annalist*.

A bibliography of 100 items is not small. It was more a case of unsystematic writing—scattered articles but not a comprehensive treatise. As Gregory (1929) noted:

> The experiences were too wide, the stimuli too many, when combined with Young's personal qualities, to make systematic writing easy. It would be the grossest injustice to his memory to suggest that he was unable to make up his mind; the trouble was that he was unable to concentrate his interests and to confine himself for any length of time to a single range of problems. A passion for thoroughness would drive him to explore every inch of the field in which he was for the time being interested; he was always convinced that economic truth was not the monopoly of a single school or a single way of thinking, and that the first duty of a teacher and thinker was to see strong points in every presentation of a point of view. Such an attitude of mind, combined with great personal modesty, made for unsystematic writing: for scattered papers and articles and not for a comprehensive treatise.

Young himself never gave special importance to a treatise over freelance writing. In a letter to his friend Frank W. Taussig, dated 23 June

1925, Young stated: "Looking over Edgeworth's volumes I am increasingly doubtful whether, after all, a large piece of sustained work, a 'Magna Opus,' (sic) is more important than the sort of thing Edgeworth has done… The man who gives years to a single book narrows his range. I have a larger range than most American economists and I am not sure but that I should make my largest contributions to economics by continuing to freelance. This does not mean that I am not going ahead with the book on money. It merely means that I do not share your opinion of the special valuation of that sort of work."

Moreover, Young had long contemplated writing a general textbook in economics as one of his preferred contributions. In a letter to Thomas S. Adams, dated 10 October 1921, he wrote: "[T]here is more reason for my writing a text-book than there is in the case of most men. In the course of my teaching I have covered more different subjects in the field of economics than anyone else I know. In any one subject there are a good many men who are more competent than I. There is no one, I believe, who has covered so broad a field… In short, I am not a specialist. I am merely a general economist. A general textbook seems to be more clearly indicated as one of my contributions."

In a letter to Richard T. Ely dated 27 October 1921, Young indicated the contents of the textbook he wanted to write:

> This book which I propose to write on my own account will differ from Outlines in that it will deal primarily with the existing economic structure as a fact of business organization. Its emphasis will be put upon an explanation of the workings of the modern business system. For example, it will be as concrete, in its way, as Outlines, but it will deal with a somewhat different range of facts. I have had the matter in my mind for a long time.

His relative lack of publications may also be attributed to his self-critical nature. One of his students, H.W. Warshow, in a letter to Young dated 16 June 1927, wrote:

> I have heard a good deal about your work at Harvard. Angell tells me that it has gotten so that every graduate student insists upon doing his thesis with you… I think also that your highly developed *critical* faculties, which

you use so excellently when reviewing other people's work, come in play in your own writing. I feel certain that if you can ever pass your own *critical tests, you will make a remarkable contribution to the science.* (Emphasis added)

Similarly, Oskar Morgenstern (1929) wrote: "Reading the entirety of his publications shows one only a fraction of his achievement. He found it difficult to decide to publish anything, being extremely modest and *self-critical in a manner which made him say something important as a casual aside*; but he greatly inspired his pupils and patiently and constantly made himself available to them… He had developed his thoughts over the years in his Harvard lectures and his theory, which would certainly have represented a milestone, *has become a part of the oral tradition at Harvard in the same way as Marshall's monetary theory at Cambridge*" (emphasis added).

Young's relative poverty and his growing family may also partly explain his unsystematic writing in obscure papers and journals. In a letter to Roger Sandilands (1999, p. 455) dated 4 June 1997, Paul Samuelson stated: "Young was wise, deep, and a great personal influence on colleagues and pupils. But he wrote so little, not only because he was so poor and so encumbered by family responsibilities but also because he had never worked out a coherent macro paradigm that differed creatively with the received notions of Marshall, Fisher, Pigou, and that crowd."

Over the years Young's family had grown. Apart from his wife Bessie and son Jack, his sister-in-law Agnes, his two adopted children and his elderly father-in-law also lived with him during his Harvard years. Virtually the same family moved to London when he was appointed Professor at the LSE in the chair vacated by Edwin Cannan. He was therefore always on the lookout for additional money to care for his growing family. That partly explains the fact that he took up whatever opportunities came his way whether they were contributions to obscure journals, encyclopaedias or chapters to *Outlines of Economics*. Consequently, he had little time left for original research.

Young loved to help others, and, when approached for an introduction or a preface to a book, he found it difficult to say no, particularly to his students and colleagues. As his friend Wesley Mitchell (1929) wrote:

For economic investigation Young was remarkably endowed. He united in rare measure mathematical powers, historical learning, and philosophical grasp. Indeed, his versatility was an ever-lurking temptation to disperse his attention. *Many were the colleagues and the students who sought his critical and his constructive advice. Because his range was so wide and his insight so quick, as well as because he loved to help others, Young found it difficult to say "No".* Few American economists of his generation are represented in so many books which bear other men's names. And Young's prefaces written to help others get a hearing would make a slender volume.... (Emphasis added)

But whatever scattered pieces he wrote for encyclopaedias or little-known journals, the quality of his writing was always first rate. As Mitchell (1929) further observed: "All of us value his published work highly, for though slender in bulk, it is of rare quality." Many of his entries were so penetrating and insightful that one is hard pressed to find comparable insights elsewhere in the economics literature. For example, in his entry 'Economics', he stated that Smith's real concern was not a hands-off approach to economic matters but establishment and maintenance of competitive conditions. He also stated that the law of diminishing returns may be true as a tendency but not as a prophecy. Similarly, in his entry 'supply and demand' he stated that Say's Law—that general overproduction is impossible—is not really erroneous but misleading as it applies as long as demand for each good is elastic, not otherwise.[4] In his entry on 'Capital', he wrote whether earnings of capital are attributed to its scarcity or to its productivity is a meaningless question for scarcity and productivity meant the same thing. In his entry on 'price', he stated: "All economic equilibria are unstable." Further: "Market price is the price which will be found in a given market at a given time. It may be regarded as the limiting form of short-time or temporary equilibrium price." In his entry on 'wages', he wrote that neither an increased supply of labour can be assumed to reduce real wages nor a reduction of real wages can be assumed to increase employment, anticipating the Keynesian insight.

---

[4] General overproduction is not possible as long as demand for each good is elastic. But, according to Young, mismatches of individual demands and supplies are possible causing business cycles.

One can go on but these examples should suffice to indicate the penetrating nature of his insights.

Young as a Teacher

Young was a brilliant and much sought-after teacher especially in graduate work. He was generally known to be absent minded, his speech was punctuated with long pauses and, while lecturing, he never consulted his notes or prepared outlines. His office was generally untidy and he often lapsed into deep thought unaware of time and surroundings. But he had vast knowledge, had mastered the whole literature of economics, and had learnt to look at various schools of thought as complementary to the discovery of economic truth. He was generally open about new ideas and shared his best ideas with others. Above all, he was an epitome of modesty and never said 'no' if approached for help. He treated his students on an equal footing and answered even their most stupid questions by reformulating them in a manner to make them feel that it was a profound question he was answering. He had a magnetic personality; not only did the students revere him, but the whole economics profession looked up to him for leadership.

Young's absent-mindedness was notorious; he often forgot or lost his hats, umbrellas, gloves or canes. Blitch (1995, p. 120) narrates an anecdote during his Harvard days: "Once when only a block from his house he was lost deep in thought and tipped his hat to his wife and sister-in-law who were walking home." In another incident, Young along with his wife and father-in-law met with an accident while turning a corner when he failed to spot a street car in time. But fortunately no one was injured but his car was a total loss.

Arthur H. Cole,[5] a younger colleague at Harvard, recounts: "Professor Young was quite absent minded. Also he had a condition of lapsing into a brown study as he lectured or, according to stories, even as he carved a turkey or roast of beef at his table—carved for his family." Eleanor Dulles[6]

---
[5] Letter to Blitch dated 1 April 1972.
[6] Letter to Blitch dated 31 December 1974.

reminisces: "A large square shouldered man with slightly rumpled tweeds, he would look into space with a long range perspective while his hands groped for a handkerchief—usually not there, and we wondered whether we should give him one. But his words never failed him." Overton H. Taylor recalls[7]: "His lectures were always lucid, penetrating, brilliant, but a bit unsystematic, being punctuated with many questions to and from the class."

Apart from his absent-mindedness Young did not consult his notes or outlines when he lectured. This gave the impression that he was poorly prepared. E.J. Hamilton[8] wrote: "Young either did not prepare his lectures or prepared them very poorly. Nothing could have been more disorganized than he was in class. Consequently, as much as 90 percent of the time I spent in his classes was wasted. But in the remaining time I got something that was so original, so profound, so meaningful and so impossible to get anywhere else that the total time I spent with him was invaluable. In the years I was at Harvard the Department of Economics was clearly the best in the United States, and Allyn Young was far and away the most innovative thinker in the Department."

Some students found his room to be extremely untidy and disorganised. Nicholas Kaldor,[9] his student at the LSE, writes: "He held…classes in his room which was extremely untidy. His desk and tables were full of letters, papers, books, notes, etc. Being a very untidy man myself I often recalled the memory of Young's desk which made one feel that untidiness in one's desk need not necessarily go together with untidiness in thought." Eleanor Dulles[10] also recounts: "When we were told he was leaving to be on the faculty of the London School of Economics, Emily Huntington, later Professor of Economics at Berkeley, and I, who knew what a mess his office was in, offered to help. He let us help him sort papers and throw some away. It was an interesting chore and one that gave me better understanding of his dedication and sense of values."

---

[7] Letter to Blitch dated 15 October 1973.
[8] Letter to Blitch dated 14 February 1973.
[9] Letter to Blitch dated June 1979.
[10] Letter to Blitch dated 31 December 1974.

Some students also found his mannerism in the class quite endearing. Melvin G. De Chazeau[11] portrays the following picture: "My most vivid mind-picture of Prof. Young in the classroom is of him wiping off the blackboard with his coat sleeve as he altered or modified notations and diagrams. He seemed always to finish his lectures well dusted with white chalk. This was an endearing mannerism in a person whose depth of understanding, breadth of knowledge and sensitivity to the reaction of others could not help but make an indelible impression on those with whom he came in contact."

By all accounts Young's range and depth of knowledge was astounding. He was a voracious reader and kept in touch with all the latest developments. Bertil Ohlin[12] recounts: "I took a very stimulating course [of] professor Young at Harvard in 1922–23. The subject was history of Economic Doctrine. He impressed me immensely. I am inclined to believe that he was a man, who knew and thoroughly understood his subject—economics—better than anyone else I have met… What characterizes Allyn Young as an economist was that he had deep understanding of all fields of economic theory while other economists knew well one third of the theory and had only superficial knowledge of the rest."

The *London Times* (8 March 1929) obituary 'Allyn Abbott Young: In Memoriam' stated:

> No man was ready to see all the sides of an argument; he had none of the intellectual arrogance which sometimes accompanies great mental gifts; and if he ever felt anger it was with those who refused to acknowledge merit in the work of other schools or of modern writers of a tendency opposite to the received tradition. These qualities of mind and character, which made him a great teacher, made him also the most sympathetic and helpful of colleagues. *No one could go to Young without receiving enlightenment, and since his range of knowledge was extraordinary, without the impression that here was a man who was an absolute master of his chosen field.* (Emphasis added)

---

[11] Letter to Blitch dated 3 October 1973.
[12] Letter to Blitch dated 21 December 1978.

Young not only excelled in theory but he also had a deep grasp of mathematical economics and statistics. E.J. Hamilton[13] wrote: "You may be interested in knowing that Irving Fisher told me several times that Allyn Young was decidedly the best mathematician among living American economists." Oskar Morgenstern (1929) observed: "He was a sovereign mathematician, and hence also statistician, acquainted with the latest methods of this discipline which gained a number of brilliant analyses from him." Young also engaged in long correspondence with Fisher and Mitchell on the subject of index numbers, and he himself made substantial contribution in the field by writing a chapter on the subject (Young 1924). He came to the conclusion that Fisher's ideal index number was not particularly ideal as all averages, whether geometric, arithmetic or harmonic, give similar results if weighted properly. In his opinion, a theoretically perfect index number was impossible.

Young was regarded by some of his students as a near perfect teacher. For example, Eleanor L. Dulles[14] wrote:

> Allyn Young was a professor who kept developing his ideas with his class. His students participated in this development—he was nearly a perfect teacher… Every year he progressed with new concepts in the field of monetary theory. None of his conclusions as to others' views were frozen, all were to be re-examined in the light of new experience. Never have I known such a combination of sound knowledge and willingness to speculate and reconsider… Allyn Young died too young and wrote too little. We who are his students owe him much.

Young was an inspirational teacher who developed his ideas as he went along. The most enduring lesson one learnt from him was that the field of economics was wide open for further improvements. Lauchlin Currie (1990, p. 11), Young's student at Harvard, wrote: "Professor Young was the most inspiring teacher I ever had. While Frank Taussig, Young's contemporary at Harvard, was a fine teacher…his impact on me was that economic theory was complete and it was up to the student not to criticise or contribute but try to master that theory. The enquiring mind of

---

[13] Letter to Blitch dated 14 February 1973.
[14] Letter to Blitch dated 31 December 1974.

Young, on the other hand, gave me a feeling that the field was wide open and it was possible and proper to criticise and explore new and different approaches. In short, he inspired as well as taught." Further: "Perhaps the most enduring lesson I learned from Young was that the subject was wide open to modifications and improvements. He gave the impression of *thinking* as he went along. He continually opened up exciting vistas" (ibid., p. 12).

Valdemar Carlson (1968) wrote of Young's habit of giving importance to his students. "Taussig tolerated no half formulated ideas in his pedagogical pursuit of developing the student's logical thinking. *Young took the least glimmer of insight or understanding expressed by a student and clothed it with an amazing amount of significance*... He was the Toscanini of the classroom, referring neither to outline nor notes while lecturing... In Young we were privileged to experience the thinking process of a great mind who shared his ideas with his students in an amazingly democratic manner" (emphasis added).

Many former students noted Young's magnetic personality. For example, Kaldor[15] wrote: "I was formally supervised by Young and was invited to one of his weekly classes. He divided his students into small groups of eight or ten, and held a two hour discussion with each group once a week in the early afternoon. *He had a magnetic personality and in a short time all of us who attended his class fell under his spell.* This was partly because his transparent sincerity and his ability to talk to young students as if they were his intellectual equals, and mainly perhaps because he talked about the things that interested him most. This way we had a running account his correspondence with Pigou on the cost controversy and of the critical line he took on...the 'rates' which is the local property tax in England... His chief quality as a teacher (which he shared with Keynes) was his ability to make the subject of economics an exciting one, by making his students feel that they were participating in forming a judgement on the main issues of economic policy" (emphasis added). Similarly, James Angell[16] recounts: "The key factor, I am sure, was some sort of warm personal magnetism (a charisma, in the literal dictionary sense?) that

---

[15] Letter to Blitch dated June 1979.
[16] Letter to Blitch dated 6 April 1973.

seemed to flow from him to his students, and that made them both trust him personally and believe in him intellectually."

Young's students loved and revered him. Currie, in a condolence letter to Mrs Young dated March 1929, wrote: "I wish that I could convey to you how deeply we students loved and revered Professor Young and what a tremendous inspiration he was to us. He was our mentor and we referred to him and talked about him constantly. He was always available and gave of his precious time all too freely. We can only try to show our appreciation and make amends for our encroachment on his time by acknowledging continually our deep debt to him for any creative work we may accomplish" (Sandilands 2009, p. 146). Similarly, Geoffrey Shepherd[17] wrote: "I took Professor Young's graduate courses in economics in 1926–27. I developed the greatest respect for him as a man as well as an eminent scholar. His erudition was tempered by kindliness and good humor. Because he had moved several times in his professional career, he referred to himself as a member of the peripatetic school of economics… *After one year of our classes with him, one of my classmates whispered to me, 'You feel you are close to greatness, don't you?' He was right*" (emphasis added).

Though Young was widely admired and even revered as a teacher there were some doubting voices as well. Frank W. Fetter was one of them. In a letter to Blitch dated 20 February 1984, he stated[18]: "When I was a graduate student at Harvard in 1923 I signed up for Young's graduate course… As I recall it he sat on his desk, talked in what I felt was rather disorganized way about the complexities of monetary theory, and in substance said that he didn't fully believe in the more simple explanation he had given in his contribution to Ely's text. As I recall it, my reaction was that I didn't want to spend a term getting the ideas of a man who didn't know what he believed, so I dropped out of the course."

Similarly Lionel Robbins (1971, pp. 120–21), while acknowledging Young's "massive" erudition, his "good grasp of the practical realities of economic life" and "his success as a graduate supervisor" at Harvard,

---

[17] Letter to Blitch dated 1 December 1975.
[18] In a letter to his Dad dated 18 May 1924, he however wrote: "Our good friends Kemmerer and Fisher had better look to their laurels as practical economists, as Harvard has a rival in the person of A.A. Young… Young certainly rates big around here."

thought that he was neither a good lecturer nor a good administrator. In Robbins's opinion, he was a difficult man to talk to, "gave me the impression of being a profoundly unhappy man, ill at ease in his surroundings and distracted by his duties" and of "complex and apparently tortured temperament". Currie suggested that this peculiar opinion may be due to Young not having similar interests as Robbins. Currie further stated that Young had a bright smile and an eager interest in the subject at hand (Sandilands 1999, p. 457).

Young as a Ph.D. Supervisor

Overton H. Taylor took "Modern Schools of Economic Thought" at Harvard, a course which Young taught. He was so much influenced by what Young said, particularly in the first part relating to Adam Smith, Physiocrats, 'natural law', 'natural rights' and 'natural order', that he decided to do his thesis on this topic. "And I recall my young pride when Young praised my thesis to [Harold] Laski, especially its part on the natural law, etc philosophy of the Physiocrats, and commended that to Laski as something that he, Laski, might well learn a good deal from!"[19]

Currie was Young's Ph.D. student at Harvard during 1925–1927. When Young signed his application for Ph.D., Currie wrote in his diary: "I fairly worship him. A five minute talk with him sets me up for the day" (Sandilands 1999, p. 463). Currie, who had started his Ph.D. 'Bank Assets and Banking Theory' under Young finished it in 1931 under John H. Williams. Subsequently he wrote extensively on monetary theory and policy in reputed journals, and dedicated his book *The Supply and Control of Money in the United States* (1934) to Allyn Young. David Laidler (1993, p. 1084) notes: "By far the greater part of that book's quantitative content documents variations in the public's currency/deposit ratio, not to mention the behaviour of excess reserves within the banking system, all very much in the spirit and style of Young (1928)."

One of Young's research students, G.T. Jones, wrote a book entitled *Increasing Returns*, which clearly showed Young's imprint. He had come

---

[19] Taylor to Blitch dated 15 October 1973.

to Harvard from England as a Rockerfeller fellow to make a study of the variations in costs and profits in different industries. Colin Clark, who was research assistant to Allyn Young at the LSE and who also edited Jones's manuscript after his untimely death in a car accident in 1928, stated that his methods were greatly in advance of his time, and clearly showed Young's influence.[20]

Young also supervised Edward H. Chamberlin and Frank H. Knight who both became famous after their theses were published. There was a widespread belief at Harvard that every worthwhile idea in Chamberlin's (1933) *The Theory of Monopolistic Competition* was expounded by Young in his classes.[21] As Earl J. Hamilton[22] wrote:

> One thing that my notes taken in 1924–26 conclusively showed was that every worthwhile idea in E.H. Chamberlin's subsequent work on imperfect competition had been clearly expounded by Allyn Young in class long before Chamberlin put pen to paper. Curiously, Young credited Cournot for most of what he said! He was the epitome of modesty.

There are many other accounts of Young's influence on Chamberlin. For example, Arthur H. Cole[23] wrote: "I have a distinct impression that Professor Young was responsible for Edward Chamberlin's innovation into monopolistic competition and the like. Mason would know this story well." Milton H. Heath[24] noted, in the margin of his personal copy of Chamberlin's (1933) book (p. 105): "This matter of excess capacity was a question grad. students discussed at length in early 20s at Harvard" (Blitch 1995, p. 119). Blitch (ibid., pp. 118–9) wrote:

> For years speculations and rumors have circulated among the American economic profession that much of Chamberlin's work originated with Young. A search of Chamberlin's and Young's papers in the archives at

---

[20] Letter to Charles Blitch dated 7 December 1972.
[21] Chamberlin submitted his thesis in 1927.
[22] Letter to Blitch dated 14 February 1973.
[23] Letter to Blitch dated 1 April 1972.
[24] Milton H. Heath, a student of Young at Harvard, was the inspiration behind Blitch's biography of Young.

8 Allyn Young's Role as an Author, Teacher and Mentor

Harvard shed no light on the matter. Since both were on the same campus while the thesis was being written, all of their communication was oral. Chamberlin attributed the origin of this theory to the debate over railway rates between F. W. Taussig and A. C. Pigou… At this late date with both protagonists deceased and with no notes, letters or memoranda bearing directly on the question available, it is not possible to delineate the full extent of Young's influence on the evolution of the monopolistic competition theory. However, the evidence suggests that Allyn Young's role in the development of the theory of monopolistic competition was far greater than has previously been recognised.

In the preface to the first edition, Chamberlin (1933) himself acknowledged Young's influence on his work:

The title of the book is apt to be misleading, since I have given to the phrase 'monopolistic competition' a meaning slightly different from that given it by other writers. Professor Young once suggested 'The Theory of Imperfect competition,' and this, although it had to be discarded as inaccurate, comes close to describing the scope of the subject. The book deals, not with a special and narrow problem, but with the whole of value theory. Its thesis is that both monopolistic and competitive forces combine in the determination of most prices, and therefore that a hybrid theory affords a more illuminating approach to the study of the price system than does a theory of perfected competition, supplemented by a theory of monopoly… But most of all I am indebted to the late professor Allyn A. Young, under whose guidance this study was first written as a doctor's thesis. He encouraged me with a lively interest in the project as it developed, and his kindly acute criticisms have contributed greatly to such validity and clarity as the theory may have.

Young had been developing a theory which conformed more closely to the economic facts of life. In his letter to Ely cited earlier, he stated that he wanted to write a different textbook on economics based "upon an explanation of the workings of the modern business system". In another letter to Ely dated 7 March 1927, in response to Ely's request for another revision of *Outlines*, Young stated:

Introduce a chapter dealing in a realistic way with the large and important field of value and price which lies between pure monopoly and pure competition. I have in mind retail trade, and, in fact, of a pretty large part of the phenomenon of modern markets. This chapter should be as realistic as possible, and pure theory should be discussed in its relation to practical problems of social policy.

As Blitch (1995, p. 132) noted, Young's textbook was never written nor any reference to it came up in any subsequent correspondence. Blitch (ibid., p. 163) further stated that a chapter on monopolistic competition was also not written, with only two pages devoted to its description in the 1930 edition of *Outlines*.

As early as 1908, Young (Ely et al. 1908, p. 195) regarded trade marks (or brands) as a feature of 'competitive businesses' to establish 'goodwill' and to escape 'the dead level of competition'. In the same edition in his chapter on profits, he stated that 'goodwill' is the difference between the valuation of a business establishment and valuation of its assets. "Those more or less definitely established kinds of profits which give rise to 'goodwill' values must not be confused with monopoly profits. Monopoly implies absence of competition. 'Goodwill' profits are to be attributed rather to imperfect working of competition, to the economic inertia and friction which result from the fact that buyers are guided to a very large extent by custom and habit rather than by conscious choice… A noteworthy feature of modern business, however, is the attempt on the part of manufacturers and wholesalers to influence the demand of the ultimate consumers of their products through the use of advertising. The trademark privilege, which enables particular brands of competitively produced goods to be distinguished, is an important factor in the efforts of such producers to gain and hold the patronage of ultimate consumers" (ibid., pp. 447–8).

Recognising that branded products may carry a higher price to gain extra profits, Young (in Ely et al. 1916, p. 196) wrote:

> *Trademarks*, like patents, are monopolies in the strictly legal sense that no one else may use them. But, unlike patents, they do not lead to a monopoly in the economic sense of giving exclusive control of one sort of business.

They are used largely in competitive business undertakings as a help in establishing and maintaining what is termed as good-will... In so far as a successful business man in a competitive field is able to induce people to believe that it is better to purchase his particular brand of goods than to take the chance of getting a possibly inferior quality by purchasing his competitors' products, he may be able to lift himself a little above the 'dead level' of competition. He may even find that he can increase his net profits by putting the price of his goods somewhat higher than that at which precisely similar goods are sold in the market... But because his power to control the price of his product is in general much more limited than that of a true monopolist, and because competition limits and conditions his activities in other ways, his business is more properly called competitive than monopolistic.

Thus there is a clear recognition that competition limits the price through, for example, entry of others or availability of close substitutes. In the same edition, in the chapter on 'Interest', he also introduced the concept of 'selling expenses' as distinguished from production costs:

[T]here is left a very important field of enterprise in which the entrepreneur may find it worth while to invest large amounts of money in 'selling expenses.' Put in a very general but roughly accurate way, these expenses are incurred, not in producing things people want, but in inducing people to want the particular things the entrepreneur has for sale. Advertising expenditures are the most obvious form of such investments. Part of the salaries paid to travelling salesmen must also be placed under this head. (ibid., p. 514)

In Ely et al. (1930, pp. 216–18), Young wrote:

The laws of normal price and monopoly price...represent two extreme norms. In the case of consumption goods, an increasing number of price transactions fall somewhere between the two... [W]e live today under a régime in which competition has been shifted, by the 'differentiation of products and sales effort,' away from price. The average producer today dreads the acid test of exact price comparison. He multiplies styles, grades, brands, and terms. He spends millions in advertising to convince purchasers that he has something that cannot be supplied by other producers... In the case of such goods, consequently, there are no definite prices mechanically fixed by the interaction of supply and demand. The producer fixes his own price in accordance with a procedure explained under monopoly price. Price determination becomes a question of individual business policy in which the principle object is to keep the customer's loyalty and divert his attention from price considerations.

But the monopoly is more apparent than real. Underneath the surface the old law of supply and demand exercises just as much control as in the past; not with as much precision but with quite as much power. We have heard a good deal of talk about the 'growth of monopoly in recent years.' On the contrary there has probably been a growth of real competition… It is only in electric power, gas, telephone, water, and street-car service that the average consumer is conscious of monopoly in any important degree… It is clear, then, that supply and demand bring about a uniform price only in a few instances. In the case of standardized goods such as wheat and cotton which are sold on the great exchanges, competition does obviously bring about a uniform or precise price, but it is temporary and flitting… Competition may thus result in either uniform or different prices, but the tendency to differentiation of product and service makes uniformity the exception rather than the rule. Competition is just as powerful as ever, but it works out through substitutes, through the offer of supplementary service or better terms of payment. Monopolistic control is probably less widespread and important than it was in the last quarter of the nineteenth century.

In his 1928 paper on increasing returns and economic progress, Young wrote: "How far 'selling expenses'…are to be counted as sheer economic waste depends upon their effects upon the aggregate product of industry, as distinguished from their effects upon the fortunes of particular undertakings." He regarded product differentiation, industrial specialisation, and fragmentation of processes and industries as an inevitable result of the forces of competition and growth.

Thus, all elements of imperfect competition—selling costs, advertising, goodwill, trade marks, brands, product differentiation, non-price competition, presence of close substitutes, entry of other firms, limited control over price, and so on—are there as a part of the general competitive process and growth. But Young never put all these elements together

8 Allyn Young's Role as an Author, Teacher and Mentor

in a coherent analytical framework as Chamberlin did. Perhaps Young was more interested in a dynamic theory of price formation linked to growth than in a static theory of price under imperfect competition.[25] Perhaps he might have done so in his proposed treatise on theory after his 1928 presidential address but unfortunately he did not live long after the address to be able to do so.

Frank H. Knight, another of Young's Ph.D. students at Cornell, similarly benefitted from Young's generosity in terms of inspiration, time and ideas. Knight was also a lifelong friend of Young who was constantly in correspondence with him even after Cornell. They generally showed their work to each other for comments before publication. Young commented extensively on Knight's thesis before it was finalised. Also, Young showed his 1928 increasing returns paper to Knight before it was delivered as a presidential address and later published in the *Economic Journal*. Blitch (1995, p. 121) noted: "Almost every paper and book which Knight wrote between 1921 and 1929, he first sent to Young for comments and suggestions. Knight and Young did not always agree on every concept and theory, but their relationship was one of open-mindedness and friendliness."

Knight's thesis 'The Theory of Business Profits' was submitted in 1916 and won a second prize ($500) in a contest sponsored by a business corporation Hart, Schaffner and Marx. Knight wanted to revise the thesis before publication and Young, soon after sending his detailed comments and suggestions, wrote[26]:

> On the whole I am not sorry that the book has progressed so far that it will be difficult to make considerable changes in view of anything that I have said. I have read the thesis from the point of view of a supposedly hostile critic, and there are a number of suggestions about which I have some doubt. On others I feel more confident, and these I have generally emphasized in the notes I have sent you.
>
> As I think I have told you before, this is by all odds the ablest thesis that has ever passed through my hands. I suspect it ought to go a long way

---

[25] See also Frank Machovec (1995, chapter 10) who criticised Chamberlin's (and Knight's) static or equilibrium theory. Young, on the other hand, had a 'process' view of competition. See also Sandilands (2000, pp. 310–11).
[26] Young to Knight dated 5 January 1921.

toward establishing your reputation as an economist. I have read it with admiration and enjoyment, and really got quite a good deal of stimulus from it.

On 5 March 1921, Young again wrote:

I have your letter of March 1. I sent off my last notes to you in a great hurry in response to what I took to be and S.O.S. from you. I am sorry they were not of assistance. I am afraid you misinterpreted their general purport,—or else I failed to make myself clear… I still think you are in error with respect to diminishing productivity. (I am fairly certain of this). But I shall not try to convince you. If I could talk with you I might at least be able to get you to understand what I mean. I fancy, however, that you are one who has to work through and out of a subject yourself. I do not say that in disparagement. It is no bad quality.

It is true that the 'exhaustion of the product' through the imputation process has no necessary relation to diminishing productivity. But without diminishing productivity the theorem has, of itself, no significance for economics.

In a letter dated 17 October 1921, Knight wrote: "Thanks again for your generous words respecting the book; also renewed assurances of my keen realization that whatever merit it has is largely owed to you and that it would have been much better if the conditions had allowed me to make fuller use of your suggestions."

Knight's book was published with the title *Risk, Uncertainty and Profit* (1921). Young was correct in his assessment that it established Knight's reputation as an economist and became a much discussed and talked about book in the economics profession. The book was about an unsettled question in economic theory—the nature of profits and their determination. In his book, Knight made a distinction between risk and uncertainty; while the former could be assimilated into the market framework through the development of insurance markets, it is the latter which was responsible for profits arising out of the violation of perfect competition in actual business life due to the absence of perfect knowledge (Emmett 2009, pp. 41–2).

But Knight had a static view of competition.[27] He thought if perfect competition is to exist, "cost must always increase as supply increases".[28] Young did not agree, and on the margins of page 36 of his thesis he noted: "Not if the increase in supply is a response to an *increased* demand. External economies[29] of certain sorts *will* be realized… The point is that certain economies are *possible only with large demand*. Take for example the installation of *automatic tools* in a machine industry. The case of 'tooling up' is too large to be distributed profitably over a small output." Knight had also stated that "New supply will then come through an increase in the number of similar establishments, not through an increase in the size of any one of them and no economies of large scale production will be realized." Young noted that this was wrong presumably because what Young talked about was specialised undertakings, and not similar undertakings, "But I admit that economies of 'large-scale production' are really economies of large-scale demand."

In a letter to Knight dated 11 August 1928, Young stated:

> Where I don't follow you, of course, is in respect of increasing returns. The reason may be that increasing returns do not exhibit themselves adequately when approached from the point of view of *equilibrium* price theory. To me it seems *obvious* that when larger output (i.e., larger *markets*) makes roundabout methods economical—or a degree of roundaboutness economical—which would be uneconomical otherwise, *potential* increasing returns exist, in the sense indicated by *your* definition of costs. That is, production can be increased while displacing a *progressively smaller* (proportionately) amount of other commodities,—quite apart from the question of whether this leads to larger-scale firms or 'industries.' The economies which show themselves in increasing returns are the economies of *large* production, not large-scale production.

---

[27] Young (1929; Mehrling and Sandilands 1999, p. 130) linked profits to dynamism in an economy. While in a stationary state there could be no pure profits, they arose due to factors that made a business successful such as foresight, fortune and quickness to see and take advantage of opportunities.

[28] Knight's thesis, page 36.

[29] It was ironically perhaps under the influence of Young's (1913) critique of Pigou that Knight did not believe in the existence of external economies. While Young later changed his position, Knight did not.

In another letter dated 6 October 1928, in response to Knight's comments on his increasing returns paper, Young wrote:

> I enjoyed your comments on my paper. The whole issue appears to be one of *exposition*. The purely static view does not interest me very much, because if it is *rigorously* adhered to, almost everything worth saying about it can be put into a very few pages. We *have* to depart from it somehow. The only question is just how. I confess that I can't see why to begin with static assumptions and *then* to inquire into the effects of changing *any* particular variables should be taboo, and consequently I don't get the point of your objection to my introducing capital accumulation. Further, I should hold that conditions of an equilibrium *rate* of change afford just as appropriate a hunting ground for '*pure* theory' as conditions of *static* equilibrium do.

Among the former students, Young was widely regarded as an inspiration and mentor to Frank Knight. Howard S. Ellis[30] reports: "Concerning Allyn Young, let me first observe that my first teacher in economics was Frank H. Knight, then at the University of Iowa, Iowa City. For some reason or other Knight 'took up' with me, a mere undergraduate, but I came to know him very well. I have no hesitation in saying that Young, as a professor at Cornell, was Frank's chief inspiration and mentor, and remained so as long as he lived."

However, there are some voices suggesting that it is important not to overstate the importance of Young's influence over Knight as well as Chamberlin. For example, in a letter to Sandilands dated 4 June 1997, Paul Samuelson stated that Young's influence on Knight and Chamberlin is manifest "but should not be exaggerated" (Sandilands 1999, p. 455).[31] Similarly, Thomas Reinwald (1985, p. 402) wrote: "There is no question but that Young was an important influence on Chamberlin, but I suspect more as a catalyst than as a main protagonist."

---

[30] Letter to Blitch dated 1 November 1973.
[31] Later, in another letter to Sandilands dated 7 April 1999, Samuelson wrote: "My words about Knight and Chamberlin were to correct an impression each of these were mere dummies who spoke with the voice of the master ventriloquist. Young himself spoke *against* such exaggerated rumors—which was not to deny that he did them lots of good." See Sandilands (1999, note 2).

Summing Up

Young did not seek success but he was a highly successful and sought-after graduate teacher. He did not seek fame, but famous he was not only in his own country but across the Atlantic as well. Sir William Beveridge (1929) in his memorial address on 11 March 1929 spoke of the reasons behind Young's success:

> First, was the high standard of scientific work that he set for himself as for others. He was at once the kindest of men and severest of judges... Second, he was by taste a great teacher, interested in young minds, able to make them share his own sense of the high issues involved in what they studied with him, believing and making them believe in the importance and the possibility of finding truth... Third, there was in him a total lack of certain things which the gods do not always remember to leave out when they mix god-like reason with human clay. He had no envy, jealousy, or harshness; of sarcasm, cynicism or flippancy he was incapable... He was ever the last person, not the first, to be persuaded of his own successes.

References

Beveridge, William (1929), 'Allyn Abbott Young: Memorial Address', *Economica*, 1 (April). Reprinted in *Journal of Economic Studies*, 17(3/4), pp. 16–17.

Blitch, Charles P. (1995), *Allyn Young: The Peripatetic Economist*, Basingstoke and London: Macmillan Press Ltd.

Carlson, V. (1968), 'The education of an economist before the Great Depression: Harvard's economics department in the 1920s', *American Journal of Economics and Sociology*, 27, pp. 101–12.

Chamberlin, Edward H. (1933), *The Theory of Monopolistic Competition*, Cambridge: Harvard University Press.

Currie, Lauchlin (1934), *The Supply and Control of Money in the United States*, Cambridge: Harvard University Press.

Currie, Lauchlin (1990), 'Recollections of Allyn Young', *Journal of Economic Studies*, 17(3/4), pp. 10–13.

Ely, Richard T., Thomas A. Adams, Max O. Lorenz and Allyn A. Young (1908), *Outlines of Economics*, New York: Macmillan.

Ely, Richard T., Thomas A. Adams, Max O. Lorenz and Allyn A. Young (1916), *Outlines of Economics*, New York: Macmillan.

Ely, Richard T., Thomas A. Adams, Max O. Lorenz and Allyn A. Young (1930), *Outlines of Economics*, New York: Macmillan.

Emmett, Ross B. (2009), *Frank Knight and the Chicago School in American Economics*, London and New York: Routledge.

Gregory, T.E. (1929), 'Professor Allyn A. Young', *Economic Journal*, 39, pp. 297–301.

Knight, Frank H. (1921), *Risk, Uncertainty and Profit*, Boston: Houghton Mifflin Co.

Laidler, David (1993), 'Hawtrey, Harvard and the origins of the Chicago tradition', *Journal of Political Economy*, 101(6), pp. 1068–1103.

Machovec, Frank M. (1995), *Perfect Competition and the Transformation of Economics*, London and New York: Routledge.

Mehrling, Perry G. and Roger J. Sandilands (eds.) (1999), *Money and Growth: Selected Papers of Allyn Abbott Young*, London and New York: Routledge.

Mitchell, Wesley C. (1929), 'Allyn Abbott Young', *Journal of the American Statistical Association*, 24, pp. 200–3.

Morgenstern, Oskar (1929), 'Allyn Abbott Young', *Zeitschrift für Nationalökonomie*, 1 (May), pp. 143–45. English translation by Susan Sirc printed in Sandilands (2009).

Reinwald, Thomas P. (1985), 'The genesis of Chamberlinian monopolistic competition theory: addendum – a comment', *History of Political Economy*, pp. 400–2.

Robbins, Lionel (1971), *Autobiography of an Economist*, London: Macmillan.

Sandilands, Roger J. (1999), 'New evidence on Allyn Young's style and influence as a teacher', *Journal of Economic Studies*, 26(6), pp. 453–80.

Sandilands, Roger J. (2000), 'Perspectives on Allyn Young in theories of endogenous growth', *Journal of the History of Economic Thought*, 22(3), pp. 309–28.

Sandilands, Roger J. (2009), 'New evidence on Allyn Young's style and influence as a teacher', in Robert Leeson (ed.), *Archival Insights into the Evolution of Economics, Volume V: Economics in the United States*, London: Palgrave Macmillan, pp. 134–79.

Schumpeter, Joseph J. (1937), 'Allyn Abbott Young', in R.A. Edwin Seligman and A. Johnson (eds.), *Encyclopaedia of Social Sciences*, 25, New York: Macmillan.

Young, Allyn A. (1913), 'Pigou's Wealth and Welfare', *Quarterly Journal of Economics*, 27(4), pp. 672–86. Reprinted in Mehrling and Sandilands (1999), pp. 86–96.

Young, Allyn A. (1924), 'Index numbers (Chapter 12)', in Henry L. Reitz (ed.), *Handbook of Mathematical Statistics*, Boston: Houghton Mifflin.

Young, Allyn A. (1928), *An Analysis of the Bank Statistics for the United States*, Cambridge: Harvard University Press.

Young, Allyn A. (1929), 'Economics', *Encyclopaedia Britannica 1928*, London: Encyclopaedia Britannica Company, pp. 925–32. Reprinted in Mehrling and Sandilands (1999).

9

Young's Estimate of His Contemporaries and Earlier Economists

This chapter will discuss Allyn Young's estimate of his contemporaries—J.M. Keynes, Francis Y. Edgeworth, Arthur C. Pigou, Wesley C. Mitchell, Irving Fisher, Joseph Schumpeter, Vilfredo Pareto, Léon Walras and earlier economists—David Ricardo, William S. Jevons and Antoine A. Cournot. Those economists who have already been discussed—Adam Smith, John Stuart Mill, Walter Bagehot, Alfred Marshall, Max Weber, Thorstein Veblen, Richard T. Ely and Ralph G. Hawtrey—will be excluded from the discussion in this chapter. His famous Ph.D. students Frank H. Knight and Edward H. Chamberlin have also been discussed elsewhere in the book (Chap. 8).

John Maynard Keynes (1883–1946)

After WWI, Keynes and Young were members of their respective delegations to negotiate peace at Paris. The Treaty of Versailles which emerged from the negotiations was negotiated in an atmosphere hostile to Germany. Keynes and Young, working independently, arrived at the same estimate of $10 billion as Germany's capacity to pay reparations as against

© The Author(s) 2020
R. Chandra, *Allyn Abbott Young*, Great Thinkers in Economics,
https://doi.org/10.1007/978-3-030-31981-6_9

their estimate of the total reparation bill to which Germany was liable—put at $10.6 billion by Keynes and close to $20 billion by Young (1920a, p. 389). Keynes and Young both realised that reparation payments had to be linked to the German capacity to pay. If the terms of the treaty were made unduly harsh then European economic and trade relations would collapse, making post-war recovery extremely difficult. Moreover, there was a transfer problem as the money for reparations had to come from the conversion of German marks into convertible currencies. If German authorities, by selling marks to purchase convertible currencies, bid up the foreign exchange price in terms of marks, exports would be facilitated and imports curbed. But Young pointed out that to export more Germany would need to import more raw materials whose prices in marks would go up as rapidly as export prices. Thus the domestic price level would increase rapidly, making exports increasingly difficult. So the possibilities of the exchange rate mechanism should not be exaggerated (Young 1927a, pp. 22–24). However, as per the actual terms of the agreement, which was essentially a political agreement, the amount of reparation was left to be decided by the Reparations Commission and no time frame for payments was set. This was a compromise agreement given that the British and French were bent on their pound of flesh.

Keynes (1919), in *The Economic Consequences of the Peace*, harshly criticised the Treaty of Versailles as a Carthaginian peace. The role played by the council of four (Georges Clemenceau, Lloyd George, Woodrow Wilson and Vittorio Orlando) was strongly indicted. He alleged that these four had arrived secretly at the terms of the agreement. President Wilson also came in for a strong criticism—Keynes alleged that the treaty was arrived at "to save the scruples or the face of the President". Furthermore, French designs to reduce the German population and weaken her financial system were "clothed, for the President's sake, in the august language of freedom and international equality". Wilson was portrayed as a Presbyterian elder outwitted by Clemenceau and Lloyd George. He also criticised the treaty for the "blank cheque" Germany was made to sign in respect of large additional potential charges on account of war pensions and separation allowances. Upon receiving a presentation copy of the book, Young wrote to Keynes that he agreed with Keynes on almost every point of fact and policy. But he disagreed with him on the role of the US President.[1]

> Most of all I feel that you concede too little to the President. He held the cards, and might conceivably have dictated the peace. But what would have come of it? The answer is implied on page 47 (of your American edition). He was beaten, not by the sophistries of Lloyd George, or the immovability of Clemenceau, but by the sheer force of circumstances. The peace of Versailles was a democratic peace in the sense that it was a fair expression of the prevailing sentiment in the victorious democracies. It was an inevitable precipitation of the slow poisons with which human souls had been drugged during the war. Perhaps the people would have responded differently to a different type of leadership, but that had nothing to do with the situation as it was.
>
> For example, I have reason to believe that the President's yielding on the war pension matter was because he felt it to be necessary, not because he was convinced. At any rate I am pretty sure that it was in accordance with a definite understanding with Lloyd George, arranged, very likely, through Colonel House.
>
> The President held all the cards, but the cards had little value. He did not have back of his program the solid sanction of public opinion in France or England, or even in the United States, and Clemenceau knew it. At a council of Vienna he could have pulled it off; at Paris he had to reckon with democracy; that is with domestic politics. His failure was inevitable. I do not believe anyone in his place could have succeeded.

In his review of the book, Young (1920a, p. 388) said that he would have been better satisfied with economic and financial clauses if they had been drafted by Keynes but he did not agree with Keynes's interpretation of the circumstances or their consequences. "What this scene lacks is a background. Mr. Keynes knows the things that should be in the background, but he tucks them away into a dim corner and forgets them. That, I imagine, is because the background is political, and Mr. Keynes is impatient of political considerations. He thinks in terms of economic

---

[1] Young to Keynes dated 11 February 1920. In his reply, dated 28 February 1920, Keynes stated: "In spite of everything I say about him, and all my disappointments, I still believe that the President played a nobler part in Paris than any of his colleagues."

right and economic wrong and personal responsibility." Young was of the opinion that, although no reparation amount or time frame for payments was specified, and although it looked as if Germans had signed a blank cheque, the provision of the Reparations Commission was important as he was convinced its powers would be used wisely. As to the cancellation of inter-allied debts and proposed loan to Germany, Young said that the initial burden would fall on the US, so should not be seriously considered, particularly at that time, even though Young had come to think this was "not only wise but probably inevitable".[2] Young's final assessment was:

> As against Mr. Keynes's brilliancy, insight, and courage, there must be put certain elements of strain, of exaggeration, of effort for dramatic consistency. But for all that his book is like nothing so much as a fresh breeze coming into a plain where poisonous gases are yet hanging. (ibid., p. 389)

Young, in the summer of 1924, in the first of a series of meetings organised by the Williams Institute of Politics at Williamstown (Massachusetts), said that apart from Russia and Germany Europe was close to 90 per cent normal. He did not agree with Keynes that since the war Europe was approaching a 'precipice' in economic matters. In the second session devoted to monetary matters, Young mentioned three important works: Gustav Cassel's *Money and Foreign Exchanges After 1914*, Keynes's *Tract on Monetary Reform*, and Ralph Hawtrey's *Monetary Reconstruction*. In Young's opinion, Hawtrey's book was much superior than the other two. He did not agree with Keynes and Cassel that inflation in Germany was deliberately plotted by its government to destroy its capacity to make reparation payments. Inflation was caused by the preference of the citizens to hold goods and foreign exchange in exchange for the depreciating mark. The best remedy, in Young's view, was to stabilise the exchange rate to control inflation, in contrast to Keynes who in *Tract on Monetary Reform* (1923) advocated stabilising domestic prices and not exchange rates.

---

[2] Young's Harvard students, Lauchlin Currie, Paul Theodore Ellsworth and Harry Dexter White called for the cancellation of those debts as part of a lengthy, urgent memorandum on anti-depression policies (Laidler and Sandilands 2002).

9 Young's Estimate of His Contemporaries and Earlier Economists

Keynes and Young had many similar ideas. For example, both favoured public works in a situation of heavy unemployment. Young (1929b) anticipated Keynes in his 'Wages' entry in the *Encyclopaedia Britannica*, where he wrote that a fall in the real wages may not lead to an increase in employment.[3] Both viewed money as integral to the real sector in contrast with classical economists who viewed money as merely a 'veil' over the real sector. For the classicals, money was just a convenient medium of exchange whose quantity affected the price level but was neutral with respect to the relative prices. Young (1928a; Mehrling and Sandilands 1999, p. 24) also praised Keynes's *Treatise on Probability* (1921) in that averages and aggregates by themselves were inadequate for inductive inference without the support of other knowledge.

After Young's untimely demise in 1929 due to an influenza epidemic, Keynes in a letter of condolence to Mrs Young, dated 17 March 1929, wrote that his influence as a teacher and a critic was far greater than his printed words. He also stated that Young always shared his best ideas with others and it was his own work which always received the least priority.

Francis Y. Edgeworth (1845–1926)

Edgeworth's most famous book was *Mathematical Psychics* (1881) in which he criticised W.S. Jevons's theory of barter exchange and showed that equilibrium was indeterminate. The degree of indeterminacy reduces as the number of players increases, and when there are an infinite number of players in the limiting case as in perfect competition, contract becomes fully determinate. In this book he also introduced the concepts of a generalised utility function and the indifference curve. Although seminal in nature, his book got lukewarm reviews by Jevons and Marshall. In 1897,

---

[3] "It cannot be assumed…that an increase in the aggregate supply of labour will normally have the effect of reducing wages. Nor can it be assumed that a general reduction of real wages would lead to the increased employment of labour…in the way that a reduction of the price of a particular commodity would generally lead to larger sales. Little or nothing is to be gained by the general formula of supply and demand for an explanation of the determination of wages" (Young 1929b, 1990, p. 138). Young believed that wages were determined by the agreement between the employer and the employee. The relative bargaining power of a worker was weak as he could not hold out indefinitely for higher wages because of the need to feed himself and his family. See also Chap. 5.

he published a survey of taxation in which he articulated his famous 'taxation paradox'—taxation of a good may lead to a fall in its price. Some economists (e.g., E.R.A. Seligman) regarded this as a 'slip' on his part until Harold Hotelling in 1932 rigorously proved that Edgeworth was correct. Edgeworth also showed the indeterminacy of the duopoly problem as against Cournot's exact solution. He was also a critic of the neoclassical theory of distribution and helped refine it. As the editor of the *Economic Journal*, he wrote a number of book reviews.

Young reviewed Edgeworth's (1925) *Papers Relating to Political Economy* and termed them as displaying 'high scientific standards' and 'unflagging intellectual energy'. Young (1925a, pp. 721–2) wrote:

> There is hardly a routine page, a banal paragraph, or a trite sentence in these three volumes. Doubtless some of the shorter papers reprinted from the Economic Journal were written as an editor's 'fillers'; but they never have qualities of hack work. Even the book reviews (or such of them, at any rate, as are printed here) are never mere abstracts. At one point or another the reviewer pushes some thesis advanced by the author a little farther, puts it under new light, or brings it under new relations.
>
> The truth is, I imagine, that Professor Edgeworth has never been interested in the commonplaces of economics. He prefers the difficult problems that lie at the very frontiers of economic analysis, where the paths are slippery and the signposts are few. More than once, it is true, he is the defender of accepted economic doctrines against criticisms born of misunderstanding or misrepresentation; but one may suspect that it is the disentangling of the confusion wrought by the critic rather than the reiterating of 'sound principles' that attracts his interest.
>
> It would be a mistake, I think, to regret that Professor Edgeworth has preferred to remain a free lance and has refrained from writing a systematic treatise. The best of treatises has its perfunctory sections. No economist can be a master, in his own right, of the whole field. It is well that Professor Edgeworth has been content to grapple with the problems which have been of most interest to him and which give room for his powers of subtle and penetrating analysis.

By and large, Young's review was appreciative of Edgeworth but there were some gently expressed disagreements or criticisms. For example, he stated that Edgeworth's solution to the problem of duopoly was not the final word. Other solutions were possible depending on the postulates. Regarding index numbers, he stated that Edgeworth had pushed the study beyond what his predecessors had done but he doubted that the advance was always in the most profitable direction. Young had sent a copy of the review to Edgeworth before sending it for publication. Edgeworth, in a letter to Young dated 8 November 1925, was very appreciative of this gesture: "Thank you for letting me see your forthcoming review… I appreciate very highly your approbation knowing what a sharpsighted and discerning critic you are, one who has successfully corrected even Pigou. I am more gratified by your general commendation of my seasonal than I am alarmed by your gently expressed dissent from my premises. For I recognise that exact uniformity is not to be expected with respect to abstract concepts and on Probability and Utility. Does not 'mode' play some part in sharpening our expressions about the intangible? I admit that utilitarianism is out of fashion. I presume I am at liberty to keep the Review—I treasure it."

Young had made use of the Marshall-Edgeworth idea of offer curves in his theory of growth. The underlying concept of reciprocal demand is the basis on which Youngian increasing returns are built. Although Young was sceptical of the use of the usual (one-thing-at-a-time) supply-demand apparatus in his theory, he thought they could be profitably used in their reciprocal senses. Among all neoclassical tools the idea of reciprocal supply-demand was, in Young's opinion, the best. Used in this sense, an increase in the supply of one sector is an increase in demand for the product of other sectors; and it could also be supposed that an increase in demand would call forth an increase in supply. But all this was premised on the elasticity of demand—there was no limit to increasing returns except the limit beyond which demand was not elastic.

Edgeworth (1925), quoting Marshall, had stated that much economic work had less need of elaborate analytical methods than of shrewd mother-wit, of sound sense of proportion, and of larger experience of life. In a similar vein, in his article on English political economy, Young (1928a; Mehrling and Sandilands 1999, p. 22) maintained that "the economist, in even greater measure than the worker in more narrowly circumscribed fields of scientific inquiry, has in need of insight, imagination, breadth of view, and complete intellectual honesty". Further, an economist always needed wisdom, and wisdom requiring a balanced view of the concrete diversities of life could most be gained by historical studies.

Arthur Cecil Pigou (1877–1959)

In his *Wealth and Welfare*, Pigou (1912) suggested that, *ceteris paribus*, in increasing-returns industries the marginal net product of investment tends to exceed the marginal net product in industries in general, while in decreasing-returns industries the reverse was true. This meant that in competitive industries of diminishing returns investment tends to be pushed too far, and in competitive industries of increasing returns, not far enough, to secure the equality of marginal products which maximises the national dividend. This led to the policy conclusion of taxing decreasing-returns industries and giving subsidies to increasing-returns industries. Young (1913; Mehrling and Sandilands 1999, p. 92) in reviewing this book stated that in diminishing returns industries increases in land and other factor prices do not represent increased use of resources but merely a transfer of purchasing power from consumers of these resources to their owners.

Young's correction to Pigou's slip in reasoning caused somewhat of a sensation in economic circles both in the US and Britain. The editor, F.W. Taussig, of the *Quarterly Journal of Economics*, on receipt of Young's review, in a letter dated 27 July 1913, stated: "Your Pigou review has come. It is A1—I take off my hat to you, as I have done before. It is a source of pleasure and pride to have such an admirable notice in an American Journal. I have read it but once, but need to read it (and Pigou) again. But I have put it into the printer's hands at once because it can probably be worked into the August Journal." Pigou at first refused to admit his error for he issued a rebuttal in the 1920 edition. But, as noted by Charles Blitch (1995, p. 39), when more criticism was levied by D.H. Robertson and Frank H. Knight, Pigou corrected his error in the 1924 edition of his book.

9 Young's Estimate of His Contemporaries and Earlier Economists

Young in his review also stated that Pigou's difficulty arose entirely because he avoided the use of a money measure for the resources devoted to the work of production. His discussion was in terms of marginal net products and apportioning of different resources which contributed to production, but these could only be discussed in terms of a money measure. Although Pigou's discussion of economic friction which prevents equality of marginal net products was admirable, he could have learnt a lot from the work of American public utility commissions. "Professor Pigou here, as elsewhere, has primarily in mind British national problems. I am inclined to think that a more intimate acquaintance with the recent work of American public utility commissions would have made Professor Pigou's conclusions as to the range and variety of the considerations that can be taken into account in the public regulation of monopoly prices and services somewhat more favourable" (Young 1913; Mehrling and Sandilands 1999, p. 93).

Young also believed that economies of large-scale production in an industry reduce the per unit cost of individual establishments but these economies cannot be treated in the same general manner as increasing expenses of agricultural production which arise from causes external to individual undertakings. Pigou (1912, p. 177) had written: "Provided that certain external economies are common to all the suppliers jointly, the presence of increasing returns in respect of all together is compatible with the presence of diminishing returns in respect of the special work of each severally." To this Young (1913; Mehrling and Sandilands 1999, p. 95, footnote 10) responded: "I cannot imagine 'external economies' adequate to bring about this result."

It appears that Young's thinking on external economies evolved over the years. While in 1913 he did not lay much store on external economies, by 1928, his theory of macroeconomic increasing returns was largely based on external economies. In his 1927 book, *Economic Problems: New and Old*, a collection of earlier published papers, his 1913 Pigou review did not find a place, as perhaps by that time Young's thinking had evolved.

Young's overall assessment of *Wealth and Welfare* was favourable. Firstly, Pigou hedged his doctrines with so many safeguards that really vulnerable points were few. Secondly, many of his results were stated as probabilities, pointing to his *courage* in pushing his analysis to the end, as well as to his inherent *caution* with which inferences were made. Thirdly, Pigou maintained that the conception of the national dividend was not a toy but a useful instrument in solving social problems.

Young (1929c) also reviewed Pigou's (1928) *A Study in Public Finance*. In this book Pigou had suggested progressive rates of taxation on the ground that the importance attached to the final increments of large incomes by their recipients is purely relative, and their sacrifice is reduced if others in the same income class are similarly treated. In response to this, Young (1929c, p. 79) observed: "Progressive taxation really rests, not upon the premise that a small taxpayer attaches (at the time of 'announcement') more importance to the marginal tenth of his income than a large taxpayer attaches to the marginal tenth, but upon the circumstance that the community as a whole, expressing its opinion through Government, regards the uses of marginal tenth of the small taxpayer's income as more important than the uses of large taxpayer's marginal tenth."

Assuming costs are constant, and therefore that it is unnecessary to treat elasticity of supply as something apart from elasticity of demand, Young reaches the conclusion: "A fairly good approximation to the optimum result could be secured by taxing only commodities which are known to be objects of distinctly inelastic demand" (ibid., p. 83). Critics have pointed out that 'Ramsey's rule' (after Pigou's student Frank Ramsey) applies where both demand and supply are inelastic, even more where supply is inelastic (implying land value taxation, an issue that will be further considered below) and not merely to objects with inelastic demand.[4] But in Young's opinion: "Mr. Ramsey's theorem does not seem to have much practical significance" (ibid., p. 82).[5]

Young's final assessment of Pigou's book was also favourable. For, in Young's opinion, it not only had the qualities which had given its author high position among world's economists, but it also dealt with real

---

[4] Frank Ramsey (1903–1930) became famous for his two widely cited articles on optimal taxation and optimal saving.

[5] Later writers (except Joseph Stiglitz) left the inelasticity of supply out of the picture, and at some point even gave up inelasticity of demand, coming back to 'uniformity' as the key to tax neutrality. Sandilands in his letter to Fred Harrison (Cc Mason Gaffney) dated 25 October 2017, suggests that Young was only considering produced goods.

problems, and therefore was more valuable than any ordinary systematic treatise on public finance.

Wesley Clair Mitchell (1874–1948)[6]

Young first met Mitchell during 1900–1901 when he took a break from his Ph.D. at Wisconsin to work under Wilcox at the US Bureau of Census at Washington. Since then Young and Mitchell were lifelong friends, constantly in touch with each other. Young not only confided in him regarding academic matters but also personal matters. In a handwritten letter to Mitchell dated 21 November 2010, Young confided about his mother's death in the following words: "I was cabled to South Dakota some weeks ago by the illness of my mother. I left her apparently out of danger but she died on Nov. 7. It was the first time death has come so close to me, and the shock was considerable. I haven't yet readjusted myself. She was a woman of very exceptional width of interest & mental power. She had always been a stimulating and encouraging factor for me, and I shall miss her sorely. This intimate matter you will forgive as putting it down in black & white relieves the tension a bit."

Charles Blitch (1995, pp. 23–24) notes that when Young was at Stanford he initially came without his family, and the presence of Mitchell at Berkeley made his life much more pleasant than it otherwise might have been. He further notes that both visited each other very frequently. Mitchell came to Palo Alto to see his former Chicago teacher Thorstein Veblen, plus Young and Harry A. Millis. At Stanford, Young and Stanford's president David Starr Jordan had a few misunderstandings, and Young was also unhappy with his salary situation. After he resigned from Stanford, Young wrote a personal letter to Mitchell dated 11 April 1911:

> I have resigned at Stanford… T. S. Adams goes to the Wisconsin Tax Commission & I will succeed him at Washington University. The position

---

[6] Mitchell along with two other American economists—Frank W. Taussig and Irving Fisher—figures as one of the ten great economists in Schumpeter (1951/2003).

is just not what I want, there is too much teaching, & I am not a good teacher,—and the facilities are limited. But Stanford is intolerable in many ways (although I am exceedingly fond of California in general). Moreover (between us) Jordan has flatly refused to carry out his definite (written) promise in the way of salary, & other things.

Mitchell benefitted immensely from Young's criticisms and comments on his work. For example, in a letter dated 8 December 1911, Young expressed his willingness to read through Mitchell's work: "I have always got much more than enough for myself in reading your work to compensate me for whatever time it took." Young, in another letter dated 5 September 1913, commended his book *Business Cycles* (1913), still in manuscript form, in the following words:

> I do not suppose that there is the slightest chance that any comments I might chance to have thought of relative to your book on Business Cycles would be of any use to you at this late day. So I shall only say now that I read the MS. with more interest than I have read anything in our line for many years; that I worked over some considerable part of it with a small class at St. Louis; that I have told a number of our mutual friends that it was a distinct pity that you had already made your reputation as a scholar; for the present book seemed so admirably designed for doing that precise thing; that I told these same persons, furthermore, that I was sure it was easily the best piece of work that any American economist had done in many years… I went over the MS. in what is (by my rather loose measure) microscopic fashion; but it seemed to me almost flawless. There are a few suggestions or questions that I would be glad to send on if you care to receive them at this late day.

Young also commented on Mitchell's (1927) book *Business Cycles: The Problem and its Setting*. In a letter dated 7 January 1927, Mitchell while thanking Young for the trouble he had taken despite being busy wrote:

> Please accept my heartiest thanks, not only for your most generous remarks about my manuscript as a whole, but also and most particularly for your detailed criticisms. They are exactly what I want. I shall take careful account of them in preparing the copy for the printer. I hope very much that you

9 Young's Estimate of His Contemporaries and Earlier Economists

can take time to deal faithfully with the remaining chapters. In the chapter on statistics, I already know of two or three points which must be amended, and I fancy that you will find numerous others.

I appreciate the trouble you are taking the more highly because I know how busy you must be. Certainly you have a great gift for criticism and I count myself fortunate in being one of the beneficiaries.

Not only did Young comment on Mitchell's work but also sought Mitchell's comments on his own work. For example, for the third edition of the *Outlines of Economics*, Young sought Mitchell's remorseless criticisms to his chapters. In a letter dated 8 December 1911, Young wrote:

> Ely is insisting that the 'Outlines of Economics' be thoroughly revised in the near future. Although the book is not of the sort I should write if I were doing all of the work, I think it has established a place for itself, and that it would be well to improve it in as many ways as possible. I should be glad of any suggestion growing out of your experience with the book, and I should especially value your criticisms on the three chapters on money. The third of these is pretty bad as it stands, I fear, and needs rewriting from beginning to end. I am especially dissatisfied with the sections on crisis, and on the value of money. But I should be glad to have rigid and remorseless criticisms on any parts of these chapters, or on any part of the book. The chapters for which I am primarily responsible are: X, XI, XII, XIV, XV, XVII (in part), XIX, XXI, XXII, XXIV, and XXV.

In the 1908 edition of *Outlines of Economics* Young had propounded his own theory of crisis. In a letter to Young, dated 7 January 1916, Ely had talked about the necessity of revising the treatment of crisis. In the reply dated 10 January 1916, Young described his treatment as exactly the same as Mitchell's except that it predated him (as well as Fisher)[7]:

---

[7] In his article on 'The trend of prices', which also had a discussion on business cycles, Young (1923a) disagreed with Mitchell that increasing costs of business would bring the expansion phase of the business cycle to an end. It had to be remembered that expenses of production were also money incomes of the consumers. The crisis occurred not due to difference in aggregate demand and aggregate supply but due to the fact that composition of demand was maladjusted with the structure of supply.

There is nothing in the present treatment inconsistent with Fisher's theory of crisis. But his theory is peculiarly incomplete and unsatisfactory, in that it is based only upon the tendency for the interest rate to lag behind the rate of business profits. My own opinion, which antedates Fisher's, is that the fundamental thing is the difference between prices and cost of production in general in their period of advance; the consequent inflation of investment, especially in fixed forms of capital; and the resulting inevitable collapse when poor crops or some other factor reduces the general purchasing power of the community,—upon which the mass of capital must depend for its ultimate profitableness. It happens that this theory is exactly that of Mitchell, although my chapter [1908] antedates his book [1913]. It is also the theory which is presented by half a dozen recent books on crisis published in Europe. I have a letter from Mitchell expressing a detailed agreement with my treatment of crisis, and as you may know, I gave Mitchell's book on crisis a very careful reading in manuscript before it went to the printer.

It is not always that Young and Mitchell agreed with each other. When Young sent him the manuscript of his article 'Economics as a field of research', Mitchell, in a letter dated 14 June 1927, objected to the first third of the draft article particularly his attribution to 'Veblen and his followers' the 'capital error' that 'the explanation of things in terms of their historical antecedents is the only really scientific mode of explanation'. In reply, dated 29 June 1927, Young stated: "I am grateful for your comments on my paper on Economics as a Field of Research. You are right in suggesting that neither Veblen nor any of his followers who needs to be reckoned with has ever held that the genetic method is the 'only' really scientific mode, etc. Very likely you are even right in suggesting that at this point my emotions got the better of my judgement." In the final printed version[8] Young substituted the words 'Veblen and his

---

[8] "Now it is a capital error to hold (with Thorstein Veblen and some of his followers) that the explanation of things in terms of their historical antecedents is in some special sense a scientific mode of explanation; that, as Veblen puts it, modern sciences are characteristically 'evolutionary sciences,' and concern themselves primarily with 'unfolding sequences' and 'cumulative causation'. The truth is, of course, that the goal towards which the natural sciences are always pressing—even though it may be an unattainable goal—is the explanation of this world of changing and evolving forms and types of organization in terms of some simple and stable mechanism" Young (1927b; Mehrling and Sandilands 1999, pp. 6–7).

9 Young's Estimate of His Contemporaries and Earlier Economists

followers' with 'Veblen and some of his followers' and 'the only really scientific mode' with 'in some special sense a scientific mode'. It appears that Young was amenable to suggestions from his friends and critics. But in this case the general drift of his statement appears to be correct even after the amendments.[9]

In his 'A Review of *The Trend of Economics*' Young (1925b, 1927a, pp. 250–1) praised Mitchell's work in general as making important and substantive contribution to economic knowledge:

> No economist of his generation has made more important substantive additions to economic knowledge than Professor Mitchell. He has shown how fruitful quantitative methods may be, when guided and supplemented by skilful analysis. He has given new meaning and significance to various short-time fluctuations and maladjustments in our exchange economy. This substantive work of his fits into and amplifies the general structure of economic knowledge that has been built up slowly and falteringly during the last century and a half. The assumptions, the modes of thought, are such as are familiar to economists. What is new is the body of concrete experience which Professor Mitchell has patiently and deftly organised and formulated in terms of general tendencies.

However, in the same review he criticised Mitchell's (1924) article 'The prospects of economics'. In 1910, Mitchell had favourably reviewed William McDougall's Social Psychology in which McDougall had stated that political economy rested on hedonistic postulates and had suggested that general instinctive propensities would afford a better basis. In a similar vein, Mitchell also stated that economic theory had always rested upon the concept of human nature posited by theorists. He further stated that it was clearly unwise for them to continue trusting and using the traditional hedonistic psychology. One of the major economic problems requiring study was the processes by which habits and institutions had grown out of instincts. Young, while criticising Mitchell, stated that economics had always been a study of human behaviour, obtaining its data

---

[9] Veblen had discarded the classical and the neoclassical theory. He had also discarded the contractual view of society in favour of a historical view. Young, on the other hand, could see the finer points of both and regarded them valid approaches to seeking economic truth.

from experience and not from psychological postulates. In any case, most postulates were just common sense; and deductive economics was just a matter of expositional form.

Young and Mitchell carried on extensive correspondence on the problem of index numbers. The earliest available reference on this subject occurs in a letter by Young to Mitchell, dated 5 October 1910, in which Young wrote: "Taussig has this morning turned over to me your paper on 'Dun-Gibson Index Number'. I have had time to give it only one reading, as it should go to the compositors today. Like all of your other work I find it admirably clear and to the point. Only one possible improvement occurs to me." In another letter to Mitchell dated 16 January 1911, Young mentioned that he would hand over his article on the 'Bureau of Labour's Index Number of Wages' to Taussig without changes as he had no suggestions for its improvement. Further: "I am glad you have done this work. This discrepancy you deal with has bothered me a little, but I never brought myself to the point of examining it in detail." Mitchell (1915) published *The Making and Using of Index Numbers* which was commented by Young. In a letter dated 1 February 1915, Young wrote to Mitchell: "I have just received your paper on the Making and Using of Index Numbers. I shall read it with very great interest and I shall send it back to you sometime this week. I am making this definite promise in order to protect you as well as myself, for, as you know, I have found by sad experience that if I postpone matters of this kind I can neither depend on myself nor ask others to depend upon me."

In a letter to Young, dated 21 November 1921, Mitchell enclosed a note on the ideal formula which he prepared for the second edition of *The Making and Using of Index Numbers*. The note mentions that the ideal formula was independently invented by three persons (although it is most commonly attributed to Irving Fisher). C.M. Walsh was the first to mention it in a footnote in his *Measurements of General Exchange Value* (1901). A.C. Pigou published the same formula in his *Wealth and Welfare* (1912, p. 46) but without the *square root* of the product. He remedied his mistake (or oversight, as Mitchell called it) in his *Economics of Welfare* (1920, p. 78). Irving Fisher presented this formula to the American Statistical Association in 1921.

9 Young's Estimate of His Contemporaries and Earlier Economists

In his reply to Mitchell dated 22 November 1921, Young observed that in *Wealth and Welfare* the omission of the radical sign by Pigou was not a typographical error as in the text as well as the formula he refers to the *product* rather than the *square root of the product*. Moreover, in the accompanying text Pigou was tackling a measure of a change in total satisfaction from changes in prices of a definite collection of goods. Young further stated that "In the Economics of Welfare, however, it is clear that Pigou has reached it." Young also said that measurement of *changes in the general price level* and the measurement of *average changes in prices* were two separate problems. Young further maintained that a completely weighted arithmetic mean was of necessity the best index number of the general level of prices because with complete weighting it *was* the general level of prices. Put into usable form, however, the weighted arithmetic mean of actual prices became the so-called ideal index number. Young continued:

> I have read with great interest the pages prepared for the revised edition of your monograph on index numbers. In general, I agree with you except that I [would] definitely limit the ideal formula to the measurement of changes of the general level of prices, interpreting that phrase rigorously. It can easily be shown, I think, that Pigou's purpose is similar. I do not believe, with Fisher, that it ought to be used in a chain index number. So used, the interpretation of the meaning and significance of the result is very different. I should limit it to the direct comparison of the price level in pairs of years…
>
> I must ask you to note that my interpretation of the meaning of the ideal index number is quite different from Walsh's. He calls it good because, to him, it combines other sorts of means. I call it good merely because it is the best workable approximation to a simple weighted average of actual prices.
>
> I do not know that we are very far apart on the matter after all. I note that you indicate your agreement with Pigou that the formula is well adapted for his purposes, and further that you suggest that it may well be adapted for use in the equation of exchange. Substitute for this last phrase the expression, 'for use in comparing the price levels of any two years, taking these price levels as defined by the equation of exchange,' and you have my own statement of the case.

In a letter to Mitchell dated 19 December 1922, Young wrote that the index number of the aggregative type was the best for measuring the average rate of change as well as the general level of prices, that he was giving up his predilection for the geometric mean, and that for measuring the rates of change his position would be closer to Fisher than to Mitchell's in the revised Bulletin. However, "For most purposes Bureau of Labour Statistics index number of wholesale prices, with whose planning you had so much to do, is distinctly the best index number published anywhere in the world."

Irving Fisher (1867–1947)

Young commented on several of Fisher's works including *Purchasing Power of Money* (1911), *Stabilizing the Dollar* (1920) and *Making of Index Numbers* (1922). Young also carried on extensive correspondence with Fisher on these matters. In *Purchasing Power of Money*, Fisher resurrected the quantity theory of money through his famous equation of exchange: $MV + M'V' = PT$; where M is currency, M' is demand deposits, V is velocity of circulation of M, V' is velocity of circulation of M', P is the general price level, and T is the total of transactions. Young (Ely et al. 1916, p. 321) described the equation of exchange as "necessarily true", "a truism" and "an identity" rather than an equation. Fisher used this equation of exchange to argue that changes in the quantity of money cause changes in the price level. To stabilise the economy therefore the total quantity of money had to be stabilised. Young, on the other hand, did not believe that money was neutral with respect to relative prices. Some prices would rise faster than the others (depending on various elasticities of demand), so an increase in money supply would more importantly change the structure of relative prices. According to him business fluctuations were not due to changes in the general level of prices but due to distortions in relative prices.

Fisher, for some time, had been advocating varying the amount of gold in the monetary unit in accordance with an officially kept index number of prices. The scheme involved the issue of gold bullion certificates by the government which were redeemable in a larger amount of gold if the

9 Young's Estimate of His Contemporaries and Earlier Economists 279

price index rose and in a smaller amount if the price index fell. In his review of Fisher's *Stabilizing the Dollar*, Young (1920b) expressed doubt and scepticism about this plan. He pointed out that the plan had wide-ranging repercussions on the economy requiring a more thorough analysis than what Fisher had attempted. "The fact is that the repercussions of the stabilizing operations upon banking, upon foreign trade, and upon business enterprise and industrial progress in general, are exceedingly complex matters. They need more accurate and more thorogoing analysis than they have yet received. Professor Fisher's unusual power of broad and yet precise generalization leads him sometimes to oversimplify his problems" (Young 1920b, p. 527).

In the review Young concentrated on two aspects of this scheme: management of gold reserves and the structure of index numbers. As regards the maintenance of adequate gold reserves to back gold bullion certificates, Young (ibid., p. 528) wrote: "If prices tend to increase, the outstanding certificates will, under the stabilization plan, be redeemable in increasing amounts of gold. The reserves might easily become less than a 100 per cent cover for the certificates. When prices tendencies are downward surplus reserves will be accumulated. If the reserves were allowed to fluctuate freely in this manner there is a possibility that in the long run surpluses might balance deficits, but there is also a possibility that the reserves might be exhausted, or reduced to a point where confidence in them would be lost."

Initially, Fisher's plan had included the use of an ordinary index of the general price level. But the objection raised was that this contained a multitude of commodities whose price movements were relatively sluggish. It was suggested that a selective index number be used in which the included commodities are particularly responsive to monetary influences. Fisher then constructed a selective index number which included imported and exported commodities as well as goods where imported or exportable commodities entered as raw materials. But Young doubted the practicability of such a plan to stabilise the dollar purely at the national level.[10] For example, with a decline in the mint price of gold, the decline

---

[10] Even before reviewing this book Young, in an undated letter probably of 1913, wrote to Fisher: "[T]he prices which would be most surely and promptly affected by a decrease in the mint price of

in the price of commodities having an international market would adversely affect exporters and benefit importers. If prices rise, exporters would gain and importers lose. This will make the plan politically unpopular and hence impracticable. Further:

> At any rate I do not believe that Professor Fisher will gain much support among economists for his proposal that the present high level of prices should be stabilized. That high level is supported by credit expansion at home, but also in part by credit expansion in Europe. A general collapse of European credit structure, with enforced liquidation, might easily drain so much gold from us that our price level could be maintained only by transforming our 'bullion certificates' into inconvertible notes. (Young 1920b, pp. 531–2)

Young and Fisher carried on extensive correspondence on Fisher's *Making of Index Numbers*. Young, apart from reviewing it, also commented on this work in manuscript form. In a letter dated 12 December 1921, Young, while returning the first three chapters, wrote: "The difference between us seems to be fundamental… As I see the matter…you reach your ideal index number on the ground not only that it meets certain tests, but also on the further ground that it is intermediate between certain faulty types of index numbers which either exaggerate or minimize the general change in prices… More concretely, I think you spend too much time on the arithmetic and harmonic means of the price relatives… I regard the arithmetic mean, in its direct or in its harmonic form, as so fundamentally unsound that I am a bit surprised that you give it serious consideration. It involves the impossible assumption that ratios are additive. In my opinion the geometric mean is the proper mean and the only proper mean to use in averaging price relatives." Further:

> When you come to the aggregative form of index number, I am more nearly in agreement with you. But you do not in these early chapters

---

gold would be the prices of those commodities which largely enter into foreign commerce. I, for one, should expect that these sudden fluctuations in these particular prices would arouse the opposition of exporters and importers, as well as of large consumers or large producers of imported or exported goods."

9 Young's Estimate of His Contemporaries and Earlier Economists

suggest the real significance of the departure involved in using actual rather than relative prices.

As you know, I derive your ideal index number from weighted averages of actual prices. I believe that this, analytically, is what it is. The fundamental point is that the ordinary weighted aggregative index number is in fact an expression of the ratio between the weighted average of actual prices in the two years compared, the weights consisting of quantities measured, not in physical units, but in the amounts that could be purchased for a dollar in the basing year.

I know that you object to the notion of an average of actual prices. But that is precisely what P in your equation of exchange is. Your objection, I understand, is that things expressed in unlike units cannot be compared. To this I reply:

1. The comparison involved is properly not between tons and yards and dozens, but between different *ratios*, between quantities of these things and quantities of money. The physical units are not comparable but their ratios are.
2. The difficulty disappears, at any rate, as soon as physical units are put into terms of dollars' worthy.

In another letter, dated 29 December 1921, while returning some more chapters, Young wrote: "I have just come across your appendix, in which you deal with the ratio of averages as contrasted with the average of ratios. I am sorry that I did not see this appendix earlier, for this brings the difference between us to a sharp focus. I cannot agree with your appendix at all, and so far as I find your work unsatisfactory, it is because of the point of view which you clearly express in this appendix."

The bone of contention between the two was the fundamental definition of an index number—whether it was an average of ratios (Fisher) or ratio of averages (Young). According to Young ratios cannot be aggregated whereas actual prices can be. It is true that in aggregating prices, if the physical unit is changed a new price level results. In Young's opinion, it is merely essential that the same physical units be adhered to for the years covered by the index number. Further, geometric mean is at once an average of ratios as well as ratio of averages. Fisher through a roundabout process eliminated all other index numbers except the ones using actual, not relative, prices. And yet Fisher in his appendix contended that all index numbers are averages of ratios.

In his review of Fisher's *Making of Index Numbers*, Young commended Fisher's work as one of the "landmarks in the history of index numbers" and as "a notable scientific achievement". Young (1923b, 1927a, p. 294), through a novel reformulation of his position, appeared to narrow the gap between himself and Fisher: "I have been forced to discard the view that there is a substantial difference between measuring an 'average change in prices' and measuring a change of the 'general level of prices'. In a way professor Fisher is right in holding that 'all true index numbers are averages of ratios.' But I should prefer to say that all true index numbers are at once averages of ratios *and* ratios of aggregates. This point has a bearing upon a virtue sometimes imputed to the geometric average." Further: "When properly constructed and properly weighted, averages of ratios, ratios of averages, and ratios of aggregates all come to be about the same thing. Arithmetic, harmonic, geometric, and aggregative types, weighted and used with due regard to their structural peculiarities, agree extraordinarily well in the results they give. That the harmonic average is always smaller than the geometric, and geometric smaller than the arithmetic, does not, in general, affect the choice of an average for use in making *comparisons*, that is, in constructing index numbers" (ibid., p. 295). Young also maintained that a theoretically perfect index number was an impossibility. As a practical problem related to practical policy issues, the problem of index number is capable of a practical working solution.

Joseph Alois Schumpeter (1883–1950)

Schumpeter was a visiting professor at Columbia from Graz in Austria during 1913–1914. At the December 1913 American Economic Association Meeting at Minneapolis, Young who at that time was Secretary-Treasurer of the Association, was a discussant of B.H. Meyer's (1914) article 'Certain considerations in railway rate making'. Schumpeter (1914), who was also on the panel of discussants, felt that discriminatory rates were required to raise capital resources for investment. He further felt that in 'charging what the traffic will bear' the railways were only

9 Young's Estimate of His Contemporaries and Earlier Economists

trying to find the slopes of their demand curves experimentally. Such discrimination may also be dictated, not by railroads as such, but by allied business interests. Young (1914), on the other hand, regarded the cost-of-service principle as the first principle in railway rate making, the departure from which is to be justified by the special circumstances of the individual case.

This was the first meeting between Young and Schumpeter, but as Blitch (1995, p. 43) writes, a friendship blossomed between the two although they had differed on railway rates. Young arranged for Schumpeter to lecture at Cornell, and on 15 January 1914 he lectured on 'The Balkan Policy of Austria'. He stayed with the Young family and upon his return, wrote to thank Young for one of the most pleasant days he ever had. Schumpeter further said that "I am glad that I met you and do hope that we shall not lose contact altogether." When Young was moving to the LSE, he arranged for Schumpeter to take his place at Harvard for a year. Schumpeter later wrote two articles on Young's work: one in the *Encyclopaedia of Social Sciences* (1937) and the other a tribute in the *History of Economic Analysis* (1954).

In a letter dated 23 March 1927, Young while recommending Schumpeter for Harvard, wrote to Dean C.H. Moore: "Schumpeter, beyond doubt, is the most distinguished of the younger generation of economists on the continent of Europe… He is, I imagine, about forty five years old. His English is good, and his special interests are such that he could handle precisely the graduate courses which I have been giving. He is well known in America, and his coming to this country would create a great deal of interest among American economists, and would be very distinctly a feather in our cap." Schumpeter was selected for the year 1927–1928, but would return later in 1932 permanently to replace Taussig upon his retirement.

Schumpeter's theory of creative destruction resembled Young's disequilibrium approach to economics. Schumpeter had emphasised the role of the innovative entrepreneur in his theory of growth, but the old inefficient ways had to be destroyed for the new innovative ways to come in. For Young the old was a stepping stone for the new leading to a cumulative spiral. However Young believed that entrepreneurship is *overemphasised* by Schumpeter: "Now genuine leadership is rare; there is a flock behind any successful leader, and the thing is overdone. But does not Schumpeter overemphasize 'originality'? It is not so important that someone should go ahead" (Young 1990, p. 82). In his 1928 article, Young talked about making better use of *existing* than *new* knowledge as the more important factor in growth as the size of the market expands. While Schumpeter emphasised the innovative role of an entrepreneur, Young gave emphasis to his mercantilist instinct of persisting search for markets. It was the commercial revolution of the mercantilist era which paved the way for the industrial revolution in Britain. For Schumpeter, the creative role of the entrepreneur is slowly replaced by the bureaucrat manager as big firms emerge. Young, on the other hand, saw diffusion of economic activity as the more dominant tendency than concentration. Schumpeter, like Marx, thought that capitalism would be ultimately destroyed. But unlike Marx, he thought that this would happen because of its success rather than its failure. Young, on the other hand, thought that capitalism's excesses could be restrained through appropriate institutions which, acting independently, would promote the public interest.

A few years after Young's untimely death in 1929, Schumpeter (1937) observed that Young's fame rested on "so little published work" and this was rare. Further, he was first and last a creative teacher, and it was through his teaching rather than his writing that he was influential. In his *History of Economic Analysis*, Schumpeter (1954, pp. 875–6) wrote:

> I take this opportunity of saying a few words on Allyn A. Young (1876–1929)… A volume of essays, *Economic Problems: New and Old*… and *An Analysis of Bank Statistics for the United States*…constitute the bulk of his published work and do not convey any idea of the width and depth of his thought and still less to what he meant to American economics and to his numerous pupils. But…the reader may form some idea of that lion from a single claw, namely, his paper 'Increasing Returns and Economic Progress,' *Economic Journal*, December 1928. He was among the first to understand the stage of transition that economic analysis entered upon after 1900 and to shape his teaching accordingly—which, so far I have been able to make out, may be described as a cross between Marshall's and Walras', with many suggestions of his own inserted. One reason why his name lives only in the memory of those who knew him personally was a habit of hiding rather than of emphasizing his own points: one must, for

example, be not only a specialist but also a very careful reader to realize that in his concise and unassuming analysis of national bank statistics, there is enshrined the better part of a whole theory of money and credit.

Léon Walras (1834–1910)

Walras, along with W.S. Jevons and Carl Menger, independently discovered the notion of marginal utility. His magnum opus was *Elements of Pure Economics* (1874) in which he developed a general equilibrium model of an economy based on a set of simultaneous equations linking products, prices and factors under conditions of free competition. Since the number of unknowns were equal to the number of equations in this system, it could be fully solved. For the actual economy, however, he postulated the concept of an auctioneer and the *tâtonnement* (or groping) process through which the system will reach equilibrium for every commodity. The auctioneer will call out prices and keep on varying them till supplies and demand perfectly match. The notion of an interdependent economic system in which each market was interlinked already existed at least since the Physiocrats, but Walras was the first to put it in a mathematical general equilibrium framework. Although described as the greatest of all economists by Schumpeter (1954), he was largely ignored in Britain, but today, as Mark Blaug (1986) points out, he is one of the three most widely read nineteenth-century economists after Ricardo and Marx.

Young recognised that the classical authors had neglected the role of demand in value theory as they had only emphasised cost of production. Jevons, Menger and Walras, by independently discovering the concept of marginal utility, had tried to cover this lacuna in the existing value theory. "One of the tasks which a newer generation of economists set for themselves was the careful examination of the mechanism of supply and demand, with special emphasis on what had been the relatively neglected factor of demand. One of the most important steps in the new analysis was taken independently but simultaneously…by W.S. Jevons…Carl Menger…and Leon Walras…although it came to be known later that they had been anticipated by some earlier but forgotten writers" (Young 1928b; Mehrling and Sandilands 1999, p. 127).

Young regarded these systems as highly abstract but thought that the use of mathematics in economics had its benefits, for example, in showing "the interdependence of the factors which determine prices, costs, supply, demand and distributive shares" (ibid., pp. 129–30). Further, for Young the principal value of these systems was that the enquirer is put on his guard so as not to oversimplify his problems, since change in any economic variable has its direct and indirect effects. By using the mathematical method, Young considered that implicit assumptions and flaws in verbal reasoning are brought to the fore. But Young warned that a perfectly abstract economics is impracticable. "A system concerned with the relations of variables which are defined only by their mathematical attributes is not economics, any more than pure mathematics is mechanics" (Young 1928a; Mehrling and Sandilands 1999, p. 25).

In general, Young was critical of the general equilibrium approach and thought it gave us nothing which was not a mere truism. In this regard he thought that Marshall's partial equilibrium approach, though flawed, had the virtue of dealing with concrete problems of economic life. He also thought that for undergraduates Marshall's approach was appropriate and offered a better tool for handling a wide range of concrete economic problems. The all-together method, though logically superior, was only for the adepts.

Vilfredo Pareto (1848–1923)

Pareto made many important contributions in the field of economics and sociology. First, he advocated a mathematical approach to economics, and along with Walras became a leading figure of the Lausanne school and its general equilibrium method. Second, he did pioneering work in the field of income distribution. Based on empirical data of many countries he discovered that if you rank families by their incomes, income does not increase proportionately but geometrically. This he called a 'law' of income distribution (Pressman 1999, p. 79). Third, he shifted from the cardinal measure of utility to an ordinal approach. Trade between two people simply showed that they wanted to acquire the good they preferred. Fourth, he also introduced the concept of Pareto optimality, a situation in which it is not possible to make someone better off without making someone else worse off. Free exchange of goods would lead to a Pareto optimal situation because people will trade only if they gain and not otherwise. This concept has been used in welfare economics and to evaluate taxation and other public policies. However, Pareto optimality has been criticised because it depends on the initial distribution of income, that is, a different income distribution leads to a different Pareto optimal result. Also, Pareto optimality may not lead to a value-free welfare economics. Finally, Pareto became dissatisfied with mathematical economics as too narrow, and later turned to sociological, political and psychological factors in understanding how real economies work.

Young (1928b), in the graphical appendix to his article on increasing returns and economic progress, writes that it owes much to Pareto. In a footnote, he further argues that the collective indifference curve is an expository device and not a rigorous conception for the different points on it represent different distributions of income. In an earlier letter to Frank Knight dated 6 October 1928, he admitted: "Pareto is not to be held responsible for the 'collective' indifference curve. Further, the conception is not free from difficulties. The collective curve might be regarded as the *weighted* sum of individual indifference curves, if it were not that, except for very small segments of the curve, the weighing cannot be regarded as constant—or, better, the weighting cannot be regarded as independent of the position of the equilibrium point, for the *distribution* of the product will vary with the position of that point. But this difficulty appeared to me to be irrelevant to my problem. Furthermore, a *rigorous* statement of conditions is possible."

In his 1917 article on the concentration of wealth, Young pointed out that Pareto's index of inequality is based on the assumption that when the number of persons with income of a given size increases as compared to the number of persons with higher incomes, the inequality in income distribution declines. While Young had no quarrel with this definition of relative equality, in Young's (1917, 1927a, pp. 98–9) opinion, Pareto made a curious slip in interpreting his index in relation to inequality. "His index does not increase, as he supposed, with what he deemed inequality in the distribution of incomes, but decreases. It can be used… in this inverted fashion. In its direct form it might conceivably be taken as a rough measure of the evenness with which income receivers are distributed through the income range. But it gives no simple and definite standard of comparison."

Young also mentioned Pareto in connection with industrial fluctuations. Pareto's was one of the earlier explanations of fluctuations in terms of psychological factors—as 'waves of optimas and pessimas'.[11] In general, Young held Pareto in very high regard. In his proposed book on methodology (discussed in Chap. 3 above), he wanted to include a chapter from Pareto's sociological writings. In the *London Times* (1929) [reprinted in Sandilands 1990, pp. 14–17] memorial to Young, dated 8 March 1929, the writer noted that "in the sphere of pure theory if he worshipped any gods at all, he was inclined, at least in those later years to rate most highly the names of Cournot, of Pareto and of Edgeworth".

Antoine Augustin Cournot (1801–1877)

Cournot's (1838) masterpiece, *Recherches sur les principes mathématiques de la théorie des richesses*, was translated by N.T. Bacon into English as *Researches into the Mathematical Principles of the Theory of Wealth* (1897). Cournot was the first economist to use calculus in economics. He was also the first to draw demand and supply curves. In his downward sloping demand curve quantity (being a function of price) is on the vertical axis while price is on the horizontal axis. In a perfectly competitive situation, he showed that in equilibrium price will equal marginal cost. In monopoly, a producer will produce at a point where marginal cost equals marginal revenue. He also developed a duopoly model where the solution is determinate.

Cournot was initially ignored but later was acknowledged by Walras, Jevons, Edgeworth and Marshall. Walras admitted that his general equilibrium was a multi-market extension of Cournot's partial equilibrium model. Jevons also hailed him as a predecessor in the later editions of his

---

[11] "Earlier investigations regarded trade cycles merely as manias, forming the basis for the later 'psychological theory' of waves of optimas and pessimas… But why should these waves coincide? This periodic movement is explicable only as a result of contagion due to some external cause and then, admittedly, mental states may accentuate 'real' fluctuations" (Young 1990, p. 76).

Theory of Political Economy. Marshall acknowledged Cournot's influence in his *Principles of Economics* (1890). Though Edgeworth took his cue on competition from Cournot, he criticised Cournot for obtaining a deterministic solution to the duopoly problem, as in his opinion the solution was indeterminate if the number of producers is small. He also criticised Cournot on the gains from trade—Cournot's conclusion that trade would result in lower revenue was based on an algebraic error.

Young commended Cournot for distinguishing between abstract and historical sciences. In the prevailing American discussions on methods of social sciences it was common to distinguish between science and history. But following Cournot, Young preferred to distinguish "between the abstract sciences and the historical sciences, between the sciences which have to do with those dependable abstract general relations which we call laws, and sciences which deal with given situations or particular events in terms of their specific relations to situations and events which have preceded them" (Young 1927b; Mehrling and Sandilands 1999, p. 6). Young, in his proposed book on methodology (discussed in Chap. 3 above), wanted to include Cournot's chapter on social environment.[12]

In his article on 'English political economy' Young noted that, although English political economy had not made much systematic use of history, those elements were woven into its general contexture. Such concrete elements, the special problems it dealt with, as well as the peculiarly British lineage of some of its conceptions made it retain the flavour of its soil. He also stated that a country's literature is its own national heritage imperfectly communicable across barriers of history and language. In this context he quoted approvingly of Cournot (1877, pp. 336–7): "The science of the economists, more than other sciences, without being, as has been wrongly said, a literature, is permeated by that flavour of its soil, marked by the stamp of time and place which distinguishes one literature from another… Other sciences also have their history, their growth, which is linked to the progress of society, but not in such degree that their physiognomy reflects, like a literature, the physiognomy of society" (Young 1928a; Mehrling and Sandilands 1999, p. 26).

---

[12] This was the first chapter of volume 2 of Cournot (1861).

Young was fascinated by Cournot's treatment of theory lying between pure competition and pure monopoly. He regarded this market form as closer to reality than those lying at the extremes. Although the detailed analysis of this market form came from the pen of Edward Chamberlin, Young had expounded it in his classes at Harvard. Strangely, he attributed most of it to Cournot, not taking any credit for himself, as one of his students, Earl J. Hamilton confirmed.[13]

At the London School of Economics, 1927–1929, a new synthesis was emerging in his mind which rejected the method of ceteris paribus. As his colleague T.E. Gregory (1929) wrote: "In mental orientation: the detailed minor problems which had hitherto interested him were beginning to recede and were making for a new synthesis: under the inspiration of Cournot and Pareto—and among the younger generation of Dr. Sraffa—he was inclined to regard the treatment of specific problems, 'other things remaining equal,' as definitely wrong."

David Ricardo (1772–1823)

Ricardo was a leading member of the London financial community and felt compelled to write three articles in the *Morning Chronicle* in 1809 on the Bullionist Controversy.[14] The parliament had suspended convertibility of bank notes into gold. Ricardo took up the Bullionist position and blamed the suspension of convertibility for the excess note issue resulting in rising prices, and urged immediate restoration of convertibility. In his famous *Essay on the Influence of a Low Price of Corn on the Profits of Stock* (1815), he showed how the proposed protectionism in the wake of the Napoleonic wars would raise food prices, increase the share of rents, and lower profits and therefore growth. But the *Essay* failed to achieve its aim as the Corn Laws were passed in 1815. James Mill, who was Ricardo's close friend, constantly urged, coaxed, cajoled and prodded him to write

---

[13] Earl J. Hamilton to Charles P. Blitch dated 14 February 1973. See Blitch (1995, pp. 118–9).
[14] These articles later appeared in his *The High Price of Bullion, A Proof of the Depreciation of Bank Notes* (Ricardo 1810).

a book on political economy.[15] The result was *Principles of Political Economy and Taxation* (1817), which was an immediate success. It received a glowing review from J.R. McCulloch in the *Edinburgh Review*. In the book Ricardo articulated his theory of value and distribution. He postulated a labour embodied approach to value in contrast to Smith's several approaches. He was the first to systematise the science of economics and became highly influential in Britain and elsewhere.

Young noted that the development of political economy after Smith arose out of the practical concerns of the nation. These problems partly arose from rapid changes in Britain's industrial structure and partly from the Napoleonic wars. Rapid rise of population, extension of agricultural cultivation, rise in land rents, expansion of industries, depreciation of currency, and economic depression after the war commanded the attention of thoughtful men. "This newer political economy was more formal and systematic than Adam Smith's, and concerned more largely with abstract general relations, but it dealt with real problems and dealt with them in what was intended to be a practical way" (Young 1929a; Mehrling and Sandilands 1999, p. 120). The group of problems which came to be emphasised was 'the theory of value and distribution'. In a period of economic storm 'normal tendencies' were emphasised in the same way as the study of pathology contributes to normal physiology.

Young was impressed by the scientific achievement of English political economy of which Ricardo was a prominent member. In his chapters in *Outlines of Economics* (Ely et al. 1908), Young tried to balance the institutional orientation of his co-authors with the scientific approach of the English political economy. He wanted to convey Ely's progressive message by rooting it in economic theory. Therefore, in the 1908 edition of *Outlines* he introduced Ricardo's theory of rent both at the intensive and extensive margin. He also introduced Jevons's theory of interest and wages based on marginal productivity of capital and labour. This of course brought him in conflict with Ely, at whose insistence, he explained that the theory of distribution had no ethical implication, and that it was only about the relationship between production and distribution. The 1908

---

[15] Apart from James Mill, his circle of friends included such names as T.R. Malthus and Jeremy Bentham.

text insisted that categories of economics were still historical in character, but English political economy was the appropriate starting point of the current stage of economic evolution (Mehrling 1997, pp. 21–2). Young did not regard the neoclassical theory as an alternative to institutionalism but liked to appreciate the strong points of every approach.

With the increase in the income-yielding power of land, land values, or what is usually called the 'unearned increment' also increases. It is commonly believed that increase in land values is not due to any special efforts put in by the owners but due to general social causes. According to Young, the phrase unearned increment is misleading. So far as the increase in land values can be foreseen, it will be discounted, so it cannot be called an unearned increment.[16] If the increase in land values is unexpected, the so-called unearned increments have to be seen against the unearned decrements. Henry George (1879) who built on the Ricardian theory of rent, proposed that a single tax be levied on land values—he did not propose to abolish rent but opposed its private receipt. His main argument was that all 'improvements in productive power of labour' accrue in the form of rent. According to Young (Ely et al. 1923, p. 420), this was akin to attributing all value to labour as in the socialist labour theory of value; it was just as reasonable to say that all improvements are due to capital or land. Taxing land values may increase the available supply of land and lower rents in the short run, but in the long run it would have little impact on rent as land would be exploited more rapidly. Moreover: "Land ownership, like any other institution, has to be judged from the viewpoint of general social interests. The 'pride of ownership,' as an incentive to accumulation and as a basis for good citizenship, cannot be lightly put aside" (Young in Ely et al. 1916, p. 425).

Young commented on Ely's article on 'The order of utilisation of various grades of land'. Regarding Ely's treatment of the Ricardian theory, Young felt that Ricardo's theory enjoyed a broad acceptance, and Ely should not discuss the impact of improvements before taking into account

---

[16] According to Young the growth of American cities and settlement of western states involved a lot of sacrifice and effort, which may not have been forthcoming had the expected rise in land values not been counted as earned reward (see Ely et al. 1916, p. 424).

9 Young's Estimate of His Contemporaries and Earlier Economists

Ricardo's own treatment of the matter. In a letter to Ely dated 23 February 1909, Young wrote:

> It seems to me a rather clear and simple and undebatable proposition that settlers always take lands which, for the time being, taking all things into consideration, are in their judgement the best lands. Some of these lands become in time poor lands, either on account of the change in relative situation or deterioration in fertility. Others become in time better lands than they were at first. Then the settlers are often short sighted and mistaken in their judgements. Still the fact that the first settlers in a new country utilize barren hill tops rather than fertile valleys, simply because, for example, the latter may require a large amount of work to make them fit for cultivation, in no way contradicts the fundamentals of the Ricardian theory. I really do not know of any economist of standing today who does not accept the Ricardian theory of rent in most of its particulars. Some writers make it broader in its application than Ricardo, but few are inclined to narrow it… I do not see why you should discuss the effect of 'improvements' on the Ricardian theory without taking into account Ricardo's own treatment of these effects. Ricardo is shown to be partly mistaken at this point (See Cannan's History of Theories), but nevertheless he has brought out important points. It seems to me that the Ricardian theory is stated with most of the limitations it needs by some of the followers of Ricardo—McCulloch, for example, who has always seemed to me to be better economist than he is usually rated… The special significance of the Ricardian doctrine seems to me to be bound up with the larger aspect of the case. The question is not whether the first farmers in Dane County get as good lands as the later comers did. The question is rather whether the world has any more Dane Counties left—whether after the exploitation of the Canadian Northwest and of the wheat fields of South America we are not going to be forced to the cultivation of poorer lands at home and a more intensive use of those already in cultivation.

In another letter to Ely dated 29 January 1913, while commenting on his *Property and Contract* manuscript, Young made a distinction between rent to a person and rent to a factor of production. While the former was a surplus, the latter was not: "Rent, as the return going to individual land owner is…largely a surplus, but as to the return going to land as factor in production, I cannot see that it is in any measure a surplus."

Young was critical of the excessive pessimism displayed by Ricardo. For example, Ricardo used conditions of agriculture, particularly scarcity of land and the law of diminishing returns, to generalise for the economy-wide tendency of falling rate of profit. If rents rise and the share of profits is squeezed, the process of accumulation may come to an end and a stationary state may emerge. Ricardo sounded like an alarmist—a prophet of impending doom. Young pointed out that the law of diminishing returns was just a tendency which could be overcome by more powerful forces such as improvements in agricultural techniques and means of transport. Ricardo, to some degree, did foresee technical improvements in agriculture but his whole attitude towards technical change was ambiguous. According to him, the use of machinery will lead to reduction of wage funds for employing workers. Some may get employed due to extra profits generated but this may not be sufficient. A pool of unemployed will exert downward pressure on wages, increasing the misery of workers.

Ricardo and Malthus engaged in a vigorous debate over the question of gluts. While Malthus attributed them to under-consumption (or overproduction), Ricardo believed in the applicability of Say's law which stipulated that general overproduction—or a general glut—was not possible. There could be mismatches of demand and supply in specific sectors, but these would be promptly corrected by the operation of market forces. This was one of the early theories in connection with business cycles. Young had his own explanation: "Crises spring from mishaps in the valuation of things; they relate to what might be called the dollars and cents aspect of economic life" (Young in Ely et al. 1908, p. 267).

Young (1929d; Mehrling and Sandilands 1999, pp. 317–8) regarded the Ricardian principle of gold movements as one of the most firmly established and important of economic doctrines. According to this principle no country could long maintain a favourable (or for that matter unfavourable) balance of trade. If a country had a trade deficit it would export gold, the general level of prices would fall, exports would increase and imports fall. In case of a trade surplus, the opposite would happen. This doctrine was not based on pure (a priori) reasoning but was related to observed facts. According to Young, actual foreign trade statistics and gold movements confirmed the validity of the doctrine.

William Stanley Jevons (1835–1882)

Young (1912, 1927a) reviewed Jevons's (1871) *Theory of Political Economy*. In 1862 Jevons had sent two articles to the British Association the first of which dealt with the use of mathematical methods and subjective utility in economics. A version of this was published as 'Brief account of a general mathematical theory of political economy' in 1866. Young pointed out that the book was not received enthusiastically by Marshall and there were many who criticised it. Further, he was not the only one or even the first in the field—the fundamentals of his theory had been anticipated in the forgotten writings of H. Gossen and A. Dupuit. But later Jevons's *Theory* did receive serious attention; he had already established himself as a logician with the publication of *The Principles of Science*; and soon he became a man to be reckoned with. Jevons himself described his own work as a bare and imperfect outline of some of the more important theorems of political economy. In Young's (1927a, p. 219) opinion, "the book does not furnish even the skeleton of a system of economics. It contains only the uneven results of Jevons's attempts to expand and correlate his brilliant suggestions of 1862." Further: "The book is not inconsistent, but rather…uneven and unsystematic… The first four chapters are, in general, more completely elaborated than the remaining four" (ibid., p. 220).

According to Young, Jevons was the first significant writer who blended English utilitarianism with abstract economics. His acceptance of hedonism with regard to economic motives was definite and unqualified. In Young's opinion his theory could be divested from its hedonistic basis without substantially altering its essential features and with a distinct gain in actuality. Even his utilitarian ethics could also be eliminated from his work. Jevons's book was a reaction to Ricardo and Mill who had neglected utility or demand in their theory of value.

Young considered that the most important contribution of the *Theory* was the concept of 'final degree of utility'. It was defined as the utility of the marginal increment divided by the size of that increment. But in Young's opinion, marginal utility was a less abstract concept, and therefore better adapted to popular exposition. Jevons's fundamental theorem stated that the ratio of exchange between two commodities was inversely proportional to their final degrees of utility. The mathematical form of this principle was the well-known 'equation of exchange'—Jevons's most substantial contribution to mathematical economics. However, it assumed direct barter and, as Edgeworth had shown, the ratio of exchange between a pair of traders would be indeterminate. The main difficulty, according to Young, was that Jevons abstracted from the use of money. He tried to overcome this by his 'law of indifference' but this, in Young's opinion, was tantamount to assuming a general medium of exchange. It appeared that he regarded the use of money as an abstraction which needed to be avoided to get below the surface view. His difficulties were further multiplied when he moved from a pair of traders to ratios of exchange between markets. He tried to avoid this difficulty by utilising the concept of a 'trading body' applying to a whole group of dealers in a commodity. If this were taken in a literal sense the market would cease to be competitive.

> With all the millers and all the bakers in England conceived rigidly as a single pair of traders, the 'law of indifference' could not be invoked, and the equation of exchange would not lead to a determinate ratio of exchange. Jevons's refusal to assume a general medium of exchange is primarily responsible for these difficulties. When the existence of money is taken into account Jevons's equation of exchange leads very naturally to the analysis of supply and demand at a price. (ibid., pp. 225–6)

As to the discussion of the relation between the costs of production and exchange ratios, again a barter economy was assumed. Here the ratio of exchange was held to be proportional to the 'degree of productiveness of labour applied in their production'. Costs of production were inversely proportional to the degrees of productiveness. In this manner new equations of exchange were developed where cost of production played the same role as was assigned to utility in the previous equations. For Jevons, however, utility was more important than cost of production. In Young's opinion, Jevons's criticism of the cost of production theory was invalid since this theory was a statement of long-period price tendencies under conditions of free competition.

9 Young's Estimate of His Contemporaries and Earlier Economists

The central point in Jevons's theory of distribution concerned the rate of interest. Gustav Cassel had credited Jevons with a marginal productivity theory of interest. Although they looked similar, Jevons attributed diminishing productivity to the period of investment rather than to the amount of capital. On the whole, his theory was closer to E. Böhm-Bawerk than to the marginal productivity theory. He accepted the orthodox theory of rent and, taking labour as fixed and capital as variable, propounded a residual theory of wages.

According to Young, Jevons's *Theory* was mathematical only in a superficial way. He was not an accomplished mathematician. He gave mathematical garb to results reached by non-mathematical reasoning. His final degree of utility, although conceived as a derivative, was treated as an algebraic ratio. Young agreed with Marshall's judgement that the book would be much improved if mathematics were left out but the diagrams retained. On the whole it was difficult to judge Jevons's influence as it was difficult to separate it from that of Walras, Menger, Böhm-Bawerk or Marshall. In England his influence was reflected in the works of Edgeworth and Phillip Wicksteed. Although Jevons did not bring about a revolution in economic theory as he had desired,[17] the body of economic doctrines would have been different had Jevons not written. His doctrines had since been absorbed in the general structure of economic theory and reconciled with the Ricardian line. "But the position of the *Theory* as one of the four or five great books of nineteenth century English political economy is secure" (ibid., p. 231).

Young (1929e, pp. 347–8) also commented on Jevons's sunspot theory of crisis. Jevons thought that the average period between severe crises in England was about 11 years which, in his opinion, agreed well with the average sunspot cycle. The link was from sunspots to trade, through climatic variations (e.g., rainfall), crops, imports and exports. According to Young, Jevons's hypothesis had not been generally accepted because the average interval between crises in England was less than 11 years while in other countries crises occurred at different dates and with a different

---

[17] Young (1928a) stated that Jevons's contribution to statistical inquiries may count for more in revolutionising economic theory than his *Theory of Political Economy*.

interval. Young (1990, p. 78) noted that if the average interval was inferred from the price changes, it seemed to be 9 rather than 11 years.

References

Blaug, Mark (1986), *Great Economists Before Keynes*, Atlantic Highlands: Humanities Press International.

Blitch, Charles P. (1995), *Allyn Young: The Peripatetic Economist*, Basingstoke and London: Macmillan Press Ltd.

Cournot, Antoine A. (1838), *Recherches sur les principles mathématiques de la théorie des richesses*, Paris: Chez L. Hachette. Translated into English by N.T. Bacon as *Researches into the Mathematical Principles of the Theory of Wealth* (1897), New York: The Macmillan Company.

Cournot, Antoine A. (1861), *Traité de l'enchainement des idées fondamentales dans les sciences et dans l'histoire*, Paris: Librairie de L. Hachette Et. Cie.

Cournot, Antoine A. (1877), *Revue sommaire des doctrines économiques*, Paris: Hachette et cie.

Edgeworth, Francis Y. (1881), *Mathematical Psychics*, London: Keegan Paul.

Edgeworth, Francis Y. (1925), *Papers Relating to Political Economy*, London: Macmillan.

Ely, Richard T., T.S. Adams, M.O. Lorenz and A.A. Young (1908), *Outlines of Economics*, New York: The Macmillan Company.

Ely, Richard T., T.S. Adams, M.O. Lorenz and A.A. Young (1916), *Outlines of Economics*, New York: The Macmillan Company.

Ely, Richard T., T.S. Adams, M.O. Lorenz and A.A. Young (1923), *Outlines of Economics*, New York: The Macmillan Company.

Fisher, Irving (1911), *Purchasing Power of Money*, New York: Macmillan.

Fisher, Irving (1920), *Stabilizing the Dollar*, New York: Macmillan.

Fisher, Irving (1922), *Making of Index Numbers*, New York: Houghton Mifflin.

George, Henry (1879), *Progress and Poverty*, New York: D. Appleton and Company.

Gregory, Theodore E. (1929), 'Allyn Abbott Young', *Economic Journal*, 39, pp. 297–301.

Jevons, Willam S. (1871), *Theory of Political Economy*, London and New York: Macmillan and Co.

Keynes, John M. (1919), *The Economic Consequences of the Peace*, New York: Harcourt, Brace and Howe (1920).

Keynes, John M. (1921), *Treatise on Probability*, London: Macmillan and Co.
Keynes, John M. (1923), *A Tract on Monetary Reform*, London: Macmillan and Co.
Laidler, David and Roger J. Sandilands (2002), 'An early Harvard memorandum on anti-depression policies: an introductory note', *History of Political Economy*, 34(3), pp. 515–52.
London Times (1929), *Allyn Abbott Young: In Memoriam*, 8 March. Reprinted in Sandilands (1990), pp. 14–17.
Marshall, Alfred (1890), *Principles of Economics*, London: Macmillan and Co.
Mehrling, Perry G. (1997), *Money Interest and Public Interest*, Cambridge and London: Harvard University Press.
Mehrling, Perry G. and R.J. Sandilands (eds.) (1999), *Money and Growth: Selected Papers of Allyn Abbott Young*, London and New York: Routledge.
Meyer, Balthasar H. (1914), 'Certain considerations in railway rate making', American Economic Review, 4(1), pp. 69–80.
Mitchell, Wesley C. (1913), *Business Cycles*, Berkeley: University of California Press.
Mitchell, Wesley C. (1915), *The Making and Using of Index Numbers*.
Mitchell, Wesley (1924), 'The prospects of economics', in Tugwell, R.G. (ed.), *The Trend of Economics*, New York: Alfred A. Knopf.
Mitchell, Wesley C. (1927), *Business Cycles: The Problem and its Setting*, NBER.
Pigou, Arthur C. (1912), *Wealth and Welfare*, London: Macmillan and Co.
Pigou, Arthur C. (1920), *Economics of Welfare*, London: Macmillan and Co.
Pigou, Arthur C. (1928), *A Study in Public Finance*, London: Macmillan and Co.
Pressman, Steven (1999), *Fifty Major Economists*, London and New York: Routledge.
Ricardo, David (1810), *A High Price of Bullion, A Proof of the Depreciation of Bank Notes*, London: John Murray.
Ricardo, David (1815), *Essay on the Influence of a Low Price of Corn on the Profits of Stock*, London: John Murray.
Ricardo, David (1817), *Principles of Political Economy and Taxation*, London: John Murray.
Sandilands, Roger J. (ed.) (1990), *Journal of Economic Studies*, 17(3/4).
Schumpeter, Joseph A. (1914), Railway rate making: discussion, American Economic Review, 4(1), pp. 81–2.
Schumpeter, Joseph A. (1937), 'Allyn A. Young', *Encyclopaedia of Social Sciences*, New York: Macmillan, pp. 514–15.
Schumpeter, Joseph A. (1951/2003), *Ten Great Economists from Marx to Keynes*, San Diego: Simon Publications.

Schumpeter, Joseph A. (1954), *History of Economic Analysis*, New York: Oxford University Press.
Walras, Léon (1874; 1954), *Elements of Pure Economics*, Homewood: Irvin.
Walsh, C. M. (1901), *Measurements of General Exchange Value*, New York: Macmillan.
Young, Allyn (1912), 'Jevons's *Theory of Political Economy*', *American Economic Review*, 2(3), pp. 576–89. Reprinted in Young (1927a), pp. 213–31.
Young, Allyn (1913), 'Pigou's Wealth and Welfare', *Quarterly Journal of Economics*, 27(4), pp. 672–86. Reprinted in Mehrling and Sandilands (1999), pp. 86–96.
Young, Allyn (1914), 'Railway Rate Making: Discussion', *American Economic Review*, 4(1) Supplement (March), pp. 82–6.
Young, Allyn (1917), 'Do the statistics of the concentration of wealth in the United States mean what they are commonly assumed to mean?', *American Economic Review*, 7(1) Supplement (March). Reprinted in Young (1927a), pp. 95–107.
Young, Allyn (1920a), 'The economics of the treaty', *New Republic*, February 25, pp. 388–9.
Young, Allyn (1920b), 'Review of *Currency and Credit* by Ralph Hawtrey and *Stabilizing the Dollar* by Irving Fisher', *Quarterly Journal of Economics*, 34(2), pp. 520–32.
Young, Allyn (1923a), 'The trend of prices', *American Economic Review*, 13(1), pp. 5–14. Reprinted in Young (1927a), pp. 63–76.
Young, Allyn (1923b), 'Fisher's *The Making of Index Numbers*', *Quarterly Journal of Economics*, 37(2), pp. 342–64. Reprinted in Young (1927a), pp. 276–301.
Young, Allyn (1925a), 'Review of *Papers Relating to Political Economy* by F. Y. Edgeworth', *American Economic Review*, 15(4), pp. 721–4.
Young, Allyn (1925b), 'Review of *The Trend of Economics*', Quarterly Journal of Economics, 39(2), pp. 155–83. Reprinted in Young (1927a), pp. 232–60.
Young, Allyn (1927a), *Economic Problems: New and Old*, Boston and New York: Houghton Mifflin Company.
Young, Allyn (1927b), 'Economics as a field of research', *Quarterly Journal of Economics*, 42(1), pp. 1–25. Reprinted in Mehrling and Sandilands (1999), pp. 3–16.
Young, Allyn (1928a), 'English political economy', *Economica*, 8(22), pp. 1–15. Reprinted in Mehrling and Sandilands (1999), pp. 17–28.

9 Young's Estimate of His Contemporaries and Earlier Economists

Young, Allyn (1928b), 'Increasing returns and economic progress', *Economic Journal*, 38(152), pp. 527–42. Reprinted in Mehrling and Sandilands (1999), pp. 49–61.

Young, Allyn (1929a), 'Economics', *Encyclopaedia Britannica 1928*, London: The Encyclopaedia Britannica Company. Reprinted in Mehrling and Sandilands (1999), pp. 115–34.

Young, Allyn (1929b), 'Wages', *Encyclopaedia Britannica 1928*, London: The Encyclopaedia Britannica Company. Reprinted in Journal of Economic Studies (1990), 17(3/4), 137–42.

Young, Allyn (1929c), 'Review of *A Study in Public Finance* by Arthur C. Pigou', *Economic Journal*, 39(153), pp. 78–83.

Young, Allyn (1929d), 'Dear and cheap money', *Book of Popular Science 1929*, New York: The Grolier Society, pp. 4705–15. Reprinted in Mehrling and Sandilands (1999), pp. 307–21.

Young, Allyn (1929e), 'Money and prices', *Book of Popular Science 1929*, New York: The Grolier Society, pp. 5109–20. Reprinted in Mehrling and Sandilands (1999), pp. 337–51.

Young, Allyn (1990), 'Nicholas Kaldor's Notes on Allyn Young's LSE Lectures', 1927–29, *Journal of Economic Studies*, 17(3/4), pp. 18–114.

10

Concluding Remarks

Allyn Young emerges as a key figure in the American economic thought in the first three decades of the twentieth century. The contemporaries he knew in America and England included Richard T. Ely, Frank W. Taussig, Irving Fisher, Wesley Clair Mitchell, Thorstein Veblen, Joseph A. Schumpeter, Alfred Marshall, A.C. Pigou, John Maynard Keynes, William Beveridge, T.E. Gregory, Lionel Robbins and Ralph G. Hawtrey. He was an inspiring teacher and mentor to his famous students such as Edward Chamberlin, Frank Knight, Lauchlin Currie and Nicholas Kaldor. The fame he attained during his lifetime was due more to his role as a teacher, mentor and critic than to his published work. He was also much sought after for his role in public and national service. After his untimely death in 1929, he continued to live for a while in the hearts and memories of his students who benefitted from his creative teaching, from his generosity in terms of time and ideas, and from his humility in making himself available whenever asked.

But soon he became a relatively forgotten figure[1] of American economic thought until he was rediscovered by post-WWII development

---

[1] Schumpeter (1954, p. 875) in his *History of Economic Analysis* wrote: "This great economist and brilliant theorist is in the danger of being forgotten."

economists, and of late by new endogenous growth and trade theorists. In between, Kaldor's (1972) attack on neoclassical theory made liberal use of Young's ideas that he picked up as a student of Young's at the LSE during 1927–1929. With the publication of Charles Blitch's (1995) biography there was a further impetus to interest in Young. This interest, as Perry Mehrling and Roger Sandilands (1999) have pointed out, springs more from his contribution to economic thought than from his contribution to the economics profession. His celebrated article on increasing returns and economic progress (Young 1928a) is well known, and has been made the starting point of the developmental and growth issues analysed by post-war development economists, as well as "new growth" and "new trade" theorists. Publication of *Nicholas Kaldor's Notes on Young's LSE Lectures 1927–29* (Young 1990) brings out his range and depth of ideas in economic theory. But it is his work in monetary theory which is relatively less well known.[2] If Joseph Schumpeter (1937) is to be believed, it is here he came closest to giving full expression to his views.

Since Young died before he completed his treatise on monetary theory, and because the manuscript of his unfinished treatise was lost after his death, his monetary theory was pieced together by David Laidler (1993, 1998) and Mehrling (1996, 1997) from his scattered writings in the *Book of Popular Science* and his entries in *Encyclopaedia Britannica*, in *Outlines of Economics* (various issues) as well as in Young (1927, 1928b) and Eugene B. Riley (1925).[3] Many of these writings on monetary issues were put together in a volume by Mehrling and Sandilands (1999). Thus Young emerges as a man with astonishing range in economic theory, economic practice, business cycles, economic growth and monetary economics. There is more to Young than being merely a sought-after graduate teacher who supervised Ph.D. theses of his students such as Knight and Chamberlin.

Allyn Young was a deep thinker. Like an iceberg, which is far more underwater than above it, much of his thought lay buried in his mind

---

[2] Milton Friedman and Anna J. Schwartz (1963) failed to take account of his monetary contribution or even mention his name in their otherwise comprehensive *Monetary History of the United States*.

[3] This book was written under the overall supervision of Young and two chapters of this book (chapter viii on 'Money and Credit' and chapter ix on 'Banking') were specifically written by him.

than was visible in his published work. Even what he published had many far-reaching implications not obvious at first. The present chapter presents concluding thoughts on Young particularly pointing to the deeper implications of his analysis, the possible elements of the Allyn Young Paradigm (as gleaned from his various writings), and his legacy.

Implications of Young's Analysis

Young discarded neoclassical equilibrium theory in favour of disequilibrium. He was against ceteris paribus (or one-thing-at-a-time) theorising and favoured instead the togetherness of the economic phenomenon. This togetherness, in turn, leads not to general equilibrium but to increasing returns. He held that growth follows the law of cumulative causation. In this regard he stated that the division of labour in large part depends on the division of labour. It is not the internal economies of scale, but external economies which are the main source of increasing returns. A typical Marshallian representative firm sooner or later loses its identity and turns into a newly specialised firm. So, increasing returns are based on specialisation: firm-level as well as industrial specialisation. It is not the advance in the methods or techniques of production which accounts for economic progress. Rather it is the prior expansion of markets which led to the industrial revolution.[4] All this is well known and well understood in the literature. However, what is not so well known are some of the deeper implications of Young's disequilibrium analysis.

1. Young suggested that since the demand and supply curves are both downward sloping in the short term, and in the long run both are

---

[4] Young was of the opinion that it was the commercial revolution which paved the way for industrial revolution. "It is dangerous to assign to any single factor the leading rôle in that continuing economic revolution which has taken the modern world so far away from the world of a few hundred years ago. But is there any other factor which has a better claim to that role than the persisting search for markets? No other hypothesis so well unites economic history and economic theory. The Industrial Revolution of the eighteenth century has come to be generally regarded, not as a cataclysm brought about by certain inspired improvements in industrial technique, but as a series of changes related in an orderly way to prior changes in industrial organisation and to the enlargements of markets" (Young 1928a, p. 536).

shifting by the same set of forces, what is required is a theory of equilibrium rate of progress (or growth) which keeps the supply curve close up to the demand curve. Such an approach would keep an economy growing at an equilibrium (or optimum) rate without undue disruptions caused by the business cycles. Since business cycles are caused by mismatches in individual demand and supply, and not in aggregate demand and supply, this would require an activist monetary policy aimed at sector-specific interventions. This would also require the central bank to collect, collate and analyse sectoral information to be able to do so. With this information the central bank is in a better position to pinpoint the specific sectors where the productive capacity is seriously misaligned with demand, and where disproportionality crisis[5] is brewing in order to take corrective action. It may however be noted that Young viewed business cycles as integral to growth, so it is neither desirable nor practicable to eliminate them totally.

2. Increasing returns in Young are transmitted in the form of reduced costs and prices in the *market system* itself. Therefore, it will pay to make the market more *competitive* by allowing more internal and external competition. Much development literature, on the contrary, has sought to promote increasing returns in an anti-market framework. Inward-looking policies aimed at import substitution advocated after WWII are a good example of this. These policies not only advocated tariff protection but also quantitative protection in the form of import licensing, quotas, outright bans and exchange controls. Even Kaldor's advocacy of increasing returns for the manufacturing sector was based on a statist framework, which involved not only tariff protection but also dual exchange rates as well as the selective employment tax (SET). More recently, there has been a revival of the big push debate notably by Paul Krugman (1993) and Kevin Murphy et al.

---

[5] See Georgio Colacchio (2005) who interprets the logic of Young's analysis in terms of "a multi-sectoral model" (p. 1) and maintains that "disproportionality crisis must have been continually in Young's mind" (p. 334). He traces situations of disequilibrium to the failure to satisfy Say's Law which in the aggregate models consists of a discrepancy between saving and investment, and in the Youngian "multi-sectoral model" of "the rupture of the correct proportionality among the various branches of the economic system" (p. 334).

(1989).[6] For example, Krugman talks about a certain core of ideas called 'high development theory' which are still relevant. Invoking Albert Hirschman's (1958) backward and forward linkages as leading to economies of scale, he argued that the central concept of high development theory circa 1958 was the idea of economies of scale at the level of the individual plant translated into increasing returns at the aggregate level through pecuniary external economies (Krugman 1993, p. 22). Krugman also stressed that there was an intellectually solid case for some governmental promotion of industries as there may be some kind of market failure. Young's analysis, by contrast, appears to suggest a much more pro-market framework as a way forward.

3. Increasing returns are transmitted through the vehicle of *pecuniary external economies*, but much of the development literature seems to argue that they are a sign of market failure. Since external economies in general are thought to bring about a divergence of private and social benefit on the one hand, and private and social cost on the other, there is deemed to be a misallocation of resources through overinvestment in some sectors and underinvestment in others. For example, Rosenstein-Rodan (1961) stated that pecuniary external economies cause a divergence between private and social marginal net product, and since they are all pervading and frequent, the price system does not put an economy on an optimal path. In the Youngian analysis, reduced costs and prices come about through a well-functioning competitive market system, so pecuniary external economies are *not a sign of its failure* but rather of its *success*.

4. In Young, increasing returns are *generalised* (or macroeconomic), rather than confined to specific sectors like manufacturing, so growth is best achieved in the framework of '*no favours, no handicaps*'. If increasing returns sectors cannot be identified for policy purposes, the best way forward then is to level the field for everyone, and let winners and losers emerge from the competitive race itself. But most development literature appears to think that increasing returns are confined to

---

[6] The idea of the big push was first put forward by Paul Rosenstein-Rodan (1943) in the context of East European reconstruction after WWII.

manufacturing, and therefore advocates protection to industry in the form of tariff and quantitative protection as well as direct subsidies. Smith had stated that the division of labour is more fully carried out in manufacturing than in agriculture, but he was against granting favours to any sector. Similarly, in Young, the broader implication of competition is to level the playing field, also in a 'no favours, no handicaps' framework. Protection to one sector constitutes disprotection to others, upsets the reciprocal exchange relationships and hence retards growth.[7]

However, since the classical economists considered agriculture to be the diminishing returns sector, there was a general gloom regarding growth prospects of the economy as a whole, particularly since David Ricardo. Ricardo had argued that an increase in population would lead to more demand for food; this in turn would require cultivation of inferior grades of land, the share of rents would rise and the share of profits will fall and may touch zero, bringing about a stationary state where accumulation and output would come to a standstill. Young pointed out that the law of diminishing returns may be true as a tendency, but was not necessarily true as a prophecy. In particular, it could be overcome by other powerful tendencies in the system such as improvements in and cheapening of the means of transport, and technical change in agriculture. The law of diminishing returns operated in an elastic manner and was not a threat to general growth prospects in the long run.

5. *Elasticities* of demand and supply play a crucial role in deciding which sectors will grow faster than the others. Sectors where demand is *inelastic*, or with an increase in supply soon becomes so, also benefit as productive resources are released for other uses. This implies that over-time sectors with inelastic demand will shrink and those with elastic demand would expand in relative importance altering the production structure of an economy. This is borne out by experience which suggests that as an economy grows in per capita income terms, the share

---

[7] Studies on the effective protection rates suggest that protection to industry constitutes disprotection to agriculture and exports.

of agriculture and mining declines, and the share of manufacturing and services increases.

6. *Institutions and laws* underlying a competitive system play a key role in growth. Adam Smith had put much emphasis on this point. In his day, mercantilism was quite widespread, and natural liberty could not be taken for granted. So he spent much time and energy in analysing various systems of political economy to arrive at the one best suited to growth. His conclusion was that the system of natural liberty was the best in this regard, and it establishes itself naturally once all preferences and restraints are removed. The state then confines itself to just a few basic tasks such as defence, justice and public works. In Young the role of the state was to be seen in an evolutionary perspective. For example, industrial fluctuations, advent of monopoly capitalism, and war imposed more responsibilities on the state. With these changes the area of public interest was enlarged. So the state had to create new and independent institutions to control monopoly and public utilities, as well as industrial fluctuations. But Young agreed with Smith that growth was better facilitated with more rather than less competition. For this reason he did not like artificially created monopolies like patents, the abolition of which, according to him, would not much retard progress. While Young did not like complete laissez-faire, he did not like unwarranted intervention either, particularly where competition could be trusted to deliver the desired outcomes.

For Young, even imperfect competition was a part of competition. Things like product differentiation, goodwill, trade marks, brands, and so on, did not mean absence of competition, but only an imperfect working of competition. Here competition took the form of nonprice competition where each producer tried to be a bit different from the others. The entry of other firms and availability of close substitutes kept a lid on producers' profits. While some imperfections were normal in the working of competition, it did not imply that artificially created market power, for example patents or protection, was a good basis for promoting growth. Despite the emergence of imperfect competition, and also of monopoly capitalism in certain areas, Young believed that competition was the rule rather than an exception. Profits in the long run tended to be zero or negative, and the case

against monopoly was overstated as monopolists did not earn as high a profit as the theory suggested.
7. Young was quick to see that the so-called laws of economics were just *tendencies*, which could be overcome by powerful counterforces. Where the preponderant influence at a given time would lie depends on the relative strengths of tendencies and countertendencies. Since the forces of disequilibrium are continuously defeating those of equilibrium, disequilibrium is the predominant tendency in an economic system. Likewise, the law of diminishing returns was not erroneous as a tendency but useless as a prophecy, as it was counteracted by more powerful forces such as improvement in agricultural technique and cheapening of the means of transport. To take another example, Young stated that concentration statistics at a given time show that forces of concentration are dominant over forces of diffusion. Both tendencies occur simultaneously in a system. One should not exaggerate the importance of one to the neglect of the other. In general, Young considered that despite the emergence of monopoly capital in certain areas (such as public utilities—railways, water transport, gas, water supply, telecommunications, etc.), competition was the predominant force.
8. Finally, Young's analysis appears to suggest that an economy is not so much resource constrained as *opportunity constrained*. This directly leads us to the 'economics of opportunity' as a more dominant paradigm than the 'economics of scarcity'. Since resources are scarce, they are thought to pose a formidable constraint on the satisfaction of human wants. Resources have opportunity costs. In a production-possibility-curve framework, if a nation wants more of one good, it necessarily implies less of the other. Post-war development economists took this problem of scarcity so seriously that they posed the problem of growth in terms of constraints such as the wage goods constraint, the foreign exchange constraint, administrative decision-making constraint or the saving constraint. Young agreed that resources are scarce, but for the same reason they are also productive. Scarcity and

productivity were two sides of the same coin.[8] So it does not pay to highlight one side of the coin to the total neglect of the other.

Young also argued that increasing returns are not negated by their costs. In that case no real economic progress would be possible, a conclusion which goes against common sense. Resources are scarce, taken individually they are subject to the law of diminishing returns, and appear to constitute a formidable constraint on the satisfaction of human wants and growth. But how is it that a competitive market system produces increasing returns, growth and improved standards of living of even an ordinary worker? Young appeared to suggest that there is a fallacy of composition involved. What appears true at the micro level is not necessarily true at the macro level. In a dynamic setting, when one lets go of ceteris paribus, and when the economic phenomenon is taken in its togetherness, the result is increasing returns, growth and a rise in per capita incomes. Even a small trading country, where natural resources may not be abundant, can transform its growth possibilities through international trade. It appears that Young was attempting a new vision of the economic process, a vision where the dominant paradigm is that of 'opportunity' provided by a growing competitive market, not that of debilitating 'scarcity'.

Allyn Young Paradigm

Paul Samuelson stated that Young wrote little not only because of his family responsibilities but also because he had not worked out a coherent paradigm which differed creatively from Alfred Marshall, Irving Fisher, A.C. Pigou and other neoclassical authors.[9] It is true that Young did not leave behind a treatise with his own paradigm based on disequilibrium, but in his last days, as William Beveridge (1929) points out, he had felt ready to write one. What that paradigm would have been is in the realm of speculation. Here we attempt to put together various elements of his

---

[8] However, he also insisted that one cannot increase productivity by artificially creating scarcity.
[9] Letter from Samuelson dated 4 June 1997 to Roger J. Sandilands. See Sandilands (1999, p. 455).

paradigm as gleaned from his various writings, which fortunately have now been largely put together in accessible volumes, and from the notes taken by some of his students such as Maurice Allen and Nicholas Kaldor. The elements of what possibly might have been the Allyn Young paradigm are sketched below:

1. Role of Money

Young pointed out that Fisher's equation of exchange was a mere truism and does not take one very far into the monetary theory. According to this equation money supply affects the general price level, leaving relative prices unchanged. By contrast, Young saw money as affecting the real economy. An increase in money supply affected the price level, but more importantly, it also affected the relative prices. For Young money was central to the study of a modern economic system. Once this is recognised prices become antecedent to values contrary to what the classical economists thought. Exchange values are determined in the actual process of exchange, and there they emerge as prices. Young believed in a monetary standard based on gold, which is directly exchangeable in gold or gold coin, and which is used in clearing all outstanding balances. Like Hawtrey, Young regarded credit (or demand deposits) as an unstable component of money supply. Credit therefore needed to be controlled if business cycles were to be moderated. This could be done by the central bank of a country which was responsible for not just its own solvency but for the solvency of the whole banking system. But unlike Hawtrey, Young favoured public works on their own merit rather than linking them with money creation.

2. Theory of Value

Young (1911) maintained that prices were antecedent to values. Like W.S. Jevons he believed that the theory of demand and the theory of supply are more properly the theory of the rate of demand and the rate of supply. The flow of demand (money) and the flow of supply (goods) from the opposite direction meet to form prices. If a snapshot of this meeting point is taken, or the flow of demand and the flow of supply are suddenly congealed at the meeting point, we have a theory of static equilibrium. From this it followed that prices applied only to the marginal units exchanged; and for the rest valuation was at best an estimate based on imputed values. Young argued that frank recognition of the primacy of prices to values would not much alter the existing static theory of value. Young however was more interested in the dynamic theory of price formation where the flows of demand and supply are not suddenly arrested but continue unabated. This disequilibrium price theory would link up the theory of value to the theory of business cycles, which themselves are a part of growth.

3. Theory of Business Cycles

By 1908, Young had outlined that business cycles arise from a mismatch in valuation of things (or relative prices). But it was only in 1923 that he wrote a full chapter on business cycles as a co-author of *Outlines of Economics*. Perhaps Young wanted to be on a firmer ground in his monetary views by rooting them in banking statistics. For this purpose he collected a vast volume of banking statistics, which were published in a series of four articles from 1924 to 1927 in the *Review of Economics and Statistics* and later collected together in Young (1928b). In the upward phase of the cycle, Young stated that the distribution of income shifts leading to change in the structure of demand in favour of luxuries. This in turn leads to the creation of large capacities in this area overshooting demand, and a point ultimately comes when the structure of demand and structure of installed capacity are mismatched. A modern business system is held together by contracts, and one man's failure to meet his obligations affects others to meet theirs. Once this happens, the system of contracts breaks down and a crisis results in which dealers are overstocked and manufacturers find themselves over-expanded and overcapitalised. Young believed that business cycles could be controlled by central banks working independently in the public interest based on discretionary monetary policy rather than on fixed rules. In Young's opinion, the central banks needed discretion to act as no two situations are alike. Young was also of the view that it was possible to moderate business cycles by building up reserves, and through open market operations. He was sceptical of the discount rate as an instrument of control particularly in the American context where trade as a proportion of total economic activity was quite low as compared to Britain. Young viewed business cycles as a part of growth; it was neither possible nor desirable to completely control them as that would slow down growth.

4. Theory of Imperfect Competition

Young had already collected various pieces of the imperfect competition theory like product differentiation, trade marks, brand names, selling costs, goodwill, freedom of entry by other firms and availability of close substitutes, excess capacity, and so on, much before Chamberlin (1933) had published his famous *Theory of Monopolistic Competition*. For example, Young pointed out that imperfect competition, the field lying between pure competition and pure monopoly, was closer to reality, and competition largely took the form of non-price competition as every seller tried to be a bit different from others. Selling costs (costs not related to production but to gaining extra market share) are competitive investments and cannot be termed as social wastes. Although they were not production costs, they formed a minuscule share of total expenses. Availability of close substitutes and entry by other firms limits the extent of profits. The price charged is a bit higher than what would prevail in pure competition, but competition still prevails and sellers cannot earn excessively high profits. Imperfect competition does not imply absence of competition, only its imperfect working. The presence of excess capacity in this market is a sign of growth where producers build capacity ahead of demand, and then wait for demand to catch up (Young 1990, p. 4). Nor is excess capacity a sign of monopoly where the producer tries to use his price policy to charge a high price. In railways and other public utilities, excess capacity was a normal feature of growth. But Young never himself put all the pieces of imperfect competition together in the form of a coherent theory, which of course was done by Chamberlin under his supervision. Many of Young's students attested to the fact that most of the concepts used by Chamberlin had been discussed by Young in class including the question of excess capacity. Young however differed from the static view of competition taken by Chamberlin.

5. Theory of Growth

Young stated that an economic system was characterised more by disequilibrium than by equilibrium. The forces of disequilibrium were continually defeating those of equilibrium. Change therefore is progressive and propagates itself in a cumulative way. Growth follows the law of cumulative causation and is based on the two-way relationship between the division of labour and market size. Increasing returns have more to do with external economies rather than internal economies of scale of individual firms. Increasing returns are not based on the relationship between prime and supplementary costs. Large production rather than large-scale production permits increasing returns (ibid., p. 54). There are no limits to increasing returns except the limit beyond which demand is not elastic. Different sectors grow at different rates depending on the elasticities of demand and supply. Young made use of the Marshall-Edgeworth idea of reciprocal demand (or offer curve) to state that if commodities are produced competitively (under conditions of elastic demand), an increase in supply of one commodity is an increase in demand for other commodities, and it must be supposed that every increase in demand will call forth an increase in supply.[10] Young stated that increasing returns will not be negated by their costs so as to secure an equilibrium of costs and advantages, as the fact of economic progress testifies. Increasing returns are economies of capitalistic and roundabout methods of production but they are limited by the size of the market. Once the process of endogenous growth is set in motion, it draws forth the necessary saving and investment.[11] Economic progress comes about by the forces engendered within the economic system. This growth is based more on differentiation of economic activity than integration. Different industries split up into a number of specialised undertakings or industries, as the size of the market expands. Thus imperfect competition based on product differen-

---

[10] Although Young stated that money was central to an economic system, he made use of offer curves or barter terms of trade while analysing growth. Among all neoclassical tools, perhaps the idea of reciprocal demand came closest to explaining the cumulative growth process. Young was aware that equilibrium under barter was indeterminate, so the use of barter (reciprocal exchange) suited him in the analysis of the disequilibrium process of growth.

[11] This implies that capital accumulation is not an independent engine of growth as use of capital in the production process is limited by the size of the market.

tiation is a part of the broader process of industrial diffusion. With increasing returns monopoly is not inevitable as many economists of standing like Piero Sraffa (1926) thought. Young believed that competition (even though working imperfectly) is the rule rather than exception. The importance of monopoly capitalism in the modern industrial system should not be overstated. Increasing returns in the system are transmitted in the form of reduced costs and prices through the vehicle of pecuniary external economies, so a competitive market system is essential to their transmission. Some market power may arise as a result of imperfect working of competition, but Young was against artificially created market power in the form of patents and protectionist privileges to promote growth.

Young also propounded the concept of an equilibrium (or optimum) rate of growth as a legitimate subject to be explored in economic theory. He considered this to be a more important field of enquiry than static equilibrium. An equilibrium rate of growth can occur if the supply curve in each sector is kept close up to the demand curve. This requires a sector-specific monetary policy; or a policy targeting those sectors where the disproportionality is brewing. Young had stated that business cycles do not result from mismatch of aggregate demand and aggregate supply but due to mismatch in sectoral demand and supply. He had also opposed Fisher's approach of targeting the general price index on the grounds that business cycles manifest themselves not in changes in the general price level but in changes in relative prices. Therefore, he had recommended targeting a price index of a few commodities which were more sensitive to the business cycles. He also favoured discretion in the conduct of monetary policy if specific sectors were to be targeted as opposed to Fisher's rule-based approach. The implication is clear: while Young had a generalised approach to increasing returns, he had a sector-specific (including a group of sensitive sectors) approach to business cycles. Thus an equilibrium rate of growth in the long run becomes possible without major upheavals in the short term through this selective approach to business cycles. In other words, the path to long-term equilibrium growth lies through the moderation of business cycles.

6. Theory of Distribution

Young believed that while marginal productivity theory was a good way of stating the problem of distribution, it was not a solution to it. At the micro level it was a good rule of thumb to equate factor rewards with their marginal contributions.[12] But this neither determined the factor prices nor their overall use. At the macro level it was the relative scarcity of a factor, its demand in relation to supply, that determined factor prices and their overall use. Young also stated that scarcity and productivity meant the same thing. So whether earnings of capital or labour are attributed to their relative scarcity or their productivity it amounted to the same thing. The fact that the resources are scarce implied that for that very reason they are also productive. Productivity is not attributed to free resources like air or oceans or rivers. But when these forces of nature are harnessed in the form of ships, boats, ports, docks, airplanes, airports, and so on, they become productive. This implies that productivity is attributed to the harness and not to the free resource. Productivity has some social aspects as well. For example if a British worker migrates to the US where land and capital are relatively abundant, his productivity increases without any corresponding increase in his technical effectiveness. So a relatively abundant factor will have a lower factor reward, while a relatively scarce factor would have a higher reward. Factor reward therefore is not a matter entirely due to that factor alone; its relative scarcity in relation to other factors is also important. So Young stated that marginal productivity theory is only a partial explanation of factor rewards. The doctrine that 'rewards tend to be proportionate to products' taken by itself has no particular significance except as a corrective to an even more misleading notion that factor rewards are in no manner related to productivity (Young 1929; Mehrling and Sandilands 1999, p. 129).

Young was influenced by the Ricardian theory of rent and discussed rent as a differential both at the extensive and intensive margins of cultivation. Rent did not arise when the best lands were available for occupation in a new territory. Rent arose as a differential only when inferior lands were brought under cultivation. Young stated that it was true both that rent was and was not a cost. From the individual point of view rent was a cost, but from the social point of view it was not. Young did not

---

[12] Currie (1997) stated that factor reward was what was *attributed* to a factor, not its *contribution*.

agree with Henry George that increases in land values are unearned increments (Ely et al. 1923, pp. 418–21). To the extent they are anticipated they are discounted. To the extent they are not anticipated one has to take into account unearned decrement as well. So there is nothing unearned about the rise in land values. Young regarded rent as neither a bounty of nature (as in Adam Smith) nor a charge due to the niggardliness of nature (as in David Ricardo) but merely a distributive problem in line with J.S. Mill.

In the explanation of wages, Young held that the formula of supply and demand was not very helpful. Neither an increase in the supply of labour will reduce wages nor a reduction of real wages would increase employment. The actual wages received are determined by an agreement between the worker and his employer. The position of a worker is relatively weaker as he cannot hold out for higher wages indefinitely because of the necessity of making a living. A worker also does not have a very accurate idea of what his services are worth to the employer. He may also have few alternative employment options. Under these circumstances, his wages are likely to be closer to the minimum he would accept than to the maximum the employer would give. If a worker is able to bargain in a group as in collective bargaining, his disadvantages may be reduced.

Interest could be a return on the advances of money or it could be attributed to the services of capital goods. A society has to divert a part of its income from producing goods for immediate requirements to the production of capital goods to satisfy future wants. This requires postponement of the present consumption or waiting. So interest is a premium or reward for this waiting. The interest rate, like any other competitive price, would be fixed at the point where the demand and supply of investment funds is in equilibrium. Short-term movements in interest rates are linked to business cycles; in the long run they show constancy and are linked to such factors as 'impatience', 'time preference' or 'sacrifice involved in waiting'.[13]

---

[13] While in Keynes money affects the real sector through changes in the interest rate, in Young money affects the real sector through its effect on relative prices. In Young's opinion, industrialists were guided by the 'market' rather than the rate of interest in the extent of their operations provided all competitors pay the same. See Young (1990, p. 82).

Profits in a stationary state are zero; in the actual world they arise because society is subject to change and competition does not work perfectly. Profits can be thought of as the 'reward for enterprise' where this may mean taking advantage of maladjustments in prices, taking chances and acting on reasoned probabilities. In the long run, pure profits may be negative or zero, so are not a cost to society. In that case they do not exert a claim on the social dividend, and the entrepreneurial function gets performed without a cost to society. Profits are in the nature of prizes of competition, so socially it is more important that they should be obtainable than obtained.

7. Circular Flow Model

In his discussion of 'social dividend', Young (Ely et al. 1908) constructed a circular flow model of an economy which depicts the togetherness of economic phenomenon in terms of various flows. In this regard, Young made a distinction between social dividend and annual product; while the former is largely the outcome of past work and effort, the latter is very largely a provision for future wants. Young linked the discussion of social dividend with the factor rewards, making entrepreneurs at the centre of the circular flow process. "There is thus a continuous flow of money income through the hands of entrepreneurs, appearing first in the form of the prices paid for an entrepreneur's goods, then emerging in the form of rent, wages, and interest that the entrepreneur pays for the service of the factors in production, then reappearing as prices paid for other goods, and so on in a continually recurring cycle of income and outgo" (pp. 448–49). While prices paid for consumers' share in social dividend constitute the fund which pays for the annual product, a part of the money may be loaned to the entrepreneurs for production aimed at future consumption. Therein lies the explanation for interest—a reward for waiting. The rate of interest thus makes possible social balancing of present and future wants. While competition among producers would ensure that labourers, landlords and capitalist are paid their marginal contribution to the total product, from another point of view, the expenditures of land, labour and capital are themselves potent factors in determining the value of things which make up the social dividend. Thus marginal productivity is both the cause and effect of wages, rent and interest.

8. Role of the State

Smith had laid much stress on the institutional arrangements underlying natural liberty which established itself once all preferences and restraints are removed. In such a system the role of the state was confined to defence, justice and public works. Young interpreted Smith as a champion of competition rather than a champion of laissez-faire. For Young the role of the state was to be seen in relation to the stage of society. As stated above, with the advent of business cycles, public utilities, monopoly capitalism in certain sectors and war, the area of public interest was enlarged and the state had to assume more responsibilities. Young, as also stated above, liked neither complete laissez-faire nor undue interference in economic matters. He had great faith in independent institutions, which acting in the public interest, would promote more competition and more communal welfare. They will therefore act as saviours of capitalism and would save it from its excesses. Unlike Karl Marx, Joseph Schumpeter or Thorstein Veblen, Young was optimistic in his prognosis of both capitalism and democracy.[14] Young had great conviction in the democratic process in meeting various challenges. Capitalism would not collapse under the weight of its own contradictions nor from its successes. The democratic process could be counted upon in moderating various strains in the form of business cycles, unemployment, inequality or monopoly. He did not expect the process to completely solve them, but the process was resilient enough to take the bite off the problems which emerge from time to time. In this Young has been proved right by events; while socialism and communism have collapsed because of their own contradictions, democracy and capitalism have thrived, albeit in a more humane form.

---

[14] Young (1990, p. 91) thought that political democracy was the result of economic democracy. Individualism in philosophy was the result of commercial change and not vice versa.

Young's Legacy

Young was as much interested in the method of economics as in economics itself. He disliked a sharp distinction between the *inductive* method of the historical school and the *abstract deductive* method of English political economy. In any practical research both were complementary. He was also against a sharp bifurcation between economic theory and practice. For theory was useless unless it was helpful in solving communal problems. As a teacher he was both creative and inspiring. The monetary thought which he developed in his Harvard lectures continued to live as an oral tradition there in much the same way as Marshall's monetary theory at Cambridge (Morgenstern 1929; Reprinted in Sandilands 2009). As a critic, he had the academic width and depth to correct some of the notions of the neoclassicals such as Pigou, Marshall and Fisher. Above all, economics was an eminently practical subject for him, and therefore at least as much an art as science.

Young avoided *extreme* views about the capitalist system or the discipline of economics. Thus he disagreed with Veblen's excessively cynical view that capitalism produced nothing but conspicuous consumption, unemployment, monopoly and social wastes. He also disagreed with him that economics was based on hedonistic psychology. The so-called psychological postulates were nothing but commonplace observations of everyday life. He also discounted the Marxian ideology of class struggle as unscientific in that he viewed it as an invitation to participate in it. He appeared to suggest that if socialism was inevitable as the next stage of historical development, why propagate the idea of a revolution or class struggle. While commending historical studies for giving us wisdom, he discounted their tendency to *decipher* universal and binding laws akin to physical sciences. While commending the use of mathematics and statistics in economic research, he cautioned that completely abstract systems divorced from practical realities were not economics. While viewing money as central to an economic system, it's more important impact was on relative prices rather than on the price level. Thus Fisher's equation of exchange did not take us very far into the monetary theory.

His views almost always tended to be rooted in *reality*. He was fascinated by the market form lying between pure competition and monopoly as closer to reality. His keen observation told him that the case against monopoly was overstated. A monopolist did not charge as high a price as the theory suggested. Profits in the long run got imputed to the other factor rewards, leaving pure profits at best a negligible sum. This implies that they make almost no claim on the social dividend, and that society gets its entrepreneurial function done at virtually no cost. While Smith was ranged against mercantilism, Young did not dismiss it out of hand, trusting businessmen's mercantilist instincts of persistent search for markets, and holding the commercial revolution to be the precursor of the industrial revolution. He saw values arising in the process of exchange where they emerged as prices, so the common sense based on common observation dictated that prices were antecedent to values in contrast to classical authors who had reversed the sequence.

Just as Young had an endogenous view of growth, he also had an *endogenous view of the democratic process*.[15] The endogenous forces unleashed by this process would cure the system of its excesses. In other words, the system would be reformed by the very forces engendered within the system. Indeed, the democratic process fostered the endogenous production of new ideas, even if they be contrary to the continuance of the system itself. The so-called socialist ideas came about in democratic societies, and specific actions aimed at giving those ideas concrete shape also happened there.[16] His abiding faith in democracy's ability to sort things out can perhaps be seen as one of the major legacies left by him in addition to his contribution to the theory of value, distribution, business cycles, growth, money and banking, index numbers and imperfect competition. Marx,

---

[15] It is the constant tension between 'the money interest and the public interest' in the American economic system, to borrow Mehrling's (1997) phrase, which in a broader sense keeps the democratic process alive and contributes to its ability to reform.

[16] Young (1912; Mehrling and Sandilands 1999, p. 84) stated that socialism as an unfolding of democracy was a socialism with its teeth drawn. Socialism as a creed was an abstraction, and if this abstraction was given a concrete content it ceased to be socialism. On the other hand, he described the idea of class struggle as 'ugly' and 'repellent' and this route to socialism was a strict 'no-no' for him. He was of the opinion that America's institutions were too deeply rooted, and too carefully selected through the long process of social evolution to suddenly collapse under the pressure of the moment.

Schumpeter, Young and Veblen had all speculated on the future of capitalism; from hindsight it is Young who appears nearer the mark than others.

References

Beveridge, William (1929), 'Allyn Abbott Young', *Economica*, 25 (April), pp. 1–3.

Blitch, Charles (1995), *Allyn Young: The Peripatetic Economist*, Basingstoke and London: Macmillan Press Ltd.

Chamberlin, Edward (1933), *The Theory of Monopolistic Competition*, Cambridge: Harvard University Press.

Colacchio, Georgio (2005), 'Reconstructing Allyn A. Young's Theory of Increasing Returns', *Journal of the History of Economic Thought*, 27(3), pp. 321–44.

Currie, Lauchlin (1997), 'Implications of an endogenous theory of growth in Allyn Young's macroeconomic concept of increasing returns', *History of Political Economy*, 29, pp. 413–43.

Ely, Richard T., Thomas S. Adams, Max O. Lorenz and Allyn A. Young (1908), *Outlines of Economics*, New York: The Macmillan Company.

Ely, Richard T., Thomas S. Adams, Max O. Lorenz and Allyn A. Young (1923), *Outlines of Economics*, New York: The Macmillan Company.

Friedman, Milton and Anna J. Schwartz (1963), *A Monetary History of the United States 1867–1960*, NBER, Princeton: Princeton University Press.

Hirschman, Albert O. (1958), *The Strategy of Economic Development*, New Haven: Yale University Press.

Kaldor, Nicholas (1972), 'The irrelevance of equilibrium economics', *Economic Journal*, 82, pp. 1237–55.

Krugman, Paul (1993), 'Toward a counter counterrevolution in development theory', *Annual Conference on Development Economics*, 1992, pp. 15–38.

Laidler, David (1993), 'Hawtrey, Harvard and the origins of Chicago tradition', *Journal of Political Economy*, 101(6), pp. 11068–1103.

Laidler, David (1998), 'More on Hawtrey, Harvard and Chicago', *Journal of Economic Studies*, 25(1), pp. 4–24.

Mehrling, Perry G. (1996), 'The Monetary Thought of Allyn Abbott Young', *History of Political Economy*, 28(4), pp. 607–32.

Mehrling, Perry G. (1997), *The Money Interest and the Public Interest*, Cambridge and London: Harvard University Press.

Mehrling, Perry G. and R.J. Sandilands (1999), *Money and Growth: Selected Papers of Allyn Abbott Young*, London and New York: Routledge.

Morgenstern, Oskar (1929), 'Allyn Abbott Young', *Zeitschrift für Nationalökonomie*, 1 (May), pp. 143–45. English translation by Susan Sirc printed in Sandilands (2009).

Murphy, K. M., A. Schleifer and R. Vishny (1989), 'Industrialisation and the big push', *Journal of Political Economy*, 97(5), pp. 1003–26.

Riley, Eugene B. (1925), Economics for Secondary Schools, Boston and New York: Houghton Mifflin Company.

Rosenstein-Rodan, Paul (1943), 'Problems of industrialisation in eastern and south-eastern Europe', *Economic Journal*, 53, pp. 202–11.

Rosenstein-Rodan, Paul (1961), 'Notes on the theory of the big push', in H.S. Ellis and H.C. Wallaich (ed.), *Economic Development of Latin America*, London: Macmillan.

Sandilands, Roger J. (1999), 'New evidence on Allyn Young's style and influence as a teacher', *Journal of Economic Studies*, 26(6), pp. 453–80.

Sandilands, Roger J. (2009), 'New evidence on Allyn Young's style and influence as a teacher', in Robert Leeson (ed.), *Archival Insights into the Evolution of Economics, Volume V: Economics in the United States*, London: Palgrave Macmillan, pp. 134–79.

Schumpeter, Joseph A. (1937), 'Young, Allyn Abbott', *Encyclopaedia of Social Sciences*, 15, New York: Macmillan, pp. 514–15.

Schumpeter, Joseph A. (1954; 1982), *History of Economic Analysis*, London: Allen and Unwin.

Sraffa, Piero (1926), 'The laws of return under competitive conditions', *Economic Journal*, 36, pp. 535–50.

Young, Allyn A. (1911), 'Some limitations of the value concept', *Quarterly Journal of Economics*, 25(3), pp. 409–28. Reprinted in Young (1927), pp. 198–212.

Young, Allyn A. (1912), *Socialism Lecture Notes*, St. Louis: Washington University, April. Reprinted in Mehrling and Sandilands (1999, pp. 74–85).

Young, Allyn A. (1927), *Economic Problems: New and Old*, Boston and New York: Houghton Mifflin Company.

Young, Allyn A. (1928a), 'Increasing returns and economic progress', *Economic Journal*, 38(152), pp. 527–42.

Young, Allyn A. (1928b), *An Analysis of Bank Statistics for the United States*, Cambridge: Harvard University Press.

Young, Allyn A. (1929), 'Economics', *Encyclopaedia Britannica 1928*, London: The Encyclopaedia Britannica Company. Reprinted in Mehrling and Sandilands (1999), pp. 115–34.

Young, Allyn A. (1990), 'Nicholas Kaldor's Notes on Allyn Young's LSE Lectures 1927–29', *Journal of Economic Studies*, 17(3/4), pp. 18–114.

Author Index[1]

A
Adams, Henry C., 34
Adams, Herbert Baxter, 34n1
Adams, Thomas S., 3, 8, 38, 39, 215n14, 216n16, 219n20, 223n26, 235, 236, 238, 271
Aghion, Philippe, 120
Allen, Maurice, 115, 312
Allison, James E., 179
Angell, James W., 2, 238, 245
Ayres, Colonel Leonard R., 199

B
Bagehot, Walter, 6, 69, 78, 83, 84n8, 86–89, 86n14, 261
  Economic Studies, 86
Baker, Ray Stannard, 203
Balogh, Thomas, 115
Barber, William J., 229
Beer, George L., 198
Bellamy, Edward, 167
Bentham, Jeremy, 291n15
Beveridge, Sir William, 11, 14, 109, 257, 303, 311
Bland, Hubert, 167n14
Blaug, Mark, 285
Blitch, Charles P., ix, x, 1, 2, 7n3, 8, 9, 11, 11n5, 14, 35, 37, 39, 42n14, 54n20, 61, 75, 84, 179, 196, 196n7, 197, 199n10, 203, 209, 212, 215n14, 224n29, 231n40, 236, 236n2, 236n3, 241, 246, 248, 250, 253, 268, 271, 283, 304

---

[1] Note: Page numbers followed by 'n' refer to notes.

Blivin, Bruce, 208
Blomström, M., 113n19
Bober, M. M., 7, 168
   Marx's Interpretation of History, 7, 168
Bohm-Bawerk, Eugen von, 34n1, 297
Bowley, A.L., 81, 134
   Mathematical Groundwork of Economics, 81, 134
Bowman, Isaiah, 196, 198
Boynton, Arthur J., 180

C

Cabet, Étienne, 167
Cairns, J. E., 69, 83
Cannan, Edwin, 8, 10n4, 239, 293
Carlson, Valdemar, 245
Cassel, Gustav, 211, 223n27, 264, 297
   Money and Foreign Exchanges After 1914, 264
Catchings, W., 231n40
Chamberlin, Edward H., x, 2, 6, 7, 26, 236, 248, 249, 253, 253n25, 256, 256n31, 261, 290, 303, 304, 314
   Theory of Monopolistic Competition, 7, 26, 248, 249, 314
Chandra, Ramesh, 100n6, 103n11, 112, 113, 121
Clapham, J.M., 112, 113
Clark, Colin, 7n3, 248
Clark, John Bates, 34n1, 41, 52, 58, 136n3
Clark, William, 167n14

Clemenceau, Georges, 262, 263
Colacchio, Georgio, 306n5
Cole, Arthur H., 241, 248
Commons, John R., 34, 35
Cooley, Charles, 87n15
Coolidge, President Calvin, 24, 196
Cooper, Lane, 50
Cournot, Antoine A., 5, 15, 18, 29, 52, 53n19, 78, 83, 129, 248, 261, 266, 288–290
   De L'Enchainement Des Idées Fondamentales, 83
   Researches into the Mathematical Principles of the Theory of Wealth, 288
Currie, Lauchlin, x, 2, 7, 19, 44, 96, 111–118, 229, 229n36, 231, 231n40, 244, 246, 247, 264n2, 303
   The Supply and Control of Money in the United States, 247

D

Day, Clive, 196, 198
De Chazeau, Melvin G., 243
Denison, E., 121
Deutscher, Patrick, 224n28
Dewsnup, Ernest R., 180
Diggins, John P., 59
Dixon, Frank H., 180
Dorfman, Joseph, 40, 58n26, 59
   Thorstein Veblen and His America, 58n26
Dulles, Eleanor Lansing, 241, 242, 244
Dulles, John Foster, 200, 201
Dupuit, A.J.E.J., 295

E

Edgeworth, Francis Y., 15, 16, 26, 27, 30, 78, 134, 180, 181, 237, 238, 261, 265–268, 288, 289, 296, 297, 315
Mathematical Psychics, 265
Ellis, Howard S., 256
Ellsworth, Paul Theodore, 264n2
Ely, Richard T., 2, 3, 7, 8, 11, 13, 17, 33–43, 61n31, 69n1, 70, 72, 75, 84n9, 89n17, 135, 139, 144, 148, 157, 158, 170n16, 185, 187n5, 188, 208n3, 210n9, 213–217, 219, 228, 228n34, 238, 249–251, 261, 273, 278, 291–294, 292n16, 303, 318, 319
Labour Movement in America, 42
Outlines of Economics, 2, 7, 17, 33, 34, 38, 39, 69n1, 156, 273, 291
Property and Contract, 293
Emmett, Ross B., 12n7, 254

F

Fetter, Frank W., 246
Fine, B., 121
Fisher, Irving, 3, 16, 25, 28, 208, 216–220, 222, 228, 229n35, 239, 244, 246n18, 261, 271n6, 273, 274, 276–282, 303, 311, 312, 316, 321
Purchasing Power of Money (1911), 278
Stabilising the Dollar, 28
Foster, William T., 209, 231n40
Fourier, Charles, 167

Friedman, Milton, 196n6, 229n36, 304n2
A Monetary History of the United States 1867-1960, 229n36

G

Gaffney, Mason, 270n5
Gay, Edwin F., 200
George, Henry, 29, 136n3, 142, 143, 146, 182n4, 292, 318
George, Lloyd, 262, 263
Godwin, William, 167
Gossen, Hermann H., 295
Gregory, T.E., 15, 26, 109, 237, 290, 303

H

Hamilton, Earl J., 109, 236n3, 242, 244, 248, 290
Harrison, Fred, 270n5
Harrod, Roy, 230, 230n38
Haskins, Charles H., 8, 12, 75
Hawtrey, Ralph G., 16, 25, 208, 220–225, 228–231, 228n34, 230n38, 261, 264, 303, 312
The Art of Central Banking, 220
Monetary Reconstruction, 220, 223, 264
Heath, Milton H., 248
Henderson, Hubert, 230n38
Hildebrand, Bruno, 35
Hirschman, Albert O., 114, 114n20, 115, 115n21, 121, 307
Hise, Charles Van, 41, 41n12
Hollander, Samuel, 98n1
Hoover, Herbert, 211
Hotelling, Harold, 266

House, Colonel Edward M., 12n8, 196, 203, 263
Howitt, Peter, 120
Hume, David, 43
Huntington, Emily, 242
Hutcheson, Francis, 43

J
Jefferson, Mark, 198
Jevons, William S., 5, 16, 28–30, 265, 285, 288, 291, 295–298, 312
The Principles of Science, 295
John Hopkins University, 34
Johnson, Douglas W., 197, 198
Jones, E.D., 8, 12
Jones, G.T., 7, 7n3, 247, 248
Increasing Returns, 7, 247
Jordan, David Starr, 38, 41, 41n12, 60, 61, 271, 272

K
Kahn, Richard F., 230, 230n38
Kaldor, Nicholas, 74, 96, 111–118, 118n22, 131, 209, 242, 245, 303, 304, 306, 312
Keynes, John Maynard, 3, 10, 13, 14, 16, 27, 92, 109, 115, 199, 203, 204n14, 211, 230, 235, 245, 261–265, 303, 318n13
General Theory, 230
Tract on Monetary Reform, 264
Treatise on Money, 230
Treatise on Probability, 92, 265
Keynes, John Neville, 69, 83, 83n7
Scope and Method of Political Economy, 83n7
Keyton, Senator William S. (Ohio), 225n32

Knies, Karl, 13, 17, 18, 34–37, 34n1, 78, 83
Die politische Oekonomie vom Standpunkte der Geschichtlichen Methode, 37
Knight, Frank H., x, 2, 3, 6, 7, 16, 26, 27, 47, 54, 57, 72, 74, 80, 82–84, 158n11, 196, 236, 248, 253–256, 253n25, 255n29, 261, 268, 287, 303, 304
Uncertainty, Risk and Profit, 7, 26, 254
Krugman, Paul, 2, 96, 120, 121, 306, 307

L
Laidler, David, 1, 2, 209, 215n14, 222n24, 229n37, 230, 236n2, 247, 264n2, 304
Lamont, Thomas W., 203
Lansing, Robert, 197, 198, 200
Laski, Harold, 247
Laughlin, J. Laurence, 25, 59, 208, 216–220, 228
Lippman, Walter, 197
Lipsey, Richard G., 113n19
Lord, Robert H., 198
Lorenz, Max O., 38
Lucas, Robert, 96, 120
Lunt, William E., 196, 198

M
Malthus, Thomas R., 110, 294
Marget, Arthur, 2
Marshall, Alfred, 3, 5, 13, 16, 17, 19, 29, 30, 33, 36, 38, 39, 52–58, 78, 95, 102, 120, 127,

149, 164, 165n13, 228, 239, 261, 265, 267, 284, 286, 288, 289, 295, 297, 303, 311, 321
Bristol University College, 52
Economics of Industry, 52
Industry and Trade, 53
Money, Credit and Commerce, 53
Principles of Economics, 17, 33, 38, 52, 53, 58, 289
Pure Theory of Domestic Values, 52
Pure Theory of Foreign Trade, 52
Marx, Karl, x, 6, 7, 21, 22, 60, 78, 100n5, 136n3, 143, 160, 167–169, 171, 253, 284, 285, 320, 322
Das Kapital, 169
McCulloch, J. R., 291, 293
McDougall, William, 64, 275
Meade, James E., 230
Mehrling, Perry G., 1, 2, 11, 37, 40, 41n11, 42, 48, 51, 51n18, 55, 63, 64, 70, 71, 73, 75–79, 80n6, 81, 82, 85–87, 85n11, 85n12, 87n15, 87n16, 89–93, 92n18, 101n7, 106n14, 136n4, 138, 138n7, 158n11, 160, 166, 169, 170, 172, 193, 208–211, 210n7, 210n8, 212n11, 213, 215, 215n14, 215n15, 220, 220n21, 225, 228, 237, 265, 267–269, 274n8, 285, 286, 289, 291, 292, 294, 304, 317, 322n15, 322n16
Menger, Carl, 28, 285, 297
Meyer, B.H., 28, 179, 180, 282
Mezes, Sidney E., 197, 198
Mill, James, 290

Mill, John Stuart, 18, 47–49, 63, 69, 72n2, 78, 84–86, 84n8, 89–91, 143, 261, 318
Essays on Some Unsettled Questions of Political Economy, 84
Miller, David Hunter, 197, 199–201
Millis, Harry A., 271
Mitchell, Wesley C., 3, 8, 11, 16, 27, 28, 34, 38, 63, 64, 128, 212, 236, 239, 240, 244, 261, 271–278, 303
Business Cycles, 27, 272
The Making and Using of Index Numbers, 276
Moore, C. H., 283
Moore, Henry L., 81
Laws of Wages, 81
Morris, William, 170n16
Murphy, Kevin, 2, 96, 120, 306
Myrdal, Gunnar, 61, 62, 115, 117

N
Newcomb, Simon, 34
Newman, Peter, 16
Nurkse, Ragnar, 2, 96, 118, 119

O
Olivier, Sydney, 167n14
Orlando, Vittorio, 262
Owen, Robert, 167, 168

P
Paley, Mary, 52, 53
Pareto, Vilfredo, 5, 29, 55, 81, 261, 286–288
Patinkin, Don, 158n11

Author Index

Pease, Edward, 167n14
Petty, William, 79n5
Pigou, A. C., 16, 27, 122n25, 127, 181, 230n38, 231n39, 239, 245, 249, 255n29, 261, 267–271, 276, 277, 303, 311, 321
  Economics of Welfare, 276
Pressman, Steven, 59, 60, 286
Proudhon, P.J., 169

Q

Quesnay, Francois, 43, 47

R

Ramsey, Frank P., 270, 270n4
Raphael, D.D., 100
Reed, Harold Lyle, 2
Reid, Gavin, 98n1
Reinwald, Thomas P., 256
Reisman, David A., 65
Ricardo, David, 4n2, 29, 47–49, 63, 78, 98n3, 110, 139, 143, 146, 261, 285, 290–295, 308, 318
  Essay on the Influence of a Low Price of Corn on the Profits of Stock, 290
  The High Price of Bullion, 290n14
  Principles of Political Economy and Taxation (1817), 291
Rickert, Heinrich John, 18, 78, 83
Riley, Eugen B., 2, 304
Robbins, Lionel, 9, 10n4, 14, 165, 165n13, 236n2, 246, 247, 303
Robertson, Dennis H., 230n38, 268
Robinson, Austin, 230n38
Robinson, Joan, 230, 230n38

Romer, Paul, 2, 96, 120, 121
Roosevelt, President Theodore, 23, 186, 230
Roscher, Wilhelm, 35
Rosenstein-Rodan, Paul, 2, 96, 113–115, 114n20, 118, 119, 307, 307n6
Ross, Edward, 40
Ruskin, John, 170n16

S

Saint-Simon, Henri de, 167
Samuelson, Paul A., 239, 256, 256n31, 311, 311n9
Sandilands, Roger J., x, 1, 2, 37, 48, 51, 51n18, 55, 63, 64, 70, 71, 73, 75–77, 79, 80n6, 81, 82, 85–87, 85n11, 85n12, 86n14, 87n15, 87n16, 89–93, 92n18, 101n7, 103n11, 106n14, 109n16, 115n21, 117, 121, 136n4, 138, 138n7, 144, 147, 157, 158n11, 160, 165, 166, 169, 170, 172, 193, 209, 210n7, 210n8, 212n11, 215n15, 220n21, 222n23, 229, 229n36, 229n37, 231n40, 236n3, 237, 239, 246, 247, 253n25, 255n27, 256, 256n31, 264n2, 265, 267–269, 270n5, 274n8, 285, 286, 289, 291, 294, 304, 317, 322n16
Schultz, Theodore W., 121
Schumpeter, Joseph A., x, 3, 6, 7, 7n3, 14, 24, 28, 45, 53n19, 83n7, 95, 109, 180, 208, 209n6, 230, 235, 261,

Author Index

271n6, 282–285, 303, 304, 320, 323
History of Economic Analysis (1954), 283, 284
Schwartz, Anna J., 229n36, 304n2
Scitovsky, Tibor, 103n10, 114n20
Scott, William A., 8, 41
Seligman, E.R.A., 34, 34n1, 266
Seymour, Charles, 196, 198
Shaw, Bernard, 167n14
Shaw, G.K., 120
Shepherd, Geoffrey, 246
Shotwell, James, 196, 196n7, 198, 199, 201
Shove, Gerald F., 230n38
Sidgwick, Henry, 18, 36, 69, 83, 84n8, 89–91, 89n17
  Principles of Political Economy, 83, 89, 89n17
Skidelsky, Robert, 230n38
Smith, Adam, 4n2, 6, 13, 14, 17, 19, 29, 33, 43–49, 61, 63–65, 74, 78, 84, 86n13, 95–101, 100n6, 101n7, 103, 104, 107–110, 116, 118–120, 127, 128, 131n1, 133n2, 212, 240, 247, 261, 291, 308, 309, 318, 320, 322
  Lectures on Jurisprudence, 43
  Lectures on Rhetoric and Belles Lettres, 43
  Theory of Moral Sentiments, 43, 64, 74
  Wealth of Nations, the, 43–45, 48, 74, 110, 116, 118
Sombart, Werner, 63
Spargo, John, 169
Sprague, Oliver, 11
Sraffa, Piero, 54n20, 290, 316

Stiglitz, Joseph, 270n5
Strong, Benjamin, 228n34
Sumner, William G., 59

T

Taussig, Frank W., 3, 9, 15, 199n9, 203, 237, 244, 245, 249, 268, 271n6, 276, 283, 303
Taylor, Overton H., 224n29, 231n40, 242
Thirlwall, Anthony P., 115, 117, 121
Thünen, Johann H. von, 53n19, 55
Tilman, Rick, 58n26
Tschuprow, Alexander, 83
Tugwell, Rex G., 48
Turgot, Jacques, 43
Turner, Frederick J., 8, 12, 34, 75, 85n11

V

Veblen, Thorstein, 13, 16, 17, 27, 33, 34, 58–65, 78, 102n8, 261, 271, 274, 274n8, 275, 275n9, 303, 320, 321, 323
  Carlton College (Minnesota), 58
  Engineers and the Price System, 60
  The Instinct of Workmanship and the State of the Industrial Arts, 60
  The Theory of Business Enterprise, 60
  The Theory of the Leisure Class, 60

W

Wagner, Adolf H. G., 36
Walker, Donald, 65

Wallas, Graham, 167n14
Walras, Léon, 3, 5, 28, 29, 53n19, 55, 81, 88, 261, 284–286, 288, 297
  Elements of Pure Economics, 28, 285
Walsh, C.M., 276, 277
Warshow, H. W., 238
Webb, Sydney (Sidney), 63, 167n14
Weber, Max, 18, 69, 78, 83, 84n8, 91, 261
  The Theory of Social and Economic Organisation, 91
Wieser, Friedrich von, 34n1
Westermann, William L., 198
Westlake, Jessie Bernice, 9
Westlake, John, 10
White, Andrew Dexter, 34n1
White, Harry Dexter, 264n2
Wicksell, Knut, 136n3, 222n24
Wicksteed, Phillip H., 30, 297
Wilcox, Walter F., 8, 37, 38, 41, 182, 271
Williams, John H., 111, 247
Wilson, President Woodrow, 27, 38, 196, 198–200, 203, 262
Working, Holbrok, 2

Y

Young, Allyn A., ix, 1, 33–65, 69, 95–122, 127–172, 175–204, 207–231, 235–257, 261–298, 303

Cornell University, 8
Currency and Credit (Hawtrey), 221, 222
Dartmouth College, 8
A Discussion of Age Statistics, 8
The Economic Consequences of the Peace (Keynes), 27, 203
Economic Problems: New and Old, 1, 269, 284
Harvard University, 8
Making of Index Numbers (Fisher), 28, 282
Papers Relating to Political Economy (Edgeworth), 27, 266
review of, 27, 28, 30, 134, 221–223, 263, 266–270, 279, 280
A Study in Public Finance (Pigou), 270
Theory of Political Economy (Jevons), 30, 74n3, 224, 295
The Trend of Economics (Tugwell), 48, 275
University of Stanford, 8
University of Washington, 8
University of Wisconsin, 34, 41
Wealth and Welfare (Pigou), 16, 27, 231n39
Western Reserve University, 8
Young, Jack, 10, 239
Young, Matilda Stickney, 7
Young, Sutton E., 7

Subject Index[1]

A

Ability to pay principle, 183, 184
Abnormal credits, 217
Academic freedom, 34, 38
Activist monetary policy, 217, 220, 231, 306
Aggregated demand, 24, 117, 214, 273n7, 306, 316
Aggregate supply, 24, 147, 214, 265n3, 273n7, 316
Agricultural Adjustment Act (1933), 24, 196
Agriculture, 23, 30, 45, 47, 48, 86, 89, 97, 98, 98n1, 108, 110, 112, 116, 131, 141, 142, 155, 162, 193–195, 223, 294, 308, 308n7, 309
All-together approach, 95
Allyn A. Young room, 236n3
Allyn Young paradigm, 305, 311–320
Alpha Delta Phi, 35
American Bureau of Industrial Research, 35
American Commission to Negotiate the Peace, 2
American Economic Association, 2, 11, 12, 12n7, 28, 34, 35, 38, 179, 282
American Peace Commission, 199
American public utility commissions, 27, 269
American Statistical Association, 12, 38, 276
Anarchism, 169
Annual product, 20, 141, 157–159, 319
Anti-market framework, 120, 306

---

[1] Note: Page numbers followed by 'n' refer to notes.

Subject Index

Anti-trust laws, 22, 23, 185–190
Applied economics, ix, 4, 50, 77, 90, 175–204
Arithmetic mean, 277, 280
Artificial monopolies, 133, 134
Art of Central Banking, 226–228
Availability of close substitutes, 26, 251, 309, 314

B

Balance of power, 169, 198
Balance of trade, 294
Balliol College, 43
Banking statistics, 24, 215, 313
Bank of England, 115, 223n26, 228n34
Bank reserves, 216, 221
Barter, 30, 117, 128, 212, 212n11, 217, 218, 265, 296, 315n10
Barter terms of trade, 315n10
Betterments, 176, 177
Big business, 12, 127, 159–164
Big push, 113, 114, 114n20, 119, 306, 307n6
Bills of exchange, 210n9, 221, 223
Bimetallism, 217, 217n18
Book of Popular Science, 10, 237, 304
Bounty of nature, 318
Brand names, 5, 314
Bretton Woods System, 231
British Association for the Advancement of Science (Section F), 3n1, 12
British National Insurance Act, 12
Bullionist Controversy, 290
Bureaucrat manager, 284
Business profits, 151, 153, 186, 274

C

Cambridge Circus, 230
Cambridge school, 52
Capital
  accumulation, 44, 96, 99, 100, 113, 113n19, 256, 315n11
  flows, 211
  goods, 136, 140, 148–152, 178, 318
Capitalisation, 140, 190
Capitalism/capitalist system, 17, 21, 60, 160, 168, 321
Capitalist class, 89, 115
Capitalistic
  methods, 103, 315
  monopoly, 20, 131
Cartel, 134
Catallactics, 130
Census and age statistics, 175
Central banks, 25, 207, 208, 210, 210n8, 217, 220, 226–228, 306, 312, 313
Central Bureau of Research and Statistics, 200
Centralised investment board, 119
Chain stores, 161, 164
Cheap money policy, 217
Circular flow of income/circular flow model, 20, 156–159
Classical school, 35
Class struggle, 22, 100n5, 168, 169, 321, 322n16
Clayton Act, 23, 185, 187, 188
Collective bargaining, 148, 318
Collective indifference curves, 29, 287
Combinations/industrial combinations, 20, 23, 64, 80n6, 112, 132–134, 156, 161, 179, 185–190, 187n5, 244

Commerce, 44, 47, 48, 87, 87n15, 89, 98, 108, 185, 186, 188, 190, 280n10
Commercial
  banks, 227
  revolution, 6, 77, 89, 284, 305n4, 322
Commission on Reparation of Damage (CRD), 200, 201, 203
Committee of Academic Freedom and Tenure, 12
Common agricultural policy (CAP), 196n6
Common law, 186
Communal welfare, 13, 18, 320
Comparative advantage, 98, 98n3
Competition, ix, 3, 5, 6, 15, 20, 23, 26, 27, 29, 46, 54, 62, 64, 65, 72, 74, 96, 99, 101, 107, 109, 116, 118, 120–122, 127, 131–134, 131n1, 133n2, 136, 136n3, 154, 159–161, 168, 180, 186–189, 187n5, 216, 248–255, 265, 285, 289, 296, 306, 308–310, 314–316, 319, 320, 322
Competitive
  equilibrium, 120, 121
  investments, 122, 150, 314
Concentration
  of economic power, 3, 21
  of wealth, 127, 159–164, 287
Conspicuous
  consumption, 60, 64, 65, 321
  leisure, 60, 64
Consumers
  income, 221
  outlay, 221

Consumer (consumers) surplus, 16, 54, 55, 56n23, 58, 127
Contractual
  relations, 88
  view of society, 76, 77, 91, 92, 275n9
Copyrights, 121, 122, 122n24, 133
Corn Laws, 4n2, 290
Corporate finance, 189
Cosmopolitanism, 36
Cost controversy, 245
Cost of production theory of price, 296
Cost-of-service principle, 22, 28, 180–182, 283
Countertendencies, 310
Creative function of markets, 116
Credit
  control, 6, 73, 84, 207, 208, 223
  creation, 221
  deadlock, 221, 229
  expansion, 117, 214, 219, 221, 222n24, 223, 225n30, 280
Crises/crisis, 24, 213, 215–217, 225, 273, 273n7, 274, 294, 297, 306, 306n5, 313
Cumulative
  causation, 17, 19, 33, 44, 61, 62, 64, 65, 95, 96, 102, 102n8, 107, 109, 116, 117, 274n8, 305, 315
  price spiral, 210, 283
Currency school, 25, 208, 218

D

Dance of the dollar, 219
Dawes Plan, 204
Dead level of competition, 250, 251

Subject Index

Debt Commission, 211
Definition of an index number, 281
Deflation, 210
Delphic Literary Society, 11
Demand and supply/demand-supply apparatus, 27, 55, 105, 267
Demand curve, 16, 21, 55–57, 56n22, 164, 165, 180, 283, 288, 306, 316
  for money, 21, 164
Democracy, 13, 171, 172, 263, 320, 320n14, 322, 322n16
Departmental stores, 161
Depreciation and rate control, 22, 175–179, 175n1
Derived demand, 105, 136n4, 144
Development theory, 121, 307
Dialectic process, 168
Differential return, 144
Diffusion, 21, 160, 284, 310, 316
Discount-rate policy, 223, 224, 226
Discount rates, 25, 135, 216, 221, 223, 223n26, 225n30, 228n34, 314
Discretionary policy, 25
Discriminating privileges, 172
Discriminatory rates, 28, 180, 181, 282
Disequilibrium, 3, 5, 6, 8, 17, 19, 44, 54, 61, 65, 86, 95, 96, 98n1, 107, 109, 115, 130, 283, 305, 306n5, 310, 311, 313, 315, 315n10
Disequilibrium (dynamic) theory of price formation, 5, 208, 313
Disposable surplus, 159
Disproportionality crisis, 306, 306n5
Distinction
  between abstract and historical sciences, 76
  between art and science, 72n2, 84
  between pure and applied economics, 4, 50, 77, 90, 175
  between rent to a person and rent to a factor of production, 293
Distribution, 40
Distribution of income/wealth, 41n11, 63, 85, 135, 136, 157, 160, 165, 167, 189, 287, 313
Distribution theory
  interest, 3, 20, 39, 170, 297
  profits, 3
  rents, 3, 20, 39, 143, 170
  wages, 3, 20, 39
Division of labour, 4n2, 6, 19, 33, 44–46, 48, 49, 61, 72, 89, 95–98, 100, 101, 104, 105, 107–109, 111, 117, 147, 305, 308, 315
Domesticated Keynesianism, 229
Double taxation, 184, 185
Dual exchange rate system, 118
Duopoly problem, 20, 27, 134, 266, 289

E

Easier credit, 217
East European reconstruction, 307n6
Economic democracy, 171, 320n14
Economic friction, 137, 269
Economic growth, 2, 27, 37, 45, 55, 98n2, 111, 114n20, 304
Economic policy, 36, 37, 245
Economic progress, 2, 3, 6, 19, 33, 44, 53, 95, 106, 132, 141, 142, 159, 231n39, 252, 287, 304, 305, 311, 315
Economic rent, 137, 144

Economics
  abstract economics, 5, 29, 30, 37, 74n3, 82, 286, 295
  deductive economics, 50, 50n17, 276
  of farm relief, 193–196
  land economics, 35
  mathematical economics, 81, 82, 244, 287, 296
  monetary economics, ix, 2, 11, 216, 304
  of opportunity, 310
  of scarcity, 310
  systematic economics, 77, 130
Economies
  external, 17, 19, 53–55, 58, 95, 96, 102, 103, 103n10, 103n11, 107, 109, 116, 119–121, 133, 231n39, 255, 255n29, 269, 305, 307, 315, 316
  internal, 19, 53, 55, 58, 95, 96, 102, 103, 103n11, 113, 120, 305, 315
Economies of scale, 19, 53, 54, 62, 96, 102n9, 103, 103n11, 109, 117, 121, 305, 307, 315
  dynamic, 102n9
Effective protection rates, 308n7
Elasticity of demand and supply, 106n14, 109, 116, 159, 270
Empty economic boxes, 112, 113
Endogenous growth, 2, 65, 96, 118–122, 304, 315
English political economy, 4, 17, 18, 29, 33, 36, 48–51, 51n18, 69, 76–78, 86–89, 87n16, 91, 267, 289, 291, 292, 297, 321
Entrepreneur, 135, 136, 138, 143, 148, 150–156, 158, 251, 283, 284, 319

Entrepreneurial function, 319, 322
Enumeration of children, 22, 190–192
Equality of competitive opportunity, 160
Equation of exchange, 30, 214, 218, 222, 277, 278, 281, 296, 312, 321
Equilibrium
  analysis, 52, 54
  of costs and advantages, 106, 315
  rate of change (or progress), 21, 57, 256, 306
Evolutionary
  approach, 65
  system, 35, 46
Evolutionary socialism, 169
Excess
  capacity, 26, 248, 314
  profits, 155
  profits tax, 156
  reserves, 247
Exchange value, 20, 24, 128–130, 207, 212–216, 220n21, 312
Exhaustion of the product, 254
Exploitation of the working class, 168
Extensive margin, 291
External economies
  pecuniary, 96, 103, 103n10, 103n11, 109, 116, 119–121, 307, 316
  technological, 119

F

Fabian socialism, 21, 115, 167, 167n14
Factor substitutability, 136n4
Fair and reasonable prices, 194
Fallacy of composition, 55, 231n40, 311

Subject Index

Falling rate of profit, 294
Federal Reserve Banks, 12, 225n30, 227
Federal Reserve Board, 219n20, 225n30, 226, 227
Federal Reserve System, 216, 216n16, 224, 226–228
Federal Trade Commission, 23, 185, 187, 188
Final degree of utility, 30, 295, 297
First principle, 50, 50n17, 182, 283
Fiscal
 deficits, 229, 231
 inflationism, 229
 monopoly, 133
 stabilisation, 231
Fixed costs, 103, 120, 121, 121n23, 132
Floor rate of interest, 230
Foreign/international trade, 6, 44, 48, 96, 98, 98n2, 98n3, 108, 115, 118, 202, 210, 279, 294, 311
Forward and backward linkages, 114, 121, 307
Freedom of entry, 314
Free resources, 317
Free silver campaign, 196
Free trade, 36, 46, 86, 89, 97, 98, 98n3, 101
Front-end loading problem, 113n18

G
Gains from trade, 289
General
 equilibrium, 3, 4, 16, 28, 29, 52, 54, 55, 82, 95, 285, 286, 288, 305

overproduction, 106n14, 165, 240, 240n4, 294
price index, 218, 316
price level, 16, 25, 207, 208, 214, 218, 220, 278, 279, 312, 316
property tax, 22, 182, 183
relations, 75, 81, 136n4, 289, 291
social interests, 292
Generalised utility function, 265
The Genius and its Influence, 50
Geometric mean, 28, 278, 280, 281
George Washington (ship), 198–200
German historical school, 17, 34–43, 48
German reparations (indemnity), 198, 199, 203
Gluts, 294
Gold bullion certificates, 278, 279
Gold-exchange standard, 210, 224
Gold reserves, 25, 28, 202, 228n34, 279
Gold standard, 25, 208–212, 210n7, 216, 218–220, 223, 224, 228, 229, 231
Goodwill, 131, 132, 202, 251
Great Crash, 229n35
Great depression, 211–212, 228–231
Great powers, 198
Gresham's Law, 92, 217n18
Growth mechanics, 107
Guild socialism, 170, 170n16

H
Hands-off approach, 46, 86, 240
Harmonic mean, 280
Harmony of interests, 100n5
Hedonism, 30, 45, 73, 74n3, 88, 92, 295

Subject Index

Hedonistic psychology, 17, 275, 321
   postulates, 16, 28, 45, 64, 88, 92, 275
Hepburn Act (1906), 176
High development theory, 121, 307
Hiram College, 7, 8, 11, 35
Holding company, 186
Human capital, 120, 121

I

Ideal index number, 28, 218, 231n39, 244, 277, 280, 281
Ideal monetary system, 210, 210n7
Imperfect competition, ix, 3, 5, 15, 26, 29, 121, 122, 131, 248, 249, 252, 253, 309, 314–315, 322
Impersonal taxation, 22, 175, 182–185
Imputed price (value), 20, 129, 213, 313
Income distribution, 29, 40, 41, 286, 287
Income inequality, 41
Increasing returns, generalised/macroeconomic, 19, 45, 57, 107, 109, 116, 269, 307, 316
Index number problem, 130, 213
Index numbers, ix, 3, 16, 28, 128, 175, 218, 231n39, 244, 267, 276–282, 322
Index of inequality, 29, 175, 287
Indifference curve, 29, 265, 287
Individual credit/personal credit, 217, 217n17
Individualism, 21, 166, 171, 320n14
Individualistic method, 92
Inductive inference, 5, 265

Industrial consolidation (integration), 62, 96, 104
Industrial differentiation/fragmentation, 62, 65, 96, 104, 107, 252
Industrial division of labour, 104
Industrial fluctuations, 29, 288, 309
Industrial operations, 62, 109, 109n15, 162
Industrial revolution, 6, 89, 145, 284, 305, 305n4, 322
Industrial (social) wastes, 17, 62, 314, 321
Industrial specialisation, 107, 109, 252, 305
Industry, 16, 24, 27, 44, 45, 47–49, 53, 57, 62, 89, 98, 101–106, 105n13, 108, 109, 109n15, 112, 116, 119, 122n25, 132–135, 136n4, 145, 148, 153, 155, 157, 160–165, 187, 188, 194–196, 202, 214, 216, 223, 226, 248, 252, 255, 268, 269, 291, 307, 308, 308n7, 315
Inflation, 151, 210, 215, 216, 219, 223, 264, 274
Input-output coefficients, 115n21
Inquiry, the, 12, 12n8, 77, 91, 192, 196–198, 267
Inquiry Concerning Political Justice, 167
Instability of credit, 222, 222n23
Instinct of workmanship, 65
Institute of Land Economics and Public Utilities, 35
Institutional arrangements, 6, 12n7, 19, 44, 228, 320
Institutional economics, 60, 63

Institutional intervention, 41
Institutionalism, 65, 292
Institutions, x, 6, 9, 10, 13, 18, 36, 38, 41n11, 42, 46, 49, 60, 62–65, 72, 73, 74n4, 76, 93n18, 96, 100, 100n6, 107–110, 112, 167, 172, 212n11, 220, 231, 275, 284, 292, 309, 320, 322n16
Instrumental value, 4, 13, 17, 48, 70
Intensive margin, 29, 139, 140, 317
Inter-allied debt problem, 211
Interlocking directorates, 188
Interlocking stockholding, 188
Intermediate products, 105, 162
International cooperation, 210, 219, 227, 228, 231
International money markets, 227
International payments, 209, 211
International pooling of reserves, 227
International settlements, 209, 210
Interregional and international inequalities, 62, 115, 118
Intersectoral demand, 111
Interstate commerce, 185, 190
Interstate Commerce Commission, 22, 176, 178, 179, 186
Interventionist monetary policy, 25, 207, 217, 218
Inward-looking (import substitution) model of development, 115

J

Jevons's law of indifference, 296
Jevons's sunspot theory of crisis, 297
Jevons's theory of interest and wages, 291
Jevons's trading body, 296

K

Keynesian aggregate demand, 111
Keynesian liquidity trap, 229
Keynesian multiplier, 111
Keynesian revolution, 230

L

Labour embodied approach to value, 291
Labour movement, 35
Labour organizations/labour unions, 186, 187
Labour theory of value, 168, 292
Laissez faire, x, 6, 13, 25, 41, 46–48, 65, 73, 84, 101, 166, 180, 208, 217, 309, 320
Land values, 24, 136n3, 140, 142, 143n8, 195, 270, 292, 292n16, 318
Laura Spelman Rockefeller Foundation, 81
Law and government, 100
Law of diminishing returns, 30, 45, 49, 86, 110, 141, 240, 294, 308, 310, 311
Laws and institutions, 108
Leading-sector strategy, 19, 112, 113
League of Nations, 12, 198
Leisure class, 60
Level playing field, 99, 308
License fee, 185
Loan-deposit ratios, 216n16
London money market, 223
London School of Economics (LSE), 7n3, 8–11, 15, 28, 74, 111, 115, 131, 224, 236, 236n2, 236n3, 239, 242, 248, 283, 290, 304

M

Machine process, 60
Mail-order houses, 161
Malthusian theory of population, 145, 146
Marginal capital goods, 149
Marginal efficiency of capital, 230
Marginalist revolution, 53
Marginal land, 140, 149
Marginal net product, 268, 269, 307
Marginal productivity of capital, 291
Marginal productivity theory, 20, 41, 136n3, 137, 138, 158, 297, 317
Marginal productivity theory of interest, 297
Marginal utility, 16, 21, 28, 39, 50, 56, 92, 128–130, 159, 285, 295
Marginal utility of money, 56
Market failure
 forms, 307
 period, 57
 place, 50, 74n4, 87, 92, 130
 power, 120–122, 309, 316
 price, 47, 129, 164, 229n35, 240
 system, 100, 100n5, 103, 120, 228, 306, 307, 311, 316
 wastes, 122
Marshallian tradition, 230n38
Marxism, 3, 21, 127, 166–172
Massachusetts Committee on Pensions, 12
McNary-Haugen Bill/Haugen Bill, 22, 23, 175, 193, 195, 196
Measurements of General Exchange Value (1901), 276
Measure of value, 212, 220, 220n21
Medium of exchange, 24, 207, 209, 212, 217, 220, 220n21, 265, 296

Mercantilism, 6, 44, 49, 100, 107, 309, 322
Mercantilist instinct, 6, 284, 322
Method of economics
 deduction, 4, 69
 historical method, 4
 induction, 4, 69
 a priori method, 36, 85
Minimum profits, 152–154
Mint price of gold, 279, 279n10
Mobility mechanism, 112
Modern Schools of Economic Thought, 247
Monetary policy, 25, 208, 218–220, 306, 313, 316
Monetary stability, 210–211
Monetary standard, 24, 208, 209, 219n20, 223, 312
Money and banking, 24, 40, 209, 224n29, 231n40, 322
Money in circulation, 222
Money of account, 222, 222n25
Money supply, 24, 25, 207, 208, 210, 214, 214n13, 218, 220, 229, 278, 312
Monopolising, 188, 189
Monopoly control
 price, 20, 134, 251, 252, 269
 spirit, 46
Moving equilibrium, 106
Multi-sectoral model, 306n5

N

Napoleonic wars, 4n2, 29, 49, 290, 291
National dividend, 157, 181, 268, 270
National money market, 227

Natural law
  order, 47, 247
  price, 47, 146
  rights, 166, 247
Natural liberty, 44, 46, 47, 49, 63, 96, 99–101, 107–109, 118, 309, 320
Natural monopolies, 23, 132–134, 186, 189
Natura non facit saltum, 52
Nature and scope of economics, 69
Neighbourhood store, 161
Neoclassical theory (economics), 3, 52, 60, 116, 121, 266, 275n9, 292, 304
New dealer, 229
New deal policies, 230
New growth theory, 19
New trade theorists, 2, 19, 304
New York banks, 215n15, 216n15
New York Federal Reserve Bank, 227, 228n34
Niggardliness of nature, 143, 318
No favours, no handicaps, 113, 116, 118, 307, 308
Non-economic factors, 71
Non-price competition, 26, 252, 314
Normal credits
  price, 217
  tendencies, 137

O

Offer curves, 27, 52, 56, 56n25, 58, 267, 315, 315n10
Old-age pension, 23, 192, 193
One-thing-at-a-time (or ceteris paribus) approach, 4, 52, 54, 55, 55n21, 65, 117, 127, 151, 267, 268, 290, 305, 311
Open market operations, 226, 313
Original and indestructible powers of the soil, 139
Outside banks, 216n15

P

Pareto optimality, 131n1, 286, 287
Particular expenses curve, 164
Passive monetary accommodation, 25
Patents, 121, 122, 133, 133n2, 250, 309, 316
Pecuniary emulation, 60
Peripatetic school of economics, 246
Perpetualism, 36
Personal and impersonal taxation, 22, 175, 182–185
Personal distribution of income, 136
Personal taxation, 183–185
Physiocrats, 43, 247, 285
Pin-factory example, 97, 103, 109
PL480 programme, 196n6
Political arithmetic, 79, 79n5
Political democracy, 320n14
Political economy, 4, 17, 30, 33–36, 40, 45, 46, 48–52, 64, 69, 70, 72n2, 76–79, 81, 84–91, 87n16, 275, 291, 295, 309, 321
Post-war agricultural boom, 195
Post-war development economists, 19, 118, 304, 310
Present consumption, 148, 318
Price discrimination
  making process, 24, 128–130, 212, 213, 218

policy of a monopolist, 193
system, 60, 103n10, 249, 307
Prime costs, 131, 132, 181n3
Principle of the hiding hand, 114
Private expenditure, 225, 225n33
Private property, 36, 72, 96, 100, 154, 168, 170, 171
Privilege tax, 185
Product differentiation, 5, 26, 62, 122, 252, 309, 314–316
Production costs, 251, 296
Productive labourers (workers), 44
Productivity, 20, 21, 39, 55, 110, 116, 117, 135–138, 138n7, 140, 144, 148, 159, 240, 254, 297, 311, 317, 320
Proletariat, 60, 65
Property rights, 137, 159, 170, 171
Protection/Protectionism, 36, 116–121, 290, 306, 308, 308n7, 309
Psychological postulates, 16, 18, 28, 45, 50, 62, 73, 92, 276, 321
Public expenditure
health measures, 46, 101
interest, x, 6, 13, 25, 45, 46, 65, 73, 99, 101, 176, 284, 309, 313, 320, 322n15
policy, 225n32
regulation, 27, 134, 269
works, 6, 25, 46, 100, 208, 220, 225, 229, 231n40, 265, 309, 312, 320
Public's currency-deposit ratio, 247
Pump priming, 231n40
Purchasing power parity, 211
Pure competition, 5, 29, 131, 131n1, 250, 290, 314, 322

Pure credit economy, 222n24
Pure profits, 122, 152–155, 319, 322

Q

Quantitative protection, 306, 308
Quantity theory
Cambridge cash-balances version, 224n29
income velocity version, 220
transactions version, 218
Quantity theory of money, 216, 218, 220, 278
Quasi rent, 149

R

Railway rate making, 22, 175, 175n1, 179–182, 283
Ramsey rule, 270
Rate of demand and rate of supply, 20, 129, 312
Rational economic man, 18, 45, 65, 74, 81
R&D expenditures, 120, 121
Real bills doctrine, 208, 217, 226
Reciprocal demand, 27, 56, 58, 267, 315, 315n10
Reciprocal exchange, 111, 122, 308, 315n10
Relative prices, 16, 24, 165, 207, 209, 213, 214, 217, 218, 220, 265, 278, 281, 312, 313, 316, 318n13, 321
Relative scarcity, 20, 138, 317
Rent as a differential, 317
Representative firm, 53, 132, 165, 165n13, 305

Subject Index

Reserves, 25, 28, 177, 178, 202, 221, 223, 226, 227, 229, 247, 279, 313
Restraint of trade, 156, 185, 186, 189
Ricardian economics, 52
Ricardian principle of gold movements, 294
Ricardian theory of rent, 29, 292, 293, 317
Risk taking, 155
Roger, 111
Role of the state, 73, 309, 320
Roundabout methods, 103, 104, 136n4, 151, 255, 315
Rule-based approach to monetary policy, 25

S

St. John's College (Cambridge), 52
St. Louis Public Service Commission, 178, 179
Saving, 8, 44, 96, 97, 99, 113, 118, 119, 148, 149, 149n9, 151, 157, 160, 192, 219, 228, 270n4, 306n5, 310, 315
Say's law, 106n14, 240, 294, 306n5
Scarcity, 20, 49, 110, 138, 138n6, 138n7, 240, 294, 310, 311, 311n8, 317
Scientific (or evolutionary) socialism, 169
Scientific knowledge, 51, 79, 110, 122, 159
Scottish Enlightenment, 43
Sector-specific interventions, 306
Selective employment tax (SET), 118, 306

Self interest, 36, 45, 46, 74, 96, 99, 101
Self-sustaining growth, 117, 119
Selling costs/expenses, 5, 11, 22, 26, 62, 122, 128, 131, 135, 136, 138–140, 142, 143, 148–155, 158, 164, 170, 176, 177, 179, 180, 194, 221, 225n30, 251, 252, 269, 273n7, 314
Settlement of debts, 220n21
Sherman Act, 22, 23, 175, 185–188
Single establishments, 164
Single tax, 142, 143n8, 182n4, 183, 292
Single tax in Missouri, 182, 182n4
Social cement, 168n15
Social control, 137
Social cost, 16, 127, 307
Social dividend, 20, 21, 127, 143, 154, 156–159, 319, 322
Social division of labour, 97, 103
Social economy, 85
Social evolution, 22, 168, 172, 322n16
Socialism, 3, 12, 21, 22, 34, 115, 127, 146, 166–172, 320, 321, 322n16
Socialism as unfolding of democracy, 172, 322n16
Socialist labour theory of value, 292
Social overhead capital, 119
Social picture, 55, 71, 103, 138
Social Science Research Council, 81
Specialisation, 107, 109, 117, 120, 252, 305
  industrial specialisation, 72
Specialized shop, 161

Speculation, 35, 90, 227, 229, 231, 248, 311
Stage of society, 35, 320
Standardisation, 103n12, 162
  standardised product, 103, 132, 155, 162
Standard of deferred payments, 128, 220n21
Standard theory of wages, 145
Static/stable equilibrium, 3, 60, 61, 65, 96, 129, 207, 212, 213, 256, 313, 316
Stationary state, 255n27, 294, 308, 319
Statistical method, 80, 83
Status goods, 60, 62
Statute of monopolies, 133
Structure of demand, 24, 214, 313
Structure of installed capacity, 24, 313
Subjective utility, 295
Subjective value, 130
Subsistence theory of wages, 145, 146
Supplementary costs, 57, 58, 132, 133, 181n3, 315
Supply curve, 7n3, 20, 21, 55, 57, 58, 164, 165, 288, 305, 306, 316
Surplus over cost, 144
Surplus value, 168
Sympathy, 74

T

Tariff protection, 306
Tâtonnement process, 285
Taxation paradox, 266
Tax-cum-subsidy approach, 122n25
Tax Law Revision Commission (New York), 12, 22, 182

Technical progress, exogenous, 120
Tendencies, 19, 30, 47, 53, 54, 61–63, 80, 86, 90, 95, 102, 110, 128, 137, 141–143, 149, 159, 160, 176, 225n30, 240, 243, 252, 274, 275, 279, 284, 294, 296, 308, 310, 321
Tension between money interest and public interest, 322n15
Theory of creative destruction, 283
Theory of distribution, 20, 91, 135–138, 136n3, 158, 266, 291, 297, 317–319
Theory of evolution, 100
Theory of value, 5, 127–130, 168, 291, 295, 312–313, 322
Time preference, 151, 318
Togetherness of the economic phenomenon, 305
Tooling up, 255
Total utility/utility, 12, 16, 21, 23, 27, 28, 38, 39, 50, 56, 56n22, 73, 74, 84, 92, 99, 128–130, 132, 155, 156, 159, 195, 200, 267, 286, 295, 296, 309, 310, 314, 320
Trade/business cycles, ix, 5, 12, 16, 24, 25, 27, 46, 49, 60, 73, 130, 151, 152, 207–231, 240n4, 272, 273n7, 288n11, 294, 304, 306, 312–314, 316, 318, 320, 322
Trade deficit, 202, 294
Trade marks, 5, 250, 252, 309, 314
Trade surplus, 294
Transactions velocity, 214n13
Transfer payment, 143
Transfer problem, 204n14, 262

Subject Index

Transmission mechanism of monetary policy, 221
Transport and communication, 45, 46, 86, 97, 101
Treaty of Versailles, 261, 262

U

Unbalanced budgets, 229
Underproduction, 132
Unearned decrement/increment, 29, 136n3, 142, 143, 150, 292, 318
Unfair competition trade practices, 187
Unified control/monopolistic control, 133, 193, 194, 252
Unified managements, 161, 162
United States Bureau of Census, 8, 37
Unproductive labour, 96
Unspent margin, 221, 224n29
Utilitarianism, 30, 45, 74n3, 88, 92, 267, 295
Utopian socialism, 167

V

Value, 4, 5, 13, 17, 20, 22, 24, 39, 48, 51, 63, 70, 79, 81, 92, 108, 127–130, 136, 136n3, 136n4, 138n7, 140, 142, 143n8, 144, 146, 148, 157, 159, 160, 166–168, 172, 176, 178–180, 195, 200, 201, 207, 208, 212, 213, 218, 220n21, 240, 242, 250, 263, 273, 286, 291, 312, 313, 318, 319, 322
and distribution, 29, 63
in exchange/exchange value, 20, 24, 116, 127–130, 207, 212–216, 220n21, 312
in use/use value, 116, 127, 128
Value theory, ix, 3, 5, 213, 249, 285
Varying dollar standard/variable standard, 25, 218
Velocity of circulation, 278
Verdoorn's Law, 19, 116
Versailles Treaty, 211
Vicious circles of poverty, 118

W

Wage-fund doctrine, 146
Waiting, 148, 149, 151, 159, 318, 319
Walras's auctioneer, 285
War Trade Board, 12, 42
Waves of optimas and pessimas, 29, 288, 288n11
Welfare economics, 287
'What the traffic will bear' rate system, 180
Wholesalers, 221, 250
Williams Institute of Politics (Massachusetts), 264
Wisconsin Railroad Commission, 41
Wisconsin Tax Commission, 41, 271

Y

Young multiplier/Currie-Young multiplier, 111
Young (Owen D.) Plan, 204
Young's 1928 Presidential Address, 2, 120